A Thoughtful Life
Essay in Philosophical Theology:

ATF Press

Adelaide

Edited by Ian Weeks and Duncan Reid

A Thoughtful Life
Essay in Philosophical Theology:
A Festshrift for
Rev Profesor
Harry Wardlaw

ATF Press

Adelaide

Edited by Ian Weeks and Duncan Reid

First published 2006

National Library of Australia
Cataloguing-in-Publication data

A thoughtful life : essays in philosophical theology

ISBN 1 920691 65 0.

1. Philosophical theology. I. Weeks, Ian. II. Reid Duncan, 1950 - . III. Wardlaw, Harry.

Published by

ATF Press
An imprint of the Australian Theological Forum
PO Box 504
Hindmarsh
SA 5007
ABN 68 314 074 034
www.atfpress.com

Cover design by Openbook Publishers, Adelaide

CONTENTS

INTRODUCTION

It was the hope of the contributors to this volume that it would be ready for Harry Wardlaw's seventy-fifth birthday, on 15 February 2004. Unfortunately that was not to be the case, though the delay has allowed the inclusion of some chapters that were late in arriving. The project is the outcome of a conversation in which Harry's long-standing conversation partner Ian Weeks undertook to contact colleagues, friends and one or two former students to invite them to write. It is a great pity that, because of illness and demanding and unanticipated family responsibilities, Ian has not been able to carry the editing process through to its conclusion, and this introduction is not by the editor himself. Harry was told of the project early on and suggested most if not all of the names of contributors. Some broad themes were suggested, though individual authors were allowed great latitude in what they chose to write about. Almost every contributor has chosen to write on a theme in which their own life's work intersects creatively with Harry Wardlaw's. Music was the only general theme to be mooted early in the planning and which unfortunately has not received any attention in the collection. An attempt was made to sort the essays collected here thematically, but any such sorting was soon found to be artificial and arbitrary. As one would expect, similar themes appear in a number of essays and the most that can be said is that some have greater emphasis on a particular theme than others. Instead of dividing the book into sections, a decision was made in favour of a movement. After Ruth Wardlaw's opening biographical piece, this broad movement is from philosophy to theological method, to biblical studies, to systematic theology, to the arts in their engagement with theology, to theological ethics. But do not ask where the lines of demarcation occur, because you will not find them. All the essays deal with matters of faith, all deal with philosophical questions, all make some reference to the questions to which Harry Wardlaw has addressed himself throughout his life with such passionate searching. John Kane's piece brings the movement back to biography. In keeping with the rather permissive guidelines followed by the Australian philosophical journal *Sophia*, authors were also given freedom to use whatever footnoting or referencing conventions they chose. Some thought was given to making these consistent before publication, but given the size of the task and the fact that the volume was already late, it was felt better, even at the risk of some untidiness, not to delay publication any further.

Fittingly the opening contribution to this volume is by the person who knows Harry best: Ruth Wardlaw. I will not presume to add anything to what Ruth has written, except to say that the inspired title she has given to her piece solved a particular editorial problem: to find a suitable title for the whole collection. The writings here encompass a life's interests and friendships. And Harry's is a life that is truly thoughtful, in the obvious, 'literal' sense of being intentionally and rigorously engaged with the task of thinking. But the word 'thoughtful' also catches another, more subtle and pastoral nuance, that of taking into consideration the needs of others.

John Howes's chapter, like many of the contributions, relates something of the writer's own story, in this case the author's departure from calling himself by the appellation 'Christian'. But what, Howes asks, of the strange hold this self-description tends to have for those who have made this departure, and just how honest is it? In short, why do so many people, even those whose lives and outlooks are quite secular, feel the need to assert their 'Christian-ness'? Howes discusses this question with reference to a number of writers whose names are well known to those who sat in Harry's classes.

Graeme Marshall's chapter on Wittgenstein touches on both a key thinker in Harry's worldview, and a key element in Harry's approach to theology: passion. Wittgenstein, according to one of Graeme's sources, was filled with 'a kind of fury' by the 'assumption that everything can be explained'. Hard as it may be to imagine Harry being filled with fury, there is certainly the passion for thinking through every question as far as thinking can possibly take us, but then – always – the recognition that thinking even rigorously pursued has its inherent limits. Harry's students learnt from him not to satisfy themselves with easy answers.

Frank Nichol asserts the evangelical power and relevance of the vocative. People do not become Christians through persuasion, but through 'overhearing' the Christian community talking to God. The essay develops this idea concisely and with philosophical precision.

Dietrich Ritschl modestly offers here a 'somewhat more radical' approach to doctrine than he did in his 1984 book *Zur Logik der Theologie*. Here he notes that particular ways of using language become, in time, markers of identity and creators of community. Such usages encompass an inner perspective that is not properly accessible to any supposedly more objective 'outer perspective' constructed outside the community of faith. In developing this theme, Ritschl criticises the extension of the use of biblical metaphors beyond their proper domain.

Eric Osborn examines the interaction of biblical faith and philosophy in Clement of Alexandria, bringing this into dialogue with a similar interaction in the works of the Melbourne philosopher A Boyce Gibson. Osborn sees Clement as being concerned with intelligent use of both the New Testament and philosophy, and argues this is an ongoing necessity for the theological task in Australia.

Geoffrey Thompson engages in an extended dialogue with the Australian cultural commentator John Carroll, and especially his identification of Jesus as the pivotal point in the 'Western dreaming'. The West's cultural malaise is the result of its having forgotten this central story, and the Christian custodians of the story would be well advised to listen carefully to Carroll's reminder of the intellectual and emotive power of this story.

Garry Trompf puts the case for anthropology to be regarded as the primary conversation partner of contemporary theology. This is already a daring suggestion in a volume that gives so much weight to theology's more traditional dialogue partner, philosophy. Where liberation theology had, by cleverly adapting a dictum from Hegel, argued that theology begins at sunset, Trompf argues more radically that theology should start 'where it hurts'.

Maurice Wiles begins, like a number of other contributors to this volume, with a reference to Harry's inimitable teaching style which conclusively makes nonsense of any supposed dichotomy between body and soul or mind and spirit. The chapter goes on to consider Harry's whole life as one of holding together the often separated styles of 'liberal' and 'confessional': Harry Wardlaw simply cannot be categorised as being one or the other. And yet the effort of holding together these two styles calls for a deeply thoughtful and at times agonised struggle for the – exactly – right word or phrase.

Robert Anderson outlines three ways in which his thinking and believing has or has not changed since his time as a student in Edinburgh in the 1950s: the influence on him of critical biblical scholarship, of the dialogue with Jewish colleagues, and the emergence of the new cosmology. The influence of each of these is discussed, and no-one who knows Robert Anderson will be surprised that it is the contact with Jewish colleagues that takes pride of place.

Louis Greenspan notes the curious phenomenon of Jewish writers and artists who feel impelled to comment on Jesus. Like the writers and artists he cites, and other examples come to mind as well, Greenspan recounts his own Jewish encounter with this Jesus, and explains why – despite the authentic Jewishness of the encounter – he chooses to remain Jewish.

Margaret Yee considers the contemporary discussion of the nature of the human person as a way into another, more precisely methodological issue: the dialogue between theology and the natural sciences. After critiquing reductionist approaches, Yee looks back to Austin Farrer as a more fruitful foundation for contemporary investigation of human personhood.

Wes Campbell offers a re-reading of Harry's doctoral supervisor, Ronald Gregor Smith, a theologian whose own work was framed by the shaking of theological foundations that followed the Second World War and led to the theological and wider cultural crisis of the 1960s. It is instructive to look back now, from a time when it is more fashionable to speak of the 'twilight of atheism' than of the 'death of God', and ask ourselves whether we have really confronted those older questions or merely relegated them to some existential filing cabinet.

Bruce Barber's chapter asks whether Christians have really yet heard the prophetic warnings of Friedrich Nietzsche. Are we too busy being mad at Nietzsche – angry at him – that we have failed to hear the uncomfortable truth spoken by one we are inclined to dismiss as mad? It may already be too late, as Nietzsche's madman proclaims, for our society to hear conventional Christian apologetics.

Christiaan Mostert addresses the relationship between Paul Tillich's existentialism and his Christian theology, arguing that, because of his 'meeting of existential questions with religious or theological answers', Tillich was in the end more than simply another representative figure of his own existentialist generation. The engagement with Tillich is particularly important in this volume because of his significance for Harry Wardlaw's own thinking. Tillich was, he once remarked, one of the thinkers who had enabled him to remain a Christian.

Catherine Laufer shares something of the quite inimitable experience of what it was like to sit in one of Harry's classes. Laufer then moves on to give a short account of what we might think of as a nineteenth century parallel to the Wardlaw phenomenon, the energetic, broad-minded but also greatly misunderstood English theologian Fredrick Denison Maurice.

John Cowburn uses the novels of Albert Camus as a way into a discussion of the problem of evil, especially moral evil. After noting Camus' failure to address this problem in his earlier novels, Cowburn argues that when Camus does eventually turn to face the matter of moral evil, his engagement with it is disappointingly superficial. Moral evil is everyone's problem, but will only be satisfactorily addressed by repentance and forgiveness.

The article by Gerard Williams addresses the question as to whether we can as contemporary human beings claim to have entered a new historical era. The author argues that no philosophical inquiry into human nature or our understanding of history can claim to be exhaustive.

My own contribution, which would have been much shorter if I had imagined that this collection would grow to be a volume of some twenty-seven chapters and over 400 pages, looks at two wisdom figures in Dostoyevsky as another way of engaging with the Jesus story. While Dostoyevsky has been mined for theological resources, the wisdom themes have in my opinion been curiously overlooked.

Patrick Hutchings like several of the authors addresses the question of human identity, the human self. After briefly considering a philosophical approach, Hutchings prefers to engage the aid of the poets. If this 'transcendental butterfly' is to be caught, it will be done with a light touch and only momentarily. So Hutchings guides us into the pursuit of self with the help of Eliot, Dickinson, Barnett Newman and WS Merwin. In the end, Hutchings defers to the theological quest, mentioned several times in his chapter, not for self as such but for the destiny of self.

Norman Young engages with the central and currently very topical but often misunderstood question: what does a it mean to believe in God as creator? Young offers four areas of implication to such belief and such a naming of God, the final emphasis falling on hope for the future and ethical action in the present.

Sandy Yule begins with a personal reminiscence of encountering Harry Wardlaw as a teacher and theological guide, before turning to address one of the burning issues confronting contemporary church life: the place of homosexual people in the church. Yule is unwilling to opt for simple answers to the complex cluster of questions that have recently emerged round this issue, but points to a balance between respect for privacy and respect for difference. Above all this chapter calls for a rediscovery of the biblical affirmation of friendship.

Nigel Watson begins his chapter with a memorable reference to what he calls Harry's 'hospitality of mind'. Watson's contribution is a study of such hospitality of mind and its opposite, tolerance and intolerance, with reference to St Paul. His conclusion, contrary to popular perception in some quarters, is that Paul offers a model of such magnanimity, reserving his intolerance only and entirely for those who refuse to show such hospitality of mind.

John O'Neill addresses the question of forgiveness: can forgiveness be exercised if the perpetrator of wrong refuses to admit the wrong-doing? Very often we hear Christians offering forgiveness, feeling they should forgive, but without any remorse on the part of the perpetrator. Such pre-emptive forgiveness is not required of Christians, O'Neill argues, though it may still be appropriate and effective to pray for wrongdoers and treat them with generosity in the hope that such treatment may be the best way to enable repentance to emerge.

As for Davis McCaughey's contribution the editor had hoped to be able to publish the sermon preached at Harry's ordination. This unfortunately has been lost, so the volume publishes here another sermon, one preached more recently. Here Davis McCaughey looks back over the past 150 years of the parish of St Andrew and St George in Edinburgh and especially at the murderous twentieth century, but more importantly, as must always be the case in either preaching or theology, forward to God's new creation.

John Kane offers a delightful tribute to Harry and Ruth's marriage and the hospitality – both of mind and of home – that characterises it. Encounters of the sort John describes are best acknowledged with gratitude as sacraments of grace.

Some words of thanks must be said in conclusion. Generous financial support for this publication was received from the journal *Sophia*, from the Uniting Church Theological College in Melbourne, from the United Faculty of Theology, and from *The Journal of Religious History*. Ian Weeks undertook to edit the volume and did most of the collecting and editing work until the final months when of necessity other priorities took over. Adrian Marshall typeset the volume and Dr Brenda Marshall read the proofs. Patrick Hutchings has been a constant guide to the project, especially in its final stages, and has raised a significant amount of money to cover the costs of publication. Finally, each of the contributors must be thanked for her or his time and effort in writing the chapter that appears under their name.

Duncan Reid
Melbourne, 2005

1

HARRY WARDLAW:
A THOUGHTFUL LIFE

Ruth Wardlaw

It is a surprise that someone who has always been excited by ideas should find the University of Melbourne alarming, even frightening.

When Harry entered its Mildura branch in 1948 intent on becoming a medical missionary, that was not yet the case. Leaving home to live in an army hut in the country and study medicine in the company of first-year science and engineering students (some of them sophisticated returned service men), was no threat. Science was interesting and he was surrounded by friends and a church congregation which took the students who had descended on the town to its heart.

Medicine was not for him though. Inevitably he gravitated to the world of ideas. His sister-in-law was studying philosphy, and that was immensely exciting. After only one year of medicine, still with the intention of serving the church, he began an arts degree and the formal study of philosophy. But here he felt he was entering hostile territory: a place where belief could be dissected and demolished. He was acutely conscious of the struggle he would have if he were to give a coherent account to himself and to others of the faith he held. The whole basis of his life could be undermined. The faith in which he had been grounded, a faith nurtured by his family, his church and his school, could be eroded. The terror of that possibility was to pervade his intellectual life, but could not loosen his engagement with philosophy. Philosophy had taken hold of him.

Throughout his life this engagement between the world of ideas and the life of faith has absorbed him: a willingness to follow an idea wherever it might lead and a passionate exploration of faith

and belief have been at the core of his personal and professional life. He could stand with Dostoevsky in saying ... 'If anyone could prove to me that Christ is outside the truth, and if the truth really did exclude Christ, I should prefer to stay with Christ and not with truth ... ' [1] But he could not allow that preference to cushion him within the church from the questions being posed by those outside it. They were his questions too.

This was a lonely position in Melbourne in the late 1950s and that no doubt explains Harry's absolute delight in Carl von Wiezsacker's Glasgow Gifford Lectures 1959–61. In those lectures Wiezsacker makes his underlying position clear.

> ... This is not a traditionalist's position. I have even found much of the Christian tradition both in thought and in life, difficult to understand and some of it impossible to follow. But if this is a possible English phrase, I have been hit by the word of Christ. In a way this word has made life impossible to me; the life I might have lived without it has been destroyed by it. In a way it has made life possible to me; I am not certain whether I would have found a possible way of life without it at all. His word means his teaching. But since this teaching refers to life, his word should be understood to include the reports we have about his life, his death and that mysterious event of which his disciples spoke as his resurrection ... [2]

A sense of vulnerability in the university millieu (which probably still makes him surprisingly uncomfortable in that setting), did not prevent Harry accepting an invitation to become a travelling secretary for the Australian Student Christian Movement after he graduated from the Ormond College Theological Hall in 1955.

He abandoned work on a Masters degree in philosophy to take up the position and it lead to his professional involvement with students from that time until his retirement in 1993 (and to us meeting on his first visit to Adelaide University). He had already had contact with the World Student Christian Federation at a conference in the Italian Alps in 1952 and the Student Christian Movement was to become an important part of his life. Later while working on a Glasgow PhD in theology he was asked by the British SCM to be senior secretary and consultant to the newly appointed

Scottish secretaries.

Harry's first attempt to begin his studies in Glasgow in 1958 had to be aborted because he succumbed to what was diagnosed at that time as a kind of encephalitis, and would probably now be described as ME. Whatever the name, the experience through his convalescence was one shared by people with chronic fatigue syndrome: a constant struggle with periods of depleted energy which have never quite gone away. That was probably the beginning of his learning to cut his coat according his cloth with regard to physical limitations. Back problems, a hyperactive thyroid, an initially undiagnosed hypoactive one which lead to him contemplating very early retirement because he seemed to be grinding to a halt in 1984, and his old and ever present enemy indigestion, all had to be lived with and worked around. They were not kicked against.

That kind of acceptance has been characteristic, not only in recognising and accepting his own limitations, but in valuing others for who they are and not for how they fit into his own expectations of them. When Ronald Gregor Smith died in 1968 Harry wrote to his widow expressing his appreciation of the contact they had had in Glasgow through Professor Smith's supervision of his thesis. He became aware from her response of how helpful it would have been to both her husband and herself to have had that kind of appreciation expressed during his lifetime. He decided then that he would try to tell some of his university teachers how they had contributed to his life. In Camo Jackson of Melbourne's Department of Philosophy, who studied with Wittgenstein in Cambridge, he recognised the challenge to make the things that he said a function of his own personal integrity. Whether in response to that challenge I am unsure, but his wholehearted acceptance of other people and his preparedness to take their ideas seriously even while not necessarily agreeing with them, together with his readiness to forgive inflicted hurt, is certainly congruent with what he sees as the central affirmation of the Christian faith: 'God was in Christ reconciling the world to himself, not counting their trespasses against them and entrusting to us the message of reconciliation'. (2 Corinthians 5:19 RSV)

Of course there have been limits to that acceptance. Where conservative politicians like Margaret Thatcher, John Howard, Peter Reith or Philip Ruddock have been unprepared to pay the price of a commitment to a humane society and the wellbeing of the less advantaged within it, they have enraged him to a level of fury even greater than that reserved for inanimate objects like a misdirected nail, a lost screw or a misbehaving computer. I have sometimes wondered whether in face to face encounters with these people he would allow himself to feel the same degree of rage he experiences when meeting them on the radio or television.

Before returning to Scotland to take up his postgraduate work in 1959, he had his first taste of theological teaching. Frank Nichol, the principal of Perth's small Presbyterian Theological Hall, who had become a close friend during Harry's visits to the West, invited him to spend some months there lecturing for him. We set off from there married and equipped with a certificate which proclaimed Harry to be a 'chap' of Oxer House and a brightly striped hood which he promised that he would wear whenever he preached in Glasgow Cathedral.

We returned to Melbourne two and a half years later with two of our three children and an almost completed thesis. Harry was responding to a call from College Church Parkville, which was then largely a student and university congregation. I was somewhat apprehensive about returning to Australia. In his thesis Harry had examined Paul Tillich's method of correlation between the questions implied in existence and the answers found in revelation. He had come to the conclusion that Tillich's method applied persistently would have led to writings more like those of Søren Kierkegaard than Tillich's own. The opportunity to discuss his work with Ronald Gregor Smith who was steeped in Kierkegaard's thought and on one occasion in Hamburg with Tillich himself (whom he was delighted to discover agreed with him that following his method meant that that there was no place for ontology within theology), contributed to the excitement and intellectual engagement which Harry enjoyed in Britain. It was good to be coming home, but I felt that all of that would contrast rather sadly with what was at that time our own anti-intellectual

and intensely secular society.

However ministering to a parish on the edge of the university, with additional responsibilities as nominal Presbyterian chaplain to the university and some lecturing in the Methodist Theological College at Queens, was stimulating enough. Just as he was getting into the swing of being a parish minister, however, a new challenge arose. One of his ministerial friends had written to him in Scotland advising him against accepting the call to College Church if as the friend assumed he would be interested in theological teaching. In a few years' time the professor of theology would retire and his friend thought that the climate of the church was such that experience in an atypical parish like this might be a disadvantage in any application Harry might make for the job. Although there were very few theological teaching positions going in Australia Harry had felt it important to respond to the call which was in front of him rather than plan a future career.

When the chair in Systematic Theology in Ormond College became vacant in 1964 Harry had been only two years in College Church and felt that to apply for the job would be unfair to the parish. Presbyteries had the right to nominate however, and when he was nominated, he decided that he would allow his name to go forward. His application was successful and at thirty-four a good deal was made of his youth and the fact that he was a home grown product. At the same time he was warned of the possibility that he might need to defend his theological position when the proposed appointment was put to the Victorian Assembly. Might the church be about to appoint an atheist to its chair of theology? There had been some concern expressed over the footnote to an article he had written. 'The proposition that God exists is so unlike any other assertion that something exists, that I would not affirm it. Neither would I deny it.' This they thought did not sound like the language of a believer.

Expectations as to what is and is not the language of faith were as frequently expressed by non-believers at that time as by those within the church. People often seemed to require that the thing they were rejecting be formulated in their own terms, or sometimes in terms of what they remembered from Sunday school. Otherwise they felt short-changed. 'You are not allowed to think that: it is not what I want to reject', seemed to be the implication. One woman attacked him at a conference of the Rationalist Society at which Harry had been invited to speak: 'And you call yourself a reverend professor? You should be ashamed of yourself!'

However it was at the same conference that another couple said to him, 'If we had known that people in the church were allowed to think like that we would not have left it'. And for many within the church there was a sense of relief in not having to bind their Christian commitment to a doctrinal structure which did not make sense to them and which was edging them out of the church. A response relayed to us after a broadcast Harry made in the early days of his appointment was that of a couple who had individually and unknown to each other been feeling very guilty about not actually being able to believe what they thought was expected of them. And the extraordinary public reaction in Melbourne to the popularising of that kind of position in Bishop Robinson's book *Honest to God*, suggests that there were a large number of people in and out of the church who could make more sense of that, than of traditional church formulae.

Harry had been charged with teaching systematic theology within the Presbyterian church. I am sorry that in one of our many moves we seem to have lost the delightful cardboard illustration of 'The Church Dogmatic' given to him by some of his students: a long low dachshund in a smart green coat attached to a set of wheels. Whatever the students intentions may have been, for me that little dog represented a joyful poking fun at a theology which was not able to explore or wander at will along unexpected pathways. Certainly Harry was never going to produce his own version of Karl Barth's *Church Dogmatic*. Even the title Professor of *Systematic* Theology was a puzzle and he was not sorry to relinquish it at the time of union, when the Uniting Church found that it had both a Presbyterian and a Methodist one of those. He was able to choose a more congenial one: Professor of Philosophical Theology.

So what was he was hoping to do in his teaching? Over the years the character of the student body changed. At first it consisted of young men training for the ministry, then women as well and older students embarking on a career change. Then came those in

secular employment or retirement who wanted to develop their understanding of the faith. His approach remained essentially the same.

For Harry the mystery of God has always been central in giving expression to any formulation of the faith, and for him the most meaningful invocation of the Trinity is expressed in terms of the Divine Mystery, the Divine Word and the Divine Presence. But he was not primarily interested in engaging students in debates on the doctrines of the church. It is his conviction that the Christian life involves immersion in the truths of the Gospel and that the purpose of theology is to enter imaginatively into those truths so that the faith and the preaching of the church can be illuminated and enriched. (Another teacher to whom he has expressed thanks is Davis McCaughey whom he credits with having first made him aware as a student of the imaginative riches of the New Testament.) He hoped to draw students into that and into an excitement in thinking through the faith, in developing an interest in apologetics, in the interaction of theology and the culture of our society, in its relationship with science and with the history of ideas.

For someone steeped in ecumenism, the formation of the Uniting Church in 1977 was a great landmark. Even more exciting to him

(perhaps partly because less painful in its inception), was the earlier coming together of Jesuits, Anglicans, Methodists, Congregationalists and Presbyterians to teach theology in Melbourne's United Faculty of Theology.

When Harry arrived in the Ormond Theological Hall in 1964 his good friends John O'Neill and George Yule, sadly both now deceased, were already teaching there. Norman Young had just been given the chair in Queens and the following year Robert Anderson and Nigel Watson were appointed to the chairs of Old and New Testament. It seemed that theological education was at last being flooded with young men. These exciting appointments were a cause for rejoicing, not least for Harry because of the rich friendships which ensued. He observed to me however that if they all stayed on until retirement the church would have a lot of old men in its teaching positions. And he resolved that if it did turn out that way he would have to look for another job.

Of course he never did that. When I once reminded him of this remark, he said that he thought that the formation of the United Faculty in 1969 had made a significant difference to the picture in introducing a variety of different teachers on to the scene. He also thought that his move away from teaching theology, so that in later years he was largely teaching philosophy, was a healthy one. My own view is, that it is a pity that as a consequence he had so little interaction during those years with the majority of men and women who were to be taking up ministry in the church. He has never related easily to people he does not know, and many students had little opportunity to engage with him as they developed their understanding of the church and their vocation within it.

Stimulating encounters and friendships developed overseas with other scholars and theologians made study leaves in Basel, New Haven and Oxford, and in particular an exciting academic year in 1972 when Harry lectured in the Department of Religion at McMaster University in Ontario and in Dunedin's Knox College, high points of our lives. Harry was always keen that students too should experience at firsthand, contact with people from outside Australia who could expand their theological horizons. He invariably returned from study leave with a plan to bring out some scholar whom he believed would make a useful contribution to the Australian scene.

The opportunity to contribute to the United Faculty's evening teaching program was something he took up with alacrity; convinced that the theological education of the laity and the wider community was important, both because of the laity's vital place within the church and in enhancing ongoing communication between the church and the secular world. And it was important for that education to happen in an independent academic faculty protected from the danger of simply becoming a department of a church. There was value too he thought in having it happen in an institution which had links to the university but was not dependent on university funding and consequently not subject to the restrictions which have been so destructive in other areas of the humanities.

Perhaps it is inevitable that many who grew up in one of the reformed church streams which came together in the Uniting Church have lingering, though guilty, regrets over the loss of some aspect of their own tradition. For Harry, attached though he is to his Presbyterian heritage, it is the Congregational contribution to union which he believes has been undervalued within our church. His suspicion of

any manifestation of power which he finds essentially inimical to the Christian gospel may be what convinces him of the importance of local autonomy for congregations who are, in Calvin's terms, 'faithfully preaching the word and faithfully administering the sacraments'. While appeal to some central authority would necessarily have to go alongside it, that would be his dream for the church: with social service, socal justice functions etc. largely tackled ecumenically.

Of course even someone who is suspicious of bureaucracy and as absent-minded and unsystematic as Harry, has not been able to escape the courts and the committees of the church altogether. While he was chairman of the national assembly's doctrine commission from 1980–86, issues surrounding baptism were in the foreground of its deliberations and discussion was vigorous. There are few questions of doctrine about which he is more passionate but I imagine that in that setting he was able to keep his cool. Not so when we were taking communion for the first time in a congregation where we would be members for more than twenty-five years. Harry had long advocated that children should be offered communion as a consequence of having been accepted into the church at baptism, and we had come from a congregation where that was practised. That was not yet the case in 1976 in our new congregation. Our three children were clearly shocked when they were passed over in the distribution of the elements and the look of paternal rage on their father's face did not go unnoticed by the elder involved. Rather shaken he came to us after the service to ask whether he had done something wrong.

While direct theological input was obviously important in places like the doctrine commission or the church hymn book committee, Harry has never looked to theology as a basis for decision making. Where a committee has been deliberating on questions of social justice or ethics, he has only been prepared to work on a theological framework in order for it to throw light on the *character* of any decision to be made, not for it to be brought to bear directly on the decision itself. The hard work of making decisions which were in character still had to be done.

When Davis McCaughey spoke at an occasion to mark the Anderson, Watson and Wardlaw retirements from theological teaching

he made reference to the fact that Harry's question was so often *the next* question. It seems to me that that contains the essence of what Harry has been about: asking the questions that others have not asked, questioning the assumptions that others have made and forseeing things that the rest of us have not yet thought about. So I suppose that it is appropriate to finish this little biographical picture by looking at what the questions are for him now. A perceptive comment made on the same occasion by his friend and colleague Graeme Griffin has some bearing on that I think. Graeme spoke of Harry's capacity for deep listening.

I do not know what questions might have been addressed over the lunches in Carlton with Ian Weeks and other friends which have sustained and delighted Harry through the years of his retirement. However I do know that at a recent workshop designed to prepare study material for older church members, he said that as an old man one is inclined to want to hold on to the things of the past, so it is important to be asking oneself which things really *are* essential to our church and our culture and how can we retain them and pass them on? And which things can we actually discard? Not new issues of course. For some time people have been expressing the fear that the church might not survive. In the 1970s Harry felt the impact of concerns about the survival of our culture as a whole. He was almost overwhelmed by the terrifying possibility of the world itself coming to an end through environmental carelessness.

Questions thrown up by fear however are rather different in character from the questions Harry is asking now. Nor are they quite the same as those which arose out of what Harry always found an extraordinarily powerful challenge: the response of Nietzsche's madman to mocking unbelievers in a world that had discovered science, slipped its moorings and denied God. '...What did we do when we loosened this earth from its sun? Whither does it now move? Whither do we move? Do we not dash on unceasingly?...' Followed by the challenge to the church goers of that world '...What are these churches now if they are not the tombs and monuments of God?...'[3] While we still have to grapple with aspects of that tirade we seem at present to be living in a world which is often looking for ways in which it can rediscover God.

As he tries to come to grips with today's questions Harry is clearly determined to focus on the source of our heritage and the things which give it life. However his ability to recognise what is going on beneath the surface, that capacity of his for deep listening, both to people and to our culture, will I think stand him in good stead as he reaches into the mysteries of our faith and draws out inspiration for the present.

He will not write anything of course. I have tried to persuade him in the past to write about some of the themes where he seems to have important things to say; about evil, about retribution, about judgement, about reconciliation, all without success. Even to see some of those old children's sermons of his written down would be good. At least these days though when he is asked to give someone a copy of a sermon he has preached he is prepared to do it without altering it too much.

End Notes

1. *Letters of Fyodor Michailovitch Dostoevsky to his Family and Friends*, translated Ethel Colburn Mayne (Peter Owen Ltd 1962), 71.
2. *The Relevance of Science, Creation and Cosmology*, CF von Weizsacker (Collins, London, 1964), 77.
3. *Joyful Wisdom*, Friedrich Nietzsche (Ungar Publishing Co, New York, 1979), 168, 125.

2

CRITERIA FOR THE APPELLATION 'CHRISTIAN'

JOHN HOWES

In his contribution to *The Way We See Things Now* (1993), Harry Wardlaw has these sentences:

> If Christian existence is determined by the relationship in which the believer stands to Jesus Christ and to the Christian community, then it would seem that one might be a Christian even though one's expressions and affirmations of belief did not fall within the bounds of Christian orthodoxy. Unitarian theology may not represent an acceptable way of expounding the Christian faith but one may be a committed member of the community of faith while holding unitarian beliefs.[1]

I note first that although the writing is tentative, 'might' is followed by 'may'; and secondly that the words 'believer' and 'belief' are prominent – and rightly, for if someone said 'I am a Christian, but I hold no Christian beliefs', that would be self-contradictory. However, I begin from these sentences because they necessitate the question I want to discuss: 'What set of criteria may reasonably be used by people who wonder whether to apply to themselves or to others, or to some principle or teaching, the appellation "Christian"?' I use 'appellation' to cover both the noun and the adjective.

Part of the interest of the question for me lies in the fact that it comes up in relation to two Oxford philosophers to whom I owe much, TH Green and RM Hare; but it is also a personal question for me, in that I did think of myself as a Christian until 1971, when I was in my mid-thirties, but have not done so since. I have continued to study a broad range of Christian literature and have advocated and arranged what I call Millian discussion, in which Christians and non-Christians, whether holding any religious beliefs or not, can join in shared exploration. How seldom such discussion has been fostered, or has occurred.

One way in which John Stuart Mill himself (in one place) uses the appellation we may immediately reject. In *On Liberty*, he says of the Roman emperor Marcus Aurelius that though by persecuting Christianity he showed how grievously a high-minded person can err, he was himself 'a better Christian in all but the dogmatic sense of the word than almost any of the ostensibly Christian sovereigns who have since reigned'.[2] The word 'Christian' should not be used as an equivalent for 'person characterised by virtues that Christianity has often emphasised', for many people who would, rightly, not want to be called Christian have been so characterised.

This paper has four sections. In the first I propose a set of three criteria as jointly necessary and sufficient; in the second and third I defend it against the views, so different from one another, that it is insufficient and that one or two of the criteria are unnecessary; finally I explain briefly why, given this set of criteria, my present 'position' (perhaps a misleading word?) is not Christian.

I

Writing a few years after Green's death in 1882, his pupil, colleague and biographer RL Nettleship said this:

> To the question . . .. Was he a christian? the answer must depend on what 'to be a christian' means. If it means to believe that every man has God in him, that religion is the continual death of a lower and coming to life of a higher self, and that those truths were more vividly realised in thought and life by Jesus of Nazareth and some of his followers than by any other known men, then without doubt he was a christian. If it means to believe that the above truths depend upon the fact that Jesus was born and died under conditions impossible to other human beings, then equally without doubt he was not a christian.[3]

The set of criteria I propose has some similarity to that in Nettleship's 'Jesus of Nazareth' sentence.

There is one passage above all in the synoptic gospels, namely Mark 12.28–34, which, with its vividness and its portrait of Jesus as endorsing and giving preeminence to basic themes in the Hebrew scriptures, deserves attention if we are asking 'What did Jesus teach?' As a young student and preacher, I delighted in it partly because of its combining of heart and mind (or understanding) and strength. Jesus, asked which is the most important of all the commandments, combines two: love the one God, and love your neighbour as yourself. The (young?) scribe enthusiastically agrees: God is one, and to love him and to love one's neighbour as oneself, 'is much more than all burnt offerings and sacrifices'. Mark adds that Jesus, seeing that 'he answered wisely', said 'You are not far from the kingdom of God'.[4] (That last phrase is also typical of Jesus's teaching, and we shall return to it in the final section.)

The very wide range of common ground between Judaism and Christianity becomes apparent if one takes, as I propose we do, as the first two necessary criteria for being a Christian (i) faith (ie, both belief and trust) in one God as uniquely worthy of the love expressed in worship and service, and (ii) commitment to the love of one's neighbour. Since, however, Judaism and Christianity are far from identical, we have to differentiate them. Harry Wardlaw's colleague Robert Anderson offers a way of doing so in a memorable companion essay in which he stresses how embedded Christianity is in the Hebrew scriptures. He mentions 'Professor Dietrich Ritschl's incisive question: Did Jesus emerge or was he sent?', says that he has to take the first of those alternatives, that only so can 'the last vestiges of a Christocentrism that forces upon the Hebrew Scriptures an extraneous figure' be abandoned, and that

> To see Jesus as one who emerges from the Jewish people and one through whom, in the course of time, the knowledge and redemption of the God of Israel are made known to Gentiles is, in fact, descriptive of what did happen.[5]

I should prefer to modify that wording as follows: one describes what in fact happened by saying that through Jesus, who emerges from the Jewish people, and in the course of time through his followers, the possibility of faith in the God of Israel as universal Redeemer is communicated to Gentiles. When we read in the prophets of what is called knowing God, the relevant distinction is not between knowledge and belief but between faithful acknowledgement and the neglect that issues in disobedience;[6] we had better avoid the juxtaposing of objective and subjective 'genitives' in 'the knowledge and redemption of the God of Israel'; and what is communicated included, if we are to give a neutral description of 'what did happen', the availability of a faith in the God in whom Israel trusted.

Much else was communicated, however, in the early Christian preaching to Gentiles, most of it concerning the status of the one who came to be called Christ or Jesus Christ even more than he was called Jesus, and much of it as regrettable to Robert Anderson as to Geza Vermes, the adherent of Liberal Judaism who has written so extensively about Jesus.[7] Nevertheless, to be a Christian is certainly to give to Jesus a special prominence. One may not go so far as to speak, with the General Thanksgiving, of 'thine inestimable love in the redemption of the world by our Lord Jesus Christ'; but one's interpretation of why and how one should love God and love one's neighbour must have been shaped by words and/or deeds of Jesus, and/or by the person of Jesus as one conceives of him, whether or not one calls him Christ or Lord. One must, in short, at least regard Jesus as the supreme exponent and/or exemplar of the great commandments and, at least in that respect, seek to follow him. There is my third criterion, which I have related to the first two. I note that Nettleship's sentence has the wording 'Jesus of Nazareth and his early followers', and I suggest that it is important to say 'and' rather than 'or'.

II

Where, among the many varieties of Christianity in which these three criteria would be regarded as insufficient for the application of 'Christian', is one to turn? Both Harry Wardlaw and I have been much influenced by the Student Christian Movement, that of Great Britain and Ireland as well as that of Australia, and it was in our youth a notable expression of all three of ecumenism, engagement with the life of the university and with national and international needs, and the attempt to expound intelligibly, for students, a liberal-minded faith that was both ecumenical and thus engaged. So I turn to two examples of a genre that has attracted me since I was a student, that of published series of such expositions given in universities. Both are from the Cambridge of the 1940s.

In 1947 Alec Vidler, an Anglican priest, gave addresses there in a mission entitled 'Christian Faith and Practice'. SCM Press published them that year under the title *Good News for Mankind*. They have the special interest for many who may read this paper that he thanks Davis McCaughey, then Associate Study Secretary of the SCM of Britain and Ireland, for reading his original drafts and for comments and encouragement. At the opening meeting he said, in words that contrast with Anderson's:

> a mission that is entitled 'Christian Faith and Practice' speaks
> pretty obviously of the belief that Christ was *sent* into the world
> to be the Head and Deliverer of mankind.

Having said in his first lecture 'I am talking about what the Christians in the main historic tradition believe', he summarises the second half of his third lecture thus:

> Christ the ground and bond of human unity, Christ the
> promulgator of a universal Law of Righteousness, Christ
> who clothes man the sinner with forgiveness and His own
> Righteousness, Christ the centre and consummation of the
> history of our race – this is what Christ can do for our world
> as men will open the door and let him in.[8]

Consider a man, A, who replies 'No wonder that, in so christocentric a statement, you do not use the name 'Jesus' at all: the Jesus of the Synoptic gospels talks in very different terms, talks constantly of his Father and of the Kingdom of God (or the Kingdom of Heaven); and it is that teaching and Jesus's self-devotion in relation to it that move me to want to follow him today, and to call myself a Christian.' It may be truly responded by B that the Pauline and Johannine writings have been more influential 'in the main historic tradition' than the Synoptics; but would B be justified in denying to A the appellation 'Christian'?

Jesus has for A a unique prominence as teacher and example, particularly perhaps in the inclusiveness with which he talks of God and of one's neighbour and in his growing willingness to challenge barriers put up by the Judaism of his day. (Vermes is less ready to emphasise that tradition concerning Jesus than is Joseph Klausner.[9]) It seems to me that if A fulfils all three of the criteria I have suggested, he should count as a Christian.

The other speaker, JS Whale, a Congregationalist, gave a series of eight open lectures at Cambridge in 1940. He too is Christocentric:

> Not only to the earliest Christians of whom we have any knowledge, but to all Christians, Christ has always been the object of faith rather than an example of faith. Here is One to believe in whom is to believe in God; to worship God is to worship Christ.[10]

A's reply is again appropriate; but we may add that the depth of acquaintance that some Christians have had, especially in recent years, with exponents of Judaism and Islam has led them to be uneasy about Christocentrism and, perhaps quietly, to abandon it. More and more, for them, Jesus himself becomes the supreme exponent, in his teaching and his life, of a radical faith in God who is worshipped also by Jews and by Muslims; but they do not think of themselves as ceasing to be Christians.

Whale has another criterion:

> Certain it is that for St Paul, and for New Testament Christianity, to be a Christian is to be a member of a living organism whose life derives from Christ. There is no other way of being a Christian. In this sense, Christian experience is always ecclesiastical experience .... In short, the Christian life is not accidentally but necessarily corporate, always and everywhere.[11]

It is one thing to hold that, at least under normal circumstances, a Christian is seriously defective if he or she has declined to be baptised or does not meet with other Christians; it is quite another to hold that he or she is not a Christian at all in the absence of baptism or of some kind of affiliation with a Christian community. Suppose that a woman named Jan, convinced that it is wrong for her to stand with others to say the Nicene Creed, does not belong to any community that calls itself Christian, but seeks to be a caring friend to many, reading the synoptic gospels and finding her primary inspiration in Jesus's example. Jan meets, let us say, the three criteria I have proposed. Is it not a failure of perspective in determining what matters most to say that she is not a Christian at all unless she is a member of an association that calls itself Christian?

I conclude that, though there are many Christians who would ask far more of people who called themselves Christians than that they met the three criteria, and many who would even insist on more for the appellation itself, the combination of the three necessary conditions I have specified is sufficient. My appeal has been to a sense of perspective, one that would, for example, lead someone to say 'Whatever view anyone, including myself, may take of Jan's set of beliefs, it is unreasonable to say that she is not a Christian.'

III

Our question now is whether our set of three criteria is too restrictive. Here I shall be particularly concerned with RB Braithwaite's Eddington lecture, 'An Empiricist's View of the Nature of Religious Belief', published by Cambridge in 1955 (but I shall refer to pages in John Hick's collection *The Existence of God* (Macmillan, New York, c1964)), and RM Hare's Wilde Lectures 'The Simple Believer', published in a revised form in his *Essays on Religion and Education* (Oxford, 1992).[12]

Summaries cannot do justice to these lectures, which deserve to be studied in full by anyone concerned to evaluate what I say about them. The lecturers have three things in common, one positive and two negative. Each sees the primary characteristic of being a Christian as having as one's basic 'policy' for behaviour towards others the kind of love towards them that in the New Testament is called *agapé*, so that each is in agreement with my second criterion; the only other criterion clearly offered as such is, to use Braithwaite's word at page

250, the 'entertainment' (the regular contemplation) of some or other Christian 'stories', ie, doctrines or parables or exemplifications of the Christian tradition that are illustrative of that love. Neither uses my first or my third criterion. Neither, in spite of their titles, has much to say about belief. The relation between the two may be summarised thus: Braithwaite is influenced by the moral philosophy of Hare (see pp 237, 251), and Hare says of Braithwaite's lecture that it is 'by far the best thing on this subject [ie, religion considered with reference to morality] that [he has] ever heard or read' (p 16), but also attends, very interestingly, to some aspects of the Christian tradition which he himself greatly values, and accordingly finds Braithwaite's account incomplete (pp 15 and 23).

Braithwaite, unlike Hare, mentions some New Testament texts and passages (pp 239–243); but he explores no Christian discussion of them. He attends only to Matthew Arnold in relation to 'the Anselmian doctrine of the Atonement' (p 245). This minimal attention to Christian writers not only means that there is almost no Millian discussion in these writings, but also partly explains that lack of support for Braithwaite's lecture which Hare calls 'distressing' (p 16), and the lack of attention to his own lectures. The rest of the explanation, indeed, lies in the paucity of real interest on the part of most theologians in studying what is going on in contemporary philosophy: the two activities generally go on with lamentably little close or personal contact.

The two sentences that are central in Braithwaite's account of his position are these:

> A man is not, I think, a professing Christian unless he both proposes to live according to Christian moral principles and associates his intention with thinking of Christian stories; but he need not believe that the empirical propositions presented by the stories correspond to empirical fact.... A moral belief is an intention to behave in a certain way: a religious belief is an intention to behave in a certain way (a moral belief) together with the entertainment of certain stories associated with the intention in the mind of the believer.
>
> (pp 246, 250)

The fundamental objection to that does not depend on one's having any religious belief at all: it is that no belief is an intention, though intentions are often based on beliefs. I may say that I believe the proposition that p, or some statement that p, or that I believe A (some person), or believe in A, or believe in X (eg some remedy). In the first two cases I mean (if I am using normal English and not engaging in unwise philosophical stretching) that I regard the proposition or statement concerned as true, but not as one that I know to be true, if to say 'know' implies, as it often does, that there is no room at all for doubt about what may be called the fact that p. In the third I mean that I believe that what A has affirmed is true. In the last two I mean that I put my trust in A or in X.[13] (That analysis, especially in its last three respects, does not take us very far from one that accounts for the various uses of 'pisteuein' in the New Testament.[14]) Instead of using 'believe', in the first two cases, we can use locutions including the noun 'belief' in its 'subjective' sense, as when we say 'I am of the belief that . . .' or 'I maintain the belief that . . .'; in the other three uses the nouns 'trust' or 'faith' would normally be preferred. 'Belief' is also used in the 'objective' sense, as an equivalent for 'proposition believed'.

Braithwaite uses or mentions the nouns 'trust' and 'faith' not at all. He often uses the phrase 'religious conviction' (pp 236, 239, 243, 249f), but leaves it unexamined, while actually saying that 'it is the intention to behave which constitutes what is known as religious conviction' (p 239). His lecture is far from being the 'empirical enquiry' said on page 236 to be required, which would have to include a study of what Christians, or other theists, say they mean when they talk about belief, or believing, in God (or in the one most Christians are willing to call Jesus Christ), or about their conviction or convictions. There is no study of any Christian text that gives a prominent place to belief, conviction, faith or trust. The lecture might better have been called 'An empiricist's replacement for religious belief'.[15]

How might Braithwaite respond? In two main ways, I think. First, he might well explain the transition to which I have objected, from talk of beliefs to talk of intentions, by referring to these remarks on page 236, which are crucial to any explanation of how he has reached his position, and in which he shows his acceptance of a revision of the earlier verificationist principle:

> The meaning of any statement, then, will be taken as being given by the way it is used. The kernel for an empiricist of the problem of the nature of religious belief is to explain, in empirical terms, how a religious statement is used by a man who asserts it in order to express his religious conviction . . . . I shall argue that the primary element in this use is that the religious assertion is used as a moral assertion.

Hence he says on page 239 that 'the intention of a Christian to follow a Christian way of life . . . is the criterion for the meaningfulness of his assertions'. But he does not provide a range of typical examples of Christian assertions and explore how Christians themselves use them or what they say about what they mean. It is as though he is content to ask himself 'How are these assertions used by those of us who are both complete empiricists and inclined to value, even to interpret, Christian statements and practices in terms of the behaviour they foster in ourselves and others?'

Two assertions that are central to orthodox Christianity and also bring out its close relation to Judaism are in the opening of the letter to the Hebrews: 'In many and various ways God spoke of old to our fathers by the prophets; but in these last days he has spoken to us by a Son' (1.1f). Two more propositions are implied to be true and linked with the verb *pisteuein* at 11.6: 'whoever would draw near to God must believe that he exists and that he rewards those who seek him'. (I have used the RSV, but would be happy to replace 'he exists' by 'he is' or 'there is God'.) We have here four propositions about God, and their acceptance has been regarded as underlying, and crucial to the motivation of, intentions to behave in certain ways. The use by Paul of *oun* or *hōste* with the meaning of our 'therefore' in a transition from assertions about God to a call to a certain kind of behaviour brings out the fact that a body of beliefs typically underlies a set of intentions but the latter do not express the meaning of the former.[16] The latter may be expressed in the form of self-directed imperatives; the former have to be stated in the indicative. But Braithwaite goes so far as to say that a Christian's assertion that God is love has to be taken as a declaration of intention (p 240), in a passage which fails to recognise the frequent place of gratitude, reverence ('the fear of God') or inspiration as, precisely, a 'connection' between what one believes and what one intends to do. (Braithwaite professes a Humean puzzlement at the connection between assertion and intention if the assertion is not itself understood as an intention.) His sudden introduction of the term 'religious principles' at page 241 obscures the fact that basic theistic assertions would not normally be called assertions of religious *principles*, for that phrase suggests that the assertions are themselves expressed in normative language, whereas they are rather presented as descriptions whose acceptance prompts such responses as gratitude.

Braithwaite's second response might be to refer to this revealing sentence on page 250:

> In disentangling the elements of this use [i.e., that of religious assertions] I have discovered nothing which can be called 'belief' in the senses of this word applicable either to an empirical or to a logically necessary proposition.

For an appropriate reply I am indebted to John Mackie's Introduction to *The Miracle of Theism*; he does not mention Braithwaite until his twelfth chapter. It is to say that the dichotomy presented here, and explained on page 231–35, leaves no room for propositions that give our answer to the question of the 'best explanation' we think we have of the universe in which we live and our life within it. Those propositions do not meet the criterion on which Braithwaite insists for scientific hypotheses, that they are accompanied by some mode of testing them that would, if they are false, show them definitively to be so. It is the combination of experience (broader or narrower) of, and thought (more or less consistent) about, the whole range of their 'world' that leads people to maintain, question, adopt or abandon particular religious or non-religious interpretations of that world, and not such supposedly decisive tests as that, mentioned by Braithwaite on page 232f, proposed by Elijah in his contest with the prophets of Baal.[17] Hence we do well to question the use of 'empirical' before 'propositions' and 'fact' in the passage I quoted from page 246.

Another reply is to note, as above, that 'belief' is not applied to propositions alone but to dispositions to assent to propositions and also to such dispositions as faith and trust. In this sense, even if a religious belief is a disposition to assent to an unfalsifiable proposition, perhaps with little to be said for it and much against, it is a belief, and it may be one that is distinctive of a particular group and even definitory for it.

Alasdair MacIntyre has given this criticism, in which the verb 'believe' deserves emphasis, of Braithwaite's approach:

> Braithwaite's way of giving a sense to religious utterances distracts us from the question, What sense do these utterances have for those who make them? And because Braithwaite deprives us of this question, he makes it unintelligible that anyone should cease to believe, on the grounds that he can no longer find a sense in such utterances.[18]

Braithwaite's lecture, however, shows that he does not use the word 'sense' but wants to explain what he takes to be 'the typical meaning of the body of Christian assertions', which he says is 'given by their proclaiming intentions to follow an agapeistic way of life' (p 241). I should prefer to express MacIntyre's question with 'How are religious utterances used by those who express their beliefs thereby?' and to invite attention to the fundamental activity of *worship*, and to replace the words beginning 'on the grounds' by the broader 'because he no longer considers the religious beliefs he has previously had to be reasonable'. One remarkable feature of Braithwaite's lecture, and this is also a feature of Hare's lectures, is that there seems to be no recognition of the fact that much of what is said in Christian worship expresses a 'world-view' so different from the person who sees things as they do that one would expect them to decline to take part in such worship. We shall find it of great interest to seek to discover why Hare did not.

What he adds to Braithwaite's lecture is of three main kinds. First, with approving reference to an article by JC Thornton of Canterbury, New Zealand, he warns against the 'palpably circular argument' whereby people assume the truth of the proposition up for discussion, 'that the traditional interpretation of Christian belief is the only admissible one', and conclude that Braithwaite must therefore be wrong.[19] Secondly, he shows how he thinks Braithwaite's position needs to be extended so as to cover more of what he thinks to be valuable aspects of Christianity. Thirdly, he warns that one cannot combine all three of philosophy, science and what he calls superstition.

I begin from what is on his first page:

> ...the problems with which I shall be dealing...have been generated...by the quite genuine perplexities of those who want to call themselves Christians, or at least theists, and yet cannot bring themselves to believe what theists are supposed to have to believe.

Nowhere else in the lectures does Hare use the word 'theist' or 'theism', and Braithwaite uses the latter term only and just once (p 242); both use 'Christian' frequently, and it is evident (especially on pp 15 and 34f) that Hare, like Braithwaite, does wish to call himself a Christian. On page 25 he points to Mackie's book as one that goes over much-trodden ground to explain why 'an educated man has to abandon superstition, ie the belief in the supernatural'. Yet Mackie, in his valuable Introduction, takes theism to be a doctrine not meaningless (for he rejects the 'strongly verificationist theory of meaning') but, as we have noted, offering an answer to the proper question of how we may best explain our experience as a whole, an answer, however, to which he considers that there are objections so insuperable that it is indeed a 'miracle' – the ironic use of the word is Hume's – that a person otherwise reasonable can be a theist. But Hare does not raise the questions with which Mackie's book begins, ie, what theism is, nor discuss whether being a Christian entails that one is any kind of theist.

He does not even acknowledge the great difficulty, recognised by Thornton, of reaching a reasonable decision on what deserves to count as, to use the latter's words, an 'interpretation of Christian belief' that is 'admissible'. Thornton, for example, is strongly inclined to the view that Christianity is distinguished by a 'logical dependence of specifically religious beliefs on certain historical beliefs', and therefore that 'any analysis of Christianity which obscures or denies this dependence will be, in that respect, misleading and perhaps incipiently reductionist'.[20] The general nature of which that move is an example is to recognise that one cannot justly give to one's position a certain appellation simply because one values some aspects of the tradition or traditions to which the appellation has hitherto primarily belonged. Our question about sufficient and necessary conditions is a difficult, even a painful, question.

On page 16–18 Hare suggests that, after the word 'Christian', 'way of life' might represent Braithwaite's view more fairly than 'moral principles' (in fact Braithwaite uses the phrase 'commitment to a way of life' on p 239), quotes his remark about change in one's wants and not only in one's conduct (p 243), and adds:

> It may be that not only our moral attitudes, but all our desires, aspirations, and ideals should be included in that total attitude to life which Braithwaite wants to call religious belief.

Then, from the point where he says that 'the Christian . . . as he must . . . believes that it is not futile to act in pursuit of these aspirations etc' (p 19), he begins to use the word 'faith' a great deal (pp 19–23). There is faith that people will respond in surprisingly positive ways if one behaves 'in a Christian way' towards them; the faith the scientist has that there are laws to be discovered, even after repeated failures to find them (cf p 13f); and a more general faith that one's endeavours, especially to love one's neighbours and to discover adequate moral policies, are not pointless.

On page 22f Hare appears much closer than Braithwaite to traditional theism:

> What I am saying is that, granted that the good man wishes above all to realise the ends of morality – moral ideals – he can hardly pursue this object unless he has faith in the possibility, as things are, of realising them. That is why faith and hope are virtues as well as charity. And I must confess that faith in the divine providence has always seemed to me to be one of the central features of the Christian religion, and one to which it is possible to cling even when much else is in doubt. This faith that all shall be well is matched by a feeling of thankfulness that all is well.

I suspect that Hare included in his thought there an awareness of his early twenties spent as a prisoner-of-war in a Japanese camp. His next sentence shows the extent of his dissatisfaction with

Braithwaite's exposition:

> So, then, I want to say that religion cannot be reduced to morality even in an extended sense, unless we include also the faith in something that saves moral endeavour from futility.

At page 33 he actually says:

> ...I do believe in divine providence....I believe, that is to say, that matters are so ordered in the world that there is a point in trying to live by the precepts to which Christians subscribe.

On page 26, however, he has presented a question he regards as crucial and realised that it might seem to involve him in an inconsistency. In the earlier lecture (p 11f) he had emphasised that there was much in even the Simple Believer that he admired:

> There seemed to me to be something about his faith that put me to shame – something whose loss would make the world a worse place. And in so far as I had a little (though perhaps only a little) of this something myself, I wanted to strengthen it rather than destroy it....Anyone who knows any people of the type I am describing will know what I mean.

There he goes on: 'I was trying...to find out what it was about his faith that really made him different – and believe me it did make him different – from other men.' If he found that out he would if possible imitate it.

Hare's mention on page 27 of Ernest Gordon's *Miracle on the River Kwai* (1963) suggests that what he has in mind is the kind of heroism, self-sacrificing care for their fellows, and refusal to despair which some Christians showed in such situations as being a prisoner-of-war without any of the orderly life that even the camp at Changi had provided.

On page 26 he writes:

> I know I said earlier that the Believer's faith made him different from other men. But the point is, Was it faith in the supernatural that made him different, or was it a faith

that could be had by somebody who did not believe in the supernatural? That really is the crux of our whole problem.

Hare acknowledges that the Believer was impressively different, says that he believes in divine providence, would prefer to call himself a Christian or at least a theist, and does not want to 'embrac[e] ... a morality without visible means of support' (p 34). He would know that Plato's Socrates (in *Apology* 27b–28a, in seeking to show that Meletus is inconsistent and without saying what he himself believes) scorns the idea that one might consistently believe in *daimonia* (spiritual things?) without believing in *daimones* (spirits?) or *theia* (divine things) and even *theoi* (gods). He needed to do more in the latter part of his second lecture than to reject belief in anything supernatural by briskly dividing that category (p 23f) into the contranatural and the transcendental (in the latter, talk of God involves no actual belief that an atheist would reject), and thereby suggesting that belief in God needed no further consideration, even by someone who might wish to call himself a theist. Though clearly and movingly showing us much that he valued, Hare did not succeed in this pair of lectures in presenting a sufficiently consistent and argued position. Even though he has sought to include more than did Braithwaite, he has, like Braithwaite, allowed his paramount concern with moral principles to loom so large that he has given an unreasonably narrow view of the criteria for being a Christian.

One might study by contrast HH Price's last chapter in his book *Belief* (1969). Price is content there to discuss what he calls Theism. He draws attention to the 'devotional practices' which he regards as criterial for being a religious or 'spiritual' person, and says of them that they 'have no direct connection with the acquisition of moral virtues'. Those virtues are necessary for the development of what he calls 'latent spiritual capacities', but are not sufficient. He goes so far as to say that the existence of the kind of person who has so developed his spiritual capacities as to be characterised by 'a certain serenity and inward peace', and a 'love of his neighbours for their own sake' that is intimately related to his belief 'that there is a God who created the universe, and that he loves each one of us', is 'in practice the most persuasive argument in favour of a religious world-outlook.'[21]

His own version of an empiricist approach to religion leads him to hold that the person who wonders whether there is anything in it should see whether some devotional practices do develop his latent spiritual capacities.[22] There is, I think, a tendency here, to which I have a Kantian aversion, to put too much emphasis on the occurrence of certain special experiences; but it cannot be denied that Price is much closer than Braithwaite or Hare to an accurate analysis of what theists are 'on about' when they talk of loving God and loving our neighbour as ourselves.

IV

Like Braithwaite and Hare, and Price, and Kant, I am impressed by the emphasis there has so often been within Christianity upon the self-giving love of one's neighbour, whoever he or she may be, for his or her own sake. On the other hand I want to stress, as they too would, the possibility of that love as something that can and does occur independently of any particular religion; and to take seriously the fact that Christians' versions of Christianity, and especially the stress on the supposed wrongness of not having certain theological beliefs, have often led them to bitter and loveless divisions between themselves and other Christians, or themselves and non-Christians, and to exclusiveness and persecution. I would emphasise the cooperative nature that so often belongs to the best kind of love, and would interpret one of Kant's remarks with reference to cooperation: 'For the ends of a subject who is an end in himself must, if this conception is to have its full effect in me, be also, as far as possible, my ends.'[23]

The reasons why I do not call myself a Christian relate to the other two criteria I have proposed. I cannot simply answer 'Yes' to the question whether I believe in God. Until 1997 I had (for twenty-six years) thought of myself as a theist of a Kantian kind. In that year, as I read and thought more about a Darwinian evolutionary conception of human and other life than I had done before, I began to recognise that I was on a spectrum between theism and agnosticism, sometimes more inclined to the one and sometimes to the other. I remain eager to study theism, but in a Millian spirit that leads one to attend to and weigh opposing arguments and considerations. (A good example of such study, of Christianity as well as theism, is Ronald W Hepburn's *Christianity and Paradox*.[24]) One major objection is that belief in God is incompatible with an unblinkered contemplation of extreme and extensive suffering, and of what mortality involves. A major difficulty is what the word 'God' is to mean, and what sense one can make of the view of the universe or universes that is expressed in the lines

> How great a being, Lord, is Thine,
> Which doth all beings keep![25]

Moreover, it seems to me that theism is committed to the conditional statement 'If there is God, then there is some kind of immortality for human beings', and, though I do not reject it, it is difficult to believe the second proposition.

I presented the third criterion in minimalist terms at the end of Section 1. My own view of Jesus does not meet it. My view is close to that of Klausner, who hoped that some of Jesus's vivid sayings and parables would one day be included among the treasures of Judaism.[26] I have elsewhere presented a crucial part of it in a statement which I repeat in the following sentence, and in whose support I would refer to Matthew, Mark and Luke.[27] Jesus was utterly sure that his mission was, through his own and his disciples' words and deeds, to proclaim as so imminent that it could be said to be already present a quite new state of things called 'the Kingdom of God' or 'the Kingdom of Heaven', in whose coming his own role was central and all were summoned to believe. Because that was his preoccupying vision, he offers little to people who see it to be unfounded and unfulfilled, and who look for an ethic, a world-view and even a fellowship of kinds that the Christian churches have never been able to offer. (I note the misleadingness of the capital-letter singular word 'Church'.) That ethic, that world-view, that fellowship would be such that people of diverse and often tentative beliefs were welcomed wholeheartedly into hospitable, cooperative and tolerant groups without being required, *if they are to be members*, to have (or to make it appear that they have) a particular set of beliefs. In such groups there would be the emphasis that is Kantian on a reverent respect for human beings because of their common humanity, and a readiness to study and discuss diverse beliefs and traditions.

Of orthodox Christianity I would say that the attempt (without which there is no such orthodoxy) to be both monotheistic and Trinitarian is incoherent; and that its doctrine of 'Jesus Christ' as both God and man is not only incoherent but also incompatible with the Jesus of the synoptic gospels. Hare once told me that he preferred Morning Prayer to the Eucharist, presumably because the former affirmed fewer Christian doctrines; I have to say that he underestimated the significance of the fact that he believed so little of what is affirmed or expressed in creeds, hymns and prayers in Christian services of worship.

As I said in the introduction, it seems to me to show a serious lack of respect towards people of other religious adherence or of none to apply to anyone the appellation 'Christian' merely because of the presence in him or her of virtues (including the love of one's neighbour) which Christianity has traditionally stressed. Nor does it make a sufficient difference to the situation if one adds that one's moral policies should be accompanied by the entertainment of Christian 'stories' of various kinds without any affirmative beliefs about God or about the significance of Jesus, traditionally called Christ. Moreover, if one finds oneself without such beliefs, then a desire to go on calling oneself a Christian reveals an extremely understandable, but in my view regrettable, clinging to past associations (in both senses of that word), a clinging better replaced by a seeking of new non-credal bases for hospitable societies that would offer friendship, cooperation, mutual help and help to others, opportunities for ongoing study, tuition and discussion, and perhaps meditation. In that connection I will mention that concerning Learningguild, the educational and social movement, we say 'It is open to everyone who wants to go on learning and help others learn'.

End Notes

1. Page 38. The booklet, published in 1993 by the Joint Board of Christian Education, Melbourne, contains lectures given at the time of their retirement by Professors Robert Anderson, Harry Wardlaw and Nigel Watson.
2. Chapter 3, in the fourteenth of forty-four paragraphs.
3. Page 100 of the Memoir that begins *Works of Thomas Hill Green,* volume III.
4. TW Manson, in *Ethics and the Gospel* (London: SCM Press, 1960), says at 60–62 that, rather than this Markan passage, which gives 'the quintessence . . . of the Jewish Law', it is the words 'As I have loved you, you are to love one another' (John 13.34) that give us 'the differentia of Christian ethics'. Apart from noting the objection to reliance on John's Gospel, I emphasise that I am here proposing three criteria for the appellation 'Christian', not for an adequate understanding of Christian ethics, and invite attention to the third criterion. At the foot of page 61, Manson takes too restricted a view of loving one's neighbour as oneself.
5. These quotations are from 23f of the booklet (see n 1).
6. See Jeremiah 22:15f and 31:31–34, and Hosea 4:1–6. MH Cressey, in his entry at 'Knowledge' in *The New Bible Dictionary* (London: Inter-Varsity Fellowship, 1962), says 'The criterion of this knowledge is obedience, and its opposite is not simply ignorance but rebellious, wilful turning away from God'.
7. I have discussed Vermes's presentation of Jesus at some length in my editorial letter in *Learningguild Letter*, 2.2000.
8. These quotations come respectively from pages 9f, 14 and 44.
9. *Jesus of Nazareth*, the English translation of Klausner's Hebrew original, was published by Allen and Unwin in London in 1925. I discuss his view in relation to Vermes's in the letter referred to in n 7.
10. *Christian Doctrine* (Cambridge: Cambridge University Press, 1941, many times reprinted), 105f.
11. *Ibid,* 128f.
12. Substantially the same version had appeared earlier in *Religion and Morality*, edited by G Outka and J Reeder (Anchor, Doubleday, 1973).
13. The second last chapter of HH Price's *Belief* (London: Allen and Unwin, 1969) deserves attention here. It needs to be supplemented by more attention to religious faith as trust and reliance. Price gives such attention to trust on pages 9–11 and 24f of his fresh and vivid lecture 'Faith and Belief' in *Faith and the Philosophers*, edited by John Hick (London: Macmillan, 1964).
14. There is a valuable survey in KP Donfried's article 'Faith' in *The HarperCollins Bible Dictionary* (New York: HarperCollins, revised

edition 1996). See also WA Whitehouse's entry 'Faith' in *A Theological Word Book of the Bible*, edited by A Richardson (London: SCM Press, 1950), in which, in contrast with the contrasting of them by Martin Buber in *Two Types of Faith* (New York: Macmillan, 1951), he links talk of faith in the Hebrew scriptures with NT uses of *pistis* and *pisteuein*.

15. Similar points have been made by Price (see n 13), 480, and A Boyce Gibson, *Theism and Empiricism*, 34.

16. See Romans 12.1 (*oun*) and 1 Corinthians 15.58 (*hōste*). Cf Gibson, *ibid*, 35f.

17. Gibson, 35f, misunderstands the intent, in its context, of Braithwaite's question 'If there is a personal God, how would the world be different if there were not?' It would be more clearly put as 'If we are to believe in a personal God, what empirical tests are there whose results would corroborate that belief or count against it?' For a valuable discussion of 'theistic interpretations of our experience', see Ian Crombie's contribution to *New Essays in Philosophical Theology*, edited by Antony Flew and Alasdair MacIntyre (London: SCM Press, 1955), 112f.

18. 'Is understanding religion compatible with believing?', in *Faith and the Philosophers* (see no 13 above), 125.

19. Hare, page 17; Thornton's article is in *Sophia*, Melbourne, October 1966.

20. *Ibid*, 9.

21. Pages 473–75.

22. Pages 476–88. See also the lecture cited above in no 3.

23. *Groundwork* (Paton's edition, *The Moral Law*), 69.

24. Watts, London, 1958.

25. *Methodist Hymn-Book*, London 1933, 78 (the first two lines are 'How shall I sing that majesty | Which angels do admire?'). I quoted and examined this use of 'being' and 'beings' in an article called 'God, "exists" and "being"', in *Sophia*, October 1968. There are articles in the same issue, by Keith Yandell and Kai Nielsen, concerned with Braithwaite's lecture.

26. See the Conclusion (413f) of the book cited in no 9: it is preferably read in relation to the seven parts that precede it in the 'Eighth Book'.

27. Page 7 of the letter referred to in no 7.

3

FAITH, PASSION AND WITTGENSTEIN

Graeme Marshall

I

In the early sixties Harry Wardlaw and I talked a lot about the still burning questions of natural theology and philosophy and especially about how properly to understand faith and its objects. I would often attempt to turn our conversations into the kind of arguments I, and without doubt Harry, was professionally committed to but while acknowledging this he kindly passed me by on his way to the heart of the matter. One of the fruits of our discussions was my early article 'Faith and Assent'[1] written, naturally enough, in the then dominant philosophical analytic mode which exploited similarities but also echoed Kent's admonition in *King Lear* 'I'll teach you differences'.

There is nothing wrong with that, far from it, but on reflection it was altogether too seductive for a young man in the full flush of post doctoral enthusiasm. Consequently I missed the point. I missed it again in quoting John Flavel of Dartmouth whom John Baillie calls one of the best of the English Puritans:

> There be three acts of faith, *assent, acceptance,* and *assurance.* The Papists generally give the essence of saving faith to the first, viz. *assent.* The Lutherans, and some of of our own, give it to the last, viz. *assurance.* But it can be neither way so .... By saving faith Christ is said to 'dwell in our hearts' (Eph.iii,17) .... But it is not by *assent,* for then he would dwell in the unregenerate; nor by *assurance,* for he must dwell in our hearts before we can be assured of it; therefore it is by *acceptance.*[2]

I warmed instead to cool John Henry Newman's view of faith as assent to assent though I was critical of its details. I argued that there could be no rationally compelling faith without religious belief in and assent to certain intelligible propositions which, in common with other believers, we accepted.

Having acquired, however, in the course of the intervening forty years a much deeper understanding and appreciation of Wittgenstein's often amazing thoughts and insights, I find myself through them now much closer I think to Harry's Kierkegaard than I could earlier have imagined. This essay is an attempt to say something of how Wittgenstein takes us in this direction and it is an invitation to Harry to continue our conversations. It goes by way, first, of a discussion of meaning governed by practices in the religious language game, and then by reflection on how that takes us to the limits of human understanding, a confrontation with the bounds of sense, and to the question how faith is the leap which might carry us over them.

II

Ten years ago there was published the last piece of philosophical work Norman Malcolm was able to complete before his death in 1990: *Wittgenstein: A Religious Point of View?* It was edited by Peter Winch and includes an excellent discussion of it by him. Alas, in 1997 Peter, too, died. Both Norman's essay and Peter's discussion are highly relevant to my present concerns. Malcolm sees a link between Wittgenstein's philosophical outlook and a religious view of the world, and comments on four 'analogies' that strike him. Behind them are language games, in particular the religious one. He says:

> Philosophy can observe a complicated linguistic practice and describe how one movement in it is related to another. But philosophy cannot explain why the practice exists; nor can the 'hard' sciences of physics, chemistry, biology; nor the 'soft' sciences of psychology, sociology, anthropology. A religious practice is itself a language game – a pattern in which words and gestures are interwoven in acts of worship, prayer, confession, absolution, thanksgiving. Religious practices are a part of the natural history of mankind and are no more explicable than are other features of this natural history.[3]

The analogies are between Wittgenstein's attitude to philosophical problems and the wonder that language games exist at all, that explanations reach a terminus in them, that it is pathological to try to push interpretation and explanation beyond the internal relations we discover within the relevant forms of human life, action and experience. Winch properly wonders whether these general features are sufficiently analogous to a religious point of view to warrant the exclusiveness of that conclusion.

There is nothing particularly mysterious about the religious language game. Wittgenstein uses the expression to gather together the large and extended conceptual family betokened by the uses of the word 'religious' whose meaning we already know and are entirely familiar with in contexts that range from High Romanticism to quotidian decency, from the felt need for grace and absolution to the desire for certainty, completeness, perfection, finality, from customs, festivals and rituals to our own private bearing in the world. That the religious language game is played shows what a large slice of life it encompasses and gives no warrant for its reduction to something other; it is not strange or perverse.

There is a manifold of particular cases which yet is different from other families such as those concerned with causal explanations. The religious language game is a congeries of sub-games that together constitute that family. There are too, of course, always borderline cases and kinship relations. Is Schiller's exhortation 'Live aesthetically!' a religious one? Are some paintings sacrilegious or just bad art? Is Zen only ethical? Is agapeistic atheism a paradox or a platitude? Is one person's piety another's self-indulgence? And so on indefinitely. It is clear not only to social anthropologists that kinship is a difficult issue.

These are hard questions but they do not illuminate, beyond casting a shadow over the mad search for necessary and sufficient conditions for family membership, what Wittgenstein thought particularly significant about language games: their showing the *primacy* of shared practices in the determination of the meaning of words and linguistic expressions that belong to them. What do the words of prayers, creeds, liturgies, rituals, greetings, confessions, hymns, and benedictions mean? See what they are used to do, the variety of feelings they engender, what emotions and desires they spring from and capture, in what directions they point, what intentions they harbour, what acts they prescribe and proscribe, and with whom all these are shared; see the life that gives them life.

This is doubtless familiar but even old masters like Malcolm sometimes forget to look and see hard enough. It is Winch's main criticism of him here that Malcolm does not make sufficiently clear the *internal* connection that exists between, for example, faith and works in the religious language game, as if the nature of the 'works' in question can be understood independently of the ways in which they are or are not connected with the particular faith of the believer and the use of the language of faith in his or her life. Despite his attention to practices Malcolm's interests here seem somewhat too cognitive, too much concerned with the *fact* that something holds firm for each of us within language games and so is beyond further explanation or justification – a point to which I shall return, rather than again the internal relation between *what* holds firm and who it holds firm for and how its holding firm is expressive of the life in which it is itself in a variety of ways expressed.

Wittgenstein advised us to look and see whether there are any overall similarities as well as similarities of detail among the particulars, any common threads – not that there must be. There are, of course, and they are some of the elements of the grammar of the game. Not that they tell us anything of substance we don't already know by reflection on the game we play. Wittgenstein asks in effect: what need have we of grand theories that want verification and the prescriptive definitions they spawn when we have our alert linguistically mediated aspectival perception of the stalwarts of nature and custom there before us? So there are two questions here: is there something that is always expressed in some way when the religious language game is played? and is it perhaps the faith of the player? It is not implausible to say *that* is what holds firm, or even: its holding firm in the way it does for each player *is* what it means to be a serious player of the game.

III

What holds firm for us anywhere 'resists the solvent influence of critical reflection' (Russell's phrase) only for as long as it does so, and has intimations of something being certain and fixed while unavoidable contingencies do not rob one of them. Hence the sense that we have at least approached the transcendent which presents a categorical difference between the religious and the non-religious. What holds firm for us does so because it absolutely survives temporal change that abounds around us, transcends it indeed, for the time of its life for us. Our faith is that it will last forever.

But not all faith is religious faith. One has faith as well in what presents to us as the certainties of life and sometimes we are shocked into awful awareness of its realities. In *On Certainty*[4] Wittgenstein has some striking images for these certainties: they are the hinges on which our doubts turn; everything speaks for them and nothing against them so there is no principle of speaking for or against here; they are the inherited background against which we distinguish between true and false; they are the river bed of thoughts; they are the element in which arguments have their life; they are *in deed* not doubted; one's *life* consists in our being content to accept many things. They are often the truths of commonsense that it would be mad to doubt – that here we are two people at home in the same world talking, for example. But the river bed also shifts, hinges sometimes no longer hold, the background we have inherited is not proof enough against contingency, our beloveds die, we stare our own death in the face. One might say that our certainties walk hand in hand with a tragic vision. We have faith through our certainties but they are not enough for religious faith.

Religious faith is perhaps alone in offering to supply the deficiencies of these certainties if we cannot live with them. Its proper objects are really transcendent and quite secure from the vicissitudes that break even our firmest holds. This is given in our languages that gather the relevant phenomena under the sortal 'spiritual' with its connotations of the immaterial, the holy, basically the intentional (including more than the religious); all of which is irreducible to the the merely physical or extensional.

We do not need to ontologise these proper objects of religious faith though our languages are saturated with metaphors that do so and many religious practices seem to require it. What would forgiveness be without one who forgives, love without one who loves, enlightenment without a source, comfort without a comforter. But religious faith does not strictly require such ontologising as I shall try to show below. What is crucial is rather the attitude we take to whatever these intentional objects may be. This comes out in the question: Why faith? Why not, for example, hope? Because hope is not motivational and staves off only despair. It does not reach the more than occasional ache for the fulfilment of desires one continually sustains. The objects of those desires are intentional objects and make their demands whether or not they actually exist. Ideals can claim the mind even though we know attaining them is hopeless. Perfection may not exist anywhere, not even as an idea with content, and yet we may strive for it. Religious faith is active like that, indeed, passionate. It is quite inappropriate to feel passionately about the things that hold firm for us in the normal course; they are quite properly taken for granted.

Let me follow this thought further. In talking of a letter Wittgenstein wrote to Drury which he quotes in full, Winch says:[5]

> There is a clear sense here of the importance – the spiritual importance, at least in certain circumstances – of philosophical clarity concerning the issue raised. Now, of course, in writings intended *purely* for philosophical clarification the surroundings are different and we do not find Wittgenstein talking in the same way. We do not find him, for one thing, speaking so directly in the first person. But at the same time the 'passion' that is so clearly present in this letter often makes itself heard. I use the word 'passion' in this context in order deliberately to make connection with certain remarks to be found in [Wittgenstein's] *Culture and Value* contrasting religion and 'wisdom':
>
> I believe that one of the things Christianity says is that sound doctrines are all useless. That you have to change your *life*. (Or the *direction* of your life.)
>
> It says that wisdom is all cold; and that you can no more use it for setting your life to rights than you can forge iron when it is *cold*.
>
> The point is that a sound doctrine need not *take hold* of you; you can follow it as you would a doctor's prescription. But here you need something to move you and turn you in a new direction (i.e. this is how I understand it). Once you have been turned around, you must *stay* turned around.

> Wisdom is passionless. But faith by contrast is what Kierkegaard calls a *passion*.
>
> Wisdom is cold and to that extent stupid .... It might also be said: Wisdom merely *conceals* life from you. Wisdom is like cold grey ash, covering up the glowing embers.

In the face of such confident and strong assertion it is impossible to insist that the proper objects of faith are propositions, mere articles of faith. Such articles require a life that gives them birth. I'm reminded of Dostoevsky's remark in his notebooks, as construed by A Boyce Gibson if I remember aright, about how crucial is actual engagement in religious experience and practices and how contrary that is to Christianity understood as any sort of apprehension of propositions or rationalising devices for streamlining humanity out of its freedom. Doctrines are entirely secondary to the religious life, and faith is only relevant to the first because it is deeply embedded in the second. Without people with passions, theses nailed to a door would be hardly noticed.

We have here a revelation of the primacy of the passions, emotions, and primitive responses, in our ability to enter any of the language games that are both available and inescapable in our continued enjoyment of life, particularly, in the present connection, the religious language game. But we must keep in mind Hume's warning that we speak not properly and philosophically when we speak of the combat of reason and passion. Without reason passion is blind (and it isn't) and without passion reason is impotent (and it isn't). The question is which dominates when. In matters of faith it is passion. John Flavel talking of saving faith makes a somewhat similar point:

> A man saith I do not assent to the being, necessity, or excellency of Jesus Christ; yet in the meantime his soul is filled with cares and fears about securing his interest in him, he is found panting and thirsting for him with vehement desires, there is nothing in all the world that would give him such joy as to be well assured of an interest in him. While it is thus with any man, let him say or think what he will of his assent, it is manifest by this he doth truly and heartily assent,

and there can be no better proof of it than the real effects produced by it.[6]

IV

No matter how much we might passionately want that things should be thus and so, however, the question remains whether our sheer faith that they will be is enough to make us intelligible to ourselves in having that faith. We are not here dealing with possibilities that are merely rosier than the realities we are already familiar with; we are concerned with great matters such as life after death in this present life, the perfections of enlightenment, happiness, peace, knowledge, true justice, all the virtues and the absence of all imperfections. We are apparently concerned with what is unlimited and therefore beyond the bounds of sense and even the imagination. There is a confronting paradox here. On the one hand we should be free to imagine and entertain whatever we like, unconstrained by what experience hitherto has taught us and the canons of actual understanding; but on the other, what else can we depend on? Fantasy would be no fun if we did not understand it at all and our airy castles no delight if we could not find our way around in them.

This is true but too straitened a view. What we have faith in is not necessarily, or not at all, the existence of certain states of affairs we desire and hope for and cannot bring about by our own efforts alone, but a particular *way of achieving them*. Someone or something else can do it and it or they are the repository of our faith. With our faith in a way, Tao, or The Way, as Jesus for one amongst many is sometimes called, we trust it or Him to open our eyes and bring us to discover what we have only been able to conjecture in our desires for something better than what we know and can now know. We do not need to cross the bounds of sense when we have faith in something or someone else who can. So we avoid the paradoxes of actually thinking both sides of the limit when we draw the boundaries of what is intelligibly thinkable. Our faith, that is, is not in anything transcendent and beyond our cognitive grasp but in the Way to it. We may understand the truths of logic and mathematics which might be thought to be unconstrained by time and space, but the same point holds – what we understand are the proofs, the ways to the truths. Besides, who can passionately want for their salvation anything merely betokened by those truths? Enlightenment hardly comes with the discovery of a necessary truth, for such truths say nothing at all.

There is a difficulty here: Can we find the Way intelligible when what it is the way to is not? Of course, when we see the conclusion we are led to. For in not crossing the limits of thought we are forced back to what is within them, to what lies open before us. The Way consists in following certain examples – the lives of the holy men, Jesus, the saints, as they are spoken of in the sacred books and interpreted by other inspired holy men; certain practices – prayer, fasting, meditation, study, contemplation; in the midst of the rich traditions of worship and service; all in the company of like-minded seekers and pilgrims, a community to help us along the Way. Why should this not be all the mystery we need in order to practise our faith? It is inexhaustible and yet within the boundaries of intelligibility. We may think we need the ontological metaphors as well but they remain metaphors. Without them the world we know would indeed be too banal to live in, but with them we still cannot leap into the incomprehensible. Our nonetheless wanting this greater mystery is itself incomprehensible. Doubtless this is too polemical but otherwise the paradox is still before us. So is our faith, however, which is not paradoxical at all.

The line of thought pursued here receives support from the reflection that if faith is a passion then like other passions and emotions its proper object is likely to be a person rather than a state of affairs or set of events. One loves a person and only then discovers the features that called it forth. One fears particular people or some other agency for the dreadful and dangerous things they do and might do. One is angry at others for what they have or have not done. Other people attract our sympathy, pity, envy, delight, disgust. Even when our emotions appear objectless, as is the case often with depression and anxiety, we find that there is a person who is the real object after all, ourselves. Hume startles us into realising that the proper object of pride is also ourselves. We are proud of our family, friends, connections, possessions, his thought is, because they enhance *us*. We ourselves as well are, I think, the proper object of grief. The loss of a beloved is our loss before it is the world's. Of course in all these cases there is more to be said, especially about what occasions or predisposes us towards the emotions and passions in question, but that is a different story from the tale of their objects. So there is good reason for thinking the same about the passion faith is claimed to be. It is not surprising that religious faith is in a person or some other agency.

It may seem a contradiction to propose such proper objects of faith which can lead us to the transcendent reality we desire when they, appearing as a Way, even capitalised, may seem just like other states of affairs, mere recipes, and no proper repository of passionate faith. But the appearance of contradiction is removed by the thought that agencies are rather originators of states of affairs and reduce in the end to people. Recipes are useless without people who know how to use them; manuals of religious exercises are of little use without an interpreter, meditation requires a master, and if the Bible calls only on the priesthood of all believers it is they who make it worthy of the faith they have in it. Mediated in these ways religious faith is still in Jesus, the prophets, the Buddha, Confucius, et al, for what they have been said to make possible. They are the Way.

This provides a ready explanation for religious differences, schisms, wars and intolerance; and it lends argument to the view. The disputes are hardly over what the Way is hoped to lead to – there is always the necessarily vague Promised Land. They are about which is the right Way to it. Here we find a dismal history littered with accounts of colonialism, imperialism, jealousy, persecution, and shouts of heresy. One party tries to neutralise another by absorbing it or just outlawing it and declaring itself the only defender of the true faith. As is painfully obvious, enormous financial, social, and spiritual capital is invested in having the right Way to ends of individual salvation, eternal blessedness, and enlightenment, because they are corrupted by base desires for profit and power. Dostoevesky's Grand Inquisitor is a chilling parable.

V

If I am right about the real analogy between Wittgenstein's point of view on problems and a religious point of view residing, as Winch suggests, in the passion possessed in both, then Wittgenstein's philosophical passion ought to be able to illuminate the passions of faith. And so it does.

Wittgenstein (a) saw clearly and had to expose those models from the past, as John Wisdom put it, which have so dominated our thinking and have led us without resolution of our problems further into error. Malcolm remarks,[7] for example, that 'the assumption that *everything* can be explained filled Wittgenstein with a kind of fury'. Wittgenstein shows again and again how problems which appear intractable depend on how they have been set up, on the first moves. We need to see them for what they are. 'Look at it this way' becomes a cry of emancipation familiar to any who have experienced conversion.

(b) By showing how insidious these models are in their ramifications – that words and sentences name our private thoughts, for instance – he hoped to break for us the seductive power of the pictures they project. This is the 'therapy' so many have commented on in his philosophy. One might even call it a mission he felt he could not escape.

(c) By contrast, solutions to philosophical problems are often to be found in what lies open before us, so obvious that we don't notice what is there. The title of an earlier book by Malcolm captures this: *Nothing is Hidden*. We hardly need a logician to bring to light the deep structures of our language before we are able to know what we mean. Wittgenstein says in *On Certainty* 'It's so difficult to find the *beginning*. Or better: it is difficult to begin at the beginning. And not try to go further back.'[8] The real beginning is the totality we are a part of, life that we share. Reasons must come to a stop somewhere and that is where faith, acceptance, begins. The Kingdom of God, as it were, is before us.

(d) He was always deeply concerned with the life in which our thoughts, acts, emotions, perceptions, problems have their place and origin. He quotes Goethe:

... and write with confidence
'In the beginning was the deed.'[9]

We are always active. We change the world insofar as we can. We change everything *in deed*.

(e) One of his dark nights of the soul he recorded in his notebook entries in October 1929:

> The philosophical region of my brain is still in the dark. And it's only when a light is again lit there that the work will go on. (8 October)
>
> The problem of the truth of a sentence eludes me. I am aware that the most magnificent problems lie next to me. But I don't see them or cannot grasp them. (9 October)
>
> Today I feel a very special dearth of problems around me; which is a sure sign that the most important and hardest problems are *in front of me*. (11 October)
>
> Today I could do a little more philosophy, thank God. (After his breakthrough).[10]

(f) Wittgenstein says in his Remarks on Frazer's *Golden Bough*:

> When Frazer begins telling us the story of the King of the Wood of Nemi, he does this in a tone which shows that he feels and want us to feel that something strange and dreadful is happening. But the question 'why does this happen?' is properly answered by saying: Because this is dreadful. That is, the same thing that accounts for this incident strikes us as dreadful, magnificent, horrible, tragic, &c, as anything but trivial and insignificant, it is *that* which has called this incident to life.
>
> One would like to say: This and that incident have taken place; laugh if you can.
>
> In the ancient rites we have the use of an extremely developed gesture-language.
>
> One could say 'every view has its charm' but that would be false. The correct thing to say is that every view is significant for the one who sees it as significant (but that does not mean, sees it other than it is). Indeed, in this sense every view is equally significant.
>
> Frazer's account of the magical and religious view of mankind is unsatisfactory: it makes these views look like errors. Was Augustine in error, then, when he called upon God on every page of the *Confessions*? But – one might say – if he was not

in error, surely the Buddhist holy man was – or anyone else – whose religion gives expression to completely different views. But *neither* of them was in error, except when he set forth a theory.[11]

Here is my answer then, following Winch's lead, to the question with which Malcolm begins his essay: What did Wittgenstein mean when he said to Drury :'I am not a religious man but I cannot help seeing every problem from a religious point of view'? It is the point of view which includes the kind of passion one finds both in religious faith and exemplified in Wittgenstein's philosophical thought, investigations and teaching. Malcolm's mistake is to dwell on the similarities of content – and I agree about how serious and of great moment to the world one sees and lives in that is – but not enough on the passionate intensity of engagement with that world.

These are mere gestures towards the wealth of evidence abounding but I don't think it is fanciful to think that in all these matters anyone possessing religious faith could fail to recognise something of their own passions. Maybe Kierkegaard of at least The Postscript would agree: the subjectively immediately felt world alone is salient and constitutes itself the proper object of such passions. Yet, since it is also the case that not all passion is religious, there arises anew the question of what the object of distinctively religious passion or faith now is. I hope Harry will tell me. I make no claim to have properly understood this at all, but for Kierkegaard, it seems, the world of paradoxical objective truths about God and eternity is too much. And though it seems too little, perhaps it really is for him, more splendidly, the revelations of unending deepening inwardness; indeed, what Wittgenstein may have had before his mind on his death bed when he said 'Tell them I've had a wonderful life'.

End Notes

1. *Sophia*, 1996, reprinted in *The Problem of Religious Language*, edited by MJ Charlesworth (New Jersey: Prentice-Hall, 1974).
2. Flavel, *The Method of Grace*, quoted by John Baillie, *The Idea of Revelation in RecentThought* (London: Oxford University Press, 1956), 88–89.

3. Norman Malcolm, *Wittgenstein: A Religious Point of View?* (New York: Cornell University Press, 1994), 85.
4. Ludwig Wittgenstein, *On Certainty* (Oxford: Blackwell, 1969).
5. Malcolm, *op cit*, 127–8.
6. Ballie, *op cit*, 91.
7. *Op cit*, 85.
8. Wittgenstein, *op cit*, 62.
9. *Ibid*, 52
10. MS 107, quoted by Merrill and Jaako Hintikka, *Investigating Wittgenstein* (Oxford: Blackwell, 1986), 170.
11. *Wittgenstein Sources and Perspectives*, edited by CG Luckhardt (Sussex: Harvester Press, 1979).

4

SPEAKING OF GOD

FRANK NICHOL

One of the thorniest problems confronting theology is that of the legitimacy and adequacy of our language about God. At the beginning of our long friendship, I vividly recall Harry Wardlaw posing to me the question, 'What is wrong with me when I talk about God?' He was not suggesting that 'God-talk', as it came to be short-handedly referred to, was some sort of symptom of a pathological state, but rather to the general absurdity of an attempt to talk sense about so great a mystery. How can we possibly know that what we say about God makes any sort of sense? How dare we imagine that our puny thoughts could possibly approach the fullness of the divine being, accurately capturing some aspect of that wonder and communicating it uncorrupted from one small mind to another?

Clearly, this problem has been with the church and her thinkers from the beginning. The best-known attempt to solve it has been the classical doctrine of *analogy* whereby it is claimed that since every created thing has its origin in God, there must be some sort of continuity between the divine being and the created being derived from it, such that properties found in the creature will also be found in the Creator, albeit in a higher and altogether surpassing mode in the latter as compared with that in the former. Thus both God and humans can rightly be said to be 'good', but the goodness of God is incomparably superior to human goodness, and we may not assume that God will be good in the ways we are, when we are.

This conviction of an essential continuity between the divine and the human held sway in theological and philosophical thinking over almost the whole of history from the beginning of the Christian era, until flaws began to appear in it in modern times, when the classical 'idealism' began to fall apart. These great systems, which dominated philosophical and theological thinking throughout the nineteenth century at any rate (with their roots reaching further back), all had in common the thought that God was the 'soul' or spiritual/rational ultimate principle of the universe and especially the human climax of it. Indeed, the human and divine Spirit were in principle identical. Hegel, for instance, saw in evolution and history the working out of a logical process of repeating thesis-antithesis-synthesis, of which his own philosophical system was no less than the spiritual/rational process coming to self-awareness.

But this flattering conviction received a mortal blow with the beginning of the twentieth century and its wars unprecedented in destructiveness and savagery. It began to dawn on human reflection that human consciousness may not, after all, be in tune with the divine harmony or reflect the comprehensive logic behind all things.

Certainly in philosophy, associated with the names of AJ Ayer and Bertrand Russell, a mounting scepticism regarding traditional talk about God came to expression, and notably linguistic philosophy with its call for the exercise of a 'principle of falsification' ('what conditions would falsify such assertions eg, the claim "God is always good"?') led to unease and discomfort in theological work.

About the same time, in theology itself, as a result of the influence of both Søren Kierkegaard and Karl Barth, who emphasised the 'infinite qualitative distinction between God and humanity' the traditional assumption of a continuity between divine and human being was thrown into sharp question, and it seemed no longer possible to make assertions about God on the strength of characteristics of human/creaturely reality.

This awareness of discontinuity appeared, too, in a sharpened sense of the reality and gravity of *sin* – something of a rediscovery, indeed, which underscored even more disturbingly the distortion of the likeness between 'the spirit of the universe' and humankind, the supposed highest expression of that Spirit in the creaturely world.

How, then, may we be confident that what we say about God is true? May it not all be a facade of hazardous guesswork, or, more likely, a blind groping in the dark, a presumptuous flying in the face of unavoidable, necessary ignorance? How can I imagine that anything

I may dare to say about God can actually accord with the divine reality? If God really is *God,* then it seems to follow plainly that he is necessarily beyond our pigmy perversity, our wildest speculations. As Isaiah 55:8 has God say in a passage often quoted to point to the transcendence of God's nature and ways, 'My thoughts are not your thoughts, nor are my ways your ways'. Here the meaning seems to be that God is strikingly *different* from us, in that, unlike us, God forgives. As theologians are wont to say, God is transcendent, far surpassing our expectations based on what we do or would do, outdoing us in every possible way.

As Heinrich Ott, Barth's successor at Basel, puts it:

> The fact we speak about God and yet are unable to do so is a fault which God himself forgives, and in doing so he takes our human words and concepts which in themselves are inappropriate and transforms them into a fitting witness to himself.[1]

Have we then, here, a way out of our embarrassment about the capacity of our language for God? Here is the proposal that Karl Barth originally made about what he called the 'analogy of faith' *analogia fidei* (to distinguish it from the *analogia entis* or 'analogy of being').

According to Barth, our language is both limited and incompetent, as well as being shot through with the perversity of our sinful state. Yet we may use it with confidence, believing that it does refer us to the reality of God thanks to the gracious condescension of God himself who listens to our babblings and deigns to use them for his own self-communication.

To summarise the matter: theological language, the language of the church about God, is justified, like us sinners ourselves (whose language it always is and always remains, falling far short of the reality of God by reason of both its creaturely limitations and natural incapacity as well as its participation in the presumptuous and corrupt perversity of all human attempts to take the measure and thus to reduce the dignity and claim of God upon us, ie our sinful condition). Church language about God is justified, not by its inherent adequacy or through the capacity of the metaphors used to reach into the divine mystery and lay it bare to human understanding, but because God in mercy and grace accepts the folly we dare to speak and permits it truly to speak of the divine reality. Like ourselves, our language about God, too, is justified by grace alone and not by any natural aptitude or penetration it may be deemed to possess.

After all, in the last resort it is before God and God alone that we and our language stand or fall. It is what is acceptable to God that in the end is true; what other human beings think of or make of it is relatively unimportant.

While I am much drawn to this account of the efficacy of theological language, I am also uncomfortably aware of at least two major difficulties with it, which, however, I hope briefly to address:

1) Perhaps this attempt to save God-language is *too* successful, in so far as it would seem to justify almost any sort of pseudo-theological babble on the strength of God's inexhaustible capacity to forgive. If I can gratefully accept the fact that *my* dubious guesswork in theological expression can be taken up and made serviceable by God, how can I deny the same outcome to all sorts of ridiculous nonsense that also claims to be sober truth about God and his ways? How now can there be meaningful discrimination between 'ways of talking' about God? How can there be meaningful argument or discussion between theologians, churches? The *analogia fidei* approach would seem to license all alike, surrendering all attempts to identify criteria for sensible speech. If God accepts us all, regardless of our credentials, where are any of us in respect of truth?

I suspect that this problem is to be resolved only by abandoning the notion of 'objective truth' in theology. To many, of course, this price will be too high to pay. But we may not shrink from it.

In common parlance, when we say 'we know' something, we think we can describe some state of affairs 'out there' in so-called 'objective reality' to which our descriptions refer ('referent' in the parlance of the 1960s).

But is this how we should understand the verb 'to know' in church language? Two theologians who have much influenced me suggest otherwise. Helmut Rex,[2] my former teacher in Hebrew and Church History, noticed an interesting turn of phrase (Karl Barth[3] noticed it, too!) where Paul writes, 'now that you have come to know God, *or rather to be known by God . . .* (Gal 4:9)".

To know God is 'to be known by God'. As many are by now aware, biblical use of the verb 'to know' quite often means not intellectual comprehension or 'grasp', but loving, claiming, choosing. It can even stand for sexual intercourse. To know God is to be found, claimed, elect of God, drawn into relationship with God, as theologians of the so-called biblical theology school used to tell us.[4] Perhaps they deserve another hearing?

2) We appear to be faced, too, with an unavoidable charge of *petitio principii,* the dreaded fallacy and unforgivable sin of *begging the question.* If I wish to be sure I am talking sense about the reality of God, how can I draw on that very reality to buttress my assertion, ie prove the truth I want to prove by assuming it?

Again, I think a high price must be paid to avoid the jaws of this dilemma.

What kind of language is theological language, anyway? As we have already remarked above, theological language is not 'ordinary language' such as we might use to describe things in the world, or give an account of states of affairs there. It does not belong to the family of languages we use in everyday human affairs for various mundane purposes. It is, rather, part and parcel of that particular language we have already called 'church language', language that also includes that of worship and prayer.

I am actually suggesting that theology is misconceived if it is thought of as some sort of authoritative account of the reality of God 'out there', a map of the 'supernatural' divine world analogous to the atlases of the natural world we have in our homes or the descriptive text-books of various sciences.

I prefer to think of theology, or a piece of theological work, as more like a hymn or a prayer, a love-song or love-poem rather than a piece of sober description. It may not look much like one, but I do not think either St Thomas or Karl Barth (who described theology as 'the *beautiful* science' would have much difficulty in seeing their many and massive volumes as extended prayers or hymns. Still less, of course, St Anselm of Canterbury, who deliberately cast his meditative[5] discourses into the language of prayer.

The most important, central and characteristic activity of the church, defining all else, is her *worship.* And the notable feature of the language of worship is its *direction:* it is directed, not to other human beings, but to God. It is the language of *address to God*. It is this feature of the language of worship that distinguishes it from ordinary language, that fundamentally modifies the question of its justification.

A strange, even alien passage at 1 Cor 14:23-25 has much to teach us. Paul describes a congregation gathered for worship, with everyone 'speaking in tongues', in the ecstatic speech of worship. Into this situation strays an 'outsider or unbeliever', who is brought to his knees at the spectacle, acknowledging, 'God is really among you'. (NRSV).

'Outsider and unbeliever' is won over not by impeccable arguments for the existence of God or detailed disquisitions on the divine nature and attributes. It is not what he or she hears directly addressed to him/her, but what he/she *overhears* as the overtones of the activity of worship that transforms them from spectator to participant.

Despite much superstition to the contrary in the practice of the modern church, it is not the direct approach whether in speech or activity that has missionary impact, but what is 'overheard' as the church addresses the object of her devotion in worship. To this language of marvelling love the outpourings of theology, too, belong.

End Notes

1. *God* (Edinburgh: St Andrew Press), 99, 100.
2. *Immortality of the Soul or Resurrection from the Dead or What?* in Reformed Theological Review, volume 17/3 (October 1958): 73-81.
3. *Church Dogmatics* (Edinburgh: T&T Clark), I/1, 244.
4. See, Alan Richardson, *Theological Word-Book of the Bible.*
5. My own little book, *Making Sense of Prayer* (Melbourne: Joint Board of CE 1985 OP) disappointed some because it so centred on intercession, apparently lacking interest in prayer as meditation. I hope I have now made some amends.

5

SOME REFLECTIONS ON SEEING THE LOOSE SEMIOTIC MANTLE ENVELOPING JEWS AND CHRISTIANS FROM AN OUTER AND FROM AN INNER PERSPECTIVE

DIETRICH RITSCHL

All systematic theologians – whatever the meaning of 'systematic' – have some roots in philosophy. Professional philosophers usually take delight in this but inevitably experience feelings of disappointment when they notice that some of their theological discussion partners have some presuppositions which – for them – are beyond critical philosophical investigation. Philosophers, therefore, have good reasons for the suspicion that theology still adheres to the attitude of mediaeval thinkers who used or abused philosophy as an *ancilla.* I, for one, would not hesitate to accept this critique for indeed I operate in theology with presuppositions which I would not like to throw into the throat of presuppositionless philosophers, provided there are those.

However, Harry Wardlaw, after philosophical and theological studies in his home town of Melbourne, drank from the fountains of modern existentialist theology in Glasgow, and continued his studies in Basel with scholars who would not hesitate to lay open their presuppositions to philosophical critique. I, on the other hand, began my studies in physics and philosophy in Tübingen and in my home town of Basel and continued in Edinburgh where, during six years, I witnessed a radicalisation of what I had learnt in Basel from Karl Barth. My other teacher in Basel, Karl Jaspers, with whom I had worked on Kierkegaard's critique of Hegel, was never mentioned in Edinburgh. Does it not shed some light on the function of philosophy in theology when, in fact, after forty and more years, the two of us find ourselves in basic agreement in matters theological? What has happened to us? Here I shall tell Harry and the readers of

61

his *Festschrift* what has happened to me.

1. Not language 'as such'

On the following pages I would like to pursue the question of the weight we should attribute to the notion of semiotic systems in the tradition of Jews and Christians, and, consequently, in theology. Could it be that a clearer distinction between inner and outer 'perspective' with regard to these traditions would open the way to a liberation from the preoccupation with the problem of 'transcendence' so typical of Continental and British philosophy of religion after Hume and Kant? The classical question of transcendence, of knowing God and of verification was persistently pursued from E Troeltsch via British authors (J Wisdom, A Flew, Ninian Smart, Don Cupitt, John Hick, to mention only a few) to the most recent 'theology of religions' (especially in the USA and on the Continent). This line of thought continued despite and against the 'theology of the word' of Barth and his followers. Why did these authors – and why did Tillich – not concern themselves with the simple fact that there are language-systems and subsystems consisting of thousands of unreflected metaphors, systems within which the believers lived and still live? Stating this so crudely may not be quite fair since some of these authors – especially those interested in 'ordinary language' – had much to say about language, however, it was language 'as such'. I shall not now discuss the many (theological authors) who had been aware of this deficiency, or better, this leaning or tendency. (Different names come to mind such as Langdon Gilkey, the early Gordon Kaufman, Paul M van Buren in his laters works, RL Hart, DM MacKinnon, F Mildenberger; and more recently Stephen Sykes and Rowan Williams, also W Pannenberg). They differed from the philosophers of religion in not investigating language 'as such' but by having the factual languages of Jews and Christians before their eyes even though, at the same time, they contributed to philosophical discussions in the 'outer perspective'. (It is noteworthy, on the other hand, that 'process theology', the only serious attempt in our days at constructing a theological metaphysics, never paid any attention to biblical scholarship and the language systems stemming from biblical books. This is perhaps why Continental theologians never showed a real interest in process theology.)[1]

2. A shift of emphasis

When I wrote the *Logic of Theology*,[2] an experiment with the theological application of what I had learnt from both analytical philosophy and phenomenology (partly stimulated by Edward Farley, my colleague in Pittsburgh) during my many years in the States, I was not aware that I would later take a somewhat more radical approach to the meaning of 'doctrine' in the church. (This is an interest not shared by philosophers of religion.) Lindbeck's book[3] appeared in the same year, and I found myself in agreement with his emphasis on the 'cultural-linguistic alternative'. Paul L Holmer[4] had earlier used the term 'grammar of theology'. My colleagues and I were content with our philosphical equipment in the circle of our theological (Protestant as well as Roman-Catholic) allies. However, we were wondering where to go from there. My interests in those years are still reflected in Heidelberg-dissertations on Wittgenstein written under my supervision[5] from which I benefited much. At that time I had already begun to deepen my knowledge of recent studies on metaphor[6] and symbols[7] as well as on system-theories.[8] This had led to some basic if not simplistic observations on the 'linguistic house' in which Jews and Christians dwell.

3. The loose Semiotic Mantle

We can list four observations from the 'outer perspective':

(a) Language used in *Israel* for recording experiences with remarkable occurences (Exodus, occupation of the land, establishing the kingdom etc) referred to both, the occurences and God. Thus the understanding of the Torah, the warnings of the prophets, the creation stories, the hymns and psalms, the books of wisdom etc were not 'words of God' in a crude, direct sense, but human words. Scholarship has shown a thousand times that these words were either borrowed from every-day language or had been taken over from neighbouring religions. We have little reason to doubt that the people of the time were aware of this; (which is not an important point). Thus the words of the Bible are not a mixture of 'words of God' and human words, but provide transparency to the awareness of God in the context of the believers' worlds of life *(Lebenswelten)*. Undoubtedly, they took and still take this transparency (which they had experienced and which they are hoping to experience again) to authenticate the recorded words. The metaphor 'word of God' indicates just this.

(b) The words, stories, interpretations, citations, reports and doxologies etc. and the corresponding ways of using language in cult, in instructing children, in private, *became marks of identity* only after they had been used over several generations, ie, had been transported into later times. Communities were thus created by clusters of words and sentences. The repeated reference to words, stories, doxological acclamations, admonitions etc. created the communal and social *identity* of the believers (hence: 'people of God').

The identity remained even after the secondary products of the words, such as buildings (eg, the temple, the ark, other sacred objects) had been destroyed. (But they too became objects of interpretation, e.g., the emergence of a 'theology of the temple'). In this process many if not all metaphorically used words and terms (there are hardly any others of significance) experienced shifts in meaning and, most of all, expansions of meaning. Uncountable metaphors generated additional ones, thus God, once named 'king', now receives a throne, a court of angels and messengers etc. (It is interesting to note that some words used for 'God', such as 'potter', three times in Is, two times in Jer; or 'physician', once in Ex 15:26, have not experienced this expansion. Is this because they were not used doxologically?)

(c) The fate of language – if this expression is acceptable – was not different in the *early church*. However, the language of the New Testament and the early authors, by fully taking over the Old Testament vocabulary, saw two huge 'language gains', as I like to call them: one through the coming and disappearing of Jesus (his teaching, death and the Easter stories), the other by its transfer into the Hellenistic world. The first gain was of one of *content*, the other one of *form*. (Avoiding a discussion on the lamentations of Harnack and others on the 'Hellenisation' of the earliest Christian language, we shall not discuss this point here.)

(d) Despite these changes and developments one can say that *the whole of the semiotic system* of Israel was rooted in the Old and that of the church in the Old and the New Testament. Although this 'loose mantle' was at all times permeable to influences from without (outflows to the outside were less frequent), it is and remains until today the chief discerning factor, the *discrimen*, between Jews/Christians and the world religions. It is, however, a fragmented semiotic 'whole' since *selections* of grave consequences have taken place within the system, thus creating sub-systems: (a) the various fashions in which the early (and later) church selected passages from the Old Testament and early Jewish tradition by both, ascribing a new meaning to them and by dropping others, (b) the breach between the Western and Eastern church, (c) the branching off of the Reformation churches from the mediaeval church. (I omit here the naming of further subdivisions which characterise the ecumenical family of churches today. Ecumenical theology attempts the re-examination and possible revision of the firm and often impermeable semiotic 'mantles' with which the subdivisions (b) and (c) have surrounded themselves; this enterprise should be carried out within the light – and shadow – of division (a).[9] I shall refer below to differences between concepts and doctrines, ie, theological systems.)

These four observations can be made in the 'outer perspective' by historical, philological and linguistic-logical investigations.

4. Dwelling within the 'Inner Perspective'

Biblical stories, reports and the naming of the persons in biblical times (and of the later church) have an 'inner aspect' within which we can dwell. By this I mean the unreflected-habitual or the reflected and willful attitude of borrowing perspectives which are mirrored in this semiotic tradition. We 'read' the phenomena in our life-words with all its hopes and fears in the horizon and perspectives of these stories, doxologies etc. We need not draw 'parallels' (such as 'we are all in one boat with Jesus in the storm') nor should we 'apply' biblical verses 'directly' to us, a risky undertaking in most cases, meaningful only with regard to exhortations or commandments (eg, to love one's neighbour, or even enemy). But we can live 'inside' the stream of language of the believers of old, within the semiotic system so to speak. The Bible (and later theological statements) are to the believers not like maps of cities in which they have never lived. It is only upon intellectual reflection that the semiotic system is called a 'system of conviction' in the manner of recent publications on perspectivism (eg, H Putnam). It is primarily a system of orientation and *Lebensgestaltung*; hence, dwelling within the originally biblical semiotic system is first of all a matter of loyalty and faithfulness (cf the original meaning of 'faith' in Hebrew and Greek). This will lead to trust and confidence rather than hopelessness and despair, to love rather than hate. 'Believing' that incredible things are 'true' is no integral part of those who live within the 'inner perspective'. 'Concepts of God' were seldom constructed, they can at best be distilled from doxologies which however were not meant for that.

The relative homogeneity of the semiotic system which stems from the Bible is in contrast illustrated by the fact that in today's Europe a generation is growing up without any knowledge or familiarity with the words and stories, the prophets, the main events in Israel, with Jesus or the apostles. The terms and concepts which explain these stories, eg, grace, righteousness and faith in the Pauline epistles, are entirely unknown to millions of people. (I realise that in Australia a secular society emerged before it did in Europe, but this is merely a quantitative difference.) Although radio and television produce programmes on a high theological level, the media in general have not succeeded in counteracting the growing ignorance. On the contrary, a wei`rd and confusing cocktail of religions is offered to the public in many of the media and in bookstores. It is in contrast with this development that the semiotic 'mantle' of Jews and Christians becomes apparent again. I do not see yet how academic theology (with its great tradition) can help overcome the disastrous situation. What appears at first sight to be an alternative to it, American fundamentalism, I would consider to be in the long run the most dangeous enemy of Christianity. I have seen it growing in Africa and in East Asia too. Only seemingly and deceptively does it take an 'inner perspective', in reality it superimposes principles upon the Bible which are alien to it.

I do not shy away from saying that those who enter into the 'inner perspective' are striving at gaining a 'God-perspective', as I like to call it, ie, an attitude of looking into their *Lebenswelten* in the light of what they hope to be God's perspective on humankind and its future. The main themes of philosophical perspectivism would have to be re-examined here. It has an interesting history from Nietzsche via Carnap, Wittgenstein and others all the way to modern 'constructive empiricism'. (In passing I would like to say that I do not find overly helpful RM Hare's concept of 'blik').[10] However, the classical problem of nominalism/realism has not been overcome by the assertion that we can assume only perspectives of persons who have lived or are alive today. Thus, in reaction to H Putnam's position in *Reason, Faith and History* of 1981, a new interest in realism has emerged, a view which I do not fully share but which I cannot discuss here further.

5. The fallacy of the concept of *Perspecuitas/Claritas Sacrae Scripturae*

Whilst it is true that the metaphors in the Bible interpret, limit and condition each other, it is also true that later harmonisations and naive generalisations have led to what in the end resulted in a non-metaphorical set of descriptive words and names. Originally, metaphors such as God as 'king', 'love', 'judge', 'creator' limited and balanced each other in such fashion that only a small portion of each of these words from everyday language was applied by way of an *analogia attributionis* to God who to the early users of such metaphors could not be defined or spoken of in descriptive language. He can only be referred to metaphorically. However, these (and thousands of other) metaphors experienced expansions, thus transgressing the limits of the portions intended to be used analogously. The clusters of metaphors concerning a certain theme became 'copy theories of truth', photographs, so to speak, of ontic realities suggesting that they existed somewhere in reality (such as God's throne and Jesus sitting on his right, heaven or hell as a place, angels as living beings equipped with wings, and, of course, God literally as Father and Jesus as Son, etc).

Moreover, during the process of the formation of the canon and in subsequent centuries, the various and differing traditions within the Bible were harmonised into a balanced whole. The harmonisation resulted in systematisations and also in further anti-Jewish thoughts when, for instance, the totally Jewish-Christian character of the gospel of Matthew was no longer recognised. So-called tensions in the Bible were ignored or debated away, a tendency we can find already in early patristic time. Formations of concepts and early forms of doctrine can be found in the Pauline epistles. It is not surprising, therefore, that the Reformation with its *sola scriptura* principle made the fullest use of St Paul's theology since it provides guidelines for the interpretation of the Bible as a whole. (Luther's hermeneutics has the advantage over Calvin's that he would allow a ranking of biblical passages and books; tragically, however, this also included certain devaluations of the Old Testament, later called 'Luther's Marcionitism'.)

It is interesting that after decades of stupendous exegetical work of the reformers, Protestant orthodoxy in defending the *sola scriptura* principle could come up with the concept of the *perspicuitas* or *claritas scripturae*. I consider this concept to be false, false in the sense of 'not helpful' (I like to use this equation). In fact, it seems to me, understanding the Bible (as a whole) is more complicated and demanding than understanding the later doctrines and theologies of the church. (Admittedly, whilst their original intent was the explanation of the biblical tradition as a whole, they often explained issues and problems which were unnecessarily or accidentally construed and which are 'not helpful' or relevant today.)[11] Talmudic tradition went other ways. No 'doctrines' resembling Christian doctrines were ever developed in Judaism. 'Teaching' refers to the *halacha*, not to explaining God. This point is of great importance and, if taken seriously, in some way relativises Christian 'doctrines'.

6. Three types of doctrines

When I was engaged in patristic studies in my days in Scotland and the first years in the States, I was aware of the problem of the illegitimate expansion of biblical metaphors and the shift of meaning they experienced. After all, patristic scholarship since the early twentieth century had thoroughly investigated the process of reducing biblical stories (or summarising the essence of them) to conceptual notions and quasi-philosophical definitions, eg, in the Christologies of the first four centuries ('incarnation', 'divine and human nature', 'anhypostasis' and 'enhypostasis'; later: *communicatio idiomatum*, and so forth). But it was only when I analysed the possibilities of ecumenical theology that I discovered that there are three distinctively different types of doctrines in the church. This observation is related to my earlier analyses of what I call 'implicit axioms', a concept that need not be explained here.[12] The church as a 'frame', mirroring the semiotic 'mantle' of Jews and Christians, has become to me a theme of great importance. The broken relationship of Christians and Jews is part of the theme. Thus Christian ecumenical theology will operate for ever with an open wound.

The three types appear in the New Testament at best in an implicit form. They are the product of the later church. They are: (a) doctrines as summations in the sense of building towers with an explanatory intention, (b) doctrines as excavatory invasions (to be compared with the digging of archeologists) into the pre-linguistic foundations of the biblical books, (c) doctrines as excursion from the 'inner perspective' into the broad realm of total explanations of God, the cosmos and of history.

Within doctrines of type (a) one can distinguish between those that are based upon large segments of the Bible (creation, election, righteousness, Christology, ecclesiology etc); those based upon only one or extremely few passages (the *imago dei* concept; the Petrine office of the pope etc); and lastly those that have no biblical basis at all (eg Maryology of the nineteenth and twentieth centuries). Some of the last must be given a chance to be understood as *modi loquendi* for another doctrine, eg Maryology in the early church as another way of speaking of Jesus Christ (or the church); others can be discarded from the number of Christian doctrines.

Obviously, there are significant differences between these doctrines within the ecumenical church even though the themes they attempt to explain may be the same. Considering the polymorphic and polycentric nature of the Bible, it is not surprising that many of the doctrines of type (a) stem from but one of the many inner-biblical traditions. This, to my mind, relativises these doctrines up to a point, which is not to say that on that account ecumenical theology should embrace a relativistic position. Re-examination, re-interpretation and revision – by showing mutual respect – is the goal, not the abolition of certain doctrines. (Parts of the third type of (a) would constitute exceptions to this tolerant attitude.)

Doctrines of type (b) I consider the most interesting and promising for future ecumenical endeavours. They are gained by asking for a network or connexions of structures, motifs, themes or axioms 'behind' the texts.[13] A prime example is the concept of the Trinity, partly also ecclesiology.

Doctrines of type (c) transgress the demarcation lines of the 'inner perspective' and embrace a broad view of God and history. Irenaeus was the first to attempt this, and he was followed of course by Origen and many others, by the mediaeval doctors, by Hegel and, to mention an example from our time, by process theology.

I shall not here discuss these types any further. It suffices to say that all three types are the subject matter of theology and are open to philosophical analysis too. It seems important to me that at least types (a) and (b) cannot be paralleled with the teachings of world religions.

The question of 'what they have in common', so hotly debated today, does not mean much to me. What they share with Jews and Christians has to do with religious issues and some customs or rites which are rather peripheral. This observation does not, of course, touch upon the issue of mutual respect.

7. A creed

I believe that there is a world of mind and spirit *(Geist)* that is continually expanded and broadened by human thought, language and feelings and which is to a small extent remembered in history, so-called good and evil included. At the end of human history it rests in its totality in God's eternal memory. This is also where we shall be after our death. Theology, therefore, is best performed in the sense of 'pneumatology' (a term which I do not find particularly attractive).[14] I undertake my theological thinking in revising or even denying classical concepts and constructing hypothetical alternatives by presenting them for a test, as it were, to God's spirit and his wisdom. This is perhaps a special form of intellectual prayer and doxology which is possible at any time when we are thinking of the 'things of God' in relation to our *Lebenswelt* and its future shape. I would like to see it distinguished from mere meditation.

What I left undiscussed in this *Festschrift* for Harry is an interpretation of what I have called above the 'transparency' of the human words of biblical books for the awarenness of God's presence. The *testimonium Spiritus Sancti internum* is indeed the matter that should be discussed here. Occasions[15] for it present themselves in worship as well as in private thought and prayer.

End Notes

1. See, however, the fine analysis by M Welker, *Universalität Gottes und Relativität der Welt* (Neukirchen: Neukirchener Verlag, 1981).
2. D Ritschl, *The Logic of Theology* (London: SCM Press, 1986 [German 1984]).
3. George A Lindbeck, *The Nature of Doctrine, Religion and Theology in a Postliberal Age* (Philadelphia: Westminster Press, 1984). See for a comparison of Lindbeck and the *Logic of Theology* Geoffrey Wainwright, 'Bemerkungen aus Amerika zu Dietrich Ritschls 'Logik der Theologie', in: W Huber *et al* (editors) *Implizite Axiome, Grundstrukturen des Denkens und Handelns* (Munich: Chr Kaiser 1990), 218–228 (also in *Evang Theologie*, 46:555–562).
4. Paul L Holmer, *The Grammar of Faith* (New York: Harper & Row, 1978). Subsequently, the term 'grammar' was widely used by later authors, eg by IU Dalferth, mostly with reference to Wittgenstein and not to Holmer.
5. Eg Th Niedballa, *Sprachspiel und religiöse Erfahrung. Wittgenstein und die Theologie* (Münster: LIT-Verlag 1993); Th Wabel, *Sprache als Grenze in Luthers theologischer Hermeneutik und Wittgensteins*

Sprach-philosophie (Berlin/New York: W de Gruyter Verlag, 1998). (Th Wabel also tested his theses in years of study in Oxford – with Rowan Williams – and in Harvard with S Cavell). Cf the earlier work by Hugh O Jones, *Die Logik theologischer Perspektiven. Eine sprachanalytische Untersuchung* (Göttingen: Vandenhoeck and Ruprecht, 1985). (Dr Jones from Dunedin, New Zealand, had come to work with me in Mainz in 1973 and this work was his *Habilitationsschrift.* He died there after a brain-tumour operation in 1985).

6. See the splendid collection of essays in R Bernhardt and U Link-Wieczorek (editors), *Metapher und Wirklichkeit. Die Logik der Bildhaftigkeit im Reden von Gott, Mensch und Natur* (Göttingen: Vandenhoeck and Ruprecht, 1999) (FS for D Ritschl), with contributions from philosophy, biblical studies, egyptology, psychosomatic medicine, physics and systematic theology.

7. At present one can observe a Cassirer-renaissance in Continental philosophy (E Rudolph and others, *Cassirer-Forschungen,* volume I ff Hamburg: Felix Meiner Verlag 1995ff); following a long period of studies on P Ricoeur, cf now with reference to biblical studies G Natt, *Symbol und Mythos. Zwei Denkbegriffe zur Bibelhermeneutik des 19. und 20. Jahrhunderts* (Münster: LIT-Verlag, 2000).

8. Cf M Welker (editor), *Theologie und funktionale Systemtheorie. Luhmanns Religionssoziologie in theologischer Diskussion,* Frankfurt: Suhrkam, 1985 and, again with reference to N Luhmann, W Krawietz and M Welker (editors), *Kritik der Theorie sozialer Systeme, ibid* 1992, second edition 1996.

9. This is the subject of my recent book *Theorie und Konkretion in der Ökumenischen Theologie. Kann es eine Hermeneutik des Vertrauens inmitten differierender semiotischer Systeme geben?* (Münster: LIT-Verlag, 2003).

10. W Pannenberg's understanding of perspective has recently been analysed by: J Kunath, *'Sein beim Anderen'. Der Begriff der Perspektive in der Theologie Wolfhart Panenbergs* (Münster: LIT-Verlag, 2002).

11. I recall early discussions with James Barr on *perspicuitas.* He has been my mentor in Old Testment matters for exactly fifty years. Cf among others the books: *The Bible in the Modern World* (London: SCM Press, 1973); *Holy Scripture. Canon, Authority, Criticism* (Philadelphia: Westminster Press, 1983); *The Scope and Authority of the Bible* (London: SCM Press, 2002) (*Explorations in Theology* 7, 1080) and *The Concept of Biblical Theology, An Old Testament Perspective* (London: SCM Press, 1999). To the New Testament see G Theissen, *Die Religion der ersten Christen. Eine Theorie des Urchristentums* (Gütersloh: Chr Kaiser, 2000). (Translation in several languages).

12. See the FS *Implizite Axiome* mentioned above in FN 3.

13. Cf my contribution to the FS for James Barr, 'Welchen Sinn hat die Suche

nach Strukturen hinter Texten?', in *Language, Theology and the Bible,* edited by SE Balentine and J Barton (Oxford: Clarendon Press, 1994), 385–397.

14. See after the important writings by K Barth *(KD IV/1 – IV/3),* P Tillich (volume III), H Berkhof, Y Congar, K Rahner, J Moltmann and many others the splendid book by my colleague in Heidelberg M Welker, *Gottes Geist. Theologie des Heiligen Geistes* (Neukirchen: Neukirchener Verlag, 1992) (also in ET). For an exegetically grounded systematic exploration cf M Press, *Jesus und der Geist. Grundlagen einer Geistchristologie* (Neukirchen: Neukirchener Verlag, 2001). (Michael Press is teaching at Suva Theological College).

15. I have used this term (originally coming from AN Whitehead) extensively (eg in *The Logic of Theology,* I, G) after discussions with my colleague in Austin, James A Wharton, 'The Occasion of the Word of God, An unguarded essay on the character of the Old Testament as the memory of God's story with Israel', in *Austin Seminary Bulletin,* no 1, 1968: 1-54.

6

CLEMENT OF ALEXANDRIA'S PHILOSOPHY OF FAITH

Eric Osborn

'Only believe!' was, according to the pagan philosopher Celsus, the common cry of Christians, who gave no grounds for the rational acceptance of their creeds. Origen replied that everyone could not be a full-time philosopher, that the scriptures were studied with utmost logical rigour, but that philosophy was not an option for most people (Cels 1:9). Furthermore, choice of philosophical allegiance is not made on rational grounds (1:10). In any case, faith in the most-high God is praiseworthy, the writers of the gospels were honest and Christian doctrines are coherent with the common notions of reasonable men (Cels 3:39f).

Clement's reply to this objection had been much more extensive, for he claimed that classical epistemology had been impoverished and that knowledge was gained in more than one way.[1]

Along lines similar to epistemology today,[2] Clement denied the exclusiveness of transcendent laws of thought. Just as scientific laws are today read off the observation of the natural world, so the rules of knowledge should be read off the practice of thought and rational belief. Knowledge, he claimed, was commonly derived from faith in several ways, as, for example, the practice of demonstration depended on ultimate premises being grasped by indemonstrable faith. This was the door through which Christian philosophy entered into discussion; it might have walked away claiming higher gnosis. Had this happened the tradition of Western culture would have had to find another beginning and we might still be doing magic and uttering spells.

Classical philosophy had followed a deductive mode. Knowledge must be inferred from higher and better known premises according to universal laws of logic; geometry provided the pattern.[3] For Plato knowledge and true belief are entirely distinct (Theaet 201c). Knowledge must always have rational grounds which persuasion cannot produce or destroy. Only the gods and a few men possess knowledge. All may possess true belief, which has no logical grounds and which results from mere persuasion. The existence of the forms makes it possible to distinguish between knowledge and true belief (Timaeus 51d). The slave who learns the solution of a mathematical problem gains knowledge when he is taken through the steps of the argument many times (Meno 85c). Faith which did not have premises beyond itself was insecure.

Arguments about the compatibility of Greek philosophy and Christian thought and about whether a particular early Christian writer is a Platonist[4] have wasted much time. Disagreements are inevitable since contributors share no common understanding of Greek philosophy or of Plato, and lack of agreement about the New Testament is even more spectacular. Instead of arguing about diverse generalities,[5] we should examine particular problems and see how New Testament and philosophy worked together.

The central problem was the adequacy of faith. Faith was inferior to knowledge in the eyes of philosophers and of Gnostic theosophists. Paul had already defended the sufficiency of faith against Jewish legalism (Rom 4; see also Heb 11). Clement's defence of faith against Greek philosophy has the same historical importance.[6] He drew on both philosophy and the New Testament and kept his two sources together, as we must in our exploration of his ideas.

We shall ask two questions: did Clement make intelligent use of Greek philosophy and of the New Testament? and, have the issues which he raised been of lasting importance for theology?

The arguments for faith[7] may be briefly listed:

> Faith was anticipation (1 Cor 1:7; 15:14, 17)[8] (Epicurus
>   – and Stoics),
> assent (2 Cor 4:13; Rom 10:9) (Stoics),
> perception (1 Cor 2:11–16; Jn 1:14)[9] (Plato, Theophrastus
>   and Stoics),
> hearing God in scripture (Rom 10:17) (Plato),

the unproved first principle (1 Cor 1:19f; 2:5; 4:21; 15:27)
   (Aristotle),
the criterion of truth (Gal 6:16) (Aristotle, Stoics, Cicero),
necessary for knowledge (1 Cor 1:4; 3:1; 3:10; 4:2) (Plato),
the source of power and stability (1 Cor 2:16) (Plato).

Paul (genuine and pseudonymous), John, Epicurus, Stoics, Plato, Theophrastus, Aristotle – what a mixture! A philological study[10] sees many parts but finds little argument. Can we take such a conglomeration seriously?

Yes, and for five reasons:

First, rules of thought are read off and not imposed on the practice of thought. If variety is ignored, the rules are not valid.

Second, the dominant philosophy of the day was a mixture. Middle Platonism mixed everything with everything to find a defence against scepticism.

Third, because all these moves in ancient epistemology were directed to a common end, that of finding a basis for knowledge and avoiding ' infinite regress'.

Fourth, Clement wanted to be all things to all philosophers, so that they might see the common ground between their ideas and Christian teaching. 'To those who ask for the wisdom which is in us, we must present what is familiar to them, so that, as easily as possible, *through their own ideas*, they may reasonably arrive at faith in the truth' (str 5.3.18). His main work, the Stromateis is haphazard in its presentation. If he had systematised his account, he would have neglected those whose concerns were made secondary.

Fifth, in casting his net so widely, Clement makes exceptional demands[11] on his readers. The miscellaneous character of the Stromateis enables him to say more than a tighter conventional form could achieve. Similarly Plato wrote dialogues, not treatises. This makes Plato and Clement elusive for any encyclopedist who tries to list their doctrines.

Clement begins his discussion in Stromateis 2 by claiming the common ground between faith and philosophy which had been won in the Wisdom literature. We follow wisdom in all our ways (Prov 3:5f). The way is found in faith and the fear of God (str 2.2.4). The

Bible presents a barbarian (non-Greek) philosophy which is complete and true. Through wisdom God gives true understanding of things that are (Wisd 7:17–21). Such knowledge is not for the many who do not believe. Heraclitus and the prophets declare that there can be no understanding without faith. The major New Testament source, Hebrews 11, declares that without faith it is impossible to please God (str 2.2.4–8).

1. Preconception and hope

Faith is a deliberate preconception or anticipation. Hebrews 11 offered the same defence of faith: faith gives substance to our hopes (str 2.2.8).

'Epicurus supposes faith to be a preconception of the mind. He explains this preconception as attention directed to something clear and a clear concept of something. He declares that no one can make an inquiry, confront a problem, have an opinion and indeed make a refutation without a preconception' (str 2.4.16). The need for preconceptions was also seen by Isaiah for whom there could be no understanding without faith (7:9) and Heraclitus who wrote 'Except one hopes for what is beyond hope, he will not find it, for it will remain impossible to examine and to understand' (Diels 18).

Epicurean preconceptions make knowledge possible, when the perceiver is confronted by a mass of sensations.[12] By means of preconception we recognise different kinds of things. Clement adds to the original empirical account (DL 10:33), the element of choice. He rejects any suggestion that faith might be innate.

The Old Stoa saw preconceptions as ingrained (Plutarch, comm. not. 1059C). The late Stoicising Academy considered them to be innate (Cic ND 1:44).

For Clement, the future reference of preconception, its anticipation of knowledge, linked it to faith and hope. As so often for Clement, Heraclitus, with his claim that hope is essential to understanding,[13] provided the link between a philosopher and the Bible. Above all, the kingdom of God had come near and the present realisation of the Eschaton enabled faith to grasp ultimate reality now; all knowledge was anticipation.

The 'substance of things hoped for' in Hebrews 11 is an extension from Pauline theology. Just as Abraham was justified by faith in the God who justifies the ungodly, raises the dead and creates out of nothing, so the whole story of Old Testament heroes presents a history of faith. Yet they were neither made perfect, nor received the promise, nor found that city of God which has foundations. The new situation of Christian hope is set out in 2 Cor 3:1-18. Paul's hope and confidence belong to a minister of the new covenant which is marked by freedom, boldness and boasting.

> Christian *elpis* therefore rests on the saving act of God in Christ and because this is the eschatological act of salvation, *elpis* itself appears as the eschatological *Heilsgut*, that is – now is the time here, when man can have assured confidence. The waiting, which belongs to *elpis*, is itself the work of the Spirit, the gift of the end-time and it rests on *pistis* and the *Heilstat* (Gal 5:5) .... *Elpis* thus constitutes, together with *pistis*, Christian existence.[14]

Bultmann, in his sermons, hammers the notion of anticipation *(vorauseilen, vorangehen, vorausnehmen)*. Preaching on Jn 16:22-33, he links prayer with an experience of the Eschaton.

> He, who believes, already to some extent anticipates in his faith that day when all is to become new. How is that possible? That day on which all is to become new is anticipated by him who has already become new, as Paul said 'If anyone be in Christ, he is a new creature, the old has passed away; behold, all has become new' (2 Cor 5:17). To be a Christian, to believe, means to have hurried on ahead of the time of this world. It means to stand already at the end of this world.[15]

In this way faith becomes that victory which overcomes the world (1 Jn 5:4).

Moltmann rejected[16] the popular misunderstanding of eschatology as the doctrine of the last things. It is rather, he said, the teaching of Christian hope, embracing both what is hoped for and the hope which it inspires. It begins from an historical reality and describes the future of that reality; it speaks of Jesus Christ and his future. He is our hope (Col 1:27) and his promises anticipate the future. Faith is the foundation on which hope rests, as faith steps over the borders which have been broken down by the resurrection of him who was crucified, seeing in him the future of mankind for whom he died – *Ave crux – unica spes*! Faith does not have a future; rather, it is the future.[17]

2. Assent and choice

The chosen preconception of faith is also the assent of godliness, or an affirmative response to God (str 2.2.8). Faith is a uniting assent, which joins the believer to God (str 2.2.9).

The scriptural command to believe is an invitation to assent or choose. With a willing spirit we choose life and believe God through his voice. We believe that his word is truth (str 2.4.12). Following Hebrews 11, the faith of Abel, Enoch, Noah, Abraham, Isaac, Jacob, Sarah, is remembered. Faith is seen in a repentance which is freely chosen (str 2.6.27)

Assent is a free choice (Chrysippus frag.phys. 992) (str 2.12.54), which determines all opinion, judgement, conjecture and learning. Unbelief is always a possible alternative; but it is simply the absence of faith. We have a disposition to truth and find error repugnant (str 2.12.55). Indeed confession *(homologia)* to God is martyrdom *(marturia)*, which is testimony and obedience to God. It sheds blood all along the way of life until it goes from earth to be with God (str 4.4.15)

Zeno described the process of knowledge in four stages. The mind, like an open hand receives *(visum)* an impression, partly closes in assent *(adsensus)* to the impression, clenches in cognition *(conprensio, Grk katalepsis)*, is grasped by the other hand in knowledge *(scientia)* (Cic Acad 2:145).

Some approximation to this account of faith is found in Newman's Grammar of Assent, where Newman distinguished between the intellectual act of inference and the assent to the truth which has been inferred.[18] Assent is an independent act and may occur when the inference has been rejected or ignored. It is essential to faith, for merely to follow an argument to its conclusion lacks the necessary, indivisible and unconditional act of assent.[19] Newman's account of assent includes more than this and differs in some detail from the complex claims of Clement and Stoics.

Hans Küng has put forward a proof of the existence of God from three successive choices of faith. He asks three questions: Yes or no to reality? Yes or no to God? Yes or no to the God of the Bible? At each stage there is good reason for answering either yes or no, and a choice must be made. Küng cites the claim of a contemporary logician, that all metaphysics rests on a 'prerational, primordial decision'.[20]

Küng's argument has great simplicity. Beginning from the nihilism of Nietszche, he offers the choice between a reasoned rejection of the world and a reasoned trust in reality. To those who choose to trust in reality, he offers a second choice for or against God as the ground of this reality. Recognising again the strength of the arguments on both sides, Küng offers a further choice to those who have chosen God. Do they choose the abstract being of the philosophers or the God and father of Jesus Christ? There is intelligent respect for the argument which goes the way not chosen, although there is some doubt as to whether fundamental distrust of the universe can be consistently carried out.

3. Perception

Faith sees clearly what is invisible (Heb 11:1). He who hopes, as he who believes, sees with his mind both *noeta* and things to come. Only the mind sees what is just, good, true (str 5.3.16). Plato's materialists grasp rocks and oaks in their hands to argue with idealists (Sophist 246a),[21] The new eye of faith sees what has never been seen before (1 Cor 2:9; Is 64:4). Faith sharpens the perception so that it quickly distinguishes counterfeit coin (str 2.4.15). Here Clement credits faith with the ability to see what remains invisible to most people. 'The artist makes us see what is, in a sense manifestly and edifyingly *there* (real), but unseen before, and the metaphysician does this too.'[22]

In scripture the language of seeing and hearing is common: Paul speaks of of looking to things unseen and eternal, even of visions in the third heaven. Hebrews 11 is full of the evidence of what is unseen. Blindness and deafness are the spiritual sicknesses of the gospels, and the prayer of the ages is 'Enable with perpetual light, The dullness of our blinded sight'. This is not an optional extra. At the last judgement, condemnation is pronounced on those who did not *see*, in the hungry, thirsty, lonely, naked, sick and prisoner, the presence of their lord.

The most recent account of this topic[23] begins from what are taken to be direct, non-sensory experiences of God and which justify M (ie manifestation) beliefs. The *presentational* character of the experiences enables them to be classed under the generic concept of perception. For 'what perception *is* is the awareness of something's appearing to one *as such-and-such,* where there is a basic unanalysable relationship, not reducible to conceptualising an object as such and such, or to judging or believing the object to be such-and-such'.[24] It is plausible that God be among the causes for these experiences, and some theories of perception support this claim. Alston does not try to *prove* the genuineness of perception of God, for such proof would require proof of the existence of God and of his causal efficacy in producing these experiences. It is possible to defend the conviction of the subjects that they are perceiving God, in their mystical experiences or mystical perceptions.

While background beliefs may play a part in some perceptual beliefs, all such beliefs possess an element of perceptual experience. How reliable are these experiences? Sense perception cannot be proved entirely reliable; epistemic circularity intervenes in many cases.

From Reid and Wittgenstein[25] we develop the notion of 'doxastic practice' which forms and evaluates beliefs and which includes sense perception, introspection, memory, rational intuition, kinds of reasoning and mystical experience. The last mentioned can, as a socially established doxastic practice, lead to beliefs in divine manifestation. The chief objections to the practice are naturalistic explanation, contradictions in results, conflicts with science and naturalistic metaphysics. It is reasonable to continue in the face of contradictions in one's experience, 'hoping that inter-practice contradictions will be sorted out in due time'.[26]

Finally how does mystical experience relate to the total basis of religious belief?[27] The different kinds of experiential grounds, revelation, and natural theology, may be reduced to two headings: 'perceptual presentation and inference to the best explanation'. Among these there is cumulative force as well subtle interaction, such as where one source may help to remove doubts about another.[28]

As a philosopher, Clement puts a simple case for non-sensory perception without falling into the abyss of Gnostic theosophy.

4. Faith and scripture

Here Clement follows Plato in turning to divine oracle (Tim 27c and 40 de). His reference to Plato is linked with the 'likely tale'[29] of the Timaeus and not with the argument of any dialogue. God, for Clement, is the first object of faith and the arguments for faith only work because God has spoken in scripture. The power of scripture, like the call of the Sirens, compels hearers, to listen to its words (str 2.2.9).

Plato says that only from God or from the offspring of God may the truth be learnt. We boast in the divine oracles which we possess and the truth we learn from the son of God, a truth which was first prophesied and then made clear (str 6.15.123).

The disciples of Pythagoras believed without hesitation in the sayings of their master. Those, who love truth, will not refuse faith to a still more credible master, the only saviour and God (str 2.5.24).

Faith is irrefutable because God speaks to us in scripture (str 5.1.5). One does not ask God to prove what he says (str 5.1.6).

The inordinate claims for scripture would not have seemed inordinate to Clement's readers, for three reasons. First, in the classical world, literature was a source of all knowledge.[30] Unlike Plato, who banished poets from his city, Clement values poetry highly. Second, Christians took over Jewish scriptures which were a universe of truth. These, said Justin and Tertullian, had become Christian property. Third, Clement is the first to speak of the New Testament as a set of writings and his enthusiasm for Sirens' voices of scripture is enhanced by novelty. He writes with the wonder of the poet John Keats, *On*

First Looking into Chapman's Homer:

> Then felt I like some watcher of the skies,
> When a new planet swims into his ken;
> Or like stout Cortez, when with eagle eyes
> He star'd at the Pacific – and all his men
> Look'd at each other with a wild surmise –
> Silent, upon a peak in Darien.

It is worth noting that many of the more rigorous critical theologians today still give the same place to the Bible. Historical research clarifies and strengthens the biblical message.[31] Conservative interpreters claim that the denial of historicity to miracles, for example, weakens the authority of scripture and reduces the claims of Christ. On the contrary, a critical examination of miracle stories shows that, in many cases, they have moved the centre of the episode away from the encounter with Christ to a discrete marvel which could be part of any religion.[32]

5. Faith and proof: argument and beyond

The faith of Abraham points to a first and universal cause, to the God who is, who justifies the ungodly, raises the dead and creates out of nothing.

Indeed, says Clement, the first principles of things are not to be demonstrated; the first principle or cause of all things is known by faith alone.[33] Greeks like Thales or Anaxagoras are plainly wrong about first principles, so we must call no man our master on earth (str 2.3.13).

Indemonstrable first principles had been central to the logic of Aristotle, 'There cannot be demonstration of everything alike: the process would go on to infinity so that there would still be no demonstration' (Met 1006 a6). Also in Posterior Analytics 2 19:100a,[34] it is insisted that there must be unproved first principles. These are of two kinds: principles on which reasoning works (non-contradiction and excluded middle) and axioms (mathematical and ethical).

However Aristotle does not give a proportional amount of space to the more important problems and the solution to his problem about first principles needs to be teased out from the new direction which he took in *Metaphysics* 4. In his account of first philosophy he uses a new method, which may be described as 'strong dialectic'. This is more selective than pure dialectic and starts from stronger premisses.[35]

In modern discussion, argument has been brought against indefinable, indemonstrable first principles. For example, it is argued that a system may be circular and regressive without being vicious. *The Oxford English Dictionary* is a monoglot dictionary which functions without any ultimate hypotheses, explaining words through mutual dependence. In response it may be noted that parts of speech, definitions and distinctions are essential to the coherence of the whole. Again, it has been objected that, within a city it is possible to indicate the position of a building by reference to other buildings. There is no need for ultimate landmarks. 'They are neither necessary nor possible.'[36] Such reflexions of an urbanised land-lubber are puzzling. How is he going to cross the Atlantic or the Sahara? How will he find his way through the bush? Ultimate landmarks, like the points of the compass, degrees of latitude and longitude, have been proved necessary.

In favour of some kind of ultimate unproved hypothesis, we may cite JS Mill, GE Moore,[37] and Gödel's theorem that there is an undecidable formula in any formal system adequate for number theory. This means that the consistency of a formal system adequate for number theory cannot be proved within the system.[38] Every adequate formal system contains at least one unprovable hypothesis within it.

Clement does not argue for the existence of God, but rather argues for faith as the only appropriate way to grasp an unconditioned, ultimate first cause. Similarly, Paul's account of faith depends on the God who justifies the ungodly, raises the dead and creates out of nothing.[39]

The same point was made by Bultmann in his discussion of what he called 'the crisis in belief'. The supreme article of the creed, is faith in God the father almighty, maker of heaven and earth;

'whoever believes that truly is helped already and is brought back so that he comes to the point from which Adam fell. But those people are few, who come so far as to believe fully that he is the God who makes and creates all things.'[40] The believer recognises that as far as good and bad, life and death, heaven and hell are concerned, in his own strength he can do nothing. 'God is the mysterious, enigmatic power that meets us in the word and in time. His transcendence is that of someone always having power over the temporal and the eternal: it is the transcendence of the power which creates and sets limits to our life.'[41] A Christian believes in God as the enigmatic power which calls him into being and makes him finite.[42]

6. The criterion of truth

Aristotle says[43] that the judgement which comes after the knowledge of a thing and declares it to be true is faith. Faith, then, is the criterion of and superior to knowledge (str 2.4.15).

A Stoic argument has simply been credited to Aristotle in error. Inaccurate citation was common in Clement's day.[44]

The Stoic origin of the argument is confirmed.[45] This version of it had been attributed by Cicero to Zeno in Acad 1:41f. Cicero comments that Stoicism must be regarded as a correction of the Old Academy rather than as something new (Acad 1:43). This makes the attribution to Aristotle almost inevitable.

Clement's summary of Zeno's argument, which he would have learnt from a similar Greek source to that of Cicero, is brief: the judgement concerning the truth of a presentation is a judgement whether it is credible; this judgement is made by faith, using its own criterion.

The quest for a canon or criterion of truth dominated hellenistic philosophy.[46] Clement speaks also of the canon of the church which includes the confession of the essential articles of faith (str 7.15.90).

From Antiochus to Albinus, dogmatic Platonism began from the Stoic teaching of the criterion and certainty, as a bulwark against scepticism.[47] For Antiochus found certainty in cognitive impressions which he identified (contrary to Stoic materialism) with the ideas of Plato.[48] Albinus proposes the criterion as the first topic of his Dialectic (did 4). He distinguishes the faculty which judges, the object of judgement and the judgement made. Both the faculty and the judgement could be seen as the criterion or the standard of judgement; the objects judged are intellectual. The world of the senses cannot go beyond opinion.

Clement's separation of the rule of faith from other claims was one answer to the infinite regress of Sceptics. It became the most important of all the arguments. Tertullian used it in his pretended ban on philosophy, as he adhered to Stoic logic and argued vigorously. For him inquiry is only possible when we follow our criterion, the rule of faith, which Christ taught and we confess (praescr 13). We may seek and find as long as we wish if we hold on to the rule. 'To know nothing against the rule is to know everything' (praescr 14).

7. The perfection of faith

Faith is neither mediocre nor inert. Clement attacks those who wish for bare faith alone, like vignerons who are not prepared to cultivate and farm the vines they plant, but want to pick fruit without delay (str 1.9.43). In contrast, the true dialectic, which is philosophy mixed with truth, ascends and descends (str 1.28.177).

Faith grows into knowledge by a process of dialectic. Faith is not just concerned with starting; it has to go on. To explain intellectual progress, Clement uses Platonic dialectic which has twofold tendencies – towards universality and towards particularity. For Plato and Aristotle, dialectic is concerned with concepts which are common to various branches of knowledge – existence, non-existence, identity, difference, similarity, dissimilarity, unity, plurality. Perhaps Aristotle is rightly incredulous of Plato's super-axioms.[49] Despite differences 'Plato and Aristotle both credit dialectic with the task of discovering some very important trans-departmental principles which hinge on the ubiquitous, non-specialist, or "common" concepts'.[50]

Faith is the royal wisdom described by Plato.[51] What is right is lawful because the law is right reason and universal king. The wise man is king and ruler according to Plato and the Stoics (str 2.4.19).

Plato (Laws 630bc and Rep 475bc) praises faithfulness, which is the mother of virtues (str 2.5.23).

Faith and knowledge are inseparably joined, just as are the father and the son (str 5.1.1). There is a 'double' faith, for Paul speaks of righteousness which is revealed from faith to faith (Rom 1:17). A common faith, says Clement, is always there. For him as for Paul there are no separate levels of faith but continuous growth within a new world.[52] The perfection of faith comes from instruction and logos. Faith saves men and removes mountains (str 5.2.1).

Faith, like a grain of mustard, stimulates the soul to growth and greatness, so that the words about things above roost upon it (str 5.2.1).

Faith is perfect and lacks nothing (paed 1 6:25–52).

For the believer there is no waiting after death, since he has anticipated life eternal by faith. All believers are equally spiritual before their lord, baptised by one spirit and members of one body (1 Cor 12:13). We are to be children in wickedness and men in understanding (1 Cor 14:20).

8. Power and stability

As in the preceding section, Clement brings together his many arguments by an account of their personal appropriation. Faith was seen by its critics as a feeble thing; Clement indicates its strength.

Faith is divine power (cf 1 Cor 2:5) and the strength of truth.

It is the mustard seed which stimulates growth. Faith can move mountains (str 2.11.48). Faith is wiser than human wisdom of men; it is the saving power of God (str 5.1.9).

Faith gives stability to the mature Christian (the true gnostic), while the man who is wise in his own conceits is driven all over the place (str 2.11.51). Faith means unity with the One in clearly Platonic terms: 'The son is not simply one thing as one thing nor many things as parts, but one thing as all things .... Therefore also to believe in him and through him is to become a unit, being indivisibly made one in him' (str 4.25.157).

Again, following Plato, faith is assimilation to God, and the end is the restitution of the promise effected by faith (str 2.22.136). Faith, is *creatrix divinitatis in nobis*.[53] Those, who are taught by the son of God, have the truth; he is himself the person of truth (str 6.15.122). The believer stands apart from others, for on him rests the head of the universe (1 Cor 2:16), the gentle word who destroys the empty craftiness of the wise (str 1.3.23; 1 Cor 3:19f).

9. Conclusion

It is evident that Clement has made intelligent use of Greek philosophy and of the New Testament and that the issues which he raises are of lasting importance for philosophical theology. Preconception is a valid part of epistemology; indeed, it might be argued that every perception is a corrected anticipation. Assent or choice is essential to Christian faith, which is always a matter of confession.

Perception of God is a part of faith. There is a tension between the claim that faith is concerned with what is not seen but anticipated and the claim that God is already heard and perceived; this is inescapable if the need for both present and future eschatology be recognised. Scripture stands as the rational link with God; at the same time there is a place for the symbolic content of scripture.

The argument to an unproved first principle does not prove God, but shows why faith and God go together.

Faith serves as a criterion to discern true from false.

The growing of faith is needed to join anticipation with perception.

The final link of faith and God guards against triumphalism and preserves the dialectic of Christian existence which lives by dying. 'Living faith is tempted faith.'[54]

How useful are Clement's arguments today? For the analytic philosopher in the tradition of Wittgenstein, Clement has certainly arranged the material in a perspicuous presentation *(einer übersichtlichen Darstellung)*, so that the connections may be seen.

'For us the conception of a perspicuous presentation is fundamental. It indicates the way in which we write of things, the way in which we see things.'[55] The objection that ancient philosophers never solve contemporary problems is always wrong, because philosophical problems are elucidated not solved, because not even what we said last year will excuse us from thinking again and because our major handicap is always conceptual parochialism[56] from which fresh minds of another time may well deliver us.

It is appropriate to end with a reference to the account of faith given by a brilliant teacher and philosopher who governed the early development of Harry Wardlaw and me. In his *Theism and Empiricism* (London, 1970), he gives an analysis, beginning from the fact that there are good reasons of an empirical sort for holding that God exists; without these reasons no amount of devotion insight or labour could carry the conclusion. The reasons, because they are empirical, do not amount to proof. They provide a high degree of suggestiveness (159). Initial faith is an assurance which leaps to personal certainty and does not bother even about the good reasons. So faith does not begin as faith in any object. 'First faith' is fixed on the future which it claims to be free from the past. It looks to forgiveness and to new life. The open, forward look of faith has nothing to do with the absence of obstacles. Here religious faith is inseparable from that displayed in any other forward looking activity. It has nothing to do with resignation to the inevitable but is opposed to such resignation. Faith is, as Aquinas put it, 'the courage of the spirit' (164). Faith in God can develop because he is not an object of faith, but its author. It defines and enlarges initial faith. It is not logically invulnerable, but grows because God is a creator who makes possible the expanding future, in which the believer, on his own initiatives, is able to cope with varied situations. Faith is not self-centred, but whole-hearted and liberating, always able to consolidate around Jesus Christ when it is confronted with discouragement. As Paul points out in 1 Cor 15, if Christ is not risen, then faith is vain. Faith indeed is directed towards the apparent disasters of the world (172). Faith *in* God cannot be reduced to belief *that* God is of a certain kind. Assent to articles of faith grows out of the trust which is the structure of faith itself. Calvin criticised the limits of the schoolmen who reduced faith to the bare simple assent of the understanding and overlooked the importance of confidence and security of heart (175). Newman distinguished between notional assent, which was purely intellectual, and real assent, which involved the whole being as well as 'right judgement in ratiocination' (173). Faith as assent is an appropriation, an activity and a decision. Descartes insisted that it is an act, not of intellect, but of will and Christian faith, as Ebeling showed, is directed in three-fold form to God and not to the trinitarian dogma.[57] Faith in Jesus Christ arises through confrontation with the counter evidence of evil and suffering. For Christ shows a concern with evil by healing the sick, especially the mentally sick. Jesus was God because he did what he did (201). While we may find 'prolongations' of God or peripheral 'fringes' of the divine, we may also find strong counter-evidence. Faith is the courage of the spirit which grapples with human fear and pride so that 'the frontiers are rolled back and the counter evidence is appropriated as the field of operations for the testing of the evidence' (207). The verification of faith is in action, just as the verification of practice is in faith. 'That the ethics of charity work, and work triumphantly, when every other device stalls at some point of the journey, is all the verification we need. But unless we have adopted the stance of practice, it might not convince us' (236). Evils do not dismay us when we move from the standpoint of theory to practice, as we follow a faith which shows how God can get rid of evils. We may put together the bits and pieces about God which come our way and see them consolidate into a developing pattern. These 'prolongations' or 'fringes' can be discerned by empirical philosophy. But then faith takes over, 'faith which underpins the necessity of action, and finds in action its vindication, supporting and completing and circulating within the more tentative constructions of the human intellect, which it dare not, for its own sake, ignore or defy' (273).

Gibson's account of faith echoes every point which Clement made. It draws upon many hundreds of years of Christian thinking and therefore states things in a different way. However the links of faith with decision, perception, will and the future confirm what Clement found in the New Testament and in philosophy.

In offering this piece to Harry Wardlaw, I express my gratitude for many hours of conversation and help. His value as Socratic midwife to Australian theologians has been inestimable. Theology in a vast continent is plagued by isolation. Most scholars have done their formative postgraduate work in different countries or at least in different universities, and work within methods, which often seem incommensurable. Physical isolation is intensified by the local cultures, which persist from six different colonies. Further, in other countries, theology is a much more parochial discipline than others, being geared to local debates and party disputes, which when flavoured by their local irony seem far from serious. The future of Australian theology depends on conversation between working scholars in a coalition against trendiness. 'For thinking is part of the human endeavour which begins and is completed in faith.'[58]

End Notes

1. It is also more extensive than most relevant discussion today. Rational faith, says Richard Swinburne, *Faith and Reason* (Oxford: Oxford University Press, 1981), 66ff, is based on evidence from investigation where the believer has subjected his standards to criticism and where he has checked that these standards made belief probable, and where the evidence, the standards and the checking were in his view adequate.

   He may strengthen his claims to rationality by lifting his standards, by talking to his minister, or by talking to atheists and reading relevant books. Elsewhere, beliefs are blameworthy only if they are reached carelessly and dishonestly. (Alan Donagan, *The Nature of Morality* (Chicago,1977), 134.

2. BD Ellis, *Rational Belief Systems* (Oxford: Oxford University Press, 1979), 100.

3. FM Cornford, *The Unwritten Philosophy and Other Essays* (Cambridge: Cambridge University Press, 1950), 87.

4. See an interesting recent study: C Nahm, 'The debate on the Platonism of Justin Martyr', *The Second Century* 9, 3 (1992), 129–151. It would be hard, in the second century, to be a Platonist, without being a Stoic and something of an Aristotelian as well.

5. Disputants resemble farmers who might argue concerning the agricultural value of a district when one is thinking in terms of wheat, another of apples and a third of pineapples.

6. Philosophy, said Clement, was to the Greeks what the law was to the

Jews, a *paidagogos* to bring them to Christ.

7. These have been set out in detail in my article, 'Arguments for faith in Clement of Alexandria', Vig Chr 48, 1, 1994, 1–24. This article examines the philosophical and theological value of the several arguments.

8. In this preliminary selection, I concentrate on Clement's favourite letter, The First Epistle to the Corinthians.

9. 'Faith, then, is a form of vision. When Christ was on earth, to have faith was to "see his glory" – to apprehend and acknowledge the deity through the veil of humanity'. CH Dodd, *The Interpretation of the Fourth Gospel* (Cambridge: Cambridge University Press, 1954), 186.

10. For example, SRC Lilla, *Clement of Alexandria* (Oxford: Oxford University Press,1971), 118–142.

11. Every writer who is worth reading makes demands. Clement acknowledges the unusual nature of his demands.

12. A Manuwald, *Die Prolepsislehre Epikurs*, 103.

13. The influence of Heraclitus on Clement is strong. See for an introductory statement, P Valentin, *Héraclite et Clément d'Alexandrie*, RSR, 46 (1958). Heraclitus was important for, and transmitted by, the Stoics.

14. R Bultmann, TWNT, 2, 528.

15. R Bultmann, *Marburger Predigten* (Tübingen, 1956), 170f.

16. J Moltmann, *Theologie der Hoffnung* (München, 1964), 9–30.

17. G Ebeling, *The Nature of Faith* (London, 1961), 175.

18. Newman, *Grammar*, (London, 1901), 189f.

19. James Collins, *God in Modern Philosophy* (London, 1960), 354f.

20. W Stegmüller, *Metaphysik, Skepsis, Wissenschaft*, second edition (Berlin, Heidelberg, New York, 1969), 1f, cited H Küng, *Does God Exist?* (London, 1980), 425.

21. JR Bambrough, *Reason, Truth and God* (London: SCM Press, 1969), 51, pointed out the modern rejection of transcendence in transcendent material substance, minds, values and universals or Platonic forms. This is no longer the case in logical theory. See J Bigelow and R Pargetter, *Science and Necessity*, Cambridge Studies in Philosophy (Cambridge: Cambridge University Press, 1991), and the Essay Review of Brian Ellis, Scientific Platonism (*Stud Hist Phil Sci* 23, 4, 1992), 665–679.

22. I Murdoch, *Metaphysics as a Guide to Morals* (London, 1992), 433.

23. William P Alston, *Perceiving God, the Epistemology of Religious Experience* (Ithaca and London: Cornell University Press, 1991).

24. *Ibid*, 5, 9–67.

25. *Ibid*, 6, 146–183.

26. *Ibid*, 7, 255–285.

27. An extended empiricist case for the belief in God has been presented in the work of A Boyce Gibson, *Theism and Empiricism* (London, 1970). This is discussed in the conclusion of this essay.

28. Alston, *Perceiving God*, 8, 286–307.
29. FM Cornford comments, 'the visible world being only a likeness of the real, no account of it can be more than a likely story'. *Plato's Cosmology* (London, 1948), 28.
30. Poetry 'represented less what we would call by that name, but an indoctrination which today would be comprised in a shelf of text-books and works of reference'. EA Havelock, *Preface to Plato* (Oxford: Oxford University Press, 1963), 27, cited by Bambrough, *Reason, Truth and God*, 122.
31. G Ebeling discusses these issues in 'The significance of the critical historical method for church and theology in Protestantism' and 'The question of the historical Jesus and the problem of Christology' in *Word and Faith* (London, 1963), 17–61, 288–304. There are difficulties, of course, within Calvinist biblicist tradition which has been strong in the English-speaking world.
32. See E Käsemann, *Essays on New Testament Themes* (London, 1964), 48–54.
33. For Aristotle, a first principle is also a cause. '*Arche* means a beginning, starting-point, first principle or cause. In one place (Met 1003b 23–24) he says that ajrchv and ai[tion are mia; fuvsi, and at 1013a17 that all ai[tia are ajrcaiv. In a physical sense it was applied to the primary substance and permanent ground of the universe postulated by the early natural philosophers – water, air, . . . In applied logic the archai are the ultimate, undemonstrable premises of apodeictic syllogism.' WKC Guthrie, *A History of Greek Philosophy*, 6, *Aristotle, an Encounter* (Cambridge: Cambridge University Press, 1981), 178.
34. The last chapter of the *Posterior Analytics* is one of the most important in all Aristotle's works. 'It is a confession of his epistemological faith, a statement of the source from which in the last resort all knowledge springs.' Guthrie, *History*, 6, 179. Guthrie notes the criticism by DW Hamlyn that the account is crude, incoherent, unclear and implausible; 'Aristotelian Epagoge', *Phronesis* 21, 1976, 167–184.
35. *Ibid*, 476.
36. Bambrough, *Reason, Truth and God*, 94.
37. Guthrie, *Aristotle*, 178.
38. See Osborn, *The Beginning of Christian Philosophy* (Cambridge: Cambridge University Press, 1981), 120f, and J van Heijenoort, Gödel's Theorem, *The Encyclopedia of Philosophy*, vol 3, edited by P Edwards (New York, 1967) 348f.
39. See E Käsemann, *The Faith of Abraham in Romans 4, Perspectives on Paul* (London, 1971),79–101.
40. Luther, cited R Bultmann, 'The crisis in belief', in *Gesammelte Aufsätze*, 2 (2 Aufl, Tübingen, 1968), 8; FT, *Essays Philosophical and Theological* (London, 1955), 8f.

41. Bultmann, *ibid*, 8; ET 9.
42. *Ibid*, 13; ET 14f.
43. Theodoret attributes this formula to Aristotle (Graec affect cur 1, 90).
44. See E Osborn, 'Philo and Clement: Citation and Influence', in *Lebendige Überlieferung* (Beirut and Ostfildern, 1992), FS H-J Vogt, editor, N El-Khoury *et al*, 231.
45. See JM Rist, *Stoic Philosophy* (Cambridge: Cambridge University Press, 1969), 138–42.
46. *Ibid*. See also Osborn, *Reason and the Rule of Faith*, FS H Chadwick (Cambridge: Cambridge University Press, 1989), 40–61.
47. See discussion in JM Dillon, *The Middle Platonists* (London, 1977), 62–9 and 273–6.
48. *Ibid*, 93.
49. 'From completely topic-neutral premisses, the truths of the special sciences *could* not follow.' G Ryle, 'Dialectic in the Academy', in Renford Bambrough, *New Essays on Plato and Aristotle* (London, 1965), 59.
50. *Ibid*, 60.
51. In *Euthydemus and Politicus*.
52. E Käsemann, *Commentary on Romans* (Grand Rapids: Eerdman, 1980), 31.
53. Luther, cited by G Ebeling, *The Nature of Faith* (London, 1961), 176.
54. G Ebeling, *The Nature of Faith* (London, 1961), 162.
55. Ludwig Wittgenstein, *Remarks on Frazer's 'Golden Bough'*, translated by AC Miles and R Rhees (Doncaster, 1979), 52. See Iris Murdoch, *Metaphysics as a Guide to Morals* (London, 1992), 424.
56. See Quentin Skinner, 'Meaning and Understanding in the History of Ideas', *HTh*, 8 (1969), 53.
57. G Ebeling, *The Nature of Faith* (London, 1961), 70f.
58. A Boyce Gibson, *Theism and Empiricism* (London, 1970), 273.

7

JESUS – THE STORY OF STORIES? ENGAGING WITH JOHN CARROLL

GEOFFREY THOMPSON

1. Culture, story and truth: Introduction

> The spirit cannot breathe without story. It sinks to a whimper, deflating its [hosts], and condemning them to psychopathology – literally disease of the soul. So it is for the young in the contemporary West – teenagers, those in their twenties, the hope and pride of their societies – and with them, swathes of their seemingly more assured elders. A malaise holds them in thrall, struggling to live in a present without vision of any future, or connection to . . . their own personal past . . . . They are dying for want of a story.[1]

So writes the Australian sociologist and cultural commentator John Carroll in his recently published book, *The Western Dreaming: The Western World is Dying for Want of a Story.*

Carroll distances himself from the postmodern celebration of the loss of a grand narrative. Indeed, he insists on confronting his readers with the cultural, social and personal costs incurred as culture has fragmented – its constituent parts unanchored by a story that would otherwise hold them together.[2]

Without story, he says, 'the temptation has been withdrawal into self'; a vision of reality in which 'each puny ego is left alone to whimper *me-me-me* at the void'. There has arisen, he claims, a 'fear of big story', a fear, that is, that your and my story will be swamped by any larger claim to truth. (p 11) 'Truth', he says, 'is a shaft of light breaking through to illuminate the mist-shrouded' life. (p 4) There is a 'grand elusive story of what it means to be human'. (p 217) In the same way that Michelangelo believed that his task was to chisel away at a piece of marble revealing the shape that already lay buried within it, this truth is buried within human existence and is piped forth not by modernity's arid rationalism but by the classical, archetypal stories that constantly recur in Western culture, including its popular expressions.

Indeed, Carroll argues that popular culture itself reveals that despite the fear of a grand narrative, the quest for it cannot be suppressed. In film, television and tabloid press, popular culture takes the ordinary and recasts it as larger than life. 'These "real-life" stories address the vital unconscious knowledge in each person that the local and particular, ordinary old me, is shadowed by a grand story, a truth shaping and vindicating its existence.' (p 11)

Carroll's intention to champion the 'higher truth' (p 11) sees him pitching out an intellectual space between the extremes of both modernity and postmodernity. Against modernity's rationalism he argues for narrative or story as the access to truth. But against radical postmodernity's relativism, he argues for the notion of a truth which is *the* truth. This engagement with the question of truth (not least in the self-conscious opposition to, and the alertness to the cultural and social consequences of, its denial) should at once attract the interest of Christian believers and thinkers with their broadly realist conceptions of truth.[3] Yet, this is not the element of the book which will most directly engage Christians. That lies with what Carroll says about Jesus.

Simply, Jesus is the book's beginning and end. At the end of his argument he identifies Jesus as the pivot of the whole enterprise: 'Jesus dwells constantly as the enigmatic *I am* pivot to the Western Dreaming.' (p 236) His story is 'the story of Western stories'. (p 207) And he insists that Jesus has again and again visited Western culture. Jesus has returned 'many, many times, his story forcing itself incessantly upon the West'. (p 208) These remarks are all set against what he said at the beginning of the book:

> We receive him ... in the form of a story. If that story is told in the right way ... and the people ... are receptive – the story cryptically intersecting with their own and then the very foundations of being may be illuminated by the light of Truth. (p 6)

John Carroll is no apologist for the Christian faith. An atheist, he mocks the churches,[4] he holds theology and theologians in contempt[5] and denies all belief in any idea of God.[6] Jesus is important to his project because he interprets him as the one who is able to tap into the fullness of human existence. In this essay, after outlining Carroll's estimate of Jesus and Jesus' relationship to the truth, I will explore precisely what it is that distinguishes orthodox Christianity's account of Jesus from Carroll's. Finally, I will make certain theological observations on how orthodox Christian faith can engage the cultural malaise highlighted by Carroll.

2. Story, truth and Jesus

The following extended passage represents what is perhaps the closest Carroll gives to a summary of what he believes about Jesus and his significance.

> [Jesus's] emphasis was simple: *I am.* But the mists lie thick over the river of the truth about the nature of being. Some of the veils he stripped away – family, tribe, property, virtue, communal ritual. The way, he also said, is not through seeing. if you can live towards me, near me, as Magdalene did, the breath will stir and you may hear it, miraculously finding yourself fitted to its form. *I am* my life, my story – that is all there is to know.
>
> He is the tragic humanness of failure – strip away that veil, too. Through this very fallibility, without God, without magical resurrection, from time to time off-balance, leaving a trail of fear, he was accompanied by some sort of knowing – such as the two at the Emmaus table learn. He was it, whatever that enigmatic *it* is. All he has, all he leaves, is *I am*, a presence, a charged thereness within the world. Of course, it is now gone, in the fleshly existential sense. It remains, however, as Story, somehow to be tapped for its *pneuma.* (p 207)[7]

Carroll's remarks about Jesus are set within an intellectual scaffolding the planks of which are provided by several key thinkers of the modern era. Jung contributes the idea of archetypal stories, but Carroll resists the idea of a universal and uniformly refracted 'collective unconscious'. Instead, with echoes of a Durkheimian sociology of religion, he insists that each culture has its own distinct set of 'one or two, perhaps three, major channels which ... are diffused through myriad tributaries forming the beliefs of a society'. (p 12) Similarly, and invoking the language of indigenous Australians: 'The sacred is universal. Each Dreaming is particular, providing its own narrative vehicles for gaining access to the general sacred order'. (p 216) [8] At the same time, Weber is invoked to highlight the *disenchantment* that accompanies modernity.[9] Nietzsche contributes the rhetoric of the death of God, but Carroll's humanist disquiet at the prospect of 'a complete collapse of meaning into nihilism' leads to an insistence that 'the force of the sacred continues to drive through the human condition'. (p 27) Nevertheless, the sacred does not refer to any objectively existing God. Rather, the sacred is paired with culture, the two mutually referring to each other. In short, culture and the sacred, or *pneuma,* are one: 'A culture is its sacred stories ... . Culture is the power to lift [humans] from their prone animal state, the power to reveal the truth'. (p 12)

The metaphysical investment that Carroll makes in story is enormous[10] – and on the surface appears to reflect the aspect of the argument that most closely parallels at least one strand of postmodern theory – specifically, a deconstructionist privileging of the text over any external referent. Nowhere is this more evident than in his stated reasons for beginning the book with Luke's story of the two disciples' encounter with Jesus on the road to Emmaus. That story was chosen because 'somewhere and somehow it bears a deep and central truth' that does its work in the telling of the story. He continues: 'Every detail remains obscure – open to question and doubt. All we are left with is the inner confidence that this story is important .... Do not press too hard for definite shape, for a definitive reading ... . The story in itself is all.' (p 17)

Inevitably with such intellectual parameters Carroll's Jesus will make little contact with the Jesus of creedal Christianity. Nevertheless, what *is* interesting to the church and its theologians, I suggest, is that Carroll has introduced Jesus to public discussion in Australia in a way that the church – and its theologians – can only dream about doing. But even more specifically than that, he has quite explicitly linked three themes: Jesus, truth and story, and he has done so in the context of contemporary culture's quest for spiritual re-enchantment.

What should be the reaction of Christian faith to Carroll's project? We could be defensive and simply pit our claims about Jesus against his. Or we could adopt the view that with our belief in God we hold the missing piece to Carroll's jigsaw puzzle: put God in the picture and Carroll's project would be ours. But it would be patronising to ignore the fact that Carroll is quite happy with his God-less understanding of Jesus and isn't fossicking around for the missing jigsaw piece: be it God- or otherwise-shaped.

It is particularly important to resist this latter option because it obscures a vital difference between the way Carroll reads the gospel narratives and the way Christian faith has read them. The difference is not merely that God enters the Christian reading of the text merely as a *supernatural* overlay to an otherwise agreed theologically-neutral or historicist reading. The difference lies much more in the respective juxtapositions of, and relationships between *Jesus, story* and *truth*. In its readings of the gospels, Christian faith aligns and weights these elements differently to Carroll. The difference between Carroll and Christian faith is as much a hermeneutical difference as it is theological one. Or, more precisely, the theological and hermeneutical factors that drive the difference mutually inform each other (just as Carroll's atheism and implicit hermeneutic mutually inform each other in the course of his work). Ultimately, these mutually informing theological and hermeneutical factors give shape to Christianity's own investment in story. Understanding the nature of that investment and the issues at stake will be the task of the next two sections of the essay.

3. Christian faith and story

Christianity is unintelligible without grasping the fact that its understanding of the relationship between story and truth is not just incidental, but is intrinsic to that which it understands reality to be. That reality is the still unfinished history of the origin and goal of creation in relation to its Creator. This is *the* Grand Narrative. Yet the plot of that grand narrative pivots around one particular chapter/episode: the story of Jesus. Whilst it is true that outside the gospels the New Testament proclaims the gospel in more formulaic and creedal terms, such formulae and creeds are always embedded in and presuppose the narrative plot and structure which the gospels make explicit.

It hardly needs commenting that the confidence that these narratives are truth-bearing was severely tested by various strands of thought bequeathed by modernity. In particular the Bible's strong dependence on narrative was taken to mean that the Bible was (at least) one remove from the truth. If the Bible was to be granted a relationship to the truth, any such relationship was made a function of the reliability of its reporting of things said and done in certain places at certain times. The cloud of suspicion which thus arose over the biblical material cast its longest shadow over the gospels. The strong nexus that formed in the modern era between 'facts' and 'truth' severely problematised the gospels' diversity and their authors' obvious use of imagination and creativity. Rather than being regarded as epistemological gains, such features of these documents became evidence of incoherence and were then used as weapons to be wielded against Christianity by its critics.

Reacting to this situation with sometimes revisionist motives and sometimes apologetic intentions, biblical scholarship saw an almost universal appropriation of the historical-critical method and a consequent privileging of historical questions in biblical hermeneutics. Arguably, the most serious casualty of this turn was the degree of theological engagement with the texts. Not only were theological readings of the biblical texts marginalised, there was also a questioning of the legitimacy of any theological reading at all. Commenting on this development, Francis Watson has written:

> [I]t is believed that theological concerns have an inevitable tendency to distort the autonomous processes of biblical exegesis – a prejudice so strong that to identify a theological motivation underlying an exegetical position is often held to be sufficient refutation.[11]

Nevertheless, just as the canons of modernity have been subject to severe scrutiny in other disciplines, so in theology narrative theologians have sought to highlight and retrieve what was lost to

Christianity during this period of preoccupation with historical-critical hermeneutics. They have argued, for instance, that prior to the modern era Christians read the Bible as a kind of textual amalgam of historical reference, doctrinal content, imaginative constructions and a general true-to-lifeness without necessarily ever privileging any one of those components as the pathway to, or guarantor of, the Bible's truth.[12] Instead, the whole text presents a portal into reality. Although for very different reasons, the point is well-made by Margaret Wertheim, the Australian-born science writer in her recent book, *The Pearly Gates of Cyberspace.*

> From Homer to Asimov, one of the functions of all great literature has indeed been to invoke believable 'other' worlds. Operating purely on the power of words, books project us into utterly absorbing alternative realities. It is no coincidence that the Bible begins with the phrase 'In the beginning was the Word.'[13]

Notwithstanding her unfortunate confusion of the Bible's forty-third book with its first, her point is well made. In the same way, the textual amalgam that the Bible is gives access to the reality it depicts precisely – and perhaps only – through the complex matrix of diverse literary genres, tropes and modes of discourse that it is. The theological implication of this hermeneutical insight is that the Bible can be taken seriously as a true account of the actual state of affairs between God and humanity, even when its 'history' or its 'science' is challenged.[14]

By moving the discussion in this direction, the impression may be given that the theological correction to historical-critical hermeneutics is to align the Christian theological investment in narrative with contemporary narrative theory, in which matters of historical reference are rendered inconsequential to a given text's multiple meanings. This is not the case. Indeed, this is not what narrative theology, at least in its theologically more mature expressions, is about. It corrects the mistaken privileging of historical questions not by jettisoning question of a text's historical referent, but by placing such questions in a larger hermeneutical framework. So, whilst it is true that faith affirms that the Bible depicts the actual circumstances of the situation between God and humanity independently of whether it is right in every matter of historical or scientific detail, it is also true that the Bible is not understood to do so without telling particular stories about Israel, its liberation from Egypt, its conquest of Canaan, its political failures and successes, its heroes, its exile, and above all, not without the particular stories about Jesus of Nazareth. It is in those events that God effects the divine purposes for all creation. In other words, the literature of Bible does not, to use Margaret Wertheim's terms, invoke just any believable other world. There are certain events, certain places and certain people who have an existence independently of their literary depiction that constitute this world.

Therefore, the way the Bible depicts a world is not like the way JRR Tolkein depicts the world of Middle Earth. That certainly is an alternative other world that people are able to enter with their imaginations and even learn its language. But Middle Earth, Gandolph and Freydo do not exist except as literary (or cinematic) phenomena. Instead, the way the Bible depicts a world is more like the way Alexander Solzhenitsyn uses fiction to truly depict life in Stalinist Russia. Solzhenitsyn was not just writing about prison in general, or about communism in general, or about totalitarianism in general. His stories depended on his imaginative powers but they *were* about Stalinist Russia in the mid-twentieth century and not some other place or some other time. The life of Ivan Denisovich and the events on Gulag Archipelago were literary phenomena, but they were not just literary phenomena.[15] The relationship between literary creativity and the depiction of reality that exists apart from its literary depiction is axiomatic for understanding the Christian investment in narrative. Nowhere is this more important than in respect to the gospels, to which I now turn.

4. Jesus and the Gospel Narratives

For all their diversity, for all the obvious use of the imagination of the gospel writers, the gospels tell the story of Jesus and not some other story, the story of Jesus who exists independently of the narratives written about him.[16] Yet to insist that the gospels tell a story about Jesus, not a fictional story or a story about something else, immediately forces us to address the question of the diversity of the gospel narratives. Does not the fact that there are four literary gospels itself feed the idea that they are not telling the story of Jesus, but that they are telling some other story: the story of the evangelists' perspectives or the story of theological and power struggles within the early church? Indeed, so strong has this suspicion been within biblical scholarship that the one biblical scholar has recently suggested that the historical critics' inability to reconstruct the *historical* Jesus has been compensated for by attempts to reconstruct the communities from which the gospels emerged.

> All the historical specificity for which historical critics long is transferred from the historical Jesus to the evangelist's community. The principle that the Gospels inform us not about Jesus but about the church is taken so literally that the narrative, ostensibly about Jesus, has to be understood as an allegory in which the community actually tells its own story.[17]

With reference to three gospels texts, I want to suggest there is an historiographical intention according to which the historical reference of the gospels, whilst not by itself determining the content of the gospel, nevertheless so disciplines the authors' writing that the gospels cannot but be understood to be primarily a depiction of Jesus. As such, the gospels are paradigmatic of the place which historical reference has in biblical narratives whose truthfulness is nevertheless neither exclusively defined nor exhausted by their historical reference. The gospel texts in question are drawn from the beginning of Luke and the end of John.[18]

> Since many have undertaken to set down an orderly account of the events that have been fulfilled among us, just as they were handed on to us by those who from the beginning were eyewitnesses and servants of the word, I too decided, after investigating everything carefully from the very first, to write an orderly account for you, most excellent Theophilus, so that you may know the truth concerning the things about which you have been instructed. (Luke 1:1–4)

> Now Jesus did many other signs in the presence of his
> disciples, which are not written in this book. But these are written
> so that you may come to believe that Jesus is the Messiah, the
> Son of God, and that through believing you may have life in his
> name. (John 20:30–31)
> This is the disciple who is testifying to these things and
> has written them, and we know that his testimony is true. But
> there are also many other things that Jesus did; if every one of
> them were written down, I suppose that the world itself could
> not contain the books that would be written. (John 21:24–25)

By citing these three particular texts I am not naively trying to make
Luke and John modern historians. But the intention of both authors
to write about someone who exists and certain events that have
happened apart from the writing of the story itself should be noted.
And note, too, their lack of embarrassment about the fact that others
have done so before and apart from them. Neither author offers their
account as definitive – and in the case of John's gospel, the author
explicitly remarks on his inability – and that of anyone else, for that
matter – ever to give a definitive and exhaustive rendering of Jesus.
And in the case of Luke, the author openly indicates the particularity
of his account and his dependence on the work of others. No claim
is made that this work supersedes the early written or oral accounts.
But also note how both writers are clear that despite their openness
to all that diversity and the valid multiplicity of interpretations of
Jesus, something particular and specific is to be said: 'something
has been fulfilled among us', writes Luke; and John declares that he
writes what he writes so that his readers may come to believe what
the narratives relate: Jesus is the Messiah.

One current Christian writer who is provoking discussion
around these issues is Francis Watson. He makes two comments
about these passages which are helpful. Firstly, he suggests that
these passages indicate that, 'These texts are not to be understood
as an enclosed fictional world, but as an imaginative rendering of a
prior reality'. Secondly, and more expansively:

> The reader implied by both John and Luke reads these texts in
> order to discover again that, outside and prior to these texts,
> Jesus is the Christ. The possibility of this discovery is dependent

on this claim to be truthful to the prior reality they seek to render – the claim that within the limits of necessary selectivity, the mediation of tradition and limited perspective, written history represents enacted history in a way that does not mislead.[19]

With these insights in mind, it is possible to begin to grasp the contours of the relationship between Jesus, story and truth in orthodox Christian faith. For Christian faith, the story of Jesus is pivotal not because it is the *story* of Jesus, but because it is the story of *Jesus*. For Carroll, as noted above, the story in itself is all there is. In his appropriation of Jesus, minimal weighting is given to the gospels' correspondence to the circumstances and course of Jesus' life. Maximal weighting is given to their correspondence to a theory of story as the access to an ultimately ineffable truth. For Christian faith, on the other hand, maximal weighting is given to the gospels' correspondence to the circumstances and course of Jesus' life. Minimal weighting is given to their correspondence to some idealised narrative form. Their narrative form is important because of their prior correspondence to the living reality that Jesus is.

Ultimately, there is nothing in *The Western Dreaming* that would make it necessary for Carroll to insist that Jesus was born a Jew, that he lived in Palestine, that he had certain disputes with certain opponents, that he healed certain people and not others, that he made decisions to go to this place and not that, or that he set himself for Jerusalem in the context of Jewish messianic hopes. For Carroll, Jesus need not have been or have done any of these things and he would still be important, he would still have pivotal significance to the Western Dreaming. For Carroll, on the basis of the argument of *The Western Dreaming,* Jesus could just have been a literary phenomenon. Where Christian faith engages with and honours the historiographical intention of the gospels, Carroll jettisons it. It is here that Christianity most decisively parts company with Carroll and his interpretation of Jesus, and indeed parts company with much radical postmodern narrative theory. I would argue that the gospels are a standing affirmation that Jesus is important and universally significant only because he was and did all these things and more.[20] In the case of the gospel presentations of Jesus, *the story in itself is **not** all.*

5. Culture, story and truth: Conclusion

In the first section of this essay, I suggested that Carroll's championing of a 'higher truth' positioned him in a socio-intellectual space somewhere between modernity's arid rationalism and postmodernity's relativism. I also suggested that Carroll's commitment to a truth which is *the* truth had a certain realist impulse, an impulse which overlapped to some extent with the realist intent of Christianity's truth claims. Certainly, the realist drive of Carroll's project was reinforced by his rejection and exposé of Nietzschean nihilism that in so many ways threatens the contemporary West. Moreover, he does not hesitate to alert contemporary culture to the injury that it does to itself when it allows the question of truth to be avoided: 'they are dying for want of a story' is his refrain throughout the first chapter.

I would suggest that if the quest for truth and the re-enchantment and spirituality that might accompany it is to succeed, it will need to happen in the space that he has mapped out. Yet I would argue that the way Carroll himself tries to fill this space, notwithstanding the preeminent place he gives to Jesus in it, is quite dangerous. His passion for truth pushes him away from nihilism, but his insistence that the story in itself is all there is does not finally lead to even a moderately realist account of the truth, but to an idealism which is of uncertain intellectual stability and of dubious value to Western society's cultural malaise. Herein, I suggest, lies the subversion of his own solution to the problem he has rightly identified. Unanchored to anything outside itself, this story (essentially the renaissance humanist story of human dignity, worth, and courage) is on the one hand ripe for ideological manipulation and on the other has nothing to stop the question of truth being reduced to a fantasy.

So, I would argue that the story of God's action in Christ, rendered to us in narrative form in the gospels, occupies the space mapped out by Carroll better than Carroll does himself. Its resistance to contemporary nihilism is more persuasive than Carroll's because of a more surely grounded claim to realism. A small element of that claim has been demonstrated in this essay through reference to the particular juxtaposition of Jesus, story and truth that accompanies the orthodox reading of the gospels.[21] Carroll declares: 'The spirit cannot breathe without story'. True. A spirituality unanchored to the truth will evaporate as quickly as it emerges and our culture will go on dying for want of a story. But I would argue that the spirit cannot breathe without a story that is true and anchored in something outside itself. The church tells the story about the calling and hopes of Israel, of Jesus's life, death and resurrection, and the bequeathing of Israel's hope to the whole world, in the confidence that it is that story. Christian faith understands this story to be the grand narrative. And it is the testimony of Christian faith that, rightly told and enacted, it is not a grand narrative that needs to be feared. It is a narrative which, far from swamping our stories, renews and restores our stories, giving them dignity and purpose.

Nevertheless, John Carroll's work remains salutary for Christian theologians. It is a reminder that the question of truth is of immense importance to contemporary culture. Indeed, in view of the tendency of the contemporary churches to understand their responsibilities for cultural engagement to be exhausted in speaking of justice, community service and spirituality (as if they were somehow neutral with regard to truth), it might be a case of Carroll being a child of the world who is wiser than the children of the light. Be that as it may, this essay has been written in the conviction, learnt in no small measure from having been a student of Harry Wardlaw, that the articulation of the gospels' truth is a perennial obligation upon the Christian theologian. Carroll's work both in its weaknesses and strengths is a reminder that this is no time to pull back from that responsibility.

End Notes

1. John Carroll, *The Western Dreaming: The Western World is Dying for Want of a Story* (Sydney: HarperCollins, 2001), 6. Hereafter all quotations from this work will be cited in parentheses within the main body of the text. This book continues themes previously developed by Carroll in *Humanism: The Wreck of Western Culture* (London: Fontana, 1993) and *Ego and Soul: The Modern West in Search of Meaning* (Sydney: HarperCollins, 1998).
2. See, for instance, the disturbing vignettes of contemporary life offered by Carroll on 6–8.

3. This admittedly rather massive generalisation about the *realist* nature of Christian truth claims is not meant to exclude any or every *idealist* element from such claims. Rather, I am pressing a Christian commitment to *realism* to distinguish the truth proclaimed by orthodox Christianity from the nihilistic *non-realism* which Carroll rightly exposes as disturbing force within contemporary culture.

4. See the various comments throughout *The Western Dreaming*, eg 17, 25f, 31, 212. And see especially his earlier and brilliantly written commentary on the funeral of Princess Diana in which he identifies the triumph of the spirituality of popular culture over a dying Christendom which was manifest in that service (see *Ego and Soul*, 209–212).

5. See *The Western Dreaming*, 6.

6. See *The Western Dreaming*, 21–43.

7. Carroll's insistence that Jesus is the personal focus of the mystery of being is further reinforced with this later comment: '[A]ll Jesus ever adds to "Courage. *I am*. Don't fear!" is "I am the Light!" and "The *pneuma* bloweth where it wills, and thou hearest its sound, but canst not tell whence it cometh, and whither it goeth."' (231)

8. In his attempts to conceptualise the relationship between the universal and the particular Carroll would appear to be staking out a novel position for which he has not quite achieved conceptual clarity. Whilst explicitly rejecting the Jungian idea of a universal unconscious *(The Western Dreaming,* 244, fn 9), he has previously drawn on Durkheim's account of a link between a particular society's 'collective conscience' and a universal sacred force *(Ego and Soul,* 87f and *Humanism*, 224f). It is the latter that seems to most inform his constructive position.

9. See *The Western Dreaming*, 221.

10. In an engaging phrase, Carroll speaks of the 'metaphysical cyclone that is Story'. (217) Story also supersedes philosophy which, Carroll writes, 'in its intellectual abstraction, at most plays a minor navigational role on the expedition beyond all chartered territory. We travel by Story.' (225)

11. Francis Watson, *Text and Truth: Redefining Biblical Theology* (Edinburgh: T&T Clark, 1997), 4.

12. The pivotal study in this regard is Hans Frei's *The Eclipse of Biblical Narrative: A Study in Eighteenth- and Nineteenth-Century Hermeneutics* (Yale: Yale University Press, 1974).

13. Margaret Wertheim, *The Pearly Gates of Cyberspace: A History of Space from Dante to the Internet* (Sydney: Doubleday, 1999), 51.

14. I am here appropriating some remarks of Brendan Byrne in his analysis of the work of George Lindbeck: 'The Bible is often "history-like" even when it is not "likely history". It can be taken seriously as a delineation of the character of divine and human agents, even when its history or science is challenged.' See Brendan Byrne, 'Gospel Narrative and the Jesus of History: Where Should Christology Begin?' *Pacifica* 13 (2000):

49–66 (54).

15. For a more detailed discussion on the analogy between Solzhenitsyn's narrative realism and Christianity's realist use of narrative see David F Ford, 'System, Story, Performance: A Proposal About the Role of Narrative in Christian Systematic Theology', in Stanley Hauerwas and L Gregory Jones (editors), *Why Narrative: Readings in Narrative Theology* (Grand Rapids: Eerdmans, 1989), 191–215 (194–196). Also see Ford's use of Solzhenitsyn in Ford's own analysis of arguably the most important theological appropriation the narrative character of biblical literature in twentieth century theology, namely Karl Barth's *Church Dogmatics* in David F Ford, *Barth and God's Story: Biblical Narrative and the Theological Method of Karl Barth in 'The Church Dogmatics'* (Frankfurt: Verlag Peter Lang, 1981), 65–71.

16. For an extended argument concerning the way the gospels tell the story of Jesus and not some other story see Hans Frei, *The Identity of Jesus Christ* (Philadelphia: Fortress Press, 1975).

17. Richard Bauckham, 'For Whom Were Gospels Written?' in Richard Bauckham (editor), *The Gospels for All Christians: Rethinking the Gospel Audiences* (Grand Rapids: Eerdmans, 1998), 9–48 (20).

18. In turning to these particular texts I am drawing on the discussion of them by Francis Watson in his *Text and Truth*, 34–37. I will make explicit use of his argument below.

19. Watson, *Text and Truth*, 36.

20. A good example of the issue at stake here would be the use Carroll makes of the Johannine account of Jesus's response to Nicodemus in John 3 concerning the unpredictability of the spirit's coming and going. Carroll introduces and comments upon this passage as follows: 'Pealing on out of eternity is the *pneuma* refrain: *The wind (pneuma) bloweth where he wills, and thou hearest his sound, but canst not tell whence he cometh.* The Greek word *pneuma* means all of spirit, breath and wind. The 'sacred breath' is potentially all around, caught in the image of the wind that bloweth. As much as ever, there is the experience of the rising out of self to conjoin with greater oneness.' (27) Carroll makes much use of *pneuma* thus interpreted (including especially further references to the Johannine passage) and Jesus's particular relationship with it in the final two chapters of the book. However, whilst not denying the appropriation of Greek thought in the gospel of John, any serious engagement with this particular text in both its historical and literary context would have to acknowledge that far from 'pealing out of eternity' or having to do with 'the rising out of self to conjoin with greater oneness', it is primarily about universalising of Israel's messianic hope that was associated with Jesus.

21. For recent (and diverse) discussions of the complex and nuanced nature of Christian realism see, for instance, Paul Avis, *God and the Creative*

Imagination: Metaphor, Symbol and Myth in Religion and Theology (London: Routledge, 1999), especially chapters 12–14; Rufus Black, *Christian Moral Realism: Natural Law, Narrative, Virtue, and the Gospel* (Oxford: Oxford University Press, 2000), especially chapter 4; Brian D Ingraffia, *Postmodern Theory and Biblical Theology* (Cambridge: Cambridge University Press, 1995) and Bruce D Marshall, *Trinity and Truth* (Cambridge: Cambridge University Press, 2000). For a less recent, but still helpful account see Ford, 'System, Story, Performance', especially his reflections on 'middle-distance' realism.

8

THEOLOGY: WHERE TO BEGIN?

Garry W Trompf

Caught in the act of lecturing during the 1960s, I remember, the Reverend Professor Harry Wardlaw conveyed suppleness of both mind and body – as if to defeat their 'phenomenal' dualism. He exemplified in his person a basic conundrum about life. Do we best begin to understand it in patent corporeality, or in probing mental exercises? because as his reasoning increased in complexity so did the moving positions of his legs, instructing us, in para-yogic fashion, that body and whatever else there is operate in an intricate partnership. There is a useful analogy here for a might-be theologian (like myself, who has hitherto barely theologised in any thoroughgoing way) confronted with the challenge of a suitable *entrée*.

In what follows, I should immediately clarify, I am mostly concerned with the discipline of theology in its most distinctive form, that is, as an *autonomous* exercise of thought to make sense of the world or construct reality theologically, not so much with hermeneutical reflection on *other* people's attempts over the centuries (scriptural studies, historical theology, etc). I inquire here concerning the most valuable point of departure, when, in our own day, we feel the impulsion, or desire to 'do the work', of representing the divine intent in a coherent, persuasively presented, even systematic manner. Does or should theology commence with the world? with the Body of God, as Spinoza would have it, or, as is probably more sensibly put, the cosmos and its diversity as the embodiments of a divine Work? Or ought we to start, as most systematisers have, with ideas and doctrines of the Almighty and work down to the humble terrestrial? For one might argue that little else than technological benefits derive from a universe that is not looked at *sub specie aeternitatis* (and thus seen, in consequence, as a creation). Again, does theology have its proper (and foregone unfathomable) starting-point in the Mind of God outside of materiality and enfleshed life; or, is it only feasible to proceed from the (better) known and work 'up', 'down', 'back' or 'onwards' to the Ultimate Source of All? These are older questions put in newer guises. Politics and philosophical trends will affect our response. Doing things from the top will look traditionalist and hierarchical, feminists would suspect also patriarchal. Doing things from the bottom opens up a pandering to earthly relativities. Where do we go for a more-than-subjective legitimacy for our chosen departure-point (if that is necessary)? To a spot somewhere between God and world? Is that indeed a key rationale for Christology – in focussing on the God-Man? And with all this questioning, how useful might be a Tillich, and the mind (and legs!) of such an exponent of his as Harry Wardlaw, to talk of being, and depth, and grounding in an 'interrelational space' between ourselves and the wholly Other! and to admit a firm connection between all talk of God and human culture.

Every beginning in any discipline will be provisional for never escaping the possible analytical charge of arbitrariness. A disturbing Derrida will tell us all speech acts inevitably do violence to reality, so our linguistic descriptors, let alone the most refined philosophical discourse, will never do justice to the world. And, if ancient apophatic theologies proscribed us from verbalising the divine essence, the daring seventeenth-century Arminian Pieter Bischop (Episcopius) was first off the mark in insisting that all theological language has and ought to be metaphoric – a point countless literalists after him chose to ignore. Once jumping out of the 'mono- and ethno-lingual trap', moreover, one will begin to appreciate how even the most obscure languages may have better means of pinpointing particular insights, enchanting lexical jetties of mental embarkation, than widely-spoken tongues. Certainly I would feel more satisfied myself referring to the Almighty with the West African Yoruba epithet 'Olodumare' than the Gothic 'God'; and I wish at this strange point I was surrounded by waiting New Guinea Bena Bena highlanders all uttering 'uyailoto!' Go ahead, 'that's it!' (there's no way out, if you are going to start, be content to begin in a suitable enough place).

As a reader you will have to understand that you are dealing with me as a cross-cultural analyst, a social critic with a residual sympathy for the Marxist accounts of human power relations, and an historian of ideas. I will not be satisfied, then, with a theology that does not attend to the riches of anthropological research, and I am especially reactive against theological systems that claim universal applicability when they are so patently Eurocentric (or pay too much homage to the European styles of philosophical discourse in their day). Protagonists for such theologies should graciously concede their contextual limitations; and I may surely be excused for such an insistence after spending most of my life trying to understand the most complex ethnic scene on earth – Melanesia. That is the region that has opened up my concern for cross-cultural study, and admittedly granted me the advantage of the finding the broadest possible grounding for my own theologising (as shall be shown later). But it is also the region in which almost every would-be (indigenous) theologian will have been 'trained' to feel inadequate before the the cultural hegemony of Western systematic thought, as if any voice from the margins would never have the right to make 'universal claims'.

One can already sense, from this last innuendo, that I would never want any theology to be read without awareness of socio-intellectual 'power play'. Aside from the general issue of ecclesiastical 'pastoral power' (as Michel Foucault called it),[1] or the pretensions made by anyone to relay dogmatic truth with an unquestioned authority, no one can afford to ignore the social dynamics in which theologies are played out. After all, old competitions still pertain – Catholic and Protestant stalwarts, higher critics versus less-than-moderate Evangelicals, advocates of would-be supra-political outlooks against politicised libertationists, and one sort of camp-following (Barthian, Tillichian, etc) challenging the rest. Let us not delude ourselves about ostensible impartiality when every act of writing has to be for and against someone else's positioning, with the least persuasive theology being one that pampers every religious viewpoint. And who does theology? One should not neglect finding out whether it is an aristocrat or an Aboriginal, a well-heeled product of bourgeois security or a struggler from some worker's harder world. And what kind of predispositions do they carry to their tasks? What kind of experiences? Will sensing God's presence on an ascetic's prayer-stool ever be enough for a decent job? Will the effects of social trauma warp or better certify their perspectives?

An historian of ideas, what is more, will always be tempted to put theology in its place. 'The history of human ideas', Giambattista Vico somewhat notoriously pronounced,[2] 'is the queen of the sciences', not (formal) theology. For, to be interpreted most satisfactorily, a theology will always to have to be placed in time and space 'by a severe analysis *(una severa analisi)* of human thought', and thus some independent discipline will be needed to establish which thinker drew on or was influenced by another, and what expressed positions bear relationships to others in a flow of ideational responses. I am not going to deduce from this that my own discipline holds a privileged position; but only that protagonists in every discipline will have – indeed should have – those in other fields to place a check on their pretensions, or to act as some kind of dialogical foil. The collective reciprocity *(universitas)* of learning already suggests that no one *collegium* of minds tastes or handles the whole cake of intelligible reality, not even those who venture into the most cosmically significant terrain.[3] A decent course in comparative sociology or political economy might even persuade one that a good deal of theology (among other commonly abstract studies, such as cosmology) is a luxury item in a materially unequal world. Furthermore, it could be that every intellectual, the theologian definitely included, requires a reality check, or recurrent opportunities for psychological (self-)assessment. But then, one would hardly want psychology, or any other given social science, to be a finally arbitrating science above other sciences, because each has thus far revealed their own very serious limitations. At least the greatest theologies have an interesting habit of better standing the test of time, perhaps for pointing to awsome durabilities rather than indulging in theoretical faddism common to modern mental competitiveness. And at least the strong residual implication of theology is that the final judgement of persons, indeed the true fulfilment of personhood (rather than fragmentations and eviscerations of it analysed by geneticists, psychologists, sociologists, economists, etc), finally resides outside human hands, and thus bears its own lessons of humility.

These harsh realities, of course, have hardly prevented others from 'starting' theology. I only introduce them because I have to face up to my own question. One cannot dictate to others that they must not begin until they have faced up to a sufficient array of preconditioning factors. It is sufficient for me to state at the onset what disturbs me about the common 'assumptive worlds' of theology,[4] so that I myself can put my cards on the table, so to speak, and defend the rigours of my own starting-point. Because, yes, the impulse to engage in theology is a highly personal business; and I take the view that one would not embark upon it as lightly as doing a piece of secular (let us say historical) analysis. In fact, I am prepared to wager that, of all disciplines, focused theology presupposes a vocation, a calling, borne out of a deeper than ordinary subjectivity[5] – to dare saying something intelligent about refractions of the Unfathomable.

But for my own part I could not imagine responding to that call without exercises of the utmost introspection, whereby all the issues I have already raised would be put through the sieve of my own ruthless self-examination. What would I be trying to prove in doing theology? Are my motives to satisfy my own ego, or to stretch my intellectual accomplishments to the limits? Can I transcend the psychological and socio-economic conditions that that I have 'fallen into' at the beginning of my own life, brought up as I was a rural, 'parochial' Australian? (expected to live down being 'a Methodist boy', as some of my academic supervisors derisively dubbed me). What, in any case, would be a sufficient amount of research into the nature of the world to satisfy my suspicions about the problems of language, ethnocentricity, in-house dogmatic prejudice, historical context and the like to allow a first step, as if I could now respond to the call because I have undergone appropriate training to answer it responsibly? Let others begin theology where they feel it appropriate to do so – for who is to police intellectual vitality? Permit me only to aver how long it has taken for me to think about plunging in at all, in case it might serve as a useful warning for those who want to test the waters too prematurely. The longer I live, indeed, the more I think theology as I am considering it is definitely for the grey-haired, and that it bests imparts a summarising wisdom after much preliminary work has been done. Lucky (or blessed), of course, are those who are gifted to expatiate it earlier or throughout their working lives! (though how remarkably few are such people in Australia, with our continent still barely making its mark in theological systematics).

Three general points apply that have slowly insinuated themselves into my urge towards a preliminary orientation. First, that a theology ought not to be undertaken in separation away from the whole 'world of religions'[6] – so that a Christian theology, which I have in mind developing myself, ought to be worked out with a clear-sighted distinctiveness of 'kerygmatic claims' *vis-à-vis* other traditions (including the great panorama of indigenous cultures). Second, that theology, as it addresses the concerns of individuals (for it surely should) must needs be brought into an early relation with the quests for healing and therapy found in the arena of medical practices, psychology, psychoanalysis, and procedures for relational healing. Third, that a theology will always be subject a dismissal of culturo-centric arbitrariness unless it provides a key to the human condition to fit both contextually and across the board of world societies. All these special requirements are likely to be resisted by those who consider theological investigation can be carried out independently of, perhaps even rescued from, the inroads of competing disciplines. Some will deem it unfair that a theologian has to spend undue time studying comparative religion, psychological theories, anthropology and other related social sciences. I will retort, with the precedent of Tillich's expansive range of interests in mind,[7] that a theology presented without this kind of 'homework' will either be doomed to a speedy irrelevance or survive only in the recognisable service of special interests. Allow me to discuss the three 'prerequisites' in turn.

Christian theology speaks within the arena of competing religious voices, and its protagonists might as well not open their mouths if they cannot from the onset distinguish peculiarly Christian claims concerning salvation, and to decide whether they make any difference beside other proffered paths of liberation. Here I will stand on what I have said elsewhere, without wishing to lock horns in the conflict over fall/redemption and creation theologies, that the Gospel proclaims Christ's cosmic role in salvation from human sin (whatever that may mean in the present context). The deepest purpose of salvation is not super-knowledge or its reverse in profound nescience (cf eg, *jnâna*, *viprîta-vijñâna, paññâ-vimutti,* etc in Vedanta and Buddhism), or activation of the highest humane moral principles (as in Chinese systems), or the final teaching to adopt God's way (*al-dîn* in Islam), although these may be entailed. The instrinsically subversive, even *anti-religious* character of the Christian *Faith,* moreover, is that it questions all religiosity, if that means a set of procedures by which to approach, manage or please the divine. The Gospel awakens one to the divine initiative for our redemption already undertaken on our behalf by the mediating role of Christ; it does not ask us to invest ourselves in a course of salvation, but rather to be affected by grace.[8] All kinds of reflection on the good, caring and holy life, of course, even those present in 'other traditions' may aid in our deepening response to the Gospel, but if they act as surrogates of the essential core of the good news they transform Christianity back into the mould of a religion that it originally surpassed.

Such a process of discernment, however, is not meant to dishonour all or any of the discrete religious impetuses known from history or around the world. It is only meant to establish the crucial point for embarking on systematic reflection upon Christian claims in the first place, even while admitting that all peoples have been 'feeling after God' in their own way (Acts 17:27), or even if wanting to affirm (with Schelling) that a 'religion can only be true if it is with us from the foundations of the earth' and has its footprints in every culture.[9] Certainly, to commence a Christian theology without grasping the uniqueness of the basic kerymatic 'revelation' would make for a sorry relativism. To move off first in a palpably New Age syncretic mode, let us say, in which all religious paths are taken as leading to the same end, is not worth the *entrée* at all, because the assumption that all so-called religions are essentially saying the same or parallel things, is not only factually incorrect,[10] but it detracts from the requirement of a 'severe analysis' of (theological) ideas we set for ourselves. A theology takes seriously the original favour of its Scriptural foundations; it does not have to pander to prevailing tastes when the world of religions might need salt, even the hot pepper of a forgotten or as-yet-unawakened sense of sin. From these beginnings, admittedly, we will have to face the fact that Christianity *shares* in a wider world of religions, which are for that reason not to be dismissed out of hand or uncharitably.[11]

But this sharing came about through processes whereby its faith was steadily turned back into what it originally circumvented. And it has not been alone in this vulnerability, considering, for instance, the Buddha's teachings, which were at first cast in a distinctly medical frame, but eventually revered as the basis for what we now term a 'world religion'.[12]

When, to turn to second prerequisite, I wrote of a necessary engagement with therapeutic and psychological pursuits, I had in mind the apparent awkwardness of overlap between Christian healing, catharsis, absolution, etc and the more secular-looking (if residually priestly) techniques to 'get us back on track' emotionally or motivationally.[13] Refined work needs undertaking to clarify the relevant issues, to lay bare the mutual grounds of suspicion between certain scientific and spiritual orientations ('religion corrupts reality', 'psychiatry and psychology are reductionistic'), and to lay out the boundary zones for an effective methodological *rapprochement*.[14] It has been tempting for me to assert that all theology must begin with some sort of psychoanalysis – in self-examination of our motives (as discussed earlier), or in a kind of psychological anthropology whereby one probes people for their own self-reckonings, or detects in earnest what is wrong with human beings that they have to be 'saved' at all. Tillich felt this pressure very intensely, because he realised how, even while engaged in the practice of a faith, 'individuals and groups can escape an unmasking' of various types of deceptions that could 'conceivably destroy them'; and how 'exposing the true condition of man [sic]' is inevitably a 'painful process' that can either be the *pre*condition for doing theology or the means by which a theologian reveals 'the ultimate meaning of the Gospel'.[15]

The trouble is, any psycho-therapeutics that is fiercely autonomous (reductionistic, atheistic, let us say) may preempt even the choice to embark on theology (deeming it a *non sequitur*); and so it follows that Christian theologians will only have use of psychological frames which fit a pre-understood religious picture of the human condition. This was the conundrum facing Søren Kierkegaard, in the writing of his masterpiece *The Concept of Anxiety* (or *Dread*) (1844), in which he essays a 'psychologically oriented' approach to 'the dogmatic issue of hereditary sin' while strongly retaining theology's own disciplinary integrity. For, it is in this remarkable opus that Kierkegaard discerns the only finally distinguishing feature of human beings is that they sin. Animals possess feelings, and some have signs of speech, powers of thought and 'self-distinction' in a group, but they cannot be blamed (even if we impute blameworthiness to them). Men and women alone are condemned to a repetition of a marredness that psychology is powerless to explain, and which cannot be put down to a traducian factor (or the passing down of a bodily contaminant, or what today we would call a genetic defect).[16] Yes, sin, that strange indelibility which only folly would argue or wish away from the assessment of affairs, that eventually inescapable sense of one's 'mixed state' or faultiness that arises in consciousness, has to be addressed head on.[17] Obviously, in view of the relevant distinctiveness I have already spotted in the Christian Gospel, I would take this nodal point as crucial for beginning theology. *Prima facie*, this might seem an old-fashioned stance, and yet, while I am prepared to wear this criticism in my concern to reassert the ancient insights of the Gospel, I would nonetheless seek an integration of the biblical understanding of sin and various contemporary approaches to psychological analysis and healing.[18] Working at such a 'wedding', I would hope, could permit both theologies and psychotherapies to fulfil complementary parts, if not their 'proper and 'highest', purposes. Here I suspect an early muddle will need to be cleared up, however, by denying (again with Kierkegaard) that psycho-therapeutics have any claim over the *kairos* of salvation; for that is purely in divine hands and irreducibly 'religious', 'spiritual', or theological in its nature. All the same, psychological and related concerns have implications for the conditions in which the salvific experience occurs – conditions which may be helpfully matured by a coupling of theological and psychoanalytical engagement.

To be sure, I am not afraid to admit the ineluctable character of sin, and I have not the slightest inclination to write it out of our vocabulary as a depressive and singularly unattractive concept bound to put off Christianity's 'cultural despisers'. On the other hand, I would want to insist that the reality of human sinfulness folds out into a thousand-and-one individual (and, as we shall see social) filaments that can be addressed on their own (or in their possibly very complex

interrelationships) to throw light on its meaning and consequences
– indeed to grasp the necessary 'point' of being 'saved' from it. To
achieve brevity, if I said theology should begin where it 'hurts' you will
soon get my message immediately. Individuals suffer from a plethora
of bad experiences, and whether they acknowledge themselves
to have 'caused' them or have (often too easily or over-sensitively)
allowed others' actions to have overtaken them, they will easily be
able to intuit something of their own problematic, their own 'stew of
resentments' and need of healing, if they acknowledge the pain of
life.[19] In this context I am naturally mindful of the frequent complaint
against conservative theologies that they typically heighten the
necessity of salvation by accentuating the need for a personal sense
of sin. I will not run away from this charge; though what I seek to do
is rehabilitate an apparently antiquated (actually New Testament)
insight about our so-called 'fallenness' through investing it with
fresh meaning; so that such an astute psychologically-oriented
suspicion ought not so much deter as be taken in one's stride here.
Just think again. It turns out, actually, that we are in as bad a need of
recovering an awareness of guilt where it has been repressed as we
are in bringing a message of grace to the guilt-ridden: both come
under the same kind of 'umbrella of interests' that need attention for
a preliminary theological orientation. The complexity of hurts and
effects of alienation we now turn to, in any case, may not necessarily
have anything to do with any kind of rejection of or distaste for 'God'
before some revelation or conversion, but could even involve being
disappointed with God *after* embarking on the Christian life.[20] We
are talking about a whole psycho-existentially charged arena that
has to be explored so that we can give a deeper account of what
the liberating power of the Good News could more fully entail – in a
world of multiculture, or one where we find many people less and less
attuned to religious sensibilities.

   In this broad context, one should not mind honouring an
intersection between Christian and other religious traditions' insights,
deeply respecting, for instance, the Buddha's first noble truth that 'all
is suffering *(dukkha)*', just like a Jew acceding to the old Edomite
maxim that 'man is born to trouble as the sparks fly upwards' (Job 5:7).
For, any teaching that throws light on the point of salvation and our

need of it will now come to have theological value (as, therefore, may a whole body of wisdom from various religious and secular quarters). To put it simply, once the Christian experiences the priceless treasure and singularity of divine redemption from our tragic state, let all sorts of tools be gathered to hand to elucidate it. Of course, if in this venture what is received as great knowledge or principles of action become surrogates for salvation, then we will have left behind the challenge of the Gospel – and the premise that only acceptance of an initiated blessing of God, embodied in the love of Christ, makes the final difference, will have lost its effect. While that premise is assumed, however, let alone embraced as the crucial force in life, then one may feel free to fill out its bearings for oneself and others with the widest range of resources. One surely need not stop at the Bible, as if 'policed' by its (admittedly astounding) range of human situations. What any or every discrete 'religion' isolates as the human predicament to be solved, or a thousand-and-one therapies proffer as answers to our problems, can all be 'placed' as possible means of assistance, pointing to a kind of 'general domain of psychology' through which theologising can really get underway. Even special attention to the particular needs of the body – its very aches – and our necessary work of self-care have roles to play; and of course the vast body of imaginative literature and televisial drama, pointing to many personal dilemmas, will render an interesting service. So much from this great 'sphere of suggestions' is waiting to be applied to specific contexts and 'real life', 'close-to-hand' problems, yet related back to the basic claims of Christian message, or shall we say 'sifted' through the wisdom of the Gospel.[21] Such theologising must obviously be clearsighted about those basic claims, yet I venture to assert that they will be lifeless if regurgitated in a vacuum: they will only come alive while the work of exploration we have envisaged goes on.

It has been part of my sense of vocation to search out a key, or interpretative 'combination lock', that opens up a window to best mirror the human condition in both its psychological and cultural dimensions, and both in their commonality and diversity. Although the word of salvation reaches out to each and every human heart, no heart beats alone. The Gospel, for a start, is never completely individualistic in tenor; and to fasten on to concerns of singular persons opens a psychologistic, even privatising 'trap'. We are what we are in relationships. If the African American scholar, Archie Smith Jr, has convincingly shown the uselessness of psycho-therapeutics in one-to-one treatments, because blacks are very decisively 'relational selves' and healing occurs among them when whole families or core groups are involved,[22] he might have been writing for everyone. Individuals do not really exist outside their place in the social world that nurtured (and usually continues to sustain) them.[23] Running alongside attention to what we have characterised as a psychological domain, we would neglect the social one at our peril – and both inevitably overlap in any case. In that case we return to the world of religions as collective and institutional, and as ostensibly solving group problems. These socio-religious forms can incorporate or sit beside visible expressions of economic and political organisation (and their like). And in terms of our argument, we are prompted to ask what purpose they serve in containing the human *problématique*. We have arrived at my third 'prerequisite'.

Social life is full of difficulties. From family life through to national and international decision-making, it is riddled with conflict. All of us 'fall' into social circumstances that are not of our choosing (to appropriate Heideggerian language[24]), and we often do not experience them to our liking. Thus when we inevitably find, whether for ourselves and others, that human affairs recurrently issue in rank inequalities, injustices, oppression, conflict, misunderstanding, irresponsibility, ineptitude and so on, we are once again facing 'hurt', ready to acknowledge what has been called 'social sin' (perhaps even tempted, when genetic defects and various 'natural aberrations' are taken into account, that the whole planet has been implicated in some kind of general 'fall').[25] In this wider set of vortices, one senses the social jump-off point complementary to that applying to the individual. Again, the role of religions in general would require investigation to assess how they have addressed and managed social ills, and whether and why the Christian message of justice, non-violent solutions, and of loving, peaceable community *(koinônia)* reflects the soteric work of Christ in a corporate and still unique way. A preliminary recognition would require to be given to the tension between the Christian acceptance of the necessity for government and institutions and the Christian right to an attitude of permanent dissent towards all human-made organisations.[26] Again, every social philosophy and science, every effort to understand the social world – its tendencies and patterns, the strengths and weaknesses of human institutions, the struggles of humans to adapt to environments, etc – may all be welcomed as potentially throwing light on social predicaments and realities. Neither Marxian nor utterly opposing Freedmanite analyses, indeed, need be excluded from view. Too often we repress the presence of a hidden 'broad assumption' behind virtually all such human endeavours: the laying out of findings to help (rather than hinder) the betterment of humanity. It is not just that they seek to teach us 'to live, to live well, to live better';[27] in fact they all tackle some aspect(s) of relational imperfection, and thus directly or indirectly provide a rationale for undertaking theology, which is meant to disclose such purposes, giving deeper meaning to them and the ubiquitous problematic they address. Indeed, in confronting evils without, not just within, and seeking some explanation for them, theology also entails theodicy in the very *Grundlagen* we seek to lay out in these few pages: we want to know why we are situated in a more 'general trouble' than the mess we ourselves feel responsible for making. But I must bend towards a conclusion.

In my life-long pursuit of some heuristic device, some rubric, or combination lock that satisfies as the appropriate 'theological starting point', I have never found anything more useful than the simplest culturo-religious complex of thought and action, and the one found present in every documented society. Appropriately, an English colloquialism captures it best: 'payback'. In my own fancier terminology, it is referred to as the logic of retribution, or retributive logic.[28] Anthropologically it operates around the most significant binary opposite: between concession and antipathy (a polarity badly neglected by Lévi-Strauss, yet one which gathers into one the conflictual elements implied by most of the others – good and bad, male and female, light and dark, etc).[29] Epistemologically, or in terms of human knowing cross-culturally, it works itself out in a tension between two kinds of 'giving', one that allows – the 'gift', a 'giving in', a 'forgiveness', to play on our lexical suggestiveness – and one that forebids – that punishes wrong, or 'gives back' to enemies the hell that is their due. In this tension Nietzsche believed he had discovered the origins of thought itself, not just the beginning of morality's *Genealogie*.[30] Ritually 'payback' manifests in the enshrouding of give and take with formalities and special gifts (such as shells, currencies, etc. that are not meant to be destroyed or be consumed), or in sacrifices – appeasing the gods, despatching enemies as victims, or giving all to aid one's fellows.[31] It is first and foremost a complex of both thought and action: in every known socialisation process children must learn friend from foe, and why they are to offer amity to some and enmity to others. Secondly, 'payback' devolves into an explanatory mode, so that what happens in our lives is accounted for in terms of praise and blame, reward and punishment. In both these guises 'logic' is present: we can always say *why* we acted the way we did, whether our acts were 'positive' or 'negative'; and we have learnt from childhood why significant outcomes are 'fitting' – why opprobrium falls on those betraying the group, and fame on those who best play according to its rules.

The interesting truth about retributive logic is that it entails both individual and social dimensions, and can therefore be approached psychologically and sociologically. It shows up in the pet hates and favouritisms of family life, in other words, or what RD Laing calls 'knots',[32] just as much as in the tit for tat between groups or nations, no better (or more terribly) illustrated than by the weekly acts of revenge taken in the recent Israeli-Palestinian crisis. It is also a very characteristic mark of 'traditional' (and especially small-scale) societies; what we may dub the basic, most fundamental, indeed perennial 'religion' depends on it, that is, the thousands of less known religions that celebrate fecundity and victory. These are the lifeways in which rituals – often great sacrifices – are performed with a view to increasing the fertility of soil, stock and women; and which lend magical power to the warrior's spear.[33] Whole empires have been constructed from the minor culturo-linguistic units sharing such outlooks, and these rarely have trouble invoking the causes of *prosperitas* and *victoria* (how Rome immediately springs to mind!) as their goals. Indeed, all the major religious traditions of the contemporary world have had to deal with this traditionalist mode of thinking – whether the mass slaughter of animals must cease, tribalist mentalities encouraged or diverted, and whether weapons can be held with honour or rejected as degrading the spiritual path. Indeed, a 'litmus test' for discerning the relative 'truth' or 'strengths' of all so-called religions, large or small, may lie in the degree to which they 'see through' and 'transform' the ubiquitous *Weltanschauung* we call 'basic religion' *(religio)*, the one whereby the gods are given to so that their support for a group's material security may be obtained.

This is the hard nexus of pressures to which the Gospel first spoke in the Galilean context, and has always spoken, whether covertly or openly, macrohistorically. It is a sphere in which personal, social and environal stability is not always secured, and battles not always won. It is a world of constant and everyday 'give and take'; a world of struggle in which people are bruised, even in their successes and let alone in their tragedies. It is a world of reckoning – of calculating how one is doing – inevitably feeling the strain of obligation, responsibility, and inevitably experiencing shame, guilt, or depression. This is the arena in which all efforts at reciprocity and managing relations can never work out for long, and in which peace is always vulnerable to the stronger forces of hostility (the pretexts and legitimations of which are all too easy to act upon). The theatre bespeaks the activations of powers invisible, not just visible, and the attendant hopes and fears of those wanting some kind of deep, immoveable, peaceful resolution in their lives. Yet this is not a settled place in which one may ask whether God exists, or even how God might have created the world. There is very little time to debate the nature of Being, the ontic state of humanness or personhood, the metaphysics of saviourhood, or even balance up the evidence for an afterlife, and what it might be like – if one can reason out its existence at all. And it is in this context where a Christian theology ought to begin, where the Gospel – as it did in its embodiment in an imperilled, eventually victimised Nazarene – was first expressed historically, in a bloodied colonial order, a landscape full of oppression, a society riddled with hurts. This is the context of basic, immediate living, in which stewards can be unjust or neglectful, widows give more mites away than they can afford, the bodies of individuals are sick and handicapped, the minds of rich men plagued by conscience or not caring a damn. So what's new? Whatever the sophistications of social management, the technological achievements of modern times, or the comforts of a leisure class in their minority, the essentials have not changed today, even for the materially lucky. Suffering, indeed, may have increased (who can measure what one can only intuit in a macroscopic vision of our troubled planet?).

In this light, we can grasp again why the singular claims of the Gospel should already be there at the very commencement of theological exploration. A core message of the New Testament strikes at the heart of pandemic retributive logic, remoulding its fossilising materials, redirecting and transforming it. What is proclaimed there is our redemption *(apolutrôsis)*, the recovery of what is 'lost', the unburdening of what is the 'heavy yoke' of pressure in the world, in which there is no apparent escape from inevitably imperfect outcomes and incessant obligations. Such epistles of Paul to the Romans and Galatians can be reread, unburdened by the historically conditioned polemics of an Augustine, Luther or Barth, and 'rediscovered' as handling humanity's most fundamental issues. Yet our distempered state is not simply wished away by soteriological pronouncements: it is revealed for what is it as the complex result of human weaknesses, soullessness, lack of moral strength, even wilful venality.[34] No amount of payback activity within the system can resolve it; no amount of *religio* – oblation, sacrifice, acts of penance, consoling verbiage – will set it permanently right; that is why religions possess their psychological and social function, and their 'necessary durability'. But it is precisely the divine actualisation of grace, the self-giving of God in Christ, that both honours this predicament yet dismantles its false solutions. We are faced with the image of a sacrifice that ends all sacrifices, in a mediatorship 'once and for all' (Heb 10:10); we are confronted with a forgiveness that overrules all systems of reciprocity, a gift or blessing that no human acts could conceivably pay back (or that the greatest of martyrs would ever presume to be 'satisfied' in the offering of one's own life). The reign of God, indeed, is the space in which the seed of an entirely new fertility applies: the unexpected harvest of the ones who, by faith, accept the way out of the morass. The Eucharist is that (ostensibly) bloodless sacrifice from which a new community gives thanks for its liberation, not to repeat a religious 'work' of piety in a closed system of requitals.

Here we discover that the Gospel works from a religious mindset, but leaves all religion – and thus particular members of the world of religions – complicit in the domain of sin that requires redeeming. The Act of Grace actually frees us from 'this world', from a totalist manacling of spirit (anything between our depressing feelings of inadequacy, let us say, to an intense fear that Satanic forces abound). Not that we can escape the hard, historical facts of hurt, discomfort, moments of loneliness and alienation, or many deep urges that must needs await a resolution of things beyond this present order. And we will not be able to cope unless we somehow 'place' and take stock of our respective arenas of circumstance, social rules, and the potential penalities applying if we impatiently resist our environal reality. (Come to think of it, the legal restraints imposed through history, if we follow the logic of our analysis, have also most often been imposed to manage the very human *problématique* we have spent time analysing, even though so many injustices and power biases have shown up when placed beside the biblical Torah). Yet our true liberty lies in the permission to live by faith, to proceed in response to the gift of new life with a firm confidence, realising that, in spite of the nature of psychological and social realities, 'the will of God is not confined to any legalism, but open to us in a thousand possibilities' – perhaps to quietism, perhaps prophetic activism.[35] Theology begun with this orientation conducts us to what essentially matters in the end, even if historical contingencies disappoint us. The singularity of the Gospel demands its own clarifying, reevaluating and reaffirming. In consequence, a deeper meaning and illumination will be shed upon the religious, psychological and social study we have found important for theology's groundwork. Indeed, would-be theologians will neglect these studies at their peril, so critical are they for explaining why it is that countless earnest voices across the planet are telling us we all need salvation. If and when we genuinely discover that 'pearl of great price', furthermore, we will have found the deepest love, which throws all human-made requirements and payback energies into crisis, harnesses them for the true Kingdom, and acts as their last judgement.

End Notes

1. M Foucault, *Power/Knowledge: Selected Interviews and Other Writings, 1972–1977*, edited and translated by C Gordon (New York, 1980).
2. *La scienza nuova* (1744), I [IV], in *Opere*, edited by P Rossi (Milan, 1959), 393–4.
3. For the cake image of knowledge, see J Needham, *Moulds of Understanding: Patterns of Natural Philosophy*, edited by G Werskey (London, 1976).
4. See JD Frank, *Persuasion and Healing* (New York, 1963), especially 27–9.
5. R Poole, *Towards Deep Subjectivity* (London, 1972). Included in this deep subjectivity is a sense of mission, which must be distinguished in (missiological) principle and self-praxis from prejudice and dogmatism.
6. Trompf and G Hamel (editors), *The World of Religions: Essays on Historical and Contemporary Issues* (Religion, Politics and Society 1), (New Delhi, 2001).
7. Start with Tillich's *The Religious Situation*, translated by HR Niebuhr (New York, 1956).
8. Trompf, 'The Incarnation and Asian Traditions, or, Do Hindus and Buddhists Carry a Christian Message?' In M Free *et al* (editors), *That Our Joy May Be Complete: Essays on the Incarnation for the New Millennium*, Adelaide, 2000, especially 120–6. Aside from non-Christian new religious movements making use of this structure, we may note how intriguingly close the Sikh position is to the Christian one, given the collective mediatorship for savings from sins in *Sausarki* texts (though these works have been strangely marginalised). I am grateful to Prof Noel King and Jasie Lal (Sohanpaal) for their observations made about Sikh views.
9. For background, EL Allen, *Christianity among the Religions* (London, 1960), especially chapter 5, section b.
10. For guidance, HD Lewis and RL Slater, *The Study of Religion: Meeting Points and Major Issues* (Harmondsworth, 1966).
11. Notice new interest in this issue, with K Cracknell's *Justice, Courtesy and Love: Theologians and Missionaries Encountering World Religions, 1846–1914* (London, 1995).
12. Here I acknowledge that original subversion of religiosity we find in Pauline theology (Rom; Gal) has already begun to be underdone by piety theologies in the New Testament itself. Cf E Käsemann, *Jesus Means Freedom: A Polemical Survey of the New Testament*, translated by F Clarke (London, 1969).
13. Cf M North, *The Secular Priests: Psychotherapists in Contemporary Society* (London, 1972).

14. For the issues, see especially P Homans (editor), *The Dialogue between Theology and Psychology* (Chicago, 1969); D S Browning, *Religious Thought and the Modern Psychologies: A Critical Conversation in the Theology of Culture* (Philadelphia, 1988); F Watts and M Williams, *The Psychology of Religious Knowing* (London, 1994); MA Jeeves, *Human Nature at the Millennium: Reflections on the Inregration of Psychology and Christianity* (Grand Rapids, Michigan: Eerdmanns, 1997); BW Grant, *A Theology of Pastoral Psychotherapy: God's Play in Sacred Places* (Binghamton, NY, 2001); JA Braakman, 'Correlation of Theology and Psychology: Implications for Pastoral Care' (Doctoral dissertation, Flinders University of South Australia, 2003).

15. Tillich, *The Boundaries of our Being*, Fontana Library of Theology and Philosophy (London, 1973), 344. Note also G W Hughes, *God of Surprises* (London, 1985), chapter 3.

16. S Kierkegaard, *The Concept of Anxiety: A Simple Psychologically Oriented Deliberation on the Dogmatic Issue of Hereditary Sin* (edited and translated by R Thomte), Kierkegaard's Writings, 8 (Princeton, 1980), especially I,2; 4ff Cf, developing from Kierkegaard, M Westphal, *God, Guilt and Death: An Existential Phenomenology of Religion*, Studies in Phenomenology and Existential Philosophy (Bloomington, Ind, 1984). Theological traducianism has a Buddhist counterpart in the Yogâcâra doctrine of *âlaya-vijñâna* (which is more an independent storehouse of unconsciousness that inevitably affects us from birth); cf Asanga, *Mahâyâsangraha*, 10.

17. Here, however, I eschew any origins theory about the (prehistorical) beginnings of a sense of sin. Such theory is still being deemed necessary by some. JS Spong, for instance, has recently and somewhat naively located it in the arising of self-consciousness (*A New Christianity for a New World*, San Francisco, 2002, chapter 3), a psychological state most theorists would put much later in macrohistory than he does.

18. As already long exemplified in work by WM Meissner (editor), *Foundations for a Pychology of Grace*, Glen Rock (NJ, 1966); P Tournier, *Guilt and Grace: A Psychological Study*, translated by A W Heathcote *et al*, (London, 1974 edition); V E Frankl *et al, Psychtherapy and Existentialism: Selected Papers on Logotherapy* (Harmondsworth, 1967).

19. For some background, M Scheler, *Ressentiment*, edited by LA Coser, translated by W H Holdheim (New York, 1972 edition).

20. Cf, eg, P Yancey, *Disappointment with God* (New York, 1988). Cf AR Sphar 111 and AA Smith, *Helping Hurting People: A Handbook of Reconciliation-Focused Counseling and Preaching* (New York, 2003). It is the author's view that most Australians who once but no longer participate in church life are disengaged from it because of specific hurt(s) waiting for healing.

21. For some related work, LE Cady, 'Resisting the Postmodern Turn: Theology and Contextualization', in *Theology at the End of Modernity*, edited by S G Davanet, 95–6 (Philadelphia, 1991).

22. A Smith Jr, *The Relational Self: Ethics and Therapy from a Black Church Perspective* (Nashville, 1982).

23. Start cautiously with C Taylor, *Sources of the Self: The Making of Modern Identity* (Cambridge, 1989).

24. Heidegger, *Sein und Zeit*, Tübingen, 1977 edition.

25. I will not pretend to unravel competing views here, from Paul's admission of a world in travail (Rom 8:22) to Gnostic and Marcionite imputations against the aeonic Sophia or Old Testament creator God; or from Godfrey Goodman's claim that the Adamic Fall set in train a planetary deterioration (*The Fall of Man, etc*, London, 1616) to George Hakewill's answer that a sufficient recurrence of things in the cosmos nonetheless bespeaks Gods's sustaining power (*An Apologie or Declaration of the Power and Providence of God, etc*, Oxford, 1627); or from more contemporary (orthodox) positions disinclined to impute nature with evil (eg, B Hebbelthwaite, *Evil, Suffering and Religion*, London, 2000) to others more willing to do so (see WB Drees [editor], *Is Nature ever Evil? Religion, Science and Value* (London, 2002).

26. Note Trompf, 'Reflections on the Origins of Christian Social Theory', *Faith and Freedom* 6/1 (1998): 23–5.

27. Thus AN Whitehead, *The Function of Reason*, Boston, 1959 edition, 5. Cf H Marcuse, *One Dimensional Man: Studies in the Ideology of Advanced Industrial Society* (New York, 1966), chapter 9.

28. Eg, Trompf, *Payback: The Logic of Retribution in Melanesian Religions*, (Cambridge, 1994); 'La logica della ritorsione e lo studio delle religioni della Melanesia', *Religioni e Società* 28, 12 (1997): 48–77.

29. On both C Lévi-Strauss and R Jakobsen behind his theory here, especially JM Benoist, 'Classicism Revisited: Human Nature and Structure in Lévi-Strauss and Chomsky', in J Benthall (editor), *The Limits of Human Nature* (London, 1973), 26–7.

30. F Nietzsche, *The Genealogy of Morals*, translated by W Kaufmann and RJ Hollingdale (New York, 1969), especially 70–4; although his interest in the interplay was remarkably isolated. Indeed, it may be a vital index to his early '*post*-modernity' as we now call it. For, if ever there was a hallmark of modernity, it is the reaction against any connection between religion and retribution, or, more specifically punishments in historical events and in the afterlife..

31. Note especially R Girard, *Violence and the Sacred*, translated by P Gregory (Baltimore, 1977). Cf M Mauss, *The Gift* [1925], translated by I Cunnison (New York, 1967).

32. RD Laing, *Knots* (New York, 1970).

33. Trompf, 'Salvation and Primal Religion', *Prudentia* (special issue on *The*

Idea of Salvation, supplementary volume) (1988): 207–31.

34. Even theologies least likely to accentuate the depravity of humanity still have to deal with it, for, however much we may admire in others the courage and ability to make something our shared, ambiguous condition, who can honestly expect a final success? And, beside all admirable efforts at 'soul-making', we still witness so much 'resentment, fear, grasping selfishness and tragic disintegration of character'. J Hick on Irenaean theodicy, in his *Christianity at the Centre* (London, 1968), 90–1. Cf also JW Woelfel, *Borderland Christianity: Critical Reason and the Christian Vision of Love* (London, 1973), chapter 4.

35. Bonhoeffer, *Ethics*, edited by E Bethge, translated by NH Smith (Glasgow, 1964 edition).

9

ON THE DIFFICULTY OF TALKING ABOUT GOD
Maurice Wiles

Attending an academic lecture by Harry Wardlaw is a remarkable and disturbing experience. (I don't describe it as a unique experience, because I have had a similar reaction to the lecturing of Donald Mackinnon.) However carefully the talk has been prepared, there is never any question with Harry of the seminar paper being read or the lecture delivered in a straightforward manner. There are agonising pauses before a key word is spoken or after some positive assertion has been made, with appropriate accompanying facial expression and bodily gestures. It is as if the struggle to find the right word and the subsequent questioning whether the word found and the sentiment expressed are really justified, that had been gone through in the process of preparation, were being gone through all over again. As no doubt they were. And all this is no affectation, no mere rhetorical device. It arises out of a deeply felt conviction of the difficulty, perhaps better the absurdity or even the impossibility, of the theologian's task of providing reasoned talk about God. That is a conviction to which almost all theologians pay lip service. We talk solemnly about the ineffability of God – but then tend to pay no further attention to that conviction as we fill book after book with accounts of God's nature and God's activity in the world. But Harry takes the conviction with a seriousness that puts the rest of us to shame. The distinctive style of his lecturing is testimony to its active presence in all that he says. And his reluctance to commit much of his wisdom to paper is, no doubt, largely due to the fact that the written word cannot convey, as effectively as the spoken, the insecure and perilous nature of all theological utterance.

What I want to do in this short paper is to take this feature of Harry's lecturing style as my starting point, and to ask what would happen if we all took the conviction that underlies it as seriously as

he does. In particular I want to suggest that it might point towards
a way out of what seems to me an unsatisfactory state of affairs in
contemporary theology. I refer to a fundamental dichotomy in the
world of critical theological scholarship between what may broadly
be described as liberal and confessional approaches. These two
approaches are described in a number of other ways with a variety
of contrasting designations, which bring out differing distinctions
within broadly the same dichotomy: 'modernists' versus 'post-
modernists'; 'foundationalists' versus 'anti-foundationalists';
'enlightenment rationalists' versus 'Wittgensteinian fideists'. The
dichotomy is, no doubt, crudely drawn; there are plenty of
variations within each general approach. And the customary
designations tend to spread more heat than light. But that there is
such a divide, and that it is not a healthy one in its present form,
seems to me beyond question.

Choosing to take a characteristic feature of Harry's theological
teaching as an aid to dealing with this particular problem is,
I want to claim, an eminently reasonable procedure. For he
himself is someone who cannot be clearly classified as belonging
to one approach rather than the other. On the one hand he is a
philosopher of religion, indefatigable in his determination to put
all our affirmations to the test by questioning in the most general
ways their claim to be true. But on the other hand he is also a
Reformed churchman who has served his church, as faithfully
as he has served the academy, in helping to determine how its
traditional confession should find contemporary expression. His
practice suggests that he is the kind of scholar whose thought
might be of value in our present situation.

Despite the rhetoric to be heard from time to time on both
sides of the divide, I find it hard to believe that any strong form
of either approach is wholly right and the other wholly mistaken.
But if one takes that view of the matter, one is left with the
question whether there is some means whereby the valid insights
of each can be held together. If there is, it is certainly not by way
of sitting on the boundary fence between the two with one foot
firmly planted on the ground on each side. What we need to look
for is something much more flexible, much more dynamic than

that image suggests – some way of showing that it is possible to pursue the positive insights of both approaches without involving oneself in inconsistency or self-contradiction. As a starting point . for that quest I propose to take the closing words of Harry's 'Karl Jaspers' lecture, delivered in Oxford in 1990. The implications of his lecturing style I shall hold up my sleeve for a later stage in the argument.

At the end of the lecture, which was entitled Theological Truth and Living Truth, he poses the question how far the insights into Jaspers' thought, that he had been describing in the course of it, could be of service to a theologian committed to a degree of pluralism in society and appreciative of the value of quite different cultural and religious traditions. The answer he gave to his own question was this:

> Ultimately I think his [Jaspers'] thought might lead us towards a recognition that the only resolution of these questions lies within the mystery of that ineffable transcendence to which our Existenz is open. But he also gives some encouragement to hold resolutely to the revelation of transcendence in our history and within our own individual lives.

In other words Jaspers' analysis of the human condition, in Harry's view, emphasises the significance of three aspects of our experience through which the reality of transcendence can be encountered. And for the theist that means three aspects of experience that make us open to an awareness of God. I don't propose to develop that suggestion in relation to the precise nature of Jaspers' thought, with its very specific sense of the term *Existenz*. I do not share Harry's expertise that might enable me to do that. I want to use it much more broadly as a way in to a more general exploration of the issues it raises.

The three ways can be broadly distinguished like this. The first is, at least potentially, universal in its scope, arising out of the fundamental nature of what it is to be a human being. The second is more limited in scope, being dependent on a person's particular cultural and religious history, which so substantially influences the form and content of every individual's specific apprehension of the world. The third relates to the distinctive character of each individual's story, with its unique way of drawing on the other two. So we might speak of two fundamental sources of transcendence, or awareness of God, which each of us brings together differently, in the light of our own particular experience of the transcendent, to form a distinctive whole. The different emphasis given to each of those first two ways seems to me to be one of the fundamental differences between the liberal and the confessional approaches to theology. For the liberal, the understanding of God, who is source and ground of all that is, is most closely correlated to the experience of what it is to be a human being; for the confessional theologian it is the presence and activity of God in the history of the faith community that is predominant and decisive. That being so, it is not surprising that the two approaches should tend to speak about God with different voices. But however important the distinction between the two may be, it cannot, logically cannot, in itself give rise to an irreconcilable conflict between them. For there is no *Existenz*, no way of being truly human, which is not at the same time part of some particular stream of historical experience; and there can be no experience of history, which is not the experience of a human being. So however different the languages in which they articulate their diverse experiences of the transcendent, there must be, in so far as they are both genuine experiences of the transcendent, some points of contact between them.

The kind of analysis that I have been drawing from Harry's reflections on Jaspers is one that has been used by a number of prominent theologians in the recent past. Harry himself alludes to Paul Tillich. Tillich distinguishes three senses of theism. It may indicate an unspecified affirmation of God; or it may imply the personalistic images of God characteristic of biblical religion; or, again, it may refer to the theological attempt to combine those two by arguing for the existence of God – a personal God whose existence stands over against our existence as human beings. The first two Tillich regards as inadequate. The third, with its suggestion that God is a being, a part of the whole of reality, he rejects as a false way of bringing them together. In place of this inadequate and misleading manner of combining the two, Tillich looks for a church which raises its message and its devotion above the God of theism without sacrificing its concrete symbols. This

God above God to whom our faith and devotion are to be directed is not, for Tillich, just an abstract, philosophical notion; it is also rooted in the preaching of the Crucified who cried to God who remained his God after the God of confidence had left him in the darkness of doubt and meaninglessness. But that is not how it has been seen by many of his readers. Those of a more confessional approach incline to see the two as in direct conflict. A recent review in the *Scottish Journal of Theology*, for example, asserts that understanding the life of Christ, in line with the New Testament, as the image of the eternal Trinity rules out the notion of some unexpressed residue of a God beyond God. And even those more sympathetic to Tillich's approach are wont to complain that he has not done much to help us see how the God beyond God and the concrete symbols of biblical faith can be held together as closely as he encourages us to do.

Fundamentally the same underlying picture is to be found in the work of another, equally prominent twentieth century theologian, who was as determined to stay true to Catholic orthodoxy as Tillich was to the Protestant principle – namely Karl Rahner. And Rahner does rather more to suggest how the ultimate and the concrete forms of religious faith can be understood to hold together. Like Tillich he insists that to understand God as a part of the whole of reality is to fail to grasp what God really is. A proper apprehension of what God really is arises, in Rahner's view, from fundamental reflection on what it is to be a human self. However fully, for example, we acknowledge the importance of our genetic inheritance and of the environment in which we have been brought up and now live, our experience of apparent freedom and of a sense of responsibility (apprehended at times as an absolute moral imperative) does not go away; it only becomes more puzzling. Questions of that kind impinge on us as inescapable, but also as unanswerable. Cumulatively they lead to an awareness of what Rahner calls 'the infinite question which encompasses us'. This process of self-transcendence shows us that human life has an ineluctable 'orientation towards mystery'. And God is the name for that 'absolute mystery' towards which this distinctively human style of reflection inevitably points. But in addition to this awareness of 'God as question', the history of religions presents a record of much more positive affirmations about God – an apprehension of what we might call by contrast 'God as answer'. For the Christian these affirmations are embodied in the biblical story of God's dealings with the people of Israel, culminating in the person of Jesus. But taken at its face value that story seems to describe a God who 'is here and not there', who has 'revealed himself here and not there'. And 'such a religion seems incompatible with our transcendental starting point, which ... we cannot abandon if we want to talk about God at all today'. In Rahner's vision there is a universal divine offer of self-communication, which is the other side of the coin of the universal human orientation towards mystery; the full story cannot, therefore, be as restricted as a superficial reading of the biblical story is liable to suggest. Potentially at least it is coextensive with the history of the world. For it is the history of human responses, however imperfect, to that divine offer. And since no human experience is a purely private or individual matter, but every human experience arises within and is significantly influenced by the cultural tradition within which it is set, these human responses to God take very different forms in different cultures – as the differences within as well as between religions bear witness.

Rahner's reflections on the cultural embeddedness of all human experience and language helps to fill out the picture indicated by Tillich's insistence on the symbolic character of all our concrete language about God if it is properly to refer to the 'God above God'. And if the way such language relates still remains puzzling, that is not necessarily the fault of either author. By definition we are bound to go beyond the ordinary use of language to speak of the God beyond God; there is bound to be something mysterious about the way we use language to speak of the absolute mystery. The most we can hope for is some justification for making the attempt at all. And on that score what Rahner has to say seems to me to make a constructive and helpful contribution.

So there are (at least) two different styles of speech to which we need to pay attention when we speak about God – and that 'we' includes not only theologians but all reflective members of the Church. Neither approach is to be ignored; but nor can the two be fully integrated. No wonder that for many sensitive minds this should give rise to a kind of verbal angst, of which Harry's lecturing style provides so vivid and uncontrived an illustration. However happy we could be with either, can we live happily with both?

I have already argued that the contrast between the two cannot be ultimately irreconcilable, even if we may never be in a position to do the reconciling. So in the first place the contrast between the two serves as a timely reminder of the provisional character of all our theology – something of which we ought not to, but in practice do need constant reminding. All theologies are incomplete and correctible, not only because they are fallible human constructions, but also because there is always another approach demanding equal attention but resisting all our best attempts at synthesis or harmonisation. But can we be content with such a situation? Have we any answer to those who find it either intellectually or religiously unacceptable – or both?

The intellectual objection is understandable enough. Theology, it argues, which claims to be offering reasoned speech about God, proceeds so far along the way following the accepted paths of reasoned reflection, but when the going gets rough it abandons the canons of reason and embraces incompatibilities of a kind that reason should eschew. That theology does sometimes behave reprehensibly in that way cannot be denied. But not all prima facie incompatibilities are to be treated as sure signs of error – and certainly not those which survive a second and third look as well. Human studies, for example, involve both physical and psychological categories. The fact that we cannot combine the two in a single synthesis, despite the fact that they relate to the same human being and the same behaviour patterns, does not persuade many that one of the two should be abandoned; and those who do respond in that sort of way are rightly criticised for their reductionist approach. Instead we puzzle about the nature of consciousness; but even that provides no way of integrating the two approaches. The parallel is not, of course, exact. But it does serve as a reminder that we have frequently to live with persisting incompatibilities in our understanding of the world. In claiming earlier that the two approaches to theology constitute an incompatibility of that kind, I incorporated the proviso, 'in so far as they are both genuine experiences of the transcendent'. That, of course, is not something that can be demonstrated; but if we accept the concept of the transcendent as developed by philosophers like Jaspers, there seem to be good grounds for affirming the presence of such experiences in both approaches. And in that case, the intellectual challenge to our uncomfortable dichotomy is not as strong as it at first appears.

The religious objection is primarily based on an anxiety that this fundamental and unresolved division in our ways of speaking about God undermines confidence in the Christian message. Insistence on the symbolic character of all religious language and on the influence that its contingent, cultural setting has had on the form taken by the Christian story seems to detract from the reliability and the universality of the Christian gospel. This too is an understandable concern for a faith which has enshrined the beliefs to which allegiance is required in propositional statements, formulated at particular moments in the course of its long, developing history. Does not the approach suggested introduce a note of uncertainty, even of unreality into what should be the bedrock faith on the basis of which Christian lives are to be lived? But however understandable, the objection is nonetheless misguided. The kind of certainty that is undermined is not something that properly belongs to the life of faith. The way of faith is grounded in an interplay between the sense of absolute mystery on the one hand and the particular instantiations of it in the biblical story and the subsequent history of the church on the other. There are dangers arising from sitting too loose to the witness of the biblical story and there are dangers from accepting it as an unquestionable given. Historically it is the evils of religious certainty that have wrought the greater havoc. Living with this dual approach has its difficulties, especially for the corporate life of the institutional church, but they do not outweigh the positive religious potential within it.

So the theoretical objections, intellectual and religious, to the dual approach that I am commending are not decisive. And if accepted, it would serve to reduce the inhibitions sometimes felt by the liberal theologian against drawing too readily from the particular insights of the tradition, while at the same time tempering the sometimes overconfident claims of the confessionalist about the particular form that it has taken. Debates between the two with their differing emphases would need to go on – but with a recognition that each, at its best, should be struggling to draw within the orbit of its own dominant emphasis the truest insights of the other approach. And the fact that we see no way of integrating them fully is no reason for not continuing to search for some overall vision that is able to do more justice to the virtues of each. Belief in one God precludes the extreme relativism of some forms of post-modernism that would abandon all such endeavours as fundamentally mistaken in principle.

But we need also to address the question of what are the implications of our acknowledgement of this duality for religious practice, the way we speak about God in reflective thought and in worship. There is nothing radically new in principle about the problem. The church has always had to come to terms with the tension between the *apophatic* and *kataphatic* aspects of its heritage. Scholars and poets can both empathise with Harry's agonising about whether the words that he has come up with are the 'right' words. But the criteria for judging the 'rightness' of our words vary. Sometimes it is a matter of whether the words are narrow enough to secure the precision of reference that we intend; at other times it is a question of whether they have the necessary breadth to indicate the range of connexions that we are seeking to convey. Both sets of criteria are relevant to the theologian and to the believer. For the way of faith is not an attempt to escape into some groundless fantasy; it is an attempt to apprehend and respond to how the world fundamentally is. So we are not free to weave our own subjective imaginings however the fancy takes us; we are controlled by that which stands over against us, and our language must reflect what we find as accurately as it can. But we can only achieve an apprehension and a response which have the ultimacy that faith demands by reaching out imaginatively beyond the limits of secure knowledge; and there the richness of the resonance of our words is all important.

So the confessional and liberal styles of theology remain

important ingredients in the whole process, but neither is as complete as it likes to think. If our speech about God is to be true to its object and avoid the disastrous outcome of absolutising the imperfect creations of our own best reflection, it needs in its final stages to adopt something of the style of the religious poet. Finding the appropriate images, enriched but not encrusted by tradition, that can also serve as vehicles of transcendence today, is no ordinary gift. But for me Harry is one of those rare theologians who at least points me towards the Promised Land.

10

THIS I BELIEVE: THAT I DO NOT
ROBERT ANDERSON

When Harry Wardlaw, Nigel Watson and I retired from our respective appointments at the end of 1993 we were each invited to deliver a lecture in a series that was subsequently published under the title, *The Way We See Things Now*. A number of years later some of my further thoughts were advanced in an address to a lay audience. The series of which it was a part was under the joint auspices of the Council of Christians and Jews and the Council for Adult Education and had the general rubric, 'This I believe'. This essay is substantially what was said on that occasion, hence its format and style.

It is with very much pleasure that I offer this as part of a published tribute to Harry Wardlaw whose intellect and ability I admire and whose friendship I greatly value.

From what I can tell, almost every ancient religion had a personal epithet for its deity. In the case of some there were many deities and therefore many epithets. Even in the case of the monotheistic ancient Hebrew faith God had what we might term an identifying name which, in the midst of polytheism, was to set the God of Israel over and against all possible competing gods.

In English translations of the Hebrew text that singularly identifying appellative is usually rendered THE LORD and so the real force and purpose of the original are lost.

For example in the central Hebraic/Jewish affirmation referred to as the *shema'* because of its opening directive the usual translation is:

Hear, O Israel: The LORD is our God, the LORD alone.

The original is thus stripped of its essential forcefulness.

What is translated as 'the LORD' is, in Hebrew, signified by four letters, indeed, four consonants. These are the Hebrew *yod, hē̄, vav* and, again, *hē̄*.

These four consonants enshrined the ancient identifying name of the God of Israel, not least as that God had become known to Moses. How it was pronounced remains, even to this day, something of a mystery, for the initial pronunciation was deliberately and very effectively repressed as the faith and the expression of the faith became more and more theologically sophisticated. When these four consonants were read they were accompanied, not by vowels that would betray the less developed understanding of God, but by vowels of a completely distinct word, namely, *adonai*, which is suitably translated as 'the LORD'.

Why this long preamble? Well, my initial purpose in raising this matter was to indicate that how we talk about God and what we mean by that seemingly simple term are mostly conditioned by our environment. In ancient Israel's case, in very early times, it made sense to have an identifying epithet for one's own God at a stage in their religious understanding and, I should say, development, when the efficacy of other gods was denied but not their existence. The environment was polytheistic – the leaders of Hebraic thought recognised that – and how the God of Israel was presented, so to speak, was in terms of that religious context.

So, then, the *shema'* is best translated:

Hear, O Israel: YHVH is our God, YHVH alone. (Deut 6:4)

That, incidentally, is the translation that the great mediaeval Jewish scholar, Rashi, would have approved.

All that I am talking about, at the moment, is the influence of the environment, the context, religiously, culturally, politically and socially. All these factors play a part in how we think.

What I am not suggesting, even though I earlier used the word 'development', is that there is, in the Bible, anything akin to an ascending, evolutionary understanding of God as though always what is late must be superior to what is early. Some of the most majestic and enduring insights have come from such luminaries as Moses, Amos, Isaiah and, of course, the psalmists.

My second purpose in speaking of the hiddenness, the *deliberate* hiddenness, of the name of God in the biblical tradition was to note a similar practice even within areas of modern, traditional Judaism. I am referring to the way in which the term God is circumvented both in speech and in writing. In speech, most often, there is substituted for the Hebrew 'elohim or the English, God, the expression ha-shem – meaning, 'the name'. In writing what happens, is that the vowel is simply omitted and so we are left with G-D. The origin of this, and its purpose in some sections of Jewish practice, I leave to others to explain. For me, although I do not adopt it, it has a symbolic significance.

In an age when we might be inclined to think we have all the answers, it is a forceful reminder that there are still some huge gaps in our knowledge. More specifically, it should warn us against any temptation to emulate the builders of the Tower of Babel. Such is human finitude that, no matter how strenuously we climb, our feet never really leave the ground. When we speak of God, of our belief in God, we should keep in check both our own claims and any tendency to sit in judgement upon the choice of others.

Throughout my teaching career I tried to impress upon my students two things:

- First, that there is NO question that may not legitimately be asked.
- Second – and this was superbly put by Sir Gerard Brennan, former Chief Justice of the High Court – 'Is truth so fragile that it cannot be openly examined and debated?'

Perhaps in stating those two points I have signalled the fact that I find myself in tension with some of the traditional beliefs and doctrines of the church.

I could not attend to the topic of this lecture series without gearing myself to speak honestly and frankly, yet mindful of what I referred to a moment ago as the finitude of human beings, not least this one.

What I have chosen to do is not to set forth a series of

propositions that might be expanded and defended (or otherwise) but to try to describe the way in which my beliefs have developed under certain influences.

There have been three main influences that have affected my thinking over a period of some four decades. These are:

1. The introduction to an engagement in an analytical, historical-critical approach to the Bible;
2. a long involvement in the area of the betterment of relations between Jews and Christians; and
3. the recognition of the importance for theology of the scientific advances of the past century or so, not least in the area of astrophysics and cosmology – what I might refer to clumsily in my own experience as 'the stretching of one's horizon'.

1. The analytical approach to the study of the bible

On the first point, then, the analytical approach to study of the Bible: does this necessarily diminish the importance of this sacred literature? That is the forerunner of a whole host of questions that comes to mind.

- Does the Bible still have a place in the determination of Christian belief?
- If so, what is its role?
- For those of us who adopt what I have been calling an analytical approach to the Scriptures, that is, a non-biblicist, non-literal, non-fundamentalist approach, what is the ground that we wish to hold at all costs?
- Is the determination of that secure ground anything more than a personal and somewhat arbitrary choice?

These are just a few of the more obvious questions that spring to mind. Have no fear, I am not going to go through them one by one.

Rather, I state them as such and leave them to stand as some indication that I take the Bible with the utmost seriousness. Indeed, it is the time and energy spent in that analytical, historical-critical approach to the Bible that indicates the seriousness with which the particular school of thought to which I subscribe does take this subject.

This is the method of biblical study to which I was introduced as a student within the Faculty of Divinity of the University of Edinburgh in the mid-fifties. Substantially I have held to it since that time, and this has enhanced thirty-three years of lecturing to students, most of whom, I trust, have learnt something.

Methods of biblical study, other than the conservative-fundamentalist, have presented themselves over the years. We have had the constructionists, the reconstructionists and the deconstructionists. Perhaps I am old-fashioned but I have always insisted that, the better our knowledge of the circumstances in which a text arose and the purpose for which it was written and transmitted, the better might we be able to discern not only its initial impact but its continuing value and validity as formative literature of a religious community. Determining this necessary initial contextual and ongoing contextual knowledge is by no means an easy or straightforward assignment and there will always be gaps in our knowledge. Competent scholarship is as much aware of these gaps as it is of the gains and the conclusions it draws will give full weight to both. But, to my mind, exacting an exercise as it is, with the ever-present possibility of imprecision, it is, nevertheless, essential if the Bible is to be used sensibly.

I should add, here, that when I speak of the Bible I mean both the Hebrew Scriptures (the Old Testament so-called) and the New Testament. The latter makes little or no sense without the former but, unfortunately, throughout most of the history of the church, the Hebrew Scriptures have been made to serve the purpose of the New Testament, not least as some kind of treasure-trove of prophesies which had to await the rise of Christianity for their fulfilment. It is only in relatively recent years that, within the church, the Hebrew

Scriptures have been studied and used *in their own right.*

On the matter of reading texts in their context, let me give an example or two of the ways in which the failure to do so may lead to misinterpretation, indeed, sometimes to damaging misrepresentation.

Take the case of the law of retaliation – the *lex talionis* – found in Exodus, Leviticus and Deuteronomy: 'an eye for an eye and a tooth for a tooth'.

The purpose of this law was that where there was no ready judicial system, where justice was meted out by means of retaliation, this would be limited in both kind and degree. Later, in the history of ancient Israel, in changed circumstances, its original purpose no longer held and so a monetary settlement was humanely invoked. To quote this law as though, somehow, it is representative of Jewish thought and practice is to use it in a mischievous and harmful way.

Reinterpretation was the means by which certain provisions within the Torah, the biblical law-code, were kept in step with changing circumstances: hence the rise of the oral Torah which eventually found its extant form in the Mishnah and Gemara which, together, constitute the Talmud.

Another example is found outside the Torah, in the historical books. In the Second Book of Samuel[1] David conducts a census of the people, ostensibly to gauge the strength of his army, thus displaying lack of faith in God. But the text explicitly says that it was God who tempted David to act in this way and this was very much in accordance with ancient belief that saw the deity as the prime force in every action. However, many centuries later, when the same episode is recounted in the First Book of Chronicles[2] it is not God who instigates the census but Satan, the avowed opponent of God. A new force, hitherto not accounted for in the Hebrew religious experience, now enters the picture and becomes an important player in ensuing Jewish and, later, Christian belief.

In like manner, it is possible to trace the means by which a belief in life after death became a possibility in ancient Israel. The first explicit statement of resurrection is as late as the book of Daniel in circa 165 BCE. Its appeal, however, was not universal. If the history of belief in life after death can be documented, does not that suggest that the imperative may have arisen within the province of human expectation rather than form part of a divinely decreed order of existence? Popular belief may see it as an essential ingredient of biblical religion, but, despite its appeal during the early centuries of the church among a Gentile population that feared death, it was relatively late on the scene.

So far, with the possible expectation of the last point, what I have said has avoided any controversy. It has moved within the parameters of the usual safe analytical approach. We have considered the charge that what is being spoken of is no more than a revision of nineteenth century liberal theology. But what if we trespass a little on the sacred territory of traditional dogma?

What if we raise questions about, say, sacrifice in its biblical context, or the use of the expression applied to Jesus in the New Testament and elsewhere, son of God?

How did Jesus' disciples react to his death? When we examine this matter, in the words of an American New Testament scholar, 'we come to the great creative contribution of Christian theology for first-century Jewish messianism'.[3] That may well be so, but what we have in the early and later Christian explanation of the tragic and premature death of Jesus moves far beyond any notion of messianism then or now entertained within Judaism. Nowhere in the Hebrew Scriptures is it even remotely suggested that an expected messiah would die, let alone die for the sins of others as an atoning sacrifice. When Paul asserts, as he does, that 'Christ died for our sins, according to the scriptures' (1 Cor 15:3) he moves far beyond any possible plain meaning of these writings. In order to explain how Paul and others came to adopt and promulgate this particular understanding of Jesus' death we have to examine the religious context of the time. I think we find some clues in the development within certain parts of Judaism, albeit on the periphery at times, of what is referred to in Jewish tradition as the *Akedah*, the 'Binding of Isaac'. It goes back to the dramatic incident recorded in Genesis chapter 22 where Abraham is tested by God and is required to offer his son, Isaac, as 'a burnt offering' on a mountain later identified as Mt Moriah, the locale of the Jerusalem Temple. In the story in Genesis it is Abraham who is the active participant whereas Isaac is the passive victim who, incidentally, is spared. But in later tradition the rôles of father and son are somewhat reversed. Isaac becomes the willing sacrifice. In one Jewish interpretation of the biblical text it is said that:

> Though he (Isaac) did not die,
> Scripture credits Isaac with
> having died and his ashes
> having lain upon the altar.

So central is Isaac's willingness in Jewish tradition that the redemptive aspect of the Temple's expiatory sacrifices become centred in the putative self-sacrifice of Isaac.

The American Jesuit scholar, Fr Robert Daly, speaks of a considerable number of possible allusions to this developed understanding of the *Akedah* in parts of the New Testament (see especially Romans 8:32, James 2:21–23 and Hebrews 11:17–20).

Daly makes this assertion:

> I would submit not only that it is now proven that there is a relationship between the *Akedah* and the NT, but also that the sacrificial soteriology of the NT can no longer be discussed without consideration of the *Akedah*.

What I have tried to suggest again, is that the explication of certain key events in the New Testament which became the foundation of later doctrinal statement are themselves contextually conditioned.

While some in the church will baulk at the suggestion that key doctrines such as the atoning death of Jesus may have to be re-examined, there are others, also in the church, and no less women and men of faith, who question the action, indeed, the morality of a God who would willingly offer a human being, his son, for the expiation of the sins of others.

We are skating on the same thin theological ice when we suggest that there is a radical movement from the use of the term *ben-'elohim*, son of God, of Jesus in the narratives of the events of his time and the later claims of the church that the expression denotes his divinity.

What has to be remembered is that within a very short space of time the Jesus movement, specifically one within Judaism, became a Gentile institution. Jesus, and what happened to him, were now proclaimed and explained, no longer in a Jewish environment, but in one that was essentially alien to his own, and decidedly Hellenistic in character. It was a world in which the great traditional Jewish divide between the human and the divine no longer held. It was a world in which human emperors, upon death, were deified.

If the Holy Scriptures of the church may be studied in the analytical way that I have attempted to describe – and that is the formal position of most mainstream churches – why is there an unwillingness to treat the fourth and fifth century credal statements in the same open manner? After all, the Scriptures are regarded as the primary definitive, some would say authoritative, writings of the church.

2. The influence of engagement in Jewish and Christian relations

This brings me to the second major influence upon my theological thinking, my long engagement, almost thirty-five years, in what is referred to as Jewish and Christian relations. This is related to the study and teaching of the Hebrew Scriptures, an endeavour which, along with the study of Biblical Hebrew, began as long ago as 1952.

When I concluded my initial theological studies in Edinburgh in 1959, also the year of my ordination, indeed, even when I began my teaching career in 1961, my understanding of Judaism was what I should now refer to as little more than a caricature. I don't think that it was entirely my own fault that that was the case. It was, in fact, the inherited position of the church in all of its communions and the scholars who presented a different understanding were very, very few in number. In the main I did not come across the works of these until several years later. If I did read them and failed to be influenced by them at the time it was because of the sheer weight of the influence of nineteen centuries of misinterpretation and, consequently, of misrepresentation of Judaism.

The essence of the scholarly Christian caricature of Judaism that held sway in the church for so long was that Judaism was a religion of arid legalism the presence of which brought about the faith's eventual demise and replacement by something infinitely superior, namely, Christianity.

The first signs of that demise were seen in the period immediately following the return from the Babylonian exile towards the end of the sixth century BCE. As Judaism moved towards the turn of the era the legalism and the nationalistic particularism became more and more pronounced and more and more stultifying to the point where the divine rejection of his ancient People Israel was only a matter of time.

Sophisticated Christian theologians have long left behind them the understanding of the Hebrew Scriptures as a repository of prophecies about an expected Messiah the fulfilment of which awaited the advent of Jesus of Nazareth. Nevertheless, the relation between the two testaments, the so-called Old and the New, was still presented in such a way as to rob the People Israel of any continuing role in the divine economy once Jesus came on the scene. It was still common for Christian scholars, even up to recent decades, to employ Emil Schürer's depiction of the Judaism of the first century CE as *Spätjudentum*, Late Judaism, that is, a Judaism in its death throes.

This portrayal of the ancient faith was dependent upon by an understanding of the writings of St Paul that most modern New Testament scholars recognise as owing more to Augustine and Martin Luther than it ever did to the first-century missionary apostle. But the classification of Judaism as a religion of works/ righteousness, that is, one by which the favour of God is earned by observance of the Torah (Law) is still very persistent. The contrast with Christianity, described most favourably as a religion of grace and faith, continues to tempt many Christian preachers.

Why this has come about cannot be understood apart from an investigation of the way in which the Jesus-movement, a movement comprising Jews and initially within Judaism, eventually moved away from and was forced to move away from the mother faith. Knowledge of the Judaism of the early and mid-first century CE, indeed, up to the destruction of the Temple in the year 70, indicates that Judaism was a relatively diverse religion. Within it, but gradually moving towards its periphery, were a number of apocalyptic groups whose writings have been preserved in the mostly Jewish Apocrypha and Pseudepigrapha. Numbered among these apocalyptic groups were the Qumran Community of the Dead Sea Scrolls and the Jesus-movement. In the case of these two, quite separate and distinct collections of literature came into existence.

What has to be noted, specially in the case of Qumran and the nascent church, was that their claims left no room for those of any other group. It is the nature of breakaway groups, which inevitably adopt a sectarian approach to the major body from which they have separated, not only to make exclusive claims to the truth, but to demean the other.

Indeed, could one possibly expect such a separated group to pull the religious mat from under its own feet, so to speak, by entertaining the claims of any other group?

The claims to exclusivity, to be the sole custodian of truth and the sole means of salvation, have to be looked at in the context in which they have emerged. What is more, these are interior claims, supported only by their own texts, and, because of that, not subject to any historical or objective verification.

It is this approach, engendered by a recognition of Judaism as a validly, continuing religion, to be understood, not in terms imposed upon it by an initially competing faith, but in its own terms that, together with an appraisal of the apologetic and polemical context in which Christianity emerged, has forced me to reassess the place of Jesus Christ in the divine redemptive purpose.

This reassessment has led me to recognise that which has occurred through the life and ministry of Jesus of Nazareth is of no less importance stated in non-exclusivist terms than has been asserted within traditional Christianity. That Hebraic religious genius which has bequeathed to the world a majestic understanding of God flows on through the witness of the New Testament beyond the borders of the historic People Israel to the larger Gentile world.

Love of God, love for one's neighbour, both injunctions of the Hebrew Scriptures, are no less binding under this theological regime than they are under any other, particularly one that denies continuing significance to the religion of their source. As for the need for forgiveness and recognition of the divine willingness to bestow it, this too is ever present, as are also the call for justice and concern for the vulnerable of society, emphases that the church finds as demands upon its own life when it turns to the Torah and the Prophets.

3. Modern Cosmology

So far, in what I have said, I have not moved beyond what one might call a biblical understanding or presentation of religion, even though my comprehension of that may be at odds with the traditional.

This biblical presentation, however, is predicated on an understanding of the universe which is vastly different to that of modern cosmology. In the Bible the world is an enclosed system created by God and subject always to the continuing activity of a deity who is described not only as Creator but as Redeemer, as one who steps in, from time to time, to order things according to his will. We speak of the acts of God as the deity pursues the role of the Lord of history. The biblical story is one that is played out on the historical scene with God ostensibly as the Chief Actor who gives purpose to all.

This is a very reassuring picture of a God who has everything within his/her control. Down through the ages, millions of people, of various faiths, have found comfort in the belief in such a deity. That it is difficult to hold together, in the light of human experience, an understanding of God as both omnipotent and all loving, has, more often than not, failed to perturb people of faith – nor even theologians of faith.

But the shape of the universe, if I might put it that way, is not, nor ever has been, that of its biblical depiction. It is not as though there is an object of divine creation, over and against a Creator who can, at will, move things along to work out a specific purpose in history. The *particularity* involved in God's choosing of a *particular* people through whom to work out his *particular* purpose becomes problematical once God ceases to be understood as over and against the universe.

What becomes even more problematic, at least for me, is the seemingly unfettered presence and perpetration of intense evil in the world. In this context I think that it is proper that we should call to mind the Holocaust, the attempt on the part of the leader of an erstwhile civilised nation with a long association with the Christian faith to eradicate an entire people. The eminent Catholic scholar Johann-Baptist Metz once confided that he could not contemplate the doing of theology except in the shadow of the Holocaust. It pervaded all his thinking. I feel no less compelled to place the Holocaust centrally within my own speculation about God. In addition, my confidence as a Christian is eroded by the undesirable fact that before that horrendous event, during it, and for a considerable time afterwards, the official response of *all* the churches was silence, a deathly silence, in some way the climax of those attitudes to which I referred.

Many theological explanations of the Holocaust have been attempted. The only ones that I would admit for serious discussion are those that call in question either the Omnipotence of God or that other central and traditional divine quality, his all-loving nature. Whatever the cost, I find I have to cling to the latter, for a God who is less than all-loving is not worthy of human consideration. For that is a quality we esteem even among ourselves. Divine Omnipotence, particularly in the context of modern cosmology, is, I think, dispensable.

Central to Christian description of God has been the doctrine of the Trinity clutched to the breast of the church as though God, himself, were dependent upon such an understanding. Woe betide anyone who should be sufficiently bold or foolish to tinker even at the edges of this notion. But, how, given the infinite nature of the Universe, that one star, alone, may contain a million galaxies, given that, how can we be adamant that even that doctrine rises above the mere human attempt to come to terms with God in a way that makes sense to us? If by the use of the expression, Triune God, Christian theologians believe that they are speaking of the essence of the deity then I must part company with them. If, on the other hand, they see the Trinitarian formula as an expression of Christian experience then I can subscribe to it. The God of whom we speak is no other than the God encountered us as a Father, who, in the context of the New Testament, sent Jesus Christ and who continues to lead and inspire us by his Spirit. That, for me, is trinitarianism.

Throughout this essay I have spoken of God in clearly personal terms referring to the deity as 'he', even though I recognise the shortcomings of the use of the third masculine singular pronoun. In light of what I have said about the influence of modern cosmology on any possible understanding of God, does it remain feasible to understand the deity in personal terms? My response to that question is 'No' and 'Yes': 'No' in the sense that an anthropomorphic God is little more than a relic of the past. To speak of the hand of God, the face of God or God having a voice was to employ what was never more than an analogy. God, in order to be God, is quite other than might be signified by the use of this type of language. But there is a sense in which the answer must also embrace a 'Yes' unless we are to abandon all possible communion with the deity; and that I do not wish to advocate for one moment. Whether or not we think of God in such impersonal terms as 'Ground of Being', 'Source of Life', 'Moral Impulse' or whatever, we are doing our thinking as *persons* and so, in that sense, if in no other, there is a personal dimension to our faith. Tempting though it is to see the only reality of God in the use of that word by human beings there has to be something more. Certainly we owe a great deal in our understanding of the composition of the Bible and in our perception of God to what must be called human creative imagination. But that is not an entirely satisfactory solution. The missing letter in G-D requires something beyond our human speculation. Perhaps we come closest to understanding what that is when we are obedient to those claims made upon us by the biblical injunctions to 'love our neighbour as our self' and to seek justice for all.

End Notes

1. 2 Samuel 24:1–14.
2. 1 Chronicles 21:1–13.
3. Paula Fredriksen, *From Jesus to Christ* (New Haven and London: Yale University Press, 1988), 136.

11

A JEWISH EXPERIENCE OF JESUS

LOUIS GREENSPAN

Jesus is rarely mentioned in classical or medieval Jewish literature, yet a number of modem Jewish writers and artists have been drawn to examine his life, his religious ideas, and his relation to Judaism. Best known among those Jewish writers who have studied Jesus are Martin Buber, Samuel Sandmel, and Joseph Klausner, but there are many more. Most have pronounced him a *bona fide* Jew. They note that his life and his teachings – including the Sermon on the Mount – are in harmony with the Judaism of his day; that he was observant of the Torah; and most significant of all, that he did not claim to be the messiah. These Jewish scholars usually maintain that the new religion, Christianity, emerged through the missions and theology of the Apostle Paul. Buber, for example, cites Paul as the real founder of the new religion. Others, such as Klausner, agree with this conclusion but argue that the break between Jesus and Paul is not so absolute. They point out that though much in Jesus's teachings is Jewish, there is a side to him – his other worldliness, his lack of a sense of the Jewish nation and its economic and social realities – that anticipates the later break.

I am not a student of Jesus. The New Testament is not my field of inquiry, but I can say there is a Jesus theme in my life. The Jesus that I have encountered is the Jesus of legend rather than the historical Jesus. The historical Jesus is, as yet, too problematic for me. And I am sure that most Jews have the opinion that the 'Jews for Jesus' and the 'Messianic Jews' (who may think that Jews can be 'saved' by the crucified and reborn Jesus) proclaim a Jesus who carries too much historical and theological baggage that separates him from Judaism. In one of his novels Dostoevsky has a character who is obsessed by Grüenwald's painting of the crucifixion. Jesus on the cross signifies for him an absolute distance from a redeeming God. As a Jew, I don't need such an image to evoke utter hopelessness and despair. I need only contemplate my aunts and uncles who perished in Treblinka.

Jews relate more easily to the Jesus of legend – the healer, the rabbi, and the storyteller. Jaroslav Pelikan conveys some of these images in the volume *Jesus Through the Centuries*. The Jesus that I have encountered can be found among those that he has uncovered, but with this reservation. My experience of Jesus is anecdotal, political, and artistic.

First, Jesus had a good name in my family. A Christian historian once wrote that he was drawn to study the history of anti-Semitism when he realised that for Jews the image of Jesus on the cross was not an image of reconciliation and love but one of oppression and fear. This was the Jesus that my father, a rabbi from Poland, had remembered in his boyhood. But, arriving in Canada, he met a new one.

One day he was travelling from one small town in New Brunswick to another small town in New Brunswick (he served both towns as a rabbi). He noticed that the other passengers were getting tipsy and a bit raucous. Suddenly he remembered that it was Christmas Eve, a dangerous time for Jews in his part of Poland. He sat terrified. When he reached his destination, he was accosted by one of the revellers who asked him where he was going and then taken rather firmly to a car and shoved inside.

Once again he was wary. When they arrived at the address that my father had signified, he was taken outside by the driver who gave him a big hug and shouted, 'Merry Christmas, Rabbi'. 'Merry Christmas, Rabbi?' My father had never heard such a phrase but it taught him that Christmas and Jesus could signify peace and good will.

This spirit pervaded the Christmas celebrations of my hometown of Halifax. These were the days before the heavy commercialisation of Christmas that we experience today. Even the Jewish community was caught up in this spirit. We, of course, were forbidden by our parents and our faith community from joining in the lovely Christmas carols. But one Christmas Eve, when I was nineteen years old, I was sitting in the back of a truck outside Nazareth with a group of Canadian Jewish students. We were not permitted in Nazareth because of the crowds of Christian pilgrims but suddenly we burst into an hour of Christmas carols.

The spirit had taken us in a country where we couldn't be accused of pandering to assimilation.

In later years I read authors, some of them mentioned above, who wrote about a Jewish Jesus. Martin Buber is an interesting example. Buber was the champion of maverick and dissident forms of Judaism such as the early Hassidim. These Hassidim were healers, seekers of a spirituality different from that which emphasised never-ending learning in legal texts. Buber's account of the Hassidim evokes images of Jesus. They lived among the simple people, they were healers, and above all they were storytellers. Let me share a Hassidic story that is not from Buber but is in the spirit of his stories. Once a king was thrown into despair because his child had lost his mind. The child imagined that he was a chicken and spent all day jumping up and down the court clucking and trying to lay eggs. Nobody could cure him. Finally, in desperation the king called in a Hassidic rebbe. The rebbe came and, to everyone's shock, bent down and jumped around the court with the young man clucking and cooing.

Eventually the young man began to communicate with the rebbe and slowly he was cured. Isn't this story similar to the parables – such as the sower in the field – tales of openness of spirit? I think that Jesus would have liked this story.

The most serious encounter I had with Jesus and the spirit of Jesus was in the Civil Rights Movement and anti-war movements of the 1960s. In their early stages, these movements practised non-violent civil disobedience and were inspired by a philosophy that held that love rather than force is the road to changing your enemy. The slogan, 'Make Love Not War', was a direct translation of the New Testament into politics. In those days I met many young Jews who told me that the Gospel rather than the Hebrew Bible spoke to them most directly. The musical *Jesus Christ Superstar* was the product of an era where youngsters allowed themselves to be carried off to prison for a just cause.

My most intense personal encounter with Jesus was through a novel by Dostoevsky – *The Idiot*. The central character of *The Idiot* was Prince Myshkin, a Christ-like Holy Fool, who was for Dostoevsky a nineteenth century embodiment of Christ. Dostoevsky's portrait was of a man of the most compelling innocence. He was in love with the tempestuous and volatile Natasya Fillipovna, and continued to love her without rancour even when she ran off with Roghozin. When Roghozin murdered Natasya, Myshkin embraces him because he was incapable of hatred. His life was an embodiment of forgiveness and was a life on the cross: a perfectly compelling and convincing portrait of Jesus and selfless love.

In the end, however, I could not become a disciple of Jesus.

Something Jewish in me rebelled from the ethic of pacifism and the ethic of Myshkin. Like the pacifist I honour the campaign of Ghandhi, of Martin Luther King, and of the Polish Solidarity movement as among the great moral achievements of the twentieth century. But I also honour the RAF in the Battle of Britain, the resistance of the Russian people to the Nazis, the fighters of the Warsaw Ghetto and many other examples of armed resistance. As for Myshkin – I still love this Christ-like figure, but I think he is an aberration. He exemplifies a life that is entangled with the world, in it but not of it, a life that seeks suffering as a means of other worldly salvation. It is a life away from the muck of this existence – an illustration of Walter Kaufman's critique of Christianity (and perhaps Nietzche's) as a life turned away from life.

The Jewish reservation about Jesus is similar to Freud's reservation about religion in general and Christianity in particular – a reservation about a quest for innocence that is as compelling as it is burdensome.

12

THE HUMAN PERSON – PICKING UP
THE DROPPED BATON

MARGARET M YEE

In paying tribute to Professor Harry Wardlaw, whose scholarship and learning was so highly commended to me before I came to Oxford by my own academic mentor at the University of Sydney, the late Revd Professor Crawford Miller, the still greater pleasure was yet to come. This arose when Professor Wardlaw was on sabbatical in Oxford, England, and the unexpected opportunity arose for me to meet him face-to-face, and to hear him lecture to a packed audience in the grand setting of the Examination Schools. His perceptive brilliance and philosophical acuteness of mind not only alerted me to the importance of Karl Jaspers' thought for serious theological enquiry, but confirmed to me the long-standing regret expressed by Professor Miller that I had not met with Professor Wardlaw much earlier! Lively exchange with Harry Wardlaw, coupled with his adept understanding of theology, left me deeply humbled. I was forcibly reminded of how invaluable ongoing enquiry into divine mysteries can prove. Inspiring and new horizons are very likely to emerge, as occurred in precious conversation together. His cordial encouragement always to probe further has brought its own rewards.

Therefore, in writing an essay in honour of Professor Wardlaw, it would seem appropriate to choose a subject matter which has been of common concern to us, and which is also currently of interest to philosophers and theologians, viz 'the human person'. Where, though, should such an enquiry begin?

I recall that at the forefront of our discussions was the question of whether, in a swiftly advancing science-world in which the neurosciences have increased our knowledge exponentially, it is possible any longer to make undisputed theological claims about the human person. This was particularly at issue when leading neuroscientists claimed that they would soon be able 'to explain all'.

At the time, the immediate task confronting theologians seemed not so much the need to respond to such brusque claims by giving an *apologetic* for Christian Doctrine. Rather, the matter demanding *prior* attention was whether theologians could ignore such claims which justified the *non-inclusion of spiritual aspects of human life* by nothing other than some brief, dismissive side-comment. The gauntlet having been thrown down, the main issue then, which has become even more pressing today, was how theologians might appropriately converse with scientific researchers in a way in which spirituality might in some way be acknowledged as integral to 'being human'.

Our initial forays at the time brought helpful agreement as to the best *'starting-point'.* If a justifiable counter position were to be offered, one would undoubtedly need to be involved in some form of *interdisciplinary* exchange. This would not only need to be conducted with the neurosciences and biogenetics but also with researchers in the social sciences, such as psychology and social anthropology, and the humanities. As will be seen from the discussion that follows, aspects in all of these areas of learning have a bearing on understanding the human person.

Thus, it was agreed that an *inclusive frame of reference* would be necessary if interdisciplinary discourse was to be undertaken adequately. In addition, theological reflection would need to be critical. On such grounds, it could be assumed that discussion with other disciplines, not least the sciences, in which theological contributions would be offered, could be conducted within a context which was *open and respectful, and allowed for two-way exchange.* Findings in the sciences on human consciousness would be treated as seriously as critical claims made from a theological stance. Given these premises, theological enquiry conducted along these lines offered enticing adventure.

Our discussion proved irresistible and unstoppable. Insights from the thought of Jaspers, countered on my part with responses, hastily culled from the thought of Austin Farrer[1] (Oxford theologian and philosopher), all helped *'fan the fire'* endlessly on one cold English winter's night. Eventually, our spouses, who had patiently awaited a moment politely to intervene to announce the lateness of the hour, were able courteously to do so! A halt was called and it was agreed that our keen exchange would need to be continued in Melbourne or back in Oxford.

Sadly, no such opportunity availed. So it has been a great delight to be given a second chance to '*bite the bullet*' and engage in discussion with Professor Wardlaw on this inescapably important topic, viz. how theologians might respond effectively to well-meaning neuroscientists who, more than ever, believe that the sciences will soon *explain all there is to know* about the human person.

In the last few years with the successful mapping of the human genome, efforts to produce replacement organs for the human body, genetic modification and advances in gene therapy, issues related to our understanding of the human person have become even more important. Closely related to these scientific developments is the moral concern of whether there is a continuing appreciation of what it means to be 'human'. It is not difficult to see how understandings of the human person could be unwittingly diminished under a cloak of 'scientific advancement' should such issues not be addressed adequately by the social sciences and humanities division of our university of which the theology faculty is a part.

This latter concern has bothered a number of scientists and theologians in Britain to such an extent that the Science and Religion Forum Conference held at Newnham College, Cambridge, in September, 2000, chose the topic 'What does it mean to be human?' as its theme. Speakers in the neurosciences and theology took part. Since that time, conferences and workshops on similar or related themes have continued to capture attention globally.

Thus, whereas we may have thought in the past that one's understanding of 'person' could be 'taken as read', in such an advancement of learning, academics are increasingly being forced to ask what their view of the 'person' is. An amazing number of conflicting positions are likely to emerge. As an illustration, let me cite quickly one such instance which occurred prior to my reading a seminar paper on 'The Human Person: Brain, Mind and Spirit' at the Ian Ramsey Centre, Oxford. These seminars are normally attended by Fellows and graduates whose main area of study is in the sciences, humanities, theology or medicine, and who have an interest in the interrelation of the sciences and religion. On this particular evening, there was a panel, comprised of a professor of medical ethics, a professor of science and religion and a Benedictine monk. These were joined at dinner by me as well as a physicist who is also an Anglican priest. During dinner the question was raised as to how each understood the term 'person'. Suddenly, congenial conversation gave way to expressions of considerable disagreement not previously apparent.

In the panel discussion later, which followed the delivery of my paper, the prime source of these disagreements about 'person' and 'what it means to be human' became more obvious. They arose from important *methodological* differences. What often is accepted as 'common knowledge' and presumed not to require definition, such as what one means by terms such as 'person' and 'human', may, upon further discourse, be found to harbour within them very different assumptions, each held for different reasons.

An even more illuminating illustration of this issue could be demonstrated if, at this moment, we also were to ask ourselves the same question, viz. what *we* understand by the term 'person'. We would very likely discover that we hold yet different *other* views. The possibilities are manifold and complex because of the multiplicity of meanings attached to these words. (If in doubt about this claim, try raising the question at your next dinner party!)

For instance, the term 'person' has often been simply taken as referring to 'a human being'. By contrast, some, with an interest in natural history, might say that the term 'person' signifies 'a member of the animal and not the vegetable kingdom'. Others might prefer an evolutionary view, using the phrase *homo sapiens* and highlighting issues such as 'development' and 'biological significance'. Still others may talk of 'conscious being' or 'thinking being' Those wishing to adopt a more socio-psychological emphasis might prefer to talk about 'person' in terms of one who feels, behaves, thinks, makes choices, relates to and with others socially, culturally and communally. Ones with a spiritual outlook, however, as occasioned at one such dinner party recently, referred to 'person' as 'that part of one that is intangible and eternal', quoting as justification the scriptural words 'before I formed you in the womb, I knew you'.[2] Another member referred to 'human' as meaning 'unique, created in God's image with a capacity for love and compassion as well as being angry or nasty'.

Supposing, at this point that we should move to a very different outlook, viz. that of the World Health Organisation. The view of 'person' implicit in their statements is normally expressed in terms of 'body, mind and human value'. Such a position is assumed as a 'given' in common medical decision-making and public policy.

From the comments so far, it should be obvious how diverse our understandings of the human person can be. The need to adopt an approach which is capable of being *all-inclusive* becomes even more pressing. Otherwise, any exploration into human consciousness is bound to meet with considerable frustration if, at the very least, fundamental assumptions about the human person and their justifiability are not adequately addressed.

Methodologically, however, neuroscientists, concerned with explorations into physiological aspects of human life, often adopt the framework of thought which is specific to their field of study as a worthwhile model also for describing *all reality*. Their subsequent claim *'that science will soon explain all there is to know about the human person'* is unwittingly defined by the limits of physiological conditions, which, applied in to wider context, results in their succumbing to a form of *reductionism*. The problem always for such approaches is that one may well close off the debate too soon, overlooking important essentials, which, though perceived, are simply bypassed and not accounted for.

A key issue for contemporary theologians deeply concerned with human life, its existence, protection, sustaining strengths and care in a fast developing scientific world, is how *'talk about God and our relation to our Creator'* might still be offered in a meaningfully significant manner. Is there a way in which theology's contribution, closely aligned to *human value and welfare,* might continue to be made effectively?

On the one hand, the need for theologians to *wrestle* with issues in which the relation of the *divine* and the *human* is central is paramount. After all, the theologian's quest is the search for truth about God and His relation to human life. The pragmatic interest of any such endeavours is vested in maintaining a moral commitment, viz. *the non-violation of human life.* On the other hand, there are many scientists, who may well concur personally with the *non-violation of human life,* but who publicly consider that their areas of study are primarily to do with the physical world. *Spiritual and moral* matters,[3] they contend, fall outside the parameter of scientific research. Latterly, however, with a greater appreciation of the value of *interdisciplinary* enquiry, such assertions are not so easily bypassed in the overall search to know, though admittedly they are not the immediate concern of the physical sciences. In addition, since the work of thinkers such as Karl Popper and John Eccles on *'states of mind'* was undertaken, social and psychological factors have been acknowledged as an essential aspect of reality.

As the widening of exploratory horizons has persisted, progressive research into human consciousness suggests that there is still 'something more' in human life which has not been satisfactorily accounted for. Thus, whilst some scientists, firmly committed to *reductionism* have defined spiritual and theological claims as mere *illusions,* there are other *non-reductionist* researchers such as Roger Penrose,[4] who have insisted that we perceive more than computation can represent. Penrose's proposal, however, is that it will most likely be mathematics that will ultimately supply the explanation for such.

Possibly one of the most significant advances in research into human consciousness and understanding of the human person has been the work of Baroness Greenfield, Director of the Royal Institution, London. Her initial explorations into human consciousness are well-recorded in her book *Journey to the Centres of the Mind.*[5] Having been involved in the neurosciences for so long, swiftly advancing studies were indicating that mind and brain were not independent concepts, nor could one strictly say they were identical. But if this was so, and such a thing as consciousness was to be given credence, the question for her was what kind of relation does the mind have to the brain or the brain to the mind?

Intuitively, her position was that as there are two sides to every coin, so in human life, the 'outside in' and the 'inside out' story were integral factors to the human person. Her keen intention was to clarify what for so long had simply been attributed to 'mystery.' In her own words:

The more I heard, read and thought about it, the more it seemed incredible that mere molecules could in some way constitute an inner vision, idea, or emotion, or even more astounding, that they could generate the subjectivity of an emotion.[6]

Particular physiological examples raised further important questions:

(a) In brain death, there is never any consciousness. Could it be that consciousness after all is *continuous* with the activity of our physical brains and in fact emerges from it?

(b) Could it be that the brain *generates* consciousness?

(c) Are the *sciences able* to undertake studies in so subjective an area of human life?

It was at this point that Professor Greenfield came to consider the necessity of interdisciplinary enquiry, which was *multi-disciplinary and inclusive* in form. Her research sought therefore to compare ideas gleaned from areas of study such as philosophy, cognitive psychology, basic neuroscience, computation, brain damage studies, animal behaviour and developmental psychology.

There is a vital difference in Susan Greenfield's methodology from that of other scientists. She recognised that in many cases both physical and biological scientists had in the past begun with the properties of the physical brain and then tried to 'tack on' consciousness *ad hoc* as an *'all-or-none entity'*. Her approach was different. Methodologically, her search was more typical of principles employed in detection and extrapolation. By considering the findings of brain chemistry and brain electricity, she sought instead to formulate the *physical base of the phenomenological sensation of consciousness.*

The emphases of her studies therefore rested upon accessible physical factors, collated respectfully from research into neuronal networks, and from these indications the task was to 'map' and 'pinpoint' the *indices* and *correlates* scientifically of consciousness. In this manner, Greenfield sought to show that previous enigmas associated with human consciousness are no longer inaccessible. In the words of Greenfield:

> ...in a sense these mythical entities exist. Our mental world,
> our consciousness, stretches beyond the physical world and
> everything observable that it contains to embrace imaginary
> concepts such as a green sky, humanoid Martians, time
> travel.... Moreover, the individual inner state of consciousness
> really is a consistent, complete, and autonomous world.[7]

In a public address in Oxford to scientists and theologians at the Ian
Ramsey Centre, she noted that though a sense of the religious was
held by many, these things were best categorised as 'private' as it
was doubtful that such could ever be accessible to scientific enquiry.
Thus though Penrose and Greenfield are more convinced of a *non-
reductionist* stance with respect to human consciousness, their
explanations do not acknowledge religious aspects. The *subjective
value* ascribed to *religion* and *spirituality* remains; explanations are
sought by appealing to other sources.

However, an interesting contrast may be made here with the
highly advanced research achieved by Lord Winston in his own
medical speciality, resulting in his publication and TV documentary,
Superhuman.[8] Winston has indicated how exploration into the
human body reveals the amazing ability and potentiality by which
healing, renewal and regeneration occur. There is much more to
the human body than that which may be directly observed. Given
the enhancement of new drugs and techniques it is now possible
to attempt to undertake what once was only dreamed about. As
a consequence, the implications of any such interventions and
experimentations need important attention. There are positive and
negative implications. Positively, genetically modified animal organs
for human transplantation, and electrodes implanted into the eye,
enabling the blind to see, indicate the *power* now accessible in
the medical science arena. However, Winston, a devout person of
Jewish background, undoubtedly has been concerned with negative
implications also of such capabilities. Ethical dilemmas inevitably arise.
In highlighting these factors he has made clear that *physiological*
limitations do not account for the fullness of human life. There is
much more open to manipulation in which ethical concerns and
respect for human life come to the fore.

In a similar *non-reductionist* vein of thought, though with a keen interest in the possible interrelation of the sciences and theology, is that of Ian Barbour,[9] Arthur Peacocke[10] and John Polkinghorne.[11] These scholars hold that since the sciences and theology need not be in conflict, openness to theology's contribution to interdisciplinary research with respect to consciousness and the human person are not precluded. Therefore, like Penrose, Greenfield and Winston, they have sought to broaden the restrictive worldview adhered to by *reductionism,* whilst proposing that a more open and comprehensive enquiry with respect to *spirituality* and *theological insight* could prove highly illuminative. Their works have commended that a *critical realist* approach be used whereby rational arguments about human life may be given just as serious consideration *via* interdisciplinary exchange with empirical findings from experimentation and scientific investigations.

One of the major benefits of this form of exchange is that whilst the constraints and checks of empirical enquiry may well limit unjustified rational claims, creative insight from critical reflection (of which theological claims form a part) may well open new horizons of exploration, previously unrecognised, which further checks by empirical enquiry may well investigate. In this way, the function for which I have coined the phrase '*empirico-cognitive principles*'[12] is applied.

These recommendations have important implications for enquiry into the multi-faceted aspects of human life. What emerges as the search into consciousness and the human person continues is an increasingly developed enunciation of the *principles of knowing* which could ensure a fuller and more critical search. However, the principles by which research is undertaken need themselves to be adequate to the task. Where a framework fails to remain open and revisable, and where principles of enquiry are not in themselves both *critical* and *empirical* in substance, unnecessary limitations could result from one's findings. In the following brief example, it will become clear why non-adherence could prove misleading, and result in limited if not distorted findings.

Steven Pinker, who is Director of the Neurosciences at MIT and Professor of Psychology, sought in his book *The Blank Slate – The Modern Denial of Human Nature*[13] to stir up world-thought by declaring pugnaciously that the social sciences and religion had 'got it all wrong' from the start, focussing on a 'nurture' or 'ghost in the machine' model respectively rather than a scientific 'nature' model of human life. Though he has harnessed an unbelievable breadth of research materials from the neurosciences and psychopharmacological studies in support of his position, his prime disagreement with such thinkers is at base *methodological*. Resting his case on biogenetic issues which he claims determine the form and development of human life, he cites findings from studies of the mind, brain and evolution as providing important additional information which needs to be incorporated into any understanding of humanity.

In offering what he has called 'a new scientific nature view' of human life, he believes that he has set aright past misunderstandings by resting his case on a more sound and scientific foundation. Pinker cites three 'bridges' which he argues enabled him to map a new understanding of human nature that encompasses both inherent and cultural aspects, bringing together biological and mental processes. The first of these are the *cognitive sciences*, which he says provide a firmer grasp of the structure and function of the mind. By understanding these mechanistic processes one is able to ascertain the form by which human beings reason, reflect, learn, and are informed. His second bridge is the *neurosciences*, especially with respect to studies of differences in brain size and shape, which can account for differences in intelligence, scientific genius, sexual orientation and impulsive violence. The third bridge he cites is the fast-developing information provided by advances in the *Human Genome Project*. Examples such as the identification of how genes can disrupt mental ability, affect behaviour, or be linked with particular aspects of cognition, language and personality, increasingly inform our understanding of potentials in the human person. These scientific findings are what can free us from past errors of thought based on theoretically questionable ideals.

Strangely, whilst insisting that these new developments in the sciences in no way undermine human values, he endeavours instead to argue that these findings enable us to sharpen our ethical reasoning and rest them on a firmer foundation.[14]

On first appearances, it could be said that his position is in accord with the multi-disciplinary and inclusive approaches of Barbour, Peacocke and Polkinghorne, given his commitment to the sciences and his openness to ethical and human values. But this is exactly where his *Achilles' heel* becomes obvious. Having acknowledged that his religious forbears had commended an understanding of human nature which was inclusive of a religious outlook, and having shown how the social sciences went on to develop this understanding more effectively and critically in a secular manner, his presumption is that spiritual things have now been adequately accounted for by these forms of enquiry. Religious values he believes will be explained in terms of chemical and neurological stimuli as the neurosciences advance. His summary dismissal of religious factors as *subjective* and justifiably discounted reveals a naively superficial and ungrounded view of religion, ethics and human values.

In his haste to offer his readers a *unified theory* for research, Pinker has instead failed to meet his own scientific demands of both *critical* and *empirical* investigation of all aspects. Ironically, his race to reach the winning post before all others has been forfeited by his 'dropping the baton'. Had Pinker been more cautious in considering the findings of more recent studies of religious phenomenon discussed below, he may have saved himself from this mishap.

This is why the research work of psychologists such as Brian Lancaster, a diligent Jewish scholar, *vide* his book *Mind, Brain and Human Potential*,[15] and more recently Eugene D'Aquili and Andrew Newberg's publication *The Mystical Mind – Probing the Biology of Religious Experience*[16] which take account of spiritual/religious aspects are significant. In each case, working directly within their fields, they have sought to pave a route towards critical, scientific enquiry in the relation of both psychological and religious factors to the biological realities of human existence. The holistic outcomes suggested have been enlightening.

Of Brian Lancaster's work, leading psychologist, Dr Susan Blackmore, has acknowledged how he has synthesised modern psychology and Jewish mysticism in an illuminative way, providing new insights into the nature of *self* and *consciousness*. Holistic accounts have the advantage of being sufficiently comprehensive as to encompass spiritual, mental and physiological factors. At the same time, attention can also be addressed to the distinctive character of these aspects, with consideration of their possible interrelation. Brian Lancaster's work does not rest on a restrictive *physical* model. In a critical manner, conscious also of important distinctions between illusion and specificity, he shows how experimentation may be employed with creative outcomes. His address of issues such as 'becoming', 'the multiplicity of "I"', 'the biology of dreaming' indicates the breadth of territory which serious scientific enquiry might productively traverse.

In addition, the diverse areas of enquiry pursued in the studies of D'Aquili more recently, and written up by his colleague Newberg following his death, suggest the possibilities of worthwhile research in the areas of biology, psychology and theology in this new century. Their offer of a neuropsychological theory of religion, dependent very much on the work in the area of mystical experience such as near-death experiences, myth-making and meditation, is certainly worthy of attention by medical and religious researchers interested in the way in which biological mechanisms may or may not be involved in mystical states and trances.

Above all, the concern of how judgements might be made adequately in this and more general study of religious experience has been greatly enhanced by the work of Caroline Franks Davis's volume *The Evidential Force of Religious Experience.*[17] Franks Davis deals with non-cognitive views and the ineffability of religious experience, raising the question of whether critical realism is applicable to such. After considering the complexities of what is to count as 'religious experience', she offers the argument for a *cumulative* case, drawing on the earlier work of Professor Basil Mitchell in *The Justification of Religious Belief.*[18] The distinctive character of spirituality is discussed in terms of the irreducible types of numinous and mystical experience and their identification. Her commendation of a non-reductionist approach to religion, examined over a number of different religions and the psychological aspect of these experiences enables readers to recognise the critical ways by which judgements in these areas may be undertaken effectively.

In the long run, it is the *convergence* of these critical findings offered by each of the disciplines as they engage in interdisciplinary exchange that is likely to enable researchers to identify with some confidence the reality of the human person: brain, mind *and* spirit in a distinctive, yet holistic form. It is at this point that theology's contribution becomes most poignant, for not only would they be 'picking up the dropped baton', but in doing so, would effectively have restored an otherwise missing link from a metaphysical approach for investigating human life that can be defended as *all-inclusive* and *critical*, and *not at variance with the demands of scientific enquiry.*

It was a noted English philosopher and theologian, Austin Marsden Farrer, who, having recognised this need many years ago, chose to raise it in his Gifford lectures, published in *The Freedom of the Will.*[19] Whereas most would have expected that he would have presented an assumed doctrinal viewpoint on the matter, no such thing occurred. In fact, cognizant of the manifold conflicts which had normally resulted from unexamined assumptions about the human person, Farrer considered that there was a prior necessity to expose these differences. In this way unnecessary disagreements could be removed, and a route towards a progressive investigation of freedom in human life could be opened up. So even though theological doctrine was not always addressed directly in his lectures, his ground-clearing endeavours achieved instead a formidable outcome, which made the case 'for' spirituality in an inescapably commanding manner.

Step by step, Farrer established that though empiricist accounts of human life could give clarity to our understanding of the *physical* aspects of the human person, these by no means accounted for everything. Knowledge of the human body, anatomically and physiologically, provided only part of the story. True, rationalist accounts could help explain the intellectual capacities of individuals and their emergence within an evolving development of the natural world. Yet enquiry such as this left one totally dissatisfied with such methodologies. There is so much more, intrinsic and accessible to daily living, such as creativity and reflective capacities, which indicates the 'something more' that still remained unaccounted for. In addition, one's sense of freedom, the ability to hope, the voluntary character of the human will, highlighted the inadequacy of positivist assumptions. It was indisputable that the human mind could explore finite thought as well as probe infinite dimensions. To exclude such factors from enquiry by mere definition disclosed if anything a blind-spot in any serious research project.

As a result, writing even in the earlier part of the twentieth century, Farrer held the view that any researcher seeking to establish an understanding of the human person as well as expose erroneous claims would require an all-inclusive, interdisciplinary approach in which *physical, mental/psychological* and *spiritual* factors were all taken into account and their relation, interrelation and interaction explored through progressive enquiry. To do otherwise, would surely leave one with a severely diminished understanding on which major decision-making would then be pursued. On such grounds, erroneous findings were indeed susceptible.

Thus in his Bampton lectures, published in *The Glass of Vision* we find him arguing for a *multi-disciplinary* and *inclusive* stance, in which a metaphysical approach which could encompass the distinctive significance of theological concepts offered a more acceptable solution:

> To reject metaphysics is equivalent to saying that there are no serious questions for the human mind except those which fall under the special sciences. We can ask historically why the crucifixion of Christ came about: physiologically, whether he died of heart-failure or by some other cause: psychologically, what train of thoughts and feeling induced him to put his neck into the noose: morally, how his action squared with a copy-book of ethical imperatives. But we cannot consider what in itself, in its intensity and elevation of being, in its divinity, the voluntary passion of Christ was. We have a first interest in keeping this road unblocked, the road by which a serious and realistic wonder advances through the contemplation of Christ's manhood into the adoration of his deity, that it may lay hold upon the Eternal Son, who, hanging on the Cross, is enthroned in Heaven; who, lying in the sepulchre, lies in the bosom of the Father; and standing in the upper room, breathes forth from the heart of all being the Paraclete, the Holy Ghost.[20]

Austin Farrer's argument was that from diligent enquiry we could establish what the facts of a case might be. In regard to the human person, we may establish anatomical and physiological factors, and also psychological/social ones. However, by definition merely to address the brain/mind factors, would fall short of taking account of the creative capacities and hopes of human reflection.

For him, it was just as essential that we look at the evidence 'for' a case, as also the evidence 'against' a case. To fail to do this, could leave one in the position of simply imposing one's own viewpoint or interpretation in an investigation, even in an unobvious manner. This he distinguished as 'reading into' rather than 'reading off' a case.[21] What he endeavoured to show was that we need instead to ascertain the established facts of a case whilst also exposing error. In this way, a case would be more convincing than one in which one simply made bland, ungrounded claims, relying on the authority normally ascribed to such offices.

Only in this manner could the serious theologian fulfil the task of examining critically the inspirational depths of divine mystery, avoiding attributing to such unwarranted, misleading claims. Thus he argued:

> The mysteries of faith must fit into one universe of sense with our natural knowledge of human personality, of history, of the form of nature, of the first principles of being: if they did not, they would not continue to be believed. The judgement on which faith is based is an *aestimatio* like that used in other fields. Faith leaps beyond it, but that happens too in common life; our faith in the goodwill of a friend goes beyond and leaves behind any weighing of the evidence for it, and becomes a root axiom of living. In the case of the friend, such an axiom may be rooted, but not be ineradicable: our friend may disappoint us. As the prophet says, the mother may forget her sucking child; but God will not forget Jerusalem.[22]

Farrer's commendations in which theologising might make its proper contribution offer a promising route forward in a world which is now largely understood in terms of the findings of biogenetics and the cognitive neurosciences. Critical exchange both *within* the discipline with other theologians is as incumbent as respectful two-way exchange *across* related studies in other areas, such as existential philosophies, social/psychological engagements and the growing body of thinkers in the cognitive neuroscience and biogenetic areas. Such can only *augment* understanding of consciousness and the human person.

On these grounds one cannot think of anything better than further exchange with a great mind committed to similar concerns. The issues are major. Perhaps these reasons will provide sufficient enticement to one deeply respected by colleagues here in Oxford to visit us once again in the English summer so that a *Jaspers-Farrer*[23] encounter may become an order of the day, since our spouses are unlikely to allow a further cold English winter reunion!

End Notes

1. A Farrer, *The Glass of Vision* (Westminster: Dacre Press, 1948).
2. Jeremiah 1:5, *The Holy Bible, Revised Standard Version, containing the Old and New Testaments* (Philadelphia: AJ Holman, 1952) (OT section), 1971 (NT section, second edition).
3. Note that some leading philosophers of science, *vide:* R Harre, *Varieties of Realism* (Oxford : Blackwells, 1986), Chapter 1, would hold that moral concerns are integral to scientific practice.
4. R Penrose, *Shadows of the Mind – A Search for the Missing Science of Consciousness*, (Oxford: Oxford University Press, 1994).
5. S Greenfield, *Journey to the Centres of the Mind* (New York: WH Freeman, 1995).
6. *Ibid,* viii.
7. *Ibid,* 3.
8. R Winston and L Oliwenstein, *Superhuman – The Awesome Power Within* (London: BBC, 2000).
9. I Barbour, *Religion and Science* (London: SCM Press, 1998).
10. A Peacocke, *Theology for a Scientific Age* (London: SCM Press, 1993).
11. J Polkinghorne, *Reason and Reality* (London: SPCK, 1991).
12. The term *'empirico-cognitive'* was first coined by me in my studies to identify the principles by which great discoveries in the sciences have been made. It became obvious that both creative insight and empirical investigation operate interactively at these times, the former enabling recognition of new links and patterns whilst the latter serves to bring checks and constraints on lively imagination. As such,. One's understanding of a subject matter is refined and more clearly pinpointed. In new discoveries, both functions operate interactively.

13. S Pinker, *The Blank Slate – The Modern Denial of Human Nature* (London: Penguin Books, 2002).
14. *Ibid*, 193.
15. B Lancaster, *Mind, Brain and Human Potential* (MA, USA: Element Inc, 1991).
16. E D'Aquili and A Newberg, *The Mystical Mind – Probing the Biology of Religious Experience* (Minneapolis: Fortress Press, 1999).
17. C Franks Davis, *The Evidential Force of Religious Experience* (Oxford: Clarendon Press, 1989).
18. B Mitchell, *The Justification of Religious Belief* (London: Macmillan, 1973).
19. A Farrer, *Freedom of the Will* (London: Adam & Charles Black, 1957).
20. *Op cit*, 78.
21. A Farrer, *A Science of God* (London: Geoffrey Bles, 1966).
22. *The Glass of Vision*, 33–34.
23. Questions related to the thought of Karl Jaspers (1883–1969), German philosopher with a particular interest in existentialism and psychopathology, are most pertinent for human consciousness. Similarly, insights from Jaspers' thought have an important relation to those of Austin Farrer (1905–1968), who was concerned with the form of revelation and the imagination, freedom of the will, and divine/human agency. In a world in which the cognitive sciences are now paramount, statements concerning the human person require much re-thinking by theologians as also other scholars.

13

REVISITING RONALD GREGOR SMITH'S DOCTRINE OF GOD

WES CAMPBELL

As befits Harry Wardlaw's integration of faith, theology and person, I begin biographically.

The year I began formal study of theology in Perth, 1968, seems like a foreign land. *Time* magazine declared God dead on the basis of American theological trends. A decade earlier Gabriel Vahanian wrote *The Death of God;* even earlier Kornelius Miskotte (1956) addressed the situation *When the Gods are Silent* and Martin Buber (1959) described the *Eclipse of God. The Secular City* (Harvey Cox) and religionless Christianity were in their ascendancy. RM Haire (SC, 188) proposed that God is a 'blik'. John Robinson's popularised amalgam of current continental theology, *Honest to God* (1963), echoed a so-called 'new theology' that busied itself with the questions posed by contemporary society. In all it seemed to a fledgling theologian, as Gordon Kaufman (1972) would say, that God was 'The Problem'.

Theologians in the English-speaking world were pressed by the claim that God had died and, indeed, took it up programmatically. Drawing on a mix of Hegel, Nietzsche and Dietrich Bonhoeffer and analytic philosophy, American theologians, particularly Thomas Altizer and William Hamilton, developed a thoroughgoing kenotic theology in which God actually died. There existed a double-edged cultural mood which simultaneously acknowledged the disappearance of a former culture and theological world in the midst of scientific and technological optimism. That double-edge was illustrated by Tillich's *The Shaking of the Foundations.* Optimism was overshadowed by a deeper anxiety, expressed in part by the so-called Cold War and its resulting conflict in Vietnam. Even more fundamentally, God was in crisis. (To today's eyes it is possible to recognise in that situation the same impulses present now which continue the liberal protestant agenda. Today the challenge and opportunity is 'postmodernity' in exactly the same way it was then 'secularity'.

(It appears to me that the theological wrestling which took place then grappled with the pressing question of how to respond as theologians to the present situation, neither denying the challenge nor failing to learn from it, but refusing to collapse Christian faith and theology into its reductions. For that reason Dietrich Bonhoeffer was a seminal figure. To retreat from the challenge of the crisis produced in the present would mean an acceptance that Christian faith had nothing to do with the present; to impose pre-modern formulations onto the present would fail to appreciate how radically the modern world has changed the human situation. To accept the present cultural self-understanding and to require that Christian theology must adopt its canons would be to give up the received Christian wisdom. Such is the theological task articulated then and still demanded.)

The first serious theological text I ever read was H Richard Niebuhr's *The Meaning of Revelation* (1941/1966). Addressing questions concerning historical relativism and faith, and thus speaking of God, Niebuhr attempts to combine the interests of Ernst Troeltsch and Karl Barth, that is, 'the critical thought of the former and the constructive thought of the latter'. As one who had been raised simultaneously within an anti-intellectual Methodist pietism and a secularised anti-intellectual Western Australian country schooling, this was my first contact with theologians who understood the full force of contemporary culture and the claim of informed and critical Christian faith. Fortunately, in those days, alongside the required curriculum's end-of-year exams, it was possible to read more widely and as I attempted to make sense of these theologico-cultural issues, I discovered Ronald Gregor Smith.

By revisiting the work of Ronald Gregor Smith for this article, it has become clear to me that my theological path has been closely intertwined with Harry's. When I first read Gregor Smith I knew neither Harry Wardlaw, nor that RG Smith had been his doctoral supervisor. Ronald Gregor Smith died in 1968.

Harry was my teacher at the United Faculty of Theology (Melbourne) in 1973 and 1974 where he was Professor of Philosophical Theology and I was completing a Bachelor of Divinity. Deeply influenced as I was at that time by Karl Barth's theological starting point and approach, Harry's philosophical spirit and espoused 'Christian humanism' drew us into to strong debate in the seminar on nineteenth and twentieth century theology. That same class assembled on one afternoon at an anti-Vietnam demonstration in Melbourne's city square. (Some years later Harry was a member of an interviewing committee as I applied for the role of directing the synod division of Social Justice, and contributed to the theological work of that division.) After several years of parish ministry and overseas study with Jürgen Moltmann I took up conversations with Harry again, this time in an attempt to deal with Ernst Troeltsch's historicist treatment of modernity's crisis for Christianity and his attempt at a radical reformulating of Christian theology.

I am struck by Harry's constant insistence on an honest theological engagement with philosophy and contemporary culture because of his faithfulness to the Christian gospel. These are the same traits in Ronald Gregor Smith, whose grounding and depth of understanding of the classical theological tradition led him to give serious attention to the contemporary scientific and cultural questions that seemed to put Christian faith and theology in crisis.

The contemporary theological and cultural crisis may be summarised as 'the death of God'. This theme was prominent in much of Gregor Smith's work, especially *The Free Man: Studies in Christian Anthropology* (1969; originally published as *The New Man: Christianity's and Man's Coming of Age*, 1956); and *The Doctrine of God* (edited and prepared for publication by K Gregor Smith and AD Galloway, 1970).

Revisiting Ronald Gregor Smith's work is to enter territory which has become quite alien. A nexus of quite different themes has replaced the issues and language addressed by Gregor Smith. Secularity has been replaced by *postmodernity*, and *history* by *culture*. In 'constructive' theology discussion formulations of God as Trinity have seemingly replaced the note of crisis. Could it be that postmodern plurality has removed the urgency? Alternatively, proposals for 'postmodern' theology (in Mark A Taylor's version *A/theology*) seem to offer accommodation to the spirit of the times. Is it that the chorus of voices prompted by the deconstruction of modernity and its theological responses (whether by critique or acceptance) have settled for their own separate melodies?

1. The doctrine of God

A series of lectures, posthumously edited, *The Doctrine of God,* was swimming against the stream. Reading it now the arguments appear obvious and the intent uncontentious. Reading it fresh from the printer, I recall, the language and arguments seemed elusive, voicing the almost unsayable.

AD Galloway says in the introduction:

> There is no point pretending *The Doctrine of God* is an easy book. Despite all the simplicity and directness of Gregor Smith's style, the argument is difficult and complex. But it is worth the effort, and will reward the effort of anyone who is prepared to try. (DG,13)

In that climate, a *doctrine* of God was most unexpected – as problematic and polemic as Karl Barth's earlier choice of a *church dogmatics*. That choice is a measure of Gregor Smith's commitment as a theologian in a time when *theo*logy seemed almost impossible. His approach shows a marked affinity with Dietrich Bonhoeffer's search for a theological voice in a radically changed world. (SC, 186)

The crisis about God (FM, 112), the possibility of 'God-language' (SC, 188–89), the death of God, the eclipse of God (DG, 21–22, FM, 154)) and the claim of history or historicity (SC, 192) form the backdrop for this work. The immediate contenders were Friedrich Nietzsche and Thomas JJ Altizer, FM, 115). In *The Free Man,* Gregor Smith understands the mid-twentieth century theologians to be going beyond Nietzsche, whom he understands as speaking of the 'death of an *idea* of God' (FM, 115, my emphasis). He notes, however, the interpretation by Ronald Carson, one of his students, (1968) that Nietzsche's concerns are ethical rather than idealist:

... that men by their actions have murdered God, but at the same time that God allowed himself, out of pity for men, to be slain. (FM, 115n2)

That is to say, here the presenting issue is not to be found in ideas and formulations of ideas but in the actual human history, and the real events of the crucifixion of Jesus.

The situation for faith is described in detail in *Secular Christianity*. Based in human freedom won by faith, the result is a human autonomy that has secularised the world (SC, 169) and brought about the 'death of God'. This contains two elements: 'the rejection of a specific metaphysic, and the idea of God which was elaborated in its terms'; and secondly, 'God is undialectically absent: he is not. This is the death of God.' (SC, 159) Gregor Smith charts each of Hegel's (speculative Good Friday), Jean Paul's (Jesus Christ's declaration that 'We are all orphans, I and you, we have no father') and Friedrich Nietzsche's declarations concerning the death of God, concluding with Nietzsche's words: 'What are the churches, if not the tombs and sepulchres of God?' (SC, 165) Heidegger's commentary on Nietzsche's proclamation of the death of God leads him to the view, that in Nietzsche's story we are 'confronted with experiential atheism as a realisation of nothingness. This is nihilism in the same sense as Jean Paul's vision is nihilism'. (SC, 165)

The 'death of God' theology of the 1960s, according to Gregor Smith, is best understood not as an undialectial withdrawal of God from the world but as the death of an idea of God (SC, 166–67, my emphasis). He recounts Altizer's view of 'a death of God which was consummated in the self-emptying of God in Christ, who was crucified, dead and buried'. This, he acknowledges, is a sophisticated theological view rejecting an exalted, distant and alien majesty of God, and by the death of such a one as Jesus Christ,

... positively finds its assurance in and through the 'historical realisation of the death of God' in Christ's death, which is then regarded as making possible 'the full unfolding of the forward movement of the Incarnation'. (FM, 116)

In this way, then, transcendence is translated into the historical actuality of our world and 'Christ has become part of the process of history, that and no more'. (FM, 116) Gregor Smith notes that if Carson is correct then Altizer and other contemporary death of God theologians are implementing the second half of Nietzsche's idea. (FM, 115n2) However, he is pressed by the way his contemporaries have implemented their 'death of God' theology. He judges they have succeeded in taking theology into the nihil. (FM, 150) What would his assessment be of an espoused 'A/theology' that argues for a theology that gives up hope and, thus, expectation of the resurrection? (Mark C Taylor, *Disfiguring*, 317–19) We may surmise that he would judge that this approach, as that of its 1960s predecessors, has lost its heart.

The Doctrine of God is thus written to deal with the crisis concerning God. He criticises that programme that dissolves theology into nothingness. He writes specifically as a theologian (FM, 114). He therefore engages the specifically *theological* problem posed by contemporary culture as addressed by Bonhoeffer and Bultmann. He also examines Paul van Buren's banning of God-language (FM, 113) according to the specific demands of analytic philosophy that statements be empirically verifiable (FM, 114). But the problem is more than a mere problem of *speaking* of God. The theological crisis is

> ... both a reflection of and an active influence upon, the underlying situation of faith. It is, once again, a question of man, of man's identity, of man's self-understanding, which faces us here. (FM, 114)

The only adequate response to this twofold question must be 'an anthropological theology, or an anthropotheology' because '(t)he crisis about God is also a crisis of faith'. (FM, 114) He will call this in *The Doctrine of God* a 'theological anthropology'. (DG, 74) It is not merely an anthropological problem – it is anthropo*theological* (DG, 110); later he will insist on the anthropological dimension (DG, 166) as 'Revelation can only take place through human experience'.

Notice that the *anthropo* precedes the *theologico*. Contrast that with Jüngel's *theo-anthropological* approach (*Theological Essays*, 1989, see 'Anthropomorphism: A Fundamental Problem in Modern Hermeneutics', 72–94; 'Humanity in Correspondence to God', 124–53) which insists upon the priority of the theological in order to provide a proper anthropology. (TE, 'Anthropomorphism', 72ff) Both, however, are addressing a hermeneutical and methodological problem permitted and prompted by the *humanity* of Jesus Christ.

Gregor Smith was seeking a radical alteration in theology. (DG, 172) This would require 'thinking everything new, including the way in which God is'. His observation is that

> This is the inwardness and pathos of the death-of-God theologians, who do see, and rightly, that God is renewed as well as man by the Christ event; he is drawn into history in such a total way that neither history nor God himself can ever be the same again. (DG 172–3)

Such a view will take the risk of patripassionism, a suffering God (Bonhoeffer), but will resist the undialectical self-emptying of the death-of–God theologians. He will seek a dialectical understanding of

> God's transcendence *and* his presence; or his presence in his absence, his being in the world without being a phenomenon in the world. But he is present in a veiled way. (DG, 173)

2. A radical historicist turn in Christian Theology

Gregor Smith articulates the demand for a radical change in Christian theology that can only be achieved if theology becomes thoroughly historical, even *historicist*. With Ernst Troeltsch and the proponent of early so-called *dialectical theology* Gregor Smith seeks a radical turn in theology. As with both of these, he responds to the concerns of Liberal Protestant theology in taking seriously the contemporary philosophical and cultural situation. With Ernst Troeltsch and Gordon Kaufman he advocates a *historicist* theology. Yet, unlike them, and his contemporaries' kenotic theologies, he refuses a reductionist path. His procedure is more akin to the Dietrich Bonhoeffer of the *Letters and Papers* who acknowledges the radically changed world and engages in an attempt at theological analysis. Gregor Smith, not unlike Friedrich

Gogarten and Carl Michelson, understands the present historicised world as also a result of Christian faith. Understanding that historicising of the world requires theology to understand its new freedom to *be* historical. Christian faith in the God, who acts historically, therefore demands a new *theological historicism*. It will require a jettisoning of former philosophical (metaphysical) categories because of intense attention to Christian faith's only starting point: *in history*.

Gregor Smith, like Ernst Troeltsch, stands at the end at the end of the great liberal protestant project, and like Troeltsch attempts to find a new form of theology. Where Troeltsch wrote in the context of late nineteenth century scientific discovery and the chaos of the First World War, and understood that the modern world represents a crisis for Christian faith *(Religionskrisis),* Gregor Smith wrote after the protest of *Dialectical Theology* and during the latter period of Karl Barth's mammoth undertaking in the *Church Dogmatics*, following the Second World War and in the apparent scientific and technological renaissance of the mid-twentieth century.

It is curious that for Gregor Smith, unlike the later Barth, Moltmann and other continental theologians, the symbols of Auschwitz and Hiroshima – as far as I can detect – do not appear. In his work there are passing references to Nazism and Marx, but apparently no attention to the political and social forms of these ideological systems. The concern with secularisation or even nationalism, on the other hand, shows little interest in the sociology or political formations of this phenomenon.

No doubt Gregor Smith's rejoinder would be that no amount of socio-political analysis is of use unless we are able to recover the capacity to speak of God who is in eclipse, and whose very nature is to be hidden. Not only is the erosion of the capacity to speak of God in crisis; the primary problem is the capacity to trust in that God. Thus the problem of God and theology is existential, and therefore must be *historical.*

> The reality of God for us is thus a historical reality, and nothing besides. But this does not mean a god who becomes, nor on the other hand does it mean a mere abstraction from the historical Christ. But the history of man appears now as the history of his dialogue with god. Sometimes this takes very strange forms,

so that God is entirely hidden behind the structures of history. Then we may speak of an eclipse of God, and all we can do is wait patiently. The form of hope may thus take the expression of agnosticism or atheism. But sometimes, again, the moment burns, and God is entirely present as fearful conviction, as a face in the midst of our encounters with our fellow men. This is the moment for which faith hopes. But in its faith does not let go of its endless criticism of all science and all controlled planning of the future. For in the last analysis there is no planning or control possible, beyond the faith that hopes for the encounter with God as the power of all history. This means that at bottom faith is responsible for history, but God is responsible for faith; everything for man lies therefore in the unpredictable future of God. (FM, 154–55)

This is a form of theology that has clearly rejected the ideologies of modernity and its heirs: fascism and communism. In the name of an *existential* faith *in history* it affirms God's realm as history and the future which is not in our hands. It would be too much, perhaps to ask that Gregor Smith is eschatological in the way Moltmann and Pannenberg are; while he values Moltmann's contribution, he criticises its 'primitive depiction of eschatological reality in terms of past apocalyptic imaginings'. (DG, 35n1). It is clear that Gregor Smith wants to take up *history* as a primary theological category, having also learned that faith is existential. Is it fair to complain that while his approach *is* existential, it does not appear to be existential *enough*? For a theology that wants to take seriously the *humanity* of Jesus Christ and the *historicity* of faith the existence and experience of the cross and the crucifixions in experienced human history seem decidedly absent. Another notable absence, apart from some general references to church history and brief analysis of some proposals for the church in secularism (SC, 197ff), is any sustained attention to the nature and form of the church.

What is evident, however, is that Gregor Smith wants to be a theologian who is contemporary, and jettisons much that will prevent his work to be properly theological. It is indeed curious that his work is as overlooked as it is. One need only look to the work of Eberhard Jüngel to find a similar emphasis on faith as existential within a sustained attempt to be rigorously theological. (See his *Theological Essays II*

(1995), 'The Emergence of the New', 'The Dogmatic Significance of the Question of the Historical Jesus', 'The Revelation of the Hiddenness of God: A Contribution to the Protestant Understanding of the Hiddenness of Divine action', 'On becoming Truly Human').

It remains for us to dig a little deeper into the way Gregor Smith deals theologically with the contemporary sense of the absence of God.

3. Responding theologically to the absence of God

As a theologian Gregor Smith refuses to capitulate to a cultural mood that declares God not only inaccessible but dead. Yet he takes seriously both the cultural and theological challenge. Behind the 1960s' death of God theology lies Nietzsche's declaration of God's death. (DG, 159f) That provides the sharpest cultural challenge. Gregor Smith is too careful a theologian to capitulate to an 'undialectical' treatment of God's absence. He knows there is a theological appreciation of God's hiddenness or otherness that precedes Nietzsche. Apophatic theology. Apophatic theology, *via negativa,* has long sought to ensure that things of this world are not divinised (DG, 55), and Gregor Smith seeks to go beyond merely negative statements (DG, 75) to affirm the experience of God as 'unbounded mystery'. He insists that an affirmation of God as involved in our history but more than our history requires the *via negativa.*

In order to address the question of God's absence, Gregor Smith requires a theological starting point in history, with human historicity. The Word itself can be nothing other than historical, and is only historical; there can be nothing additional. (DG, 144ff) The metaphysics of God as *being* must thereby be rejected. Theology's task is not to '*express* God, but rather to address him'. (DG, 145) This leads directly to God's otherness. Yet, this otherness is experienced 'in terms of [God's] historical being-for-men'.

It follows, then, that the sense of absence of God experienced in the contemporary world is a direct expression of God's hiddenness. Here Gregor Smith is an heir of Martin Luther for whom the only way God is present in history is hidden under alien forms. (See Eberhard

Jüngel, 'The Revelation of the Hiddenness of God', *Theological Essays II*, 120–144)

Hiddenness is thus a correlate of God's otherness. That otherness is how God is known and experienced in the historical situation. There can be no 'direct expression' of God. It is possible to affirm then that God is encountered in history but is not confined to or assimilated into any part of the world (DG, 147). Because God is experienced historically, God is not to be treated as 'wholly other' in such a way as the world is 'left to itself'.

The treatment of God's hiddenness demonstrates how Gregor Smith is both a Christian theologian and contemporary. In dialogue and criticism of Paul van Buren and Thomas Altizer, Herbert Braun and Schubert Ogden, confining himself to what may be said in a radically historical way, Gregor Smith makes a case for continuing to speak of God who is known historically in the Word. (see 154–59) Equally, because he speaks of *God* it is necessary to affirm and to preserve the transcendence of God. (DG, 151–53) With the 'death of God' theologians he insists upon Jesus Christ as the centre of faith over against conceptualities of the past. Equally, in affirming the transcendence of God, he refuses merely to reaffirm 'concepts of a bygone age'; he does not want to entrap theology into a contemporary protest in which theological meaning is ' exhausted within the historical process'. (153)

Is the name God to be relinquished? Is it still possible to speak of God?

> The word God, which was originally a name, has become so misused, as a battle-cry, as a symbol for a retreat from historical responsibility, as the conclusion of a philosophical analysis and as the representation of a private pietistic experience, that we might well decide to get along without this name. For through man's arbitrariness and hatefulness the name has become so soiled that it sometimes seems as though it can never be made clean. (DG, 160)

Is silence then the necessary option? His approach is too subtle for that solution.

> One thing seems to me to be necessary in this context, and that
> we recognise the necessity for silence, or at least for a certain
> reserve, before we dare to use the name of God. We must not
> pretend that we can expose the whole mystery of this name.
> A *theologia negativa* still has a most important part to play.
> Nor can we hope to force God out of his hiddenness. We cannot
> expect that we can bring God to light by means of our little bit
> of reason or of faith. There are mysteries which can never be
> solved. (DG, 160)

It is worth noting that in a contemporary discussion of deconstruction
and God, Kevin Hart employs the resources of apophatic theology
through the *via negativa* in order to respond to the challenge
of the experience of the absence of God and a philosophy that
seems to leave no possibility of God. *(The Trespass of the Sign:
Deconstruction, Theology and Philosophy, 1989.)*

For the theologian there can be no option of silencing talk
of God, just as there can be no return to 'traditional ways of
thinking about God, man and the world'. (DG, 159) It is necessary
to recognise the radically altered world and to hold fast to the
historical centre of faith in Jesus Christ.

> So we cannot dispense with the attempt to use the name of
> God. Whatever the difficulties, this is not possible, precisely
> because we are involved in history and because God himself,
> God as a name, comes to us only in and through this history.
> God is embodied in human history.

So our task must be to lift the Name of God out of the dust again
and to set it over the hour of our responsibility. (DG, 161)

4. Finally

Since we first read those words the theological challenge has not
lessened. If, because theologians are speaking more confessionally it
seems easier to speak of God and, if, because of an apparent greater
acceptance of the 'Spirit' and 'spirituality' we have taken pause, a re-
reading of Gregor Smith makes clear that the challenge of lifting up

the name of God has not lessened but is actually more pressing.

Certainly this re-visiting of Ronald Gregor Smith shows how different the world is now, and how theological discussion has developed and moved on. We might speculate how his work would have developed had he lived into his theological prime and faced with us the further development trends he identified in his own work. As it is, he – like Bonhoeffer – has left us the basic building blocks of major work that was yet to come. The purpose of this return visit was not an attempt to revive his work. Yet that visit does remind us of the passion with which Gregor Smith struggled to confront the crisis of faith and demonstrates the clarity with which he saw the challenge of the *theological* task in this radically altered world.

Finally, a revisiting of Ronald Gregor Smith's work has served as a reminder of Harry Wardlaw's early formation as a theologian and uncovers one source of those theological passions which have driven his life's work.

14

THEOLOGICAL RABIES: ON BEING MAD WITH NIETZSCHE

Bruce Barber

God guard us from those thoughts men think
In the mind alone.
He that sings a lasting song
Thinks in the marrow-bone.

WB Yeats

Have you not heard of the madman who lit a lantern at noonday, ran to the market place, and cried unceasingly, I am looking for God! I am looking for God! Since it happened that there were many standing there who did not believe in God, he roused great laughter. Is he lost? said one. Or gone astray like a child? said another. Or has he hidden himself? Is he afraid of us? Has he gone on a voyage? Or emigrated? So they shouted and laughed. The madman leaped into their midst, and pierced them with his glance. Where has God gone? he cried. I will tell you. We have slain him – you and I. We are all his murderers. But how did we do it? How could we drink up the sea? Who gave us the sponge to wipe out the whole horizon? What did we do, when we unchained this earth from its sun? Where is it moving to now? And where are we moving to now? Away from all suns? Do we not stumble all the time? Backwards, sideways, forwards, in every direction? Is there an above and below any more? Are we not wandering as through infinite nothingness? Does empty space not breathe upon us? Is it not colder now? Is not night coming, and ever more night? Must we not light lanterns at noon? Do we not hear the noise of the gravediggers, as they bury God? Do we not smell God decaying? – Gods too decay! God is dead. God stays dead. And we have slain him. How shall we console ourselves, chief of all murderers. The holiest and the most powerful that the world has ever possessed has ebbed its blood away beneath our knives – who will wipe this blood from our fingers? What water can make us clean? What propitiations and sacred rites will we have to invent? Is not the greatness of this deed too great for us? Must we not ourselves become gods, in order to seem worthy of them? There was never a greater deed, and because of it all who were born after us are part of a higher history than ever was before!

The madman fell silent, and looked at his hearers again. They too were silent, and looked at him with shocked eyes. At last he threw his lantern on the ground, so that it broke in pieces and went out. I come too early, he said, it is not yet my time. This monstrous event is still on the way – it has not yet penetrated human ears. Lightning and thunder need time, the light of the stars need time, even after they have been done, in order to be seen and heard. This deed is still further from men than the remotest stars – and yet they have done it. The story goes that the madman went into several churches on the same day and sang his requiem to the eternal God. Led out and questioned, he replied just the one thing: What are the churches, if not the tombs and sepulchres of God?

F Neitzsche, *Joyful Wisdom*

1. A reflection on becoming who one is

One should not conceal and corrupt the facts of how our thoughts have come to us.

F Neitzsche, *Will to Power*

I remember the day I got bitten; a cloudless May day in spring – it was the northern hemisphere. I was twenty-six. In retrospect, there was an inevitability about it. Intellectually awakened as a late teenager by Bonhoeffer (*The Cost of Discipleship*); secreting *Letters and Papers from Prison* into a city office when a career in oil seemed promising; a neo-Orthodox theological formation; hearing John Robinson deliver in St Giles Cathedral, Edinburgh, what turned out a few months later to be *Honest to God*; the shaking of the foundations in Geneva reading Paul van Buren, *The Secular Meaning of the Gospel* concurrently with Vols 3:1 and 3:2, *The Doctrine of Creation, in the Church Dogmatics*; an introduction by a Dutch colleague to Gogarten's secularisation thesis, soon to be revealed as one source for Harvey Cox, *The Secular City*; a course on the Parables with Robert Funk at Drew in the USA in the days when we were all 'hermeneuts'. The ingredients were being assembled, though I knew it not.

The day of this haunting parable I recall the hair on the back of my neck rising as it has for a few, although regrettably perhaps not so many theological students down the years. Not only Englishmen, it seems, were destined to 'go out in the midday sun'. There seemed to be no alternative but to throw in one's lot with those theologians who, having ventured into that sun, explicitly set out to do their work in the after-noon.

Since parables are nothing but extended metaphors, they are never finished. The fundamental theological task from this point on could only be a continual conversation with this parable, attempting to understand and 'answer' these extraordinary lines which interpreted a world being left behind and a world emerging. The madman has remained elusive, and that is its perennial attraction as well as its potential danger, for it is easily open to abuse and vulgarisation. At worst, the 'Death of God' can, and has, become a slogan, being made to mean whatever one rejoices in or seeks to evade. Nevertheless, just as a kaleidoscope creates a colourful new pattern every time it is taken up, so the parable suggests itself to the imagination. Compare prosaic utterance, where we believe we know what is being said as we grasp the meaning. Inarticulate then and largely ever since in the face of this parable, I knew from that first encounter that I too was now destined to be 'mad'. This was confirmed on returning to Australia, as friends and colleagues expressed their irritation as I ricocheted around. Eventually I found Harry. Harry understood, and in his gentle way, as so many students have discovered over the years, always expands the field of discourse to ever greater understanding. But we must all go our own way.

2. Which God died?

There are, in the consciousness of man, two bodies of knowledge: the things he tells himself, and the things he finds out. The things he tells himself are nearly always pleasant, and they are lies. The things he finds out are usually rather bitter to begin with.

DH Lawrence

It is a commonplace to acknowledge that no-one in the history of philosophy has launched such a radical attack on the religious, moral and intellectual foundations of Western society as Friedrich Nietzsche. It is also certain that Nietzsche intended his hearers to identify the figure of the madman in the parable with himself. Further, it may well be that his legacy is only now becoming realised in everyday life. The leading letter in *The Age* newspaper at this time of writing came with an imprimatur which Nietzsche himself could have written: 'The glorious world of belief – without God'.

To adopt Lawrence's distinction: Was the death of God something Nietzsche told himself, or did he find it out? It is an important question, since the answer will dictate the significance we attribute to him. Some clearly believe he was working out his own pathology in view of his ultimate insanity, and, for that reason, believe that he need not be taken seriously. If, on the contrary, the death of God was something he 'found out', then he perhaps ought not too quickly be cast aside by theologians, not least for the power of his diagnosis, if not for his attempts at reconstruction. It is surely pertinent in this connection to note that, as Hegel had done before him, Nietzsche appropriated 'the death of God' from his Lutheran confessional heritage, and applied it to his philosophical endeavours. The burden of this essay is to attempt to return the compliment by now retrieving Nietzsche's cultural critique encapsulated in the parable as a positive prospect for theology beyond the strictures both of modernity and postmodernity.

However the questions posed in the parable are to be answered, the God whose death the madman announces is undoubtedly the God of theism, the monotheistic ontotheological God of Western culture – the philosophically projected omnipresent, omniscient, omnipotent deity, whose 'Christian' face had long since evaporated, as Nietzsche so perceptively observed. Witness the solemn and splendid sentences in Chapter Two of the *Westminster Confession of Faith* of 1646 which already, by means of the *via negativa*, the *via eminentiae* and the *via causalitatis*, maps out a path that was to end with Nietzsche's conclusion. The first paragraph reads as follows:

> There is but one only living and true God, who is infinite in
> being and perfection, a most pure spirit, invisible, without
> body, parts, or passions, immutable, immense, eternal,
> incomprehensible, almighty, most wise, most holy, most free,
> most absolute ...

These words conclude with a semi-colon, to be followed by a description of 'God with a human face', recognisable as the God of the biblical tradition. Nietzsche, of course, made no distinction regarding the prospective viability of either of these bifurcated deities. Rather, he regarded this deity in either incarnation as the greatest threat confronting human beings. For Nietzsche, the totalitarian deity of Christendom must die for the human to flourish. Yet in denouncing this Platonic/Christian idea of transcendence, there is always the suspicion that he feared its departure, as the parable clearly indicates. It is clear, however, that he cannot be described as any sort of latent believer.

Notwithstanding his early enthusiastic pious outpourings, it is apparent that Nietzsche had never become a mature Christian. The death of his ministerial father early in his life must have been a formative factor in his development. Consequently, it appears that Nietzsche inherited Christianity in quite formal terms without internalising it. Certainly there are major theological doctrinal errors in his later fulminations, particularly in relation to his understanding of the person and work of Christ. For example, he unequivocally asserted that Jesus wanted to die, disregarding, to cite but one text: 'Let this cup pass from me ...' (Luke 17:21). Further, it is apparent that Nietzsche was dishonest in his choice of weapons to attack his enemy. For while he had no difficulty excusing his own crusades, he was perfectly happy to attribute Christian crusades to resentment.

An intriguing question is whether or not Nietzsche was searching for a modern post-Christian religion? It is significant that although personally he had 'given up' God, he nevertheless did permit one meaning for the concept: 'God not as the driving force, but God as a maximal state, as an epoch – a point in the evolution of will to power ...' (*Will to Power*, 639). Moreover, at the end of his life, after he had rejected Yahweh and Christ, Nietzsche nevertheless held to the religious belief that 'Being is gracious'. Though he called this conviction *amor fati*, the love of fate, it remained fundamentally an affirmation of the goodness of existence and human life, even as it illustrates a disinterest in any cognitive content concerned as it was primarily with feelings and emotions. It is hardly surprising, then, that, even for Nietzsche, if the ontotheological God of Christianity is dead, and if the human spirit abhors a vacuum, then a new 'religion' is inevitable, as the newspaper headline cited above demonstrates. Such a conclusion does not negate Bonhoeffer's well-known aphorism that modern man cannot be religious anymore. Indeed, it may well demonstrate its truth. In any case, the new 'religion' advocated by Nietzsche is the creative caricature of a new trinity – Eternal Return replacing the Father, Übermensch, the Son, and Dionysus, the Spirit, in a secular eschatological heaven beyond guilt and punishment.

3. Nietzsche in Australia

> The curses of the godless sometimes sound better in God's ear
> than the hallelujahs of the pious.
>
> Martin Luther

The proposition of the heading is preposterous, of course. Although Nietzsche was writing almost 100 years after European settlement in Australia, unlike Lawrence, he never made the journey. But if his parable suggests retrospectivity as well as prospectivity, we might expect some congruence of the parable's claim with this founding event.

The thesis could, I believe, readily be maintained that Australia is the most genuinely secular, enlightened country in the world. Certainly, European settlement took place when the sun was thought to be at its zenith. Consider some of the epochal events surrounding 1788 when Captain Arthur Phillip sailed into Botany Bay – the American Revolution (1775); the Jeffersonian draft of the American Declaration of Independence (1776); Hume's *Dialogue Concerning Natural Religion* (1779); Lessing's *Education of the Human Race* (1780); Kant's *Critique of Pure Reason* (1781); Herder's *Ideas for* the *Philosophy of the History of Mankind* (1784); the French Revolution, 1789.

In this respect, it has become a commonplace to contrast the antithetical nature of European settlement in the United States of America and that in Australia. When the Pilgrim fathers and mothers reached New England, their first act was to participate in a service of worship; when the first convicts arrived in Australia, initial celebrations began with an orgy on the beach.[1] So it is that our colleague Ian Breward could entitle a history of church and state from the beginning of this settlement quoting James Denney's description of Australia to a prospective settler as 'the most Godless place under Heaven'.[2] Given the evangelical 'revival' of eighteenth century England, compulsory Sunday religious services in the new colony, and the strong Irish Catholic constituency in the early settlement, what vacuum with regard to God was existentially being experienced in a land similarly vacant, as the condescending European description of *terra nullius* supposed?

One need not look any further for evidence of that vacuum in what was later to be given formal and intellectual expression in the arena of tertiary education. Thus the United Faculty of Theology, of which Harry Wardlaw has been such a significant founding father, and its parent body, the Melbourne College of Divinity through which he has exercised his teaching, are in their situation and composition a direct consequence of the decision to exclude the teaching of theology from the University of Melbourne.

These observations may help to explain something of the fundamental problem Australian society has with a religious tradition it shares with other Western nations. Consequently, if one may again quote the Melbourne *Age* – and where better can one register the pulse of a society than a newspaper – in a Visual Arts review the critic wrote: 'The most obvious fact ... is the one that causes most embarrassment: he was a religious artist. More embarrassing still, he was a Christian artist ...'. We do not know whether the reviewer personally rejoiced in, or regretted, this observation. The crucial matter is the joining of religious and Christian with embarrassment in a public medium. It conforms to the sort of anecdotal evidence which abounds for those of us sooner or later forced to reveal at social gatherings our occupation. The downcast eye, the evocative pause, the ejaculation of surprise, the muttered apology for some harmless expletive, and then the fateful confession: 'I'm not religious ...'! In the face of that, and in disobedience of the apostle Paul's injunction to become all things to all people, it hardly seems fair to offer the rejoinder: 'Neither am I', identified as one is by the occupational title 'Minister of Religion'. All this fundamentally corroborates the reviewer's sentiments; religion, and therefore the Christian faith, is in the public realm a matter of curiosity at best, irrelevance in practice, and embarrassment at worst.

With the character of such a history behind us, it is understandable that Australia has been well placed to embrace, with apparent intellectual imperturbability, what is purported to be a 'value free' climate in education, and a ruthless 'managerialism' in commerce. In this it is in good company with other secularised Western nations. The concept both of 'value free' and 'managerialism' is a direct outcome of the death of that God who was understood to have effectively embodied both the apotheosis of values and the office of supreme manager. Those who advocate such a 'level playing field' may not consciously be aware of their debt to Nietzsche and the death of God – at least to the nihilistic half of Nietzsche before the eschatology of the 'superman' unfolds – but such is their progenitor. Inevitably, though regrettably, there is some evidence that this culture, at least in the form of managerialism, has infiltrated church structures, one would hope unconsciously. On a wider front, the contemporary universal and even more vicious phenomenon of rapidly expanding global inequality demonstrates the outcome of the death of the monotheist God of Western developed nations, and that deity's concomitant cultural values, for perhaps the most beneficent gift of that God was the recognition that before Him all human beings were understood to be equal.

4. God's departing shadow and the demise of truth

It is our taste which now decides against Christianity, not our reason.

F Neitzsche, *Joyful Wisdom*

Men as they are now simply cannot be religious any more.
D Bonhoeffer, *Letters and Papers from Prison*,
30 April 1944

Nietzsche greeted the death of God with gratitude, optimism, and expectation, but rejoicing was soon tempered by the realisation of the long shadow cast by God's real but slow demise. A recent study of Nietzsche has identified five arenas where God's shadow lingers: in morality, in teleology, in language, in science, and in truth.[3] Each has its recognisable contours in the public realm today.

With regard to morality, for example, Nietzsche was scathing about those who, having ostensibly given up God, nevertheless held on to love, or altruism, or pity, or some ethical remnant of Christian theism. For him, Christian morality only has truth if God is the truth – it stands or falls with faith in God. Likewise for all secular eschatologies; strong, free spirits do not need an end or goal for existence, since after God, there are no eternally enduring substances. In the same way, both science and language are equally fraudulent as vehicles substituting for departing deity. Science for Nietzsche is mostly mathematical reductionism, and language all too easily occupies the place formerly occupied by God. He called reason in language, 'an old deceptive female' – somewhat less strident, even if more comprehensive in this description than Luther's well known aphorism contrasting whoring reason and speculation with faith and being damned.

One of the more enduring categorisations which continues to be maintained in a postmodernist climate that one would have thought would hardly sustain such anachronistic bifurcations is that of fideism[4] and its contrary. Such a claim of anachronism is, of course, contestable, and largely hinges on the degree of significance one attaches to Nietzsche and his project. Further, the nature of that contrary is frequently difficult to ascertain. The conventional Enlightenment antinomy is that between 'reason' and 'faith', but the term 'rationalism' scarcely suggests itself as the contrary of 'fideism'. Paul Avis, for one, knows exactly where he stands in this matter. Writing under the chapter heading of 'The

Implausible Antichrist: Friedrich Nietzsche', he fulminates against deconstructionists, those anarchists of learning, who:

> choose to throw in their lot with Nietzsche by an act of intellectual suicide, despairing of rhyme or reason in our common discourse; or like the Christian fideists, they convince themselves that the Christian faith, as a conceptuality revealed vertically from above (as Barth put it), creates its own narrative world – one that is impervious to Nietzsche's acids ... They enrol Nietzsche as an ally against the critics and rivals of Christian belief, hoisting them with their own petard.[5]

That is some rebuke. This essay is certainly not intended to be impervious to Nietzsche's acids. Indeed, though the parable be another of Nietzsche's 'lies', it qualifies perhaps as being the most noble of lies, and therefore is to be understood as of the utmost seriousness for any subsequent theological endeavour. Consequently, such an enterprise might well seek to demonstrate what the rationality of faith this side of Nietzsche's critique would look like. Presumably what critics of fideism like Avis have to propose is some form of foundationalism;[6] the pathos of their critique is surely that now (after the death of God?) foundationalism is as imprecise a category as fideism has always been. Both putative foundationalism and a naked fideism are thus anachronistic terms. The contemporary methodological pursuit is better to be described as a quest for a convincing 'non-foundationalist foundation'[7] explicated by the 'rationality *of* faith'.

5. A lantern at dusk? A transvaluative flicker of radical Christology

> ... theology is not perishing at the bastions of unbelief but as a result of its own sleepiness. The symptoms of drowsy theology can easily be observed in our own day. Whenever theology awakens from its historical twilight zone, it develops all the more excited hectic activity and grasps at anything, which appears remotely relevant in order to regain the course, which it lost while sleeping.
>
> E Jüngel

Nietzsche was the most radical philosopher to draw out the consequences of a post-Kantian legacy in the transition from cognitivism (the Ontotheological God) to perspectivism (the Death of God). What does this move mean for Christian theology? If a flaming sword demonstrates that there is little prospect of a return to the paradise of theological cognitivism with respect to belief in God, is it not the case that theological perspectivism is the only recourse, east of Eden? And is not this perspectivism fundamentally the meaning of the biblical witness in its struggle against opposing claims to deity?[8]

Ironically, for the early Church this perspectivism was not enough. Seeking to ground this confession in a purportedly reliable foundationalism, the 'idea' of God became unassailable by means of a cognitive, foreign, 'unbaptised' (R Jenson) linguistic terminology derived from Hellenistic philosophy – notwithstanding the attempt by, and considerable success of, Patristic theologians to subvert that language from within. Yet just as for the First Testament, Yahweh's correspondence with Hebrew experience was problematic given polytheistic options, so what became problematic out of the Hellenistic/Christian amalgam was the correspondence of Jesus precisely with that theological construction. We can witness this difficulty, which was scarcely resolved by the Chalcedonian Definition in Christology, since the integrative resolution of the two natures achieved there was effectively re-enculturated into dualistic ways of thinking. It is scarcely surprising that Christians today have to deal with that legacy – while 'Jesus' more or less remains as the embodiment of the human, it is 'God' who, as the parable declares, has become dispensable.

Thus the prevailing, virtually universal, theological effort after the death of God has been to accept Nietzsche's agenda and to construct an experiential anthropological foundation for a 'revival' of God. Nietzsche had already anticipated this move. He believed that the appeal of Christianity in his day lay in the fact that it contributed to one's enjoyment, which presumably he condoned because it signalled the death throes of classical Christianity. The appeal of Christianity today is widely encouraged in the Churches such as to provide a 'faith journey' of self-discovery. This might well qualify for Nietzsche as a modern form of enjoyment. In similar vein, though some in our culture may assert: 'I don't go to church because I don't believe it any more', a good many more are likely to say: 'I don't go to church any more because it does not do anything for me'. That is to say: I don't enjoy it.

One should not infer from this observation any necessary judgement of either approval or disapproval. What it does do is to illustrate the enormous expenditure of effort required as the consequence of that conclusion in the hope that the Christian enterprise will begin to 'do something' for contemporary Australians. It is not therefore surprising to observe the growing attraction of new non-denominational gatherings where success is measured by appeal to enjoyment, contra the boring and irrelevant churches of the parents of these participants – or should that not read, grandparents? It ought not to be surprising in this context that so little is thought to be of use out of the Church's tradition in liturgy, doctrine and creed. So long as experience, and specifically pleasurable experience, is the criterion of effectiveness, little light is to be expected from linguistic appeal to historical texts, except insofar as they might provide precedents for normative pleasurable experiences.

Nevertheless, it remains to be seen for how long appeal can be made to the essentially *modern* category of human experience appealed to by both Nietzsche and post-Kantian theology in their quite different ways. What if we arrive at the point at which there remains no experience left of recognisable theological significance? What warrant do we then have for naming God, either as the presupposition, or the consequence, of our experiences? How do we know that God is intrinsic to these experiences? Indeed, it appears already the case that only by a Herculean effort of imagination can contemporary Australia's secular, religiously immanental, privatised experience be correlated with 'God', notwithstanding the still reasonably impressive census figures indicating a tacit 'belief in God' in the community. Much less can such a diffuse religiosity convincingly be correlated with any positive biblical category.

Nietzsche insisted on what might be called ontological realism, that is, that precedence must be given to encountered reality over perceptions that human beings might bring to that reality; there is no reality outside of reality itself. As a formal statement, this does not take us far. It is not, however, much removed from the biblical insistence that there should be no idols in the presence of truth, or, to put it in more theological terms so far as Christian faith is concerned, there is no God but the God found in the scriptural canon.

Hence, a radical Christology rather than an overworked anthropology may, after Nietzsche, prove to be no more radical than the gospel itself. We recall the imagery of the parable: the lantern which the madman lit in his failed search for God was dashed to the ground, broken, and its light extinguished, following the reception by the hearers of the announcement of the death of God. If Christology is to serve as the reignition of that flame, it will likely appear initially only to be an originating flicker. But the promise is that that flicker may again become as radiant as the sun. For it was once said of that incandescence that it is, and will show itself to be, the light of the world.

Let two experiments, which may permit an emergence of God after God, suggest themselves by way of illustration.

The first is grounded in the sophisticated testimony of the Hebrew people to the nature of the presence of JHWH, as confessed in the symbolism of the Ark of the Covenant.[9] A full account of this construction is to be found in Chapter 25 of the book of Exodus. What follows is a brief summary of the significance of the command to 'make two cherubim of gold at the two ends of the mercy seat. They shall face one to another, their faces turned towards the mercy seat. There I will meet with you' (18–22). This is a pregnant text, replete with radical proposals, not least those which attach to the mercy seat. What is the meaning of that location for the people of God, both then and now? Two things might be said in answer. First, the cherubim flanking the ark define a space where God would be if God was capable of being located anywhere. We are told that the God of Judah is the one who sits, literally dwells, between the cherubim, but – and this is crucial – there is no image between the cherubim. If you wish to encounter the God of Judah, this is where he both is and is not simultaneously. To see God is literally to look into the gap between the holy images. What is tangible and accessible is the empty throne of God. This presence of an absence can not only be carried in procession – the ark has rings to accommodate poles so that the people can carry it around, taking it into battle for instance – but, more significantly for our purpose, what is represented in it is not the image of God, but the place where God is not. And the second observation is a consequence of the first. The mercy seat is the location of the place into which our forebears and we ourselves are invited to project all our human understandings and misunderstandings of deity, only to discover that there they encounter a void – a void of true definition. That must surely be the greatest mercy that human beings can experience!

We have to do here with the presence of an absence, not the absence of a presence. The difference is crucial. Atheism after Nietzsche can only testify to the absence of a presence, and that is banal. Faith, on the other hand, understands why it is that God is always experienced as the presence of an absence, and we can all live with that. Humanly speaking, it may well be the case that the future of the Church now rests on grasping that distinction as the foundation for theological retrieval for the future.

In any event, the heart of Christian faith is to be found in an analogous representation in the New Testament. Why does the gospel of John seize on this image when it transforms the gold cherubim into white angels sitting one at the head and one at the feet where the body of Jesus had been lying (20:12f)? Presumably, they, too, testify to what is not there, the presence of an absence. Presumably, also, their faces are turned towards a new incarnation of the mercy seat, but now the space formerly occupied by JHWH – a present absence – is occupied by the empty space where the body of the crucified son of the Father had lain. Only on a foundation like this does the subsequent narrative receive its force. We now know why Mary sees Jesus, but does not know who he is – she thinks he is the gardener. In this she is the archetypal believer. Jesus is present before Mary as the one absent in his presence – until he speaks. And what does he say? Mary! And what does she reply, but an answering recognition: Rabboni! The lost has been found in the word of recognition. The absent one has become present in the name.

The second, and shorter, experiment in Christology also involves another reading of the Gospel of John, now in its testimony to the eventfulness of the Word made flesh before the physical presence occurs, and concluding with the vindication of that presence in the final words of the risen Lord to Mary at the tomb. The hiatus between these boundary announcements serves to reconfigure God by means of just this Christology. Jesus Christ alone fills the space between 'No-one has ever seen God; the only Son who is in the bosom of the Father has "exegeted" him.' (1:18) and 'Do not hold me, for I have not ascended to the Father; but go to my brethren and say to them, I am ascending to my Father and your Father, to my God and your God' (20:17). The gospel events between these chiastic markers essentially demonstrate the fundamental gift of Christian faith, namely, the disclosure through historical events that the Father of Jesus is God. However, as if we do not have difficulties enough, as this essay has attempted to describe them, we make this discovery at the very time – and its pathos is palpable – when the freedom to name God 'Father' is increasingly denied. Thus this disclosure – not to speak of the fruitful consequences of an equally radical Trinitarianism – is confronted by the misplaced attribution of so-called cultural patriarchal language to this evangelical linguistic revolution.

Our conclusion, finally, must be a sober one. Whether these exegetical experiments may be deemed to engage, if not overcome, the revolution disclosed by Nietzsche's madman is, of course, open to debate. If they do nothing more, however, than encourage renewed conversation between Nietzsche's descendants, and those who believe that it is not yet all up with a reconfigured Christian God, then this may be as much as one can hope for. There will doubtless be many who may remain unconvinced by the attempted constructive prospects adumbrated here. If such can do better, all power to them. But then the onus is on them to demonstrate that the *method* of traditional apologetics, even if suitably repristinated in content, will be adequate to provide a hearing for God in the contemporary climate. Evidence is mounting that long standing Australians, who for generations have for the most part lived well outside religious institutions, are moving from either practical apathy or even overt hostility to the conventional portrayal of God. The situation now is increasingly more serious. Nietzsche's voice more and more has become a culturally condoned and strident voice witnessing to the demise of any God recognisable as conforming to modern Christian tradition.

In human terms, therefore, it may be too late for traditional apologetics, since by accepting the modernist agenda Western churches have, despite every contrary intention, collaborated in the project of marginalising themselves. In Nietzsche's terms, they have consented to become 'occupied' tombs by allowing God to be converted into the god of ontotheology. Consequently, a Christian church discernible as being in continuity with the apostolic tradition may well be a contemporary church embracing the implications of living out of the reality of an empty tomb as proposed above. With the death, and thus consequent deprivation of the longstanding ontotheological deity, we may have to settle for an indeterminate period of time for a perspectivism that one hopes, sooner rather than later, may culturally be grasped as a newly appropriated Trinitarian ontology which will bear the weight required for transformative speech about God.

This essay began with a personal confession concerning the power of Nietzsche's parable. At the very time that it so powerfully described our contemporary world, the writer also encountered what was the most beautiful theological paragraph which to that point he had experienced. There has been no reason over the past forty years to revise that judgement:

> Faith makes the world what it truly is, the creation of God. It rids the world of demons and myths, and lets it again be what God wills it to be. Because faith frees us from the world, it frees us for the world. Because it does not live on the world, it makes it possible for us to live for the world. Because it puts an end to the misuse of the world, it opens the way to the right use of the world. Because it breaks the domination of the world, it gives domination over it and responsibility for it. And because it drives out the liking and the misliking of the world, it creates room for pure joy in the world.[10]

One likes to think that, even though as his life unfolded Nietzsche came not to believe a word of this confession, it may not be too far fetched to imagine that the other side of his madness he now in principle understands. But even if this is not the case, something like this must surely be the word to free all who experience the madness of Nietzsche's legacy.

End Notes

1. This is open to dispute. There is some basis in fact, but perhaps too much was made of it by Robert Hughes in *The Fatal Shore*. I am indebted to Katharine Massam for the information that it took something like two weeks for a formal (perfunctory?) service of worship to take place. Is this sufficient qualification of the observation?
2. The title of the book included a question mark. Breward leaves the question open.
3. AJ Hoover, *Friedrich Nietzsche* (Wesport: Praeger, 1994), 91.
4. Fideism is a pejorative term used to describe those theologies which sit lightly to the purported 'foundations' offered by a contemporary culture, and thus they incur the accusation of evading the intellectual challenge involved in the use of the word God.
5. P Avis, *Faith in the Fires of Criticism* (London: Darton Longman Todd, 1995), 38.
6. Foundationalism may be defined as the doctrine that knowledge constitutes a structure the foundations of which support all the rest but themselves need no support. Two categories have historically offered themselves as such a foundation: that of the rational and the empirical.
7. C Gunton, *The One, the Three and the Many* (Cambridge: Cambridge University Press, 1993), 134.
8. So for example, 1 Corinthians 8:5–6 where Paul writes: 'Indeed, even though there may be so-called gods in heaven or on earth – as in fact there are many gods and many lords – yet there is for us one God, the Father from whom are all things and for whom we exist, and one Lord, Jesus Christ, through whom are all things and through whom we exist.'
9. I am indebted to Rowan Williams for this exegetical insight. See 'Between the Cherubim: The Empty Tomb and the Empty Throne' in *On Christian Theology* (Oxford: Blackwell Publishers, 2000). He is not, of course, responsible for the application.
10. Gerhard Ebeling, *The Nature of Faith* (Philadelphia: Fortress Press, 1961), 161.

15

PAUL TILLICH AS EXISTENTIALIST AND MORE

CHRISTIAAN MOSTERT

I

It is beyond dispute that Paul Tillich was one of the most influential Christian theologians of the twentieth century, who spoke to many struggling to hold on to Christian belief in the culture that developed in the Western world after the Second World War. Tillich was a troubled soul, whose distinctive theological voice and – even more – his 'sometimes unconventional lifestyle'[2] – also made many more conventional Christians dismiss him and his interpretation of the Christian faith. I was first introduced to Tillich's theological ideas in 1965 by Harry Wardlaw, whom this essay seeks to honour, when I was a first-year theological student.[1] Before that I had heard the name of Tillich in connection with the kind of theology which I should at all costs avoid, a theology which was 'unsound', even dangerous.[3] In the event, Tillich made a deep impression on me for the best part of a decade, both in the method and the content of his theological work. These days I am a more distant and critical admirer, but I regard him as standing head and shoulders above almost all his contemporaries in the theological world. I am convinced that, even after his close contact with Japanese Buddhism late in his life, he remained a thoroughly Christian theologian; I have no doubt that he 'had a Gospel to proclaim'.

In this essay it is not my concern to substantiate this claim, nor to set out the reasons why other, later theologians came to speak more persuasively to me. It is rather to consider what kind of thinker Tillich was and whether there is a single category into which his thought can best be fitted. I wish to argue that Tillich is properly and deservedly called an existentialist, but that this is only part of the truth. 'Existentialism' does not encompass his wide-ranging interest, and does not exhaust his rich theological and philosophical ideas. Fundamentally, he is as preoccupied with the character and power of *being* – and with its structure and ground – as he is with the analysis of *existence,* though these should not be set dualistically over against each other. It must be asked whether, in addition to being an existentialist, he is best described as an ontologist or as an essentialist, and what this might mean. Certainly, he is a Christian theologian, which makes him a particular kind of existentialist thinker, very different from the best-known existentialists of the twentieth century, Jean-Paul Sartre and Albert Camus. In this respect, despite many differences, he has more in common with that incomparable nineteenth century existentialist, Søren Kierkegaard.[4] As a theologian, Tillich lived and thought from the position of discerning a theological answer to the existential questions, indeed the questionableness of existence as such. In Tillich's own terms, there is a place where the negative, estrangement, 'non-being' is overcome, *viz.* in the picture of Jesus as the Christ.[5]

Walter Kaufmann is on the right track when he describes the heart of existentialism as a 'refusal to belong to any school of thought, the repudiation of the adequacy of any body of beliefs whatever, and especially of systems, and a marked dissatisfaction with traditional philosophy as superficial, academic, and remote from life.'[6] It would be better to speak of a family of cognate views of human existence or the human self, understood – as Kaufmann, again, puts it, with particular reference to Kierkegaard – in terms of 'possibilities, dread, and decisions'.[7] The term 'existentialism' is difficult to use with precision. If the non-religious or anti-religious versions of it are more characteristic of the twentieth century and better known, there are certainly religious versions of it as well. For religious existentialists, despair and meaninglessness do not have the last word; the world is not characterised by absurdity and pointlessness but by mystery and meaningfulness (Gabriel Marcel). For Tillich, the power of the new being overcomes the abyss of non-being. He is, arguably, the existentialist theologian *par excellence.*

II

Tillich was born in August 1886 in Starzeddel, a small town in the province of Brandenburg, Germany, and lived in Berlin from about the age of fourteen. He died in October 1965 in Chicago, at the age of seventy-nine. His academic and literary career spans two cultures, the German and the North American. He was one of the first intellectuals to be suspended from his professorship (in Frankfurt) in 1933, and by the end of that year he was in New York, where he had been offered a position at Union Seminary and Columbia University. After more than twenty years at Union Seminary, he had had distinguished professorial positions at Harvard and Chicago, right up to the time of his death. Tillich grew up in a strongly religious family; his father was a Lutheran pastor. He speaks of 'the experience of the 'holy", which he received early in his life, as 'an indestructible good and as the foundation of all my religious and theological work'.[8] He was moved by poetry, particularly that of the German Romantics (Hölderlin, Novalis, Eichendorff, Rilke). He had a great love of nature –speaking of a 'romantic relation to nature'[9] – and, unsurprisingly, was much moved by the 'philosophy of nature' of Friedrich Schelling, the philosopher of Romanticism, whom he discovered early in his student years. Later he did his doctoral study on Schelling's philosophical development. He regards Schelling as moving toward a philosophy of existence, while also holding on to a philosophy of essence, i.e. a vision of the essential structure of reality. From Schelling Tillich learnt the 'principle of identity', which he never surrendered. In our experience subject and object are separated, but there is actually some underlying unity within which they are held together. He recalls the purchase of the collected works of Schelling during his student days in Berlin. 'This spending of non-existent money was probably more important than all the other non-existent or sometimes existing money that I have spent. For what I learned from Schelling became determinative of my own philosophical and theological development.'[10]

One of Tillich's very formative experiences was his appointment as Army chaplain, and his military service on the Western front, for which he left three days after his marriage. Here, over four years, Tillich shared with many other young men the end of optimism and the beginning of despair; their God turned to ashes.[11] Here, with many others, he knew suffering. He read the 90th Psalm – 'Lord, you have been our refuge from generation to generation' – with 'the thunderous roar of cannon in the distance'.[12] He was a Lutheran pastor; he was also a grave-digger, and constantly in the presence of death. One can only speak of an emotional and mental anguish beyond words. and yet, as he wrote later, the hope of the Gospel was stronger 'than the sound of exploding shells, of weeping at open graves, of the sighs of the sick, of the moaning of the dying'.[13] He knew fear and the force of the demonic and the tragic, but he did not lose his faith, as many did. It did help to turn him into an existentialist. He found great solace in art. He philosophised in his spare time, and even wrote theological papers. Despite all this, the devastation and demonic violence of war left their mark on him.

After the war, Tillich read and wrote, studied and lectured, having been appointed *Privatdozent* in the University of Berlin. He had read Nietzsche during the war, and this had given him, on the one hand, a strong sense of the vibrancy of life; it 'lured him back to passion and to life', as his biographers put it.[14] On the other hand, Nietzsche confirmed his dissatisfaction with the traditional concept of God, especially a God who would simply ensure that everything turned out for the best. The problem of articulating an alternative understanding of God preoccupied Tillich greatly, probably all his life. He had wide interests apart from philosophy and theology, and these included politics, religious socialism, art and depth psychology. To quote his biographers again, 'Freud's psychoanalysis, Cézanne's 'Expressionism', Marx's socialism, all became material for his Christian apologetic theology'.[15] He wanted to understand what was happening socially and politically in Germany. He argued for a combination of Christianity and socialism. Politically, religious socialism did not make much impact, especially when faced with the so-called National Socialism, but Tillich was an articulate spokesperson for it in those early years after the First World War.

From Schelling Tillich had learnt the close relation between philosophy, aesthetics and religion. As he wrote later, 'Religion stands between aesthetics and philosophy . . . In one period of Schelling's development, the aesthetic was the great miracle of the divine self-manifestation. In the aesthetic vision the Kantian dualism between theoretical and practical reason was overcome.'[16] During the war, painting had been a form of escape from horror and destruction, but it became something of lasting importance for him. Not only was it a medium through which to arrive at a fuller understanding of himself, but he saw it – not unlike Schelling – as a vehicle for the holy and the absolute. Religion and art were inseparable; through a work of art, especially in the Expressionist style, one could be grasped by the absolute as powerfully as through religious symbols, or more so. When he saw Botticelli's painting of the *Madonna with Singing Angels*, he was not merely moved by its beauty and aesthetic power; he felt grasped by the reality of the absolute and 'felt he was looking not merely at angels but at the holy itself'.[17]

One other piece of background information deserves emphasis and underlines Tillich's existentialism, *viz.* his interest in depth psychology. In later years Tillich turned away from explicitly political writing and gave expression to a concern to understand the interior dynamics of the human person. His interest in Freud overshadowed his earlier interest in Marx.[18] He discussed the relation of religion and psychology and formed friendships with some leading psychotherapists, who were influenced by his views. He analysed the phenomenon of anxiety, and made an important distinction between *neurotic* and *ontological* anxiety. A few years before his death the Academy of Mental Health and Religion honoured him for the importance of his work. But long before that he had regarded existentialist thought as offering the best point of contact between theology and psychology.[19]

This outline of Tillich's life locates him in time and space and indicates his cultural and intellectual heritage. It stands to reason that his experience of the First World War had the most momentous effect on the shape and dynamics of his life. It confronted him not just with human 'loneliness in the physical universe of modern cosmology', to use a phrase from Hans Jonas, with reference to Pascal,[20] but with such depths of anxiety and fear and such a pervasive sense of the senselessness of the human condition as to connect him strongly with the mood of modern existentialism. We must now make these oblique references more direct, and turn to Tillich's writings on existentialism and the fundamental dynamics of human existence. The question why Tillich's existentialism was so different from that of Sartre or Camus will be left in the background for now.

III

Tillich's theological system, the three-volume *Systematic Theology*, published between 1951 and 1963, comprises five parts: Reason and Revelation, Being and God, Existence and the Christ, Life and the Spirit, and History and the Kingdom of God. Tillich, existentialist though he was, could only think systematically.[21] If the second part suggests ontological concerns, the third part takes up questions about existence. Here too we have a discussion of existentialism, as well as the characteristic themes of existentialism: estrangement, self-loss and world-loss, death, finitude and guilt, suffering and loneliness, doubt and meaninglessness. Here, using the theological symbol of 'the fall', Tillich deals with the transition from essential to existential being.

Tillich distinguishes between the 'existential' attitude and the philosophical school of 'existentialism', though they are obviously connected. The *existential attitude* is one which rejects the idea of cognitive detachment. The engagement of the subject is not suppressed in the interest of some spurious 'objectivity'. Tillich sees involvement and detachment as polar opposites, not as conflicting alternatives. In fact, there are 'many mixtures of detachment and involvement'.[22] Theology, in Tillich's view, is by its very nature *existential*.[23] *Existentialism*, on the other hand, is something more specific, *viz.* a philosophical 'school' or movement of protest. It is, as noted earlier, very diverse, but it arose in opposition to the 'essentialism' of Hegel's grand system of thought and reality. The existentialism of the twentieth century had its roots in the decades 1830–50, when 'the historical destiny and the cultural self-expression of the Western world in the twentieth century' was prepared.[24] Tillich is particularly interested in the nature of this existentialist revolt, first in its own terms and then in order to confront it with the religious symbols which point beyond it. A long quotation makes the point well:

> The common point in all existentialist attacks is that man's existential situation is a state of estrangement from his essential nature. Hegel is aware of this estrangement, but he believes that it has been overcome and that man has been reconciled with his true being. According to all the existentialists, this belief is Hegel's basic error. Reconciliation is a matter of anticipation and expectation, but not of reality. The world is not reconciled, either in the individual – as Kierkegaard shows – or in society – as Marx shows – or in life as such – as Schopenhauer and Nietzsche show. Existence is estrangement and not reconciliation; it is dehumanisation and not the expression of essential humanity. It is the process in which man becomes a thing and ceases to be a person. History is not the divine self-manifestation but a series of unreconciled conflicts, threatening man with self-destruction. The existence of the individual is filled with anxiety and threatened by meaninglessness. With this description of man's predicament all existentialists agree and are therefore opposed to Hegel's essentialism. They feel that it is an attempt to hide the truth about man's actual state.[25]

Strictly speaking, existentialism concerns itself with the nature of human existence, inasmuch as it is questionable or problematic; it does not offer answers to the problematic structure of existence. Insofar as existentialist thinkers do so, they draw on religious or quasi-religious traditions which go far beyond their analysis of the human condition. However, Tillich sees existentialism as a great help to Christian theology, for it has given support to the classical Christian interpretation of human existence. Christian theology should regard existentialism as an ally, for it offers much help from 'the practical explorers of man's predicament'.[26] Tillich himself received an enormous amount of help from poets, novelists, psychoanalysts, artists, philosophers and the like. However, his existentialism owes at least as much to his own deep and sensitive reflection on his own experience.

Tillich offered his own statement of human existence as a state of estrangement, which he relates closely to the biblical concept of sin, though the two terms are not co-terminous. Human beings are estranged from their true being; they are not what they ought to be. They are estranged from others, both individually and collectively, as people's lives and the relations of communities and nations demonstrates *ad nauseam*. In religious terms, they are also estranged from God, who is the source (or ground and power) of their being. Paradoxically, what we are estranged from is precisely that to which we essentially belong. 'Man is not a stranger to his true being, for he belongs to it. He is judged by it but cannot be completely separated, even if he is hostile to it. Man's hostility to God proves indisputably that he belongs to him.'[27] Estrangement is our universal and inescapable condition; that is its tragic side. But we are also its agents; that is its personal side. There is a sense in which we choose it, which makes us in part responsible for it. However, even before we come into the world and make choices, the cards are, as it were, stacked against us; our choices alone do not bring about estrangement. There are powers or structures that embody and create estrangement and keep humankind in their grip.

Tillich's understanding of estrangement gains its distinctive shape from the concepts of Christian theology, in which it is embedded. It is also influenced by existentialist writers and it draws on novels and poetry, psychology and sociology. Fundamentally, however, estrangement is identified with the three classical elements of sin. First, it may be understood as *unbelief.* By this Tillich does not mean the inability to accept particular Christian doctrines, but a fundamental turning away from God, cognitively, in terms of will, and emotionally.[28] It is not the denial of God so much as the loss of union with God. It is already implied in the polarity of finite and infinite, in particular the finite's loss of its grounding in the infinite. This situation of estrangement characterises both the world into which we are born and the personal choices and decisions people make. It comes to expression in the restlessness, emptiness and meaninglessness that are thematised in the literature of existentialism. However, Tillich also describe estrangement in terms of the possibility of reunion. Unbelief as the loss of God has within it the possibility of reconciliation with God, but only as a matter of gift and grace.

Second, estrangement can be understood in terms of *hubris,* in which the human being makes itself the centre of its world.[29] The capacity to be 'centred' beings, through self-consciousness, is part of the dignity of human life, but the capacity to see ourselves as being a centre to which other things and other people relate extends to the temptation to make ourselves the centre of all things, and thus to stand in the place of God. In *hubris* human beings elevate themselves beyond the limits of finite being. The Greeks knew this phenomenon well and made it a central theme in their tragedies. It is not adequate to equate *hubris* with pride. It is the natural extension of the qualities that give humankind its greatness. In theological terms, it is the tendency to seek our autonomy apart from God rather than in relationship with God. The Old Testament also knows *hubris,* already in its opening pages. It is about humankind's 'self-elevation . . . into the sphere of the divine.'[30] The serpent's promise to Eve that eating from the tree of knowledge will make her and Adam equal to God (Gen 3:5) illustrates the temptation, as does the construction of the tower of Babel, reaching into the heavens (Gen 11:1–9).

Third, estrangement can also be understood in connection with *concupiscence,* the drive to draw the whole world into oneself.[31] It is there for us – there to be had, possessed, consumed. Far from being reducible to lust, or the desire for sexual pleasure, concupiscence covers the whole range of human desires, from physical hunger and sexual desire to knowledge and power, from material wealth to the highest spiritual values. Tillich is particularly interested in Freud's notion of *libido* and Nietzsche's concept of the *will to power.* They are the symbols of concupiscence inasmuch as they are all-consuming. He cites the figures of Don Juan and the Emperor Nero, both as portrayed by Kierkegaard, as exemplifying the all-consuming and insatiable character of concupiscence. In themselves, the yearning to unite with another person and the self's affirmation of itself are necessary elements in human wellbeing. They become expressions of concupis- cence when, respectively, libido is detached from love and when self-affirmation becomes a striving for power without limit. Another example of concupiscence is Goethe's Faust, whose unlimited striving is directed toward the knowledge of everything. 'It is the 'everything', not knowledge as such, which produces the demonic temptation.'[32]

These, then, are the marks of estrangement as understood with the help of some fundamental Christian theological concepts. In using these, Tillich emphasises the universal scope of this existential estrangement. He sees no conflict between the analysis of the human situation offered by the classical tradition of biblical and Christian thought, on the one hand, and that provided by modern existentialism, on the other. But he is not restricted by his theological categories, and moves outside them in a further elaboration of the depth and meaning of estrangement. The tragic consequence of estrangement is what he calls 'self-loss'.

> Self-loss ... is the loss of one's determining centre; it is the disintegration of the centred self by disruptive drives which cannot be brought into unity. So long as they are centred, these drives constitute the person as a whole. If they move against one another, they split the person. The further the disruption goes, the more the being of man as man is threatened. Man's centred self may break up, and, with the loss of self, man loses his world.[33]

If *we* fall apart, our world also falls apart, whether through moral conflict or psycho-pathological disruption. The potential for this 'falling apart' is there for all of us as individuals, as our society is beginning to acknowledge. Mental illness and various neurological conditions have brought it home to us powerfully. Equally powerfully, the 'falling apart' of empires and ideological systems, of social and economic institutions, of political alliances and organs of multi-lateral co-operation is no longer foreign to our experience. The breakdown of ecological systems is not a distant reality but a perilously present threat. What Tillich wrote about self-loss and world-loss resonated powerfully in the middle decades of the twentieth century.

IV

The reality of estrangement expresses itself in a number of forms which have become thematic in the literature of existentialism. One of these is the experience of mortality and death; nothing is more certain that the fact that we shall all die at some time. Death is an immovable boundary at the end of our existence; we come from dust and to dust we return. We are finite and mortal beings. The human person is 'under the domination of death and is driven by the anxiety of having to die'.[34] When Tillich describes the human condition in this way, he has in mind not neurotic but ontological anxiety, an anxiety which belongs unavoidably to our existence.[35] What Tillich is describing is akin to the more detailed, more technical philosophical description of *Dasein* as a 'Being-towards-death', which we find in Heidegger.[36] Death is the horizon within which our lives are lived, and for some it renders life futile, even absurd. Not so for Tillich, though he is sharply aware of its negative power. He writes, 'In estrangement man is left to his finite nature of having to die. Sin does not produce death but gives to death the power which is conquered only in participation in the eternal'.[37]

We know the reality of estrangement also in the experience of time and space. They belong to the structure of being; they are fundamental categories for our perception of the world. But time, when disconnected from any sense of the presence of the eternal, can become 'transitoriness without actual presence'. Space can be experienced as 'spatial contingency', the sense that there is no space in which one belongs.[38] Time can be experienced as a demonic power, and human beings resist it, if they can afford to, by trying to prolong the small stretch of time given to us for as long as possible or by filling it up with all kinds of diversionary strategies. Likewise with the category of space: people try to overcome the element of estrangement by absolutising particular places, or by becoming part of, or acquiring, as many places as possible. But it does not overcome our finitude; we come and we go, and 'our place does not know us any more' (Job 7:10).

Nowhere is Tillich's existentialism more apparent than in his discussion of despair. A major section of his *Systematic Theology*, Vol 2, is entitled 'The Meaning of Despair and its Symbols'. However, some years earlier, in 1952, he published a little book entitled *The Courage to Be*,[39] which became a best-seller. The book is a discussion of courage in the face of anxiety and despair. There are different types of anxiety, and at different times anxiety has taken the form of ontic anxiety (in ancient times), moral anxiety (the end of the Middle Ages) or spiritual anxiety (the end of the modern period). By spiritual anxiety he means the anxiety manifested in the sense of emptiness and meaninglessness. All types of anxiety contribute to despair, which Tillich describes as 'an ultimate or 'boundary-line' situation'.[40] It contains no way forward into the future; it is devoid of hope. Elsewhere he writes of despair, 'it is the final index of man's predicament . . . . In despair, not in death, man has come to the end of his possibilities.'[41] He also discusses the problem of suicide, the sharpest expression of human estrangement. The significance of suicide cannot be over-stated, for here the temptation to escape pain or suffering means getting rid of one's self; the threatening annihilation can no longer be resisted. It should not be singled out for moral or religious condemnation, but neither can it, in Tillich's view, be regarded simply as an escape from despair. It can mean escape from despair on the temporal level, but as a religious person he wants to consider also the dimension of the eternal or the ultimate, and on this level suicide does not bring escape from the despairing self. Actually, Tillich believes that one cannot escape from despair; one can only overcome it, in an act of courage, the courage to *be*. The courage to *be* has to be understood not just in moral but in ontological terms, as an affirmation of being over against non-being. He finds support here in Nietzsche's notion of the will-to-power, which he interprets as a very strong sense of the self-affirmation of life. In this self-affirmation of life 'the power of being actualises itself. But in actualising itself it overcomes that in life which, although belonging to life, negates life.'[42]

Clearly, Tillich sees in existentialism not merely a protest against abstraction and objectification in thought, and against all 'systems' of thought which ignore 'the deserts and jungles of the human soul'.[43] He also sees in existentialism an expression of 'the self-affirmation of the self, in a situation in which the self was more and more lost in its world'.[44] This is identical with the courage to *be*. This courage has three forms or aspects: (1) the courage to *be* as part of larger wholes to which we belong but from which we are also separated; (2) the courage to *be* as oneself, ie as a free, centred and determining self; and (3) the courage to accept acceptance. This is the courage that is 'rooted in a power of being that is greater than the power of oneself and the power of one's world.'[45] This is courage in relation to transcendence. 'Courage', says Tillich, needs the power of being, a power transcending the non-being which is experienced in the anxiety of fate and death, which is present in the anxiety of emptiness and meaninglessness, which is effective in the anxiety of guilt and condemnation.'[46] These forms of courage comprise the courage to *be*. Common to all three is the desire to conquer anxiety by taking it up into the courage of self-affirmation, the courage to *be*. This is not merely a moral quality which a person might summon up in a situation of threat. It is rather an affirmation of *being*, an ontological courage, an affirmation of life in the face of whatever threatens the sense that life is worthwhile. It is made possible by the power of being itself, its power to negate and overcome its negation.[47]

It is reasonable to conclude that Tillich's existentialist credentials are strong. The major preoccupations of existentialist writers engaged Tillich also. The structure and dynamics of human existence are a major part of his theological agenda. As a theologian, his theological method is a method of correlation, in which the 'kerygmatic' content of Christian faith is brought into correlation with the human situation, especially in its character of estrangement. In does not matter at what point one begins – with the message or the situation – as long as the correlation of the two sides occurs. Tillich begins with the situation, the human predicament, the actual experience of human existence, especially as empty and meaningless. This justifies calling him an existentialist.[48] His analysis of 'existence' in Part III of his system precedes the answer of the New Being in the picture of Jesus as the Christ. His analysis of 'life' in Part IV precedes the answer of the Spiritual Presence. However, the question arises whether it is sufficient to regard him as an existentialist thinker. He is certainly an unusual kind of existentialist. Arguably, he should be seen as something more than an existentialist, though this assumes that the label 'existentialist' has an agreed determinate meaning. Two things might be said in support of such a suggestion. First, Tillich is as much an 'essentialist' as he is an existentialist, possibly even an ontologist. This combination is unusual, although something similar should be said of

Heidegger, whose existentialist credentials are not in question.[49] For Heidegger the analysis of *Dasein* is the first stage of an ontological enquiry, an enquiry into being.[50] The suggestion should at least be given consideration. Second, Tillich is also a Christian theologian and a preacher; as such he has a word to address to the situation of estrangement which so deeply characterises human existence. In short, he has something called 'Good News' to announce. In this respect he is quite unlike Heidegger, for Heidegger did not bring his theological convictions – to the extent that he had any – into his ontology.[51] But precisely because he is a Christian theologian he is also unlike his contemporaries, Sartre and Camus.

V

It is not easy to determine whether Tillich should be regarded as an ontologist. If one were to consider only the first volume of his *Systematic Theology* the judgement would very likely be in the affirmative. In Tillich's view, theology can no more avoid the fundamental ontological questions of being than philosophy can: what is being? What is the structure of being? What is the meaning of being? Theology is particularly concerned with the latter question, but in order to think about this question it must develop its own ontology – and become, in effect, philosophy – or it must borrow an ontological system from somewhere else. There can be no doubt that Tillich is fascinated by ontological questions. The question of being-itself – why there *is* anything at all, rather than just nothing? – arises through the shock of possible non-being.[52] The question about God – if it is asked at all – must be asked in connection with the question of *Being*. For Tillich, God is not simply *a* being, but *Being-itself*, or the power of being over against non-being. Tillich is interested in *Being:* its structure, its elements, its ground, its power over *Non-being*. He is particularly interested in the difference between *essential* and *existential* being, the duality in which being manifests itself. Both the difference and the relation between these two aspects of being can be – and have been, in the history of philosophy – described in very different terms.[53] However, the quest to understand the relation between them is the task of ontology. Clearly, in Tillich's view, theology cannot ignore this and related questions, the fundamental structure of being and its basic categories.

In the first volume of *Systematic Theology* Tillich concerns himself with these questions with a high degree of interest. Part II of the System is called 'Being and God', with two sub-parts, 'Being and the Question of God' and 'The Reality of God'. The two chapters in the first of these two sub-parts are devoted to ontological questions. John Macquarrie's judgement that 'Tillich has gone on from existential to ontological analysis in his treatment of theological problems'[54] seems to be well-founded. But it is noticeable that in the second and third volumes of *Systematic Theology* the ontological questions have receded into the background, if indeed they have not disappeared altogether.[55] Better justice is done to Tillich's real interest if he is regarded as an 'essentialist'; this is a term which he happily applies to himself, for it is impossible, in his view, to be an existentialist without being an essentialist, someone who seeks the essential structure of reality.[56] He writes,

> Existentialism is not a philosophy which can stand on its own legs. Actually, it has no legs. It is always based on a vision of the essential structure of reality. In this sense it is based on essentialism and cannot live without it. If you say that man is evil, you must have a concept of man in his essential goodness, otherwise the word 'evil' would not make any sense ... And if you say that man's structure is distorted in time and space, or that it is 'fallen', then you must have something from which he is fallen ... So mere existentialism does not exist ... Thus all existentialism presupposes that from which it breaks away, namely, essentialism.[57]

Macquarrie's judgement about Tillich's ontological analysis is, it seems, not entirely correct, though it is understandable.[58] It would be more correct to say, first, that Tillich has moved away from ontological questions than that he has moved on to them and, second, that he is better described as an essentialist than as an ontologist. The ontological questions are certainly no longer in the forefront by the time the later parts of Tillich's system are written, though this is not to deny their importance. At every point, theology – no less than philosophy – rests on ontological assumptions of one kind or another.[59] It is clear that Tillich sees himself more as an essentialist. Everything that is said about the character of human existence presupposes an essential structure of being. It is akin to Plato's theory of the forms, though Tillich does not hypostasise it into an actual realm of being. The biblical symbol of 'the fall' expresses the truth that human existence, in its brokenness or disintegration, is a 'falling away' from something whole and integrated, even if this is not to be understood as an event in time.

Tillich is well aware of the problematic nature of the notion of 'essence', certainly of its ambiguity.[60] But the distinction between essential and existential being is, in his view, inescapable, whether one means by 'essence' the essential nature *(ousia)* or ideal of something, on the one hand, or the norm by which an actual thing is judged. 'Whenever the ideal is held against the real, truth against error, good against evil, a distortion of being is presupposed and is judged by essential being. It does not matter how the appearance of such a distortion is explained in terms of causality.'[61] One way or another, for Tillich, existence is preceded by essence, a point which Sartre famously denied. It precedes temporality; it belongs to paradise, or 'the dreaming', not the 'real world', in the normal sense of this term. It has no time or place.[62] But just as essence anticipates existence, so the actual has its existence in some relation to the essential. Tillich attributed this last conviction to the strong influence on him of Lutheranism, with its doctrine that the finite is capable of the infinite *(finitum capax infiniti)*, over against the Calvinist denial of this.[63] In any case, for Tillich this relation and distinction are fundamental in his ontology (or onto-theology). It was part of the philosophical air which he breathed as a young student and it remained determinative of his thought all his life. The influence of Schelling was undoubtedly most formative, and Tillich regarded him as being both an essentialist and an existentialist. Tillich says that 'there is hardly one category in twentieth-century existentialist poetry, literature, philosophy, and indirectly the visual arts, which you cannot find in [Schelling's] lectures [in Berlin in the middle of the nineteenth century].[64] (Kierkegaard attended these lectures.) If Tillich is more than an existentialist, the 'more' is his essentialism. Far from detracting from his existentialism, it gives rise to it and enriches it. Preoccupied though he is with the nature of human existence and life in the world, this is but a form of the ultimately fascinating mystery of Being-itself, essential being.

The other way in which Tillich is more than an existentialist – or at any rate different from the most well-known existentialists of his time – is in his meeting of existential questions with religious or theological answers. The best-known existentialist writers of the twentieth century have concerned themselves with the analysis of human existence. They do not provide answers of a religious or quasi-religious kind; perhaps their 'answer' is that there are no answers. By his own definition, Tillich is, strictly speaking, more than an existentialist.

> Existentialism gives an analysis of what it means to exist. It shows the contrast between an essentialist description and an existentialist analysis. It develops the question implied in existence, but it does not try to give the answer, either in atheistic or in theistic terms. Whenever existentialists give answers, they do so in terms of religious or quasi-religious traditions which are not derived from their existentialist analysis. Pascal derives his answers from the Augustinian tradition, Kierkegaard from the Lutheran, Marcel from the Thomist, Dostoevski from the Greek Orthodox. Or the answers are derived from humanistic traditions, as with Marx, Sartre, Nietzsche, Heidegger, and Jaspers. None of these men was able to develop answers out of his questions. The answers of the humanists come from hidden religious sources. They are matters of ultimate concern or faith, although garbed in a secular gown.[65]

The extent to which non-theistic existentialists give 'answers' at all, and whether they have religious roots, are debatable matters. In an extended discussion of existentialism Tillich comments on the philosophical existentialism of Heidegger and Sartre. Heidegger offers a precise analysis of non-being, finitude, anxiety, death and the like, and then analyses the phenomenon of 'resolve' (Entschlossenheit), on the basis of which one can act. But, says Tillich,

> Nobody can give directions for the actions of the 'resolute'
> individual – no God, no conventions, no laws of reason, no
> norms or principles ... Our conscience is the call to ourselves.
> It does not tell anything concrete, it is neither the voice of God
> nor the awareness of eternal principles. It calls us to ourselves
> out of the behaviour of the average man, out of daily talk, the
> daily routine ...[66]

If the phenomenon of 'resolve' is Heidegger's answer – at least
the early Heidegger's answer – it is an answer without particular
content, except such content as one may choose to give it. There
are no norms with any force other than their being chosen.

Sartre takes this line of thinking further, in a way which Heidegger
could not, in Tillich's view, have done. 'In the background of Heidegger's
ontology lies the mystical concept of being which is without
significance for Sartre. Sartre carried through the consequences of
Heidegger's Existentialist analysis without mystical restrictions.'[67] What
distinguishes Sartre, as Tillich sees it, is not the originality of his basic
concepts but the radicalism and consistency with which he worked
with them. This makes him the person most readily associated with
existentialism, especially its twentieth century version. Tillich says
that Sartre's most telling statement is that 'the essence of man is his
existence', a sentence which 'illuminates the whole Existentialist scene.'
Tillich regards it as 'the most despairing and the most courageous
sentence in all Existentialist literature.'[68] There is no essential human
nature; all there is is what an individual makes of it. This is, of course,
an answer to the question of meaning, an answer of sorts. And it
cannot be condemned as lacking in courage, the courage to *be*.
But in such a position it cannot be of any consequence whether one
chooses to be or whether, at a certain point, one chooses not to be.

Predictably, Tillich has a different answer. Hints of it have been
given at various points in this essay. Essentially it has to do with
the conquest of existential estrangement by the power of being,
which he calls the *New Being*. This *New Being* has appeared in
the picture of Jesus as the Christ. To see what it is about one should
consider Tillich's sermons, although he also says a good deal about
in the second volume of his *Systematic Theology*.[69] Formally
speaking, 'New Being is essential being under the conditions of

existence, conquering the gap between essence and existence'.[70] In three collections of sermons[71] Tillich communicated the content of Christian faith to believers, unbelievers and those in between in powerful, non-technical language, and did so with an imaginative power and a depth of insight into the human condition that won him an enormous reputation. The titles of the last two collections already suggest the shape of Tillich's answer. As he says himself, 'the title, "The Eternal Now" . . . indicates that the presence of the Eternal in the midst of the temporal is a decisive emphasis in most of the sermons'.[72] What is new about it is, on the one hand, that essential being is manifested in an undistorted way in the conditions of existence and, on the other hand, that it is a renewal of the estranged character of existential being, existence in the world.[73] It is a way of speaking about the Pauline idea of a new creation *in Christ*. He concludes the sermon on 'The New Being' with these lines:

> Reconciliation, reunion, resurrection – this is the New Creation, the New Being, the New state of thing. Do we participate in it? The message of Christianity is not Christianity, but a New Reality. A New state of things has appeared, it still appears; it is hidden and visible, it is there and it is here. Accept it, enter into it, let it grasp you.[74]

This is Tillich's answer to the problem of existence. This is the point at which Tillich is both existentialist and Christian theologian. Here the inescapable tension between essential and existential being, between essence and existence, finds resolution. The resolution is not an unbroken one; in fact, it breaks through, now and then, here and there. But there is a power at work, the power of the New Being, which *has* broken through and which *does* break through in the condition of estrangement. Sometimes subtly, almost imperceptibly, sometimes powerfully, it transforms persons and situations. It is the promise of Easter; it is also the power of Pentecost. The last word cannot then be about estrangement but about reconciliation, not about despair but about freedom and hope, not about the negation of being but the negation of negation. Tillich ends a characteristic sermon with these words:

We can stand the Yes and No of life and truth because we participate in the Yes beyond Yes and No, because we are *in* it, as it is *in* us. We are participants of His resurrection; therefore we can say the ultimate Yes, the Amen beyond *our* Yes and *our* No.[75]

End Notes

1. An earlier form of this material was given as a paper to the Existentialist Society, Melbourne, in April 2003. I am grateful to Harry Wardlaw for his comments on the paper, which gave rise to some re-thinking.
2. WL Sessions, 'Tillich', in Robert Audi (editor), *The Cambridge Dictionary of Philosophy* (Cambridge: Cambridge University Press, 1995), 803. This is a rather euphemistic description. For two detailed (and quite different) accounts of Tillich's complexity as a human being, see Hannah Tillich, *From Time to Time* (New York: Stein and Day, 1973) and Rollo May, *Paulus: Reminiscences of a Friendship,* revised edition (Dallas: Saybrook, 1988), originally published as *Paulus: Tillich as Spiritual Teacher* (Harper & Row, 1973).
3. Tillich was once asked the question, 'Are you not a dangerous man?', to which his answer was, 'Yes', though he distinguished himself from 'the really dangerous people', the Enlightenment critics of theology. See P Tillich, *Ultimate Concern: Tillich in Dialogue,* edited by D Mackenzie Brown (London: SCM Press, 1965), 188–93.
4. It is perhaps better to regard Kierkegaard as the 'father' of existentialism; at least its precursor.
5. P Tillich, *Systematic Theology,* Vol 2 (London: James Nisbet, 1957), 132f (Please note that page references in the British and American editions do not always coincide exactly.)
6. W Kaufmann (editor), *Existentialism from Dostoevsky to Sartre* (Cleveland and New York: The World Publishing Company, 1956), 12.
7. W Kaufmann (editor), *Existentialism from Dostoevsky to Sartre,* 17.
8. P Tillich, 'Autobiographical Reflections', CW Kegley and RW Bretall (editors), *The Theology of Paul Tillich* (New York: Macmillan, 1961), 6.
9. P Tillich, 'Autobiographical Reflections', 4f.
10. P Tillich, *Perspectives on Nineteenth and Twentieth Century Protestant Theology,* edited by Carl E Braaten (London: SCM Press, 1967), 142.
11. See W and M Pauck, *Paul Tillich: His Life and Thought,* Vol 1 (New York: Harper & Row, 1976), chapter 2.

12. W and M Pauck, *Paul Tillich,* Vol 1, 43.
13. W and M Pauck, *Paul Tillich,* Vol 1, 49.
14. W and M Pauck, *Paul Tillich,* Vol 1, 52. 'He became wildly addicted to life's vivid joys while on leave.'
15. W and M Pauck, *Paul Tillich,* Vol 1, 59.
16. P Tillich, *Perspectives,* 127.
17. W and M Pauck, *Paul Tillich,* 76.
18. W and M Pauck, *Paul Tillich,* 223.
19. W and M Pauck, *Paul Tillich,* 224.
20. H Jonas, *The Gnostic Religion,* second edition (Boston: Beacon Press, 1963), 322.
21. A declaration to this effect is made in the opening sentences of the Preface of *Systematic Theology,* Vol 1 (London: James Nisbet, 1953), ix.
22. P Tillich, *Systematic Theology,* Vol 2, 29.
23. P Tillich, *Systematic Theology,* Vol 2, 29.
24. P Tillich, *Systematic Theology,* Vol 2, 27.
25. P Tillich, *Systematic Theology,* Vol 2, 27f.
26. P Tillich, *Systematic Theology,* Vol 2, 31.
27. P Tillich, *Systematic Theology,* Vol 2, 52.
28. P Tillich, *Systematic Theology,* Vol 2, 53ff.
29. P Tillich, *Systematic Theology,* Vol 2, 56ff.
30. P Tillich, *Systematic Theology,* Vol 2, 57.
31. P Tillich, *Systematic Theology,* Vol 2, 59ff.
32. P Tillich, *Systematic Theology,* Vol 2, 60.
33. P Tillich, *Systematic Theology,* Vol 2, 71.
34. P Tillich, *Systematic Theology,* Vol 2, 77.
35. M Heidegger distinguishes 'anxiety in the face of death' from 'fear in the face of one's own demise'. See *Being and Time* (London: SCM Press, 1962), 295.
36. M Heidegger, *Being and Time,* 296–311.
37. P Tillich, *Systematic Theology,* Vol 2, 77.
38. P Tillich, *Systematic Theology,* Vol 2, 79 and 80 respectively.
39. P Tillich, *The Courage to Be* (London: Collins, Fontana edition, 1962).
40. P Tillich, *The Courage to Be,* 60.
41. P Tillich, *Systematic Theology,* Vol 2, 86.
42. P Tillich, *The Courage to Be,* 37.
43. P Tillich, *The Courage to Be,* 136.
44. P Tillich, *The Courage to Be,* 137.
45. P Tillich, *The Courage to Be,* 152.
46. P Tillich, *The Courage to Be,* 152.
47. 'Courage participates in the self-affirmation of being-itself, it participates in the power of being which prevails against non-being. He who receives this power in an act of mystical or personal or absolute faith is aware of

the source of his courage to be.' P Tillich, *The Courage to Be*, 175.

48. P Tillich, *Ultimate Concern*, 1f.

49. The qualification is that Heidegger is clearly an ontologist, rather than an essentialist.

50. N Melchert notes that many commentators classify Heidegger as an existentialist, but adds that 'the analysis of existence is not what he is mainly interested in. Heidegger is, from first to last, intent on deciphering the meaning of Being.' *The Great Conversation: A Historical Introduction to Philosophy*, fourth edition. (Boston: McGraw-Hill, 2002), 660.

51. J Macquarrie describes Heidegger's philosophy as 'definitely religious and mystical in tone, though it would not coincide with any of the commonly accepted forms of Christianity.' *Twentieth-Century Religious Thought* (London: SCM Press, 1963), 352.

52. P Tillich, *Systematic Theology*, Vol 1, 181, 207.

53. See P Tillich, *Systematic Theology*, Vol 1, 183.

54. J Macquarrie, *Twentieth-Century Religious Thought*, 353, 366.

55. Harry Wardlaw tells the fascinating story of a conversation between Tillich and himself around 1960, in which he asked Tillich where ontology really fitted into his system. Tillich's answer was along the lines that ontology did not have a very significant place in the system at all! It is to be hoped that this conversation will be set down in writing some time.

56. P Tillich, *Ultimate Concern*, 56.

57. P Tillich, *Perspectives*, 142f.

58. Macquarrie's judgement does not stand alone. See JH Randall, 'The Ontology of Paul Tillich', in CW Kegley and RW Bretall (editors), *The Theology of Paul Tillich*, 132–61.

59. P Tillich, *Systematic Theology*, Vol 1, 23.

60. P Tillich, *Systematic Theology*, Vol 1, 225.

61. P Tillich, *Systematic Theology*, Vol 1, 224. The transition from essence to existence and the symbol of 'the fall' is the subject of chapter 13 of the system (Vol 2).

62. P Tillich, *Systematic Theology*, Vol 2, 38.

63. P Tillich, *My Search for Absolutes* (New York: Simon and Schuster, 1967), 26. Arguably, the more formative influence here is Romanticism, with its view that the finite and the infinite are not only antithetically related but also belong together; the finite is *in* the infinite, and vice versa.

64. P Tillich, *Perspectives*, 150. He has in mind Schelling's so-called 'Negative Philosophy'.

65. P Tillich, *Systematic Theology*, Vol 2, 28.

66. P Tillich, *The Courage to Be*, 146.

67. P Tillich, *The Courage to Be*, 147.

68. P Tillich, *The Courage to Be,* 147.
69. See in particular chapters 18 and 21.
70. P Tillich, *Systematic Theology,* Vol 2, 136.
71. P Tillich, *The Shaking of the Foundations* (London: Penguin Books, 1949), *The New Being* (London: SCM Press, 1956), and *The Eternal Now* (London: SCM Press, 1963).
72. P Tillich, *The Eternal Now,* 159.
73. P Tillich, *Systematic Theology,* Vol 2, 137.
74. P Tillich, *The New Being,* 24.
75. P Tillich, *The New Being,* 104.

16

BEHOLD AN ISRAELITE IN WHOM THERE IS NO GUILE

CATHERINE E LAUFER

The title of this chapter is the quote with which I began a speech to Harry Wardlaw on his retirement from the United Faculty of Theology (UFT). I was honoured to be the student asked to speak of Harry as lecturer on that occasion; I am honoured once again to have the same privilege, this time in print.

Harry was an extraordinary teacher. He was passionate about conveying the thought of philosophers and theologians of the past to his current students in ways they could understand. To this end, Harry would use anything he could lay his hands on. This went far beyond the teacher's traditional tools of books or blackboard or even, in later years, computer or palm organiser. Harry used all these, with enthusiasm. But anything at all could become a teacher's aid in Harry's hands. I well remember him placing crockery around the floor as he explained Kant's understanding of 'the thing perceived' and 'the thing in itself'.

Passion and enthusiasm were the hallmarks of Harry's teaching. His energy seemed to have no limits as he moved around his office, seizing on a book for a pertinent quote, or sitting at his desk and simultaneously lecturing, keying notes into his organiser and making a pot of tea.

As a student, one generally came to know of Harry well before one met him, for 'Harry Wardlaw stories' were legion at the UFT. They were stories of an absent-minded professor so absorbed in thought – his own or others' – that he was liable to forget where he was or what he was doing. Yet within these tales one could also sense a genuinely humble man who was uninterested in self promotion or personal image. These characteristics were evident when one finally met the subject of the stories and discovered that Harry was the chief teller of these tales on himself.

I recall the day on which I hobbled into class and pulled up an extra chair on which to rest my recently sprained ankle. 'You'd better keep an eye on me', said Harry. 'The last time a student did that, I nearly broke his leg again!' Harry went on to describe how, some years earlier, a student with a broken leg had also propped his injured limb on a chair. Harry was teaching Kant and needed a prop of another kind. He looked around, seized what seemed to him to be a spare chair, and the student's plaster-encased leg hit the floor.

This anecdote could give the impression of a scholar unaware of the needs of ordinary people; nothing could be further from the truth. Harry was pastor as well as teacher for his students. Often, the two roles overlapped, to the great benefit and encouragement of students, as I can attest. I was struggling with Kierkegaard. No, not struggling: that implies some comprehension. I was floundering, lost in language that may as well have been the original Danish for all I understood of it. To find a written work impenetrable was a new and very disconcerting experience for me. I sought reassurance from fellow students and from staff in my own (Anglican) tradition. The response was less than helpful, along the lines, 'It's about time you found something difficult!' Then I went to Harry, ready to withdraw from the class. He was generous with his time, and more than sympathetic. He treated me as an equal: 'Kierkegaard's purpose was to challenge theologians like you and me. We find him difficult because we're meant to.' Harry was not too proud to admit to his own struggles. He told me that, although he had done his doctorate on Kierkegaard, he too had found him incomprehensible at first. Harry helped me to understand at least part of what I was reading, but he did more: he gave me back my self confidence, my self esteem as a growing theologian. That is worth more than grasping Kierkegaard.

Harry's great love was nineteenth century theology. He introduced the class on this subject to the UFT and made it his own. He knew the philosophers and theologians of that era intimately. Their writings were his friends; he could as easily grab the right book for the apposite quote from his shelves as he could identify a friend in a crowd. Yet Harry was always modest, willing to learn from his students as well as teach them. I saw Harry become as excited as a small child with a new toy when someone wrote an essay about an obscure nineteenth century cleric whom Harry had not met before. When I suggested that CS Lewis may have written a children's story as a response to Feuerbach,[1] Harry noted down the details and, I am sure, not only read but enjoyed it.

The United Faculty of Theology was a pioneer in ecumenical theological education. At the time of its inception in 1969, it was almost unthinkable for reformed, Anglican and Roman Catholic ordination candidates to study together, and to be taught by faculty from all three traditions. When this 'experiment' began, many doubted its wisdom; the faculty involved were taking a brave and radical step in ecumenical relations. Such a challenge was meat and drink for Harry Wardlaw, however. Ecumenism in its best sense was second nature to Harry: he encouraged his students to discuss their denominational differences openly, honestly and with mutual respect. In this, as in so much else, Harry was an ideal role model. He knew where he himself came from, and loved and valued his heritage. He expected others to feel the same way about their own traditions, and he delighted in hearing them expounded. Of course, as a true scholar, Harry questioned what he did not understand and challenged anything he disagreed with, yet always with genuine respect for both the person and the tradition concerned.

Harry's respect for other people and his commitment to the Gospel met in his concern for society as a whole. Harry's class on nineteenth century thought included discussions of Marx and socialism, in which he reminisced about his involvement in the Student Christian Movement in his youth. Harry was clear about his own position as a Christian and a minister of the Gospel; his clarity and conviction allowed him to be equally confident about Christian obligations to the poor and the marginalised. Here too, Harry was both teacher and exemplar.

I was privileged to be in Harry's final nineteenth century theology class. I learnt a great deal, not all of it theology, although the theology was always at the forefront of our discussions. I had come into that class with only a rudimentary understanding of the place of history in systematic theology. Harry taught me to look for and treasure the roots of current theology, not just in Scripture and the Church Fathers, but in the more recent past. From Harry, I learnt to trace the origins of an idea, walking back through time like a detective, seeking the fingerprints of a concept. I am now writing my doctoral thesis in the field of the history of doctrine.

I recently spent the better part of a year researching nineteenth century writings on the four last things, including an investigation of the life and work of FD Maurice (1805–72). As I read, I was often reminded of Harry Wardlaw. Maurice was primarily an educator, but one concerned with students as whole persons, not just embodied intellects. In the mid-nineteenth century, tertiary education was restricted to the sons of the wealthy. This was an affront to Maurice's Christian faith. He believed it was the church's duty to provide education for all, as such education would improve social conditions. Maurice was one of the founders of the Christian Socialist movement. One of its goals was to provide education for the working class. Maurice himself was instrumental in founding Queen's College, London, a college for women, and the Working Men's College, both of which still exist. Maurice's concern for working men and women was grounded in his faith: Christ has redeemed all humanity, therefore all aspects of human life should reflect redemption.[2]

Maurice cared for his students as whole persons. When he was dismissed from his chair, many of his current and former students wrote letters commending, not just his scholarship and teaching, but also his preaching and pastoral care. Similar letters came from the law students of Lincoln's Inn whom he served as chaplain. Maurice was far more than a professor of theology: he was an advocate for equal educational opportunities for all, a pastor, a preacher, a true educator, and above all a profoundly Christian man. It should not be surprising, then, that Maurice reminds me of Harry Wardlaw, for in all these ways, Harry is a Maurician. The late Revd Dr Richard McKinney, one of Harry's Anglican colleagues at the UFT, once described him as, 'The most Christian man I have ever known'.[3]

A *Festschrift* is both a tribute and a gift. As such, it includes descriptions of the scholar who is its subject and also essays which are dedicated to the scholar concerned. My tribute is written above. As my gift to Harry, I append a short piece on Frederick Denison Maurice, one of those nineteenth century theologians so appreciated by Harry, and one whose writing and biography remind me of Harry Wardlaw.

FD Maurice and the State of Eternity

The seventeenth to nineteenth centuries saw a gradual shift in theological discourse about the afterlife. The change was slow; it was influenced, even driven, by new scientific discoveries, by enlightenment philosophy, by the development of historical criticism, and most especially, by the changes in people's understanding of justice. This last, a profound sociological change, demanded a corresponding review of Christian concepts of justice, especially in regards to eternal reward and punishment. Traditional notions of hell were criticised on the grounds that it is inherently unjust to condemn a person to infinite punishment for a finite crime. No matter how wicked an individual is, no matter how wide reaching that person's evil becomes, it still remains finite. How, then, can infinite punishment be just? One possible way out of the difficulty is to deny hell altogether. This would mean that evil remains unpunished, which is also unjust for it would allow the wicked to continue perpetrating evil and gives no justice to their victims. It would seem, therefore, that if one believes in an afterlife at all (and many rejected any such belief on the grounds that the concept of hell is unjust), then the wicked must be punished, but not for ever. The punishment must be finite, just as their evil deeds were finite. When punishment ends, the wicked can either be annihilated, or else admitted to heaven. Either way, there is a problem: Scripture refers to both heaven and hell with the same adjective, 'eternal'. If hell is not endless, then neither is heaven. Thus, the Church found herself forced to defend an endless hell, at least publicly, and as a result many left the traditional churches for sects.

Then, in the mid-nineteenth century, an eminent theologian argued that the concept of 'eternity' has nothing to do with time, and all hell broke loose.

England's cause célèbre of the century began in 1853 with the publication of a book of essays. Its author was Frederick Denison Maurice, a man who held two separate professorships at King's

College, London, was chair of the Committee of Education at its sister college, Queen's, was chaplain to the law students of Lincoln's Inn, and who regularly preached to the 'working men' of London. It is unfortunate that Maurice, a social reformer, educator and advocate for women as well as a prominent theologian, is best remembered for losing his professorship over a theological argument characterised by the lack of perspicacity of his adversaries.

> I regard Frederick Denison Maurice as having been by far the most important and significant personality – the most potent and pervasive influence – in the religious life and thought of England during the past century. A very great man, he owes his pre-eminent importance and influence to his marvellous – I am inclined to say unique – combination of prophetic witness, systematic thought, and creative endeavour, unified and inspired by the ceaseless aspiration and pursuit of a wholly consecrated and truly saintly life. His influence has been far-reaching and is still abundantly fruitful in every realm of Christian concern.[4]

While J Scott Lidgett's 1934 tribute may somewhat overstate the case, it is true that Maurice's work has had far reaching consequences. Theologians such as FJA Hort, BF Westcott and Michael Ramsey acknowledged their debt to him.[5] Queen's College and The Working Men's College, both of which he founded, remain today as monuments to his efforts to provide education to all irrespective of gender or social status. His desire for social reform, epitomised in the founding of the Christian Socialist movement, was based in an incarnational theology which would not be out of place in the late twentieth century.

> Maurice defined reality itself in terms of the Christ of the creeds through whom all things were made...this meant for Maurice a closing of the gap between creation and redemption, a definition of the human person through Christ and not through Adam, and priority for the Incarnation over the fall.[6]

It is not surprising, then, that there is a branch of Anglican scholarship devoted to 'Maurician studies'; Hort even coined a

Greek word, Maurikizien, to describe those whose theology followed Maurice's.[7] Yet, despite the breadth of Maurice's contribution, limitations of space mean that this essayist must reluctantly focus solely on that one infamous episode in his life.

Maurice was an Anglican priest. However, amongst his diverse contacts were many Unitarians, not surprisingly as his father was a Unitarian minister. His book, *Theological Essays*, was addressed to Unitarians, with the overall purpose of responding to Unitarian disagreements with orthodox Christian faith. One such was that Christianity maintains that there will be no end to the punishment of the wicked, a belief which, on the face of it, contradicts the love and justice of God. Maurice's final essay, 'Eternal Life and Eternal Death', was intended as a response to this criticism. It was this essay which became the impetus for the debate which cost Maurice his professorship. A second edition of the book followed, in which there was a new preface and the last essay was considerably expanded.[8]

In 'Eternal Life and Eternal Death', Maurice makes two fundamental points: Christ saves us from *sin* not *hell*, and 'eternal' is a descriptor, not of time, but of God.[9] Maurice was misunderstood by many to be arguing that hell is not everlasting; however, to associate duration with hell or, for that matter, heaven, was absurd from Maurice's viewpoint. He argued cogently that 'eternal' refers, first and foremost, to God. Its use to describe one's state in the afterlife is subservient to this primary usage. If, when we describe God as 'eternal', we mean that God has no beginning or end, then that meaning must also apply to 'eternal life' and 'eternal punishment'. However, this is a nonsense: both certainly have a beginning, if not an end. Therefore, whatever 'eternal' means, it is not 'without beginning or end'.

> Shall we say that Eternal means, in reference to God, 'without beginning or end'? . . . . [Is] man's bliss or misery . . . without beginning as well as without end? 'Oh no! you must leave out the beginning. That of course has nothing to do with this case.' Who told you so? . . . . How dare you fix the standard by which the signification of a word is to be judged, and reject that very standard a moment after?[10]

Eternity has nothing to do with time or with endlessness. Rather, it refers to the being and nature of God. Eternal life is sharing in that nature; eternal death is being excluded from it.

> The eternal life is the righteousness, and truth, and love of God which are manifested in Christ Jesus; manifested to men that they may be partakers of them . . . This is held out as the eternal blessedness of those who seek God and love Him. . . eternal punishment is the punishment of being without the knowledge of God, who is love . . . If it is right, if it is a duty, to say that Eternity in relation to God has nothing to do with time or duration, are we not bound to say that also in reference to life or to punishment, it has nothing to do with time or duration?[11]

While this understanding of eternity is, essentially, what the ensuing furore was about, Maurice actually took his argument further. If 'eternal punishment' means being without the knowledge of God, then it means remaining in sin. To be without God means to be separate from all the attributes of God, and to be left with only the attributes of sin. This is hell, where people 'are in eternal misery, because they are still covetous, proud, loveless'.[12] This immersion in sin is what Christ saves us from, not the punishment that the term 'hell' is commonly taken to mean. To suggest that humankind should fear divine punishment rather than sin is the very distortion of the Gospel which Martin Luther sought to redress.

> But dilettanti popes . . . were establishing, once for all, the doctrine that the thing men have to dread is punishment and not sin, and that the greatest reward which the highest power in the Church can hold out is deliverance from punishment, not deliverance from sin. Let us understand it well; it was against this doctrine that Luther protested in his theses at Wittenberg.[13]

Maurice was well aware that the common understanding of 'eternal' is 'endless', and fully expected to be accused of 'departing from the simple intelligible meaning'[14] of the word when he insisted otherwise. He also seems to have realised that his insistence that 'eternal punishment' does not mean 'endless punishment' would lead many to assume that he was a universalist, and to condemn him on that ground alone. However, that was certainly not

Maurice's position.

> I ask no one to pronounce, for I dare not pronounce myself,
> what are the possibilities of resistance in a human will to the
> loving will of God. There are times when they seem to me
> – thinking of myself more than of others – almost infinite.
> But I know that there is something which must be infinite. I
> am obliged to believe in an abyss of love which is deeper than
> the abyss of death: I dare not lose faith in that love. I sink
> into death, eternal death, if I do. I must feel that this love is
> compassing the universe. More about it I cannot know. But
> God knows. I leave myself and all to Him.[15]

The publication of the *Essays* led to complaints being made to the
principal of King's College, RW Jelf, along the lines that someone
holding Maurice's views was not a fit and proper person to hold the
position of Professor of Theology, a position which involved teaching
theology to future clergy of the Church of England. Jelf wrote a 'please
explain' letter to Maurice, reproduced here in full.

> My Dear Professor Maurice,
> My attention has been called by high authority to the
> conclusion of the last of your Theological Essays lately
> published.
> It is alleged that you therein deny the eternity of future
> punishments.
> I have read the Essay with attention, and confess that
> it appears to me to bear that interpretation; at least the
> impression it gives seems to throw an atmosphere of doubt
> on the simple meaning of the word eternal, and to convey a
> general notion of ultimate salvation for all.
> I am of course most anxious to ascertain your real meaning.
> Yours very truly,
> RW Jelf[16]

As the letter indicates, the extended row which followed hinged
on the ability of the members of King's College Council to think of
'eternity' without simultaneously thinking of time. This most of the
Council members, including Jelf himself, were unable to do. One of
the minority was WE Gladstone, then Chancellor of the Exchequer
and, by virtue of this position, a member of the College Council. On

his copy of *Theological Essays*, available in the Library which is his memorial,[17] Gladstone wrote: 'In the main, a noble document. WEG Sept. 76'.[18] The same Library contains four documents related to the King's College Council's protracted deliberations on the question of whether Maurice should continue to hold his professorship. They include the correspondence between Jelf and Maurice, with Jelf's footnotes, and a description of the Council's proceedings by a London barrister.[19]

The letters highlight both the intensity of the emotions involved and the depth of Jelf's incomprehension of Maurice's argument, that eternity has to do with God and God's goodness. Eternal life is knowing God; eternal death or punishment is not to know God, to be in rebellion against him. Maurice states repeatedly that the term 'eternity' must be divorced entirely from any notion of time or duration. This may or may not include the word 'everlasting': if it means lasting endlessly, then it has nothing to do with eternity; if it is the Saxon word for the Greek eon and Latin eternal then it is a legitimate translation. Jelf seems incapable of understanding these fine distinctions: he keeps insisting that, in saying that 'eternal' does not mean 'everlasting', Maurice is denying the doctrine of eternal punishment and is a universalist; this despite the fact that Maurice repudiates universalism in all its forms at every opportunity. Maurice simply did not see that he could limit the goodness of God, or comment upon what limits there are on rebellion, if any.

Maurice explains his position clearly in Letter III, written to an unnamed friend some three years before the controversy.[20] He sent a copy to Jelf and asked to have included in the correspondence given to the College Council. (The passage referred to is Matt. 25:31–46, the parable of the sheep and the goats, often used in nineteenth century debates on the afterlife.)

> ...I am bound to believe that the eternal life into which the righteous go is that knowledge of God which is eternal life; I am bound to suppose that the eternal punishment into which those on the left hand go, is the loss of that eternal life – what is elsewhere called 'eternal death'

Now if you ask me on the strength of this passage, or of any similar one, to dogmatize on the duration of future punishment, I feel obliged to say, 'I cannot do so...I cannot apply the idea of time to the word eternal.'..But do I then dogmatize on the other side? Do I fall back on the theory of Universal Restitution...No...I know that we may struggle with the Light, that we may choose death. But I know also, that Love does overcome this rebellion...I am sure that Christ's death proves that death, hell, hatred, are not so strong as their opposites. How can I reconcile these contradictory discoveries? I cannot...But I can trust in Him, who has reconciled the world to Himself. I can leave all in His hands. I dare not fix any limits to the power of His love. I cannot tell what are the limits to the power of a rebel will...I am taught to expect 'a restitution of all things...' I am sure that restored order will be carried out by the full triumph of God's loving will. How that should take place while any rebellious will remains in the universe I cannot tell...I wish to trust God absolutely, and not to trust in any conclusion of my own understanding at all.[21]

This would seem to be clear enough – but not to Jelf who, with other members of the Council, genuinely did not comprehend Maurice's argument on the meaning of eternity. They seem to have felt that Maurice was being deliberately obscure in order to hide universalist beliefs. But Maurice was no universalist. I do not think he can be held to any specific position, either that some remain in rebellion or that ultimately God's love prevails. He says he does not know because Scripture has not revealed it, a thoroughly Christian position.

The correspondence between Jelf and Maurice was presented to a meeting of College Council on 27 October 1853, which a number of members were unable to attend. Three resolutions were passed: that Maurice's views were of a 'dangerous tendency, and calculated to unsettle the minds of the theological students'; that Maurice's continued employment as a Professor of the College would be 'seriously detrimental to its usefulness'; that the Council 'laments' the need for the former resolutions, and commends Maurice for the way he has discharged his duties and his loyalty to the College. Gladstone moved that the Chair of the Council, the Bishop of London, should appoint competent theologians to examine Maurice's theology but this was lost.[22]

On 7 November, Maurice wrote to the Council in response. He took the view that, in its resolutions, Council was effectively condemning him as having 'departed from the orthodox faith'. Given that Maurice was a priest of the Church of England, such a charge was extremely serious and could result in him losing his livelihood. Maurice therefore asked the Council to 'declare what Article of our faith condemns my teaching'. This request was ignored when Council met again on 11 November. Instead, it was resolved to declare both Maurice's chairs vacant.[23]

While the majority of Council agreed to this resolution, there was quite some dissent. Three members who had been absent from the earlier meeting objected to the haste of the proceedings, and especially to ascribing 'the brand of "dangerous doctrines" – a very strong censure indeed – to Mr. Maurice'.[24] After his dismissal, various testimonials and letters in support of Maurice were sent to the Council from such diverse groups as the Committee of Education of Queen's College; Lincoln's Inn (that is, the city lawyers to whom Maurice was, and remained, chaplain); former students; the 'working men' of London; a group of clergy.[25]

Some postscripts to the drama are worth noting. Although dismissed by King's College London, Cambridge gave Maurice a chair in 1866 which he held until his death in 1872. Maurice was never brought before any body of the Church of England to defend his views, and he now has a place in the Church of England's Calendar of Lesser Feasts (1 April)! Almost eighty years after Maurice's dismissal, and some sixty years after his death, King's College instituted the FD Maurice Lectures, an annual series of three lectures which continue to the present day. The first lectures were presented in 1933 by the Dean Inge of St Paul's, London. So perhaps, in the case of Maurice versus King's College, Maurice has had the last word after all.

Throughout the dispute, Maurice continued to maintain his orthodoxy, and to affirm his belief in the Creeds and the Thirty-Nine Articles. Despite his rejection of universalism, he went so far as to point out that even this extreme position is not contrary to the formularies of the Church of England. While the last of the Forty-Two Articles of 1553 condemned universalism, this

Article was not included in the final form of the Thirty-Nine Articles.

> ...careful considerate omission...made by persons who probably were strong in the belief that the punishment of wicked men is endless, but who did not dare to enforce that opinion upon others; above all, who did not dare to say that the words Eternal and Everlasting, which they knew had such a profound and sacred meaning in reference to God Himself, and to the revelation of his Son, could be shrivelled and contracted into this signification.[26]

It is a fascinating exercise to read these documents with the eyes of one who has grown up post Einstein, who quite naturally sees time as part of the created universe. Post Einstein, it is self evident that eternity has no more to do with time than heaven does with space.[27] To the twenty-first century mind, Maurice appears to be stating the obvious. But in 1853, Maurice saw with faith and sound theological reasoning the mathematical insight which Einstein himself described, some seventy years later, as 'thinking God's thoughts after him'. In this light, Maurice's perspicacity and contribution to theology must be assessed as both significant and well ahead of its time.

Bibliography

Correspondence Between the Principal of King's College, London, and the Rev Professor Maurice. Privately printed, 1853.

King's College and Mr Maurice. No 1 The Facts, by a Barrister of Lincoln's Inn (London: D Nutt, 1854).

Brose, OJ *Frederick Denison Maurice: Rebellious Conformist* (Cleveland: Ohio University Press, 1971).

Jelf, RW *Grounds for Laying Before the Council of King's College, London, Certain Statements Contained in a Recent Publication, Entitled, 'Theological Essays, by the Rev FD Maurice, MA, Professor of Divinity in King's College'* (Oxford and London: John Henry Parker & Rivington, 1853).

Lewis, CS *The Silver Chair* (Harmondsworth: Penguin, 1953).

Maurice, F *The Life of Frederick Denison Maurice Chiefly Told in his Own Letters*. (2 vols) (fourth edition) (London: Macmillan, 1885).

Maurice, FD *Answer to the Prinicpal's Final Letter* (London: Wilson and Ogilvy).

Maurice, FD *Theological Essays* (second edition) (Cambridge: Macmillan, 1853).

Ramsey, AM *FD Maurice and the Conflicts of Modern Theology* (Cambridge: Cambridge University Press, 1951).

Scott Lidgett, J *The Victorian Transformation of Theology* (London: Epworth, 1934).

Vidler, AR *FD Maurice and Company* (London: SCM Press, 1966).

Wolf, WJ, Booty, JE, and Thomas, OC (editors). *The Spirit of Anglicanism* (Edinburgh: T&T Clark, 1979).

Wood, HG *Frederick Denison Maurice* (Cambridge: Cambridge University Press, 1950).

End Notes

1. *The Silver Chair* (Harmondsworth: Penguin, 1953). Lewis has a character argue that, if Christianity is just a mental game (as Feuerbach maintained), then this game, or dream, is far better than so-called reality (148–157). Lewis then 'includes' Feuerbach in the story as a fire-river from which beasts called salamanders speak, 'wonderfully clever with their tongues: very witty and eloquent' (175–76).

2. WJ Wolf, 'Frederick Denison Maurice', in WJ Wold, JE Booty, and OC Thomas (editors), *The Spirit of Anglicanism* (Edinburgh: T&T Clark, 1979), 63–66.

3. Personal communication to the author, circa 1993.

4. J Scott Lidgett, *The Victorian Transformation of Theology* (London: Epworth, 1934), 13.

5. AR Vidler, *FD Maurice and Company* (London: SCM Press, 1966), 7, 259ff and 8 respectively.

6. WJ Wolf, 'Frederick Denison Maurice', 74, in WJ Wolf, JE Booty and OC Thomas (editors), *The Spirit of Anglicanism* (Edinburgh: T&T Clark, 1979), 49–98.

7. Vidler, *Maurice and Company*, 7. For Maurician Studies, aside from books already mentioned, the reader is referred to OJ Brose, *Frederick*

Denison Maurice: Rebellious Conformist (Cleveland: Ohio University Press, 1971); F Higham, *Frederick Denison Maurice* (London: SCM Press, 1947); F Maurice, *The Life of Frederick Denison Maurice Chiefly Told in his Own Letters* (2 vols, fourth edition)(London: Macmillan, 1885); AM Ramsey, *FD Maurice and the Conflicts of Modern Theology* (Cambridge: Cambridge University Press, 1951); HG Wood, *Frederick Denison Maurice* (Cambridge: Cambridge University Press, 1950), amongst numerous others.

8. FD Maurice, *Theological Essays* (second edition) (Cambridge: Macmillan, 1853). This edition is the one which is now most readily available.
9. *Theological Essays*, 442-78.
10. *Theological Essays*, 447-48.
11. *Theological Essays*, 449-50.
12. *Theological Essays*, 455.
13. *Theological Essays*, 456-57.
14. *Theological Essays*, 465.
15. *Theological Essays*, 476.
16. RW Jelf, *Grounds for Laying Before the Council of King's College, London, Certain Statements Contained in a Recent Publication, Entitled, 'Theological Essays, by the Rev FD Maurice, MA, Professor of Divinity in King's College'* (Oxford and London: John Henry Parker & Rivington, 1853), 1.
17. St Deiniol's Library, Hawarden, North Wales. Gladstone was a bibliophile and donated some 40,000 volumes from his private collection to what he hoped would become a residential library dedicated to 'divine learning'. The library was completed after Gladstone died, as his national memorial. Gladstone's donation forms the basis of its now 250,000 volume collection.
18. *Theological Essays*, xi, in the copy in St Deiniol's Library.
19. The four documents are bound together in a book with 'Case of Mr Maurice' printed on the spine. The first two documents it contains are, respectively, *Correspondence Between the Principal of King's College, London, and the Rev Professor Maurice* (60 pages), and then a thirty page letter from Maurice to Jelf entitled, *Answer to the Prinicpal's Final Letter*. The third document is Jelf's *Grounds for Laying Before the Council* (cited above). This contains a brief preface and the correspondence of the first document, with footnotes by Jelf. Finally, there is *King's College and Mr Maurice. No 1 The Facts, by a Barrister of Lincoln's Inn* (London: D Nutt, 1854). On the title page of this last, anonymous, document, underneath the words 'Barrister of Lincoln's Inn', is written, in pencil, 'JM Ludlow'. The handwriting is definitely not Gladstone's. It is the professional opinion of Ms Patsy Williams, Librarian of St Deiniol's Library, that these four documents were

Williams, Librarian of St Deiniol's Library, that these four documents were bound together by a librarian who may well have been the attributor of the last document.

20. The recipient has been identified as FJA Hort by various Maurician scholars.

21. *Correspondence Between the Principal of King's College, London, and the Rev Professor Maurice*, 5–8.

22. *King's College and Mr Maurice. No 1. The Facts*, 25–26.

23. *King's College and Mr Maurice. No 1. The Facts*, 30–33.

24. *King's College and Mr Maurice. No 1. The Facts*, 32.

25. *King's College and Mr Maurice. No 1. The Facts*, 36–49.

26. *Theological Essays*, 461.

27. Some weeks after writing this paragraph I discovered the following statement in Florence Higham's *Frederick Denison Maurice*, 85: 'To the theologians of to-day nourished on Von Hügel, to scientists accustomed to Einstein's theories, Maurice's conception of time and eternity are without any startling novelty.' Higham takes this no farther, however.

17

ALBERT CAMUS AND THE PROBLEM OF EVIL

JOHN COWBURN

Philosophers have different ideas about what constitutes philosophy and many of them do not accept people like Albert Camus as philosophers. However, a non-religious search for the meaning of life and for how to cope with life's major problems is a search for wisdom if anything is and it is what most people think of as philosophy. Many thinkers in the past have put their search for wisdom into words by writing novels like Voltaire's *Candide* and plays like Plato's *Dialogues* as well as essays of various kinds and Camus was in their company. At one time he wanted to republish the novel *The Outsider*, the play *Caligula* and the book *The Myth of Sisyphus* together in one volume, to be called *The Absurd*, because they dealt in different ways with the same problem. I intend to show how in three novels Camus wrestled with what we call the problem of evil, and how his thought developed through the years during which he wrote them. To a considerable extent, his thoughts were affected by his experience and it was his practice not to deal directly with his own life-situations but, as I hope to show, to deal with them in his novels by means of analogies.

1. *The outsider:* death[1]

Camus was born in November 1913 into an extremely poor family in Algiers and grew up there. Though he was baptised he grew up without religion and later said that he had not lost the Christian faith but had never had it. He went to a good school. When he was sixteen he showed signs of tuberculosis but he seems not to have been greatly affected by it then and he went on to university and on graduation worked in journalism and the theatre. Later his tuberculosis got worse and when he was twenty-three he went into a sanitorium for a month. On the one hand, he recovered sufficiently to be able to live a fairly normal life; on the other hand, the disease was always there and he suffered some serious attacks, so that his grasp on life was never secure.

He had begun to write a novel before the attack which sent him to the sanatorium and when he came out he put it aside and began to write *The Outsider*. This is the story of Mersault, a working-class French Algerian young man who, without feeling emotion, attends his mother's funeral and who, after his return, takes his girlfriend, Marie, to a comic film. Later he shoots an Arab on a beach. He is put in gaol and in due course is put on trial and condemned to death. I believe that Marie stands for a girl whom Camus knew but did not love, the gaol stands for the sanatorium, the lawyers stand for the doctors, Mersault hearing himself being discussed by others as if he was not there (95) stands for Camus hearing the medical staff discussing his case, the chaplain stands for the chaplain at the sanatorium, and (to come to the point) the situation of the man who is waiting to be sentenced to death or not is that of Camus waiting to be told whether he is going to die or not. There are differences between Mersault and Camus: Mersault never went to university, Camus's mother was still alive when he wrote the book, and he survived the sanatorium whereas at the end of the novel Mersault is going to be executed. More significantly, a man gets tuberculosis through no action of his own whereas to be tried for murder, and to plead guilty as Mersault does, a man must kill somebody. Camus endeavoured to solve this problem by describing the killing in such a way that it seems to be not so much something that Mersault does as something that happens to him. The most he feels about his deed is a kind of annoyance (69) and it is with no sense of guilt that he faces the probability of his own death, which of course is precisely what Camus was going through.

In the novel, Mersault is strangely indifferent to whether he will be executed or not. This angers his lawyer (65) and puzzles everyone else. One can, I think, picture other patients in the sanatorium pleading with the doctors and nurses for good news about their prospects, and Camus puzzling everyone greatly by seeming to be indifferent to life or death. In the novel, Mersault is emotional on only one occasion, which is when the chaplain, whom he had three times refused to see, comes to him with the aim of preparing him to meet God. Mersault quite fiercely refuses to talk about God, saying of the chaplain that 'none of his certainties was worth one strand of a woman's hair'. I assume that that is what Camus thought and felt at that time about religion.

If there is a message which this book communicates it is that 'nothing, nothing matters' (115). Early in the book, when Marie asks him to marry her, he replies that it really doesn't matter (44). When he is sentenced to death he says to himself that 'everybody knows that life isn't worth living' and that 'given that you've got to die (sooner or later), it obviously doesn't matter how or when' (109). His whole life, he thinks, has been 'absurd' (115); by absurdity he means meaningless or (to use a Biblical term) vanity. Instead of finding this a cause for despair, Mersault finds it liberating and he opens his heart to the 'benign indifference' of the universe (117). With this belief in his mind and heart, Mersault as he awaits his execution says to himself that he is happy (117). These are almost the last words of the book.

Soon after he came out of the sanitorium in 1937 Camus met Francine Faure. They came to be seriously in love and they were married in 1940. In Francine, Camus discovered someone who mattered, as the girl he had not been in love with had not mattered, and life, indeed the world, became important. On the one hand, Camus wrote *The Outsider* during this time but he came to believe that, as he said in a letter, 'absurd thought is not possible'. By 1942, when it was published, he regarded the book as the expression of a world-view which was no longer his own. It is, I believe, unfortunate that many students read *The Outsider* at school, find it liberating, and go no further in their reading of Camus – I hope to goodness that, like Camus, they go further in their search for value.

2. *The plague:* suffering

In 1940 France was invaded by Nazi Germany and after a short fight surrendered. From then until 1944, when it was liberated, France was directly or indirectly subject to the Nazis.

After their marriage in 1940 Camus and his wife lived in Algeria, where she was a teacher. Because of his tuberculosis, in July 1942 they went to France and in October she returned to Algeria to resume her work there. When he became well enough to leave the sanitorium, he could not join her but went to Paris, where openly he worked for a publisher and in secret he wrote for the underground paper *Combat*.

From his experience of life in France under Nazi-German occupation came the novel *The Plague*. On the surface, so to speak, it is about an outbreak of bubonic plague in the city of Oran in Algeria and how different people deal with it. As was obvious to everyone in France who read the book when it was published in 1947, however, at a deeper level it was about Nazism in France. In it, when the first cases of plague appear and are reported to the government, the authorities are at first unwilling to inform the people and take any action: they behave as the French authorities did when they saw that France was going to be invaded and occupied. In the novel, when the authorities can no longer conceal the truth, they put up notices all over the city; these reminded Parisian readers of the notices that were posted in the city when the Germans took over there. In the novel, people are not allowed to leave Oran for fear of spreading the plague; correspondingly, no French person was allowed to leave France. In the novel, the wife of the central figure, Dr Rieux, is away when the outbreak occurs and he and she are kept apart; in an analogous way, Camus and his wife were kept apart during the occupation. In the novel, a big camp for plague victims is set up in a sportsground (195); in Paris almost all Jews were suddenly arrested at the same time and taken to a bicycle-riding stadium, the Vélodrome d'hiver, where they were imprisoned before being taken to concentration camps. In the novel, some men actually take advantage of the plague to make money and they are actually pleased about it (118, 132); they correspond to the black-market profiteers who made money in France. In the novel, when the plague ends some profiteers are punished (249), as in France after the liberation collaborators and profiteers were punished. These are only some of the correspondences.

While *The Outsider* is about death, it is not about suffering.

In his first few months in gaol Mersault experiences 'a tormenting desire for a woman' and he feels sick because he cannot smoke (76), but he gets used to his situation and it is no longer a punishment for him (77). It seems that he does not even expect his execution to be painful. If I am right, this is because tuberculosis is not a painful disease. In The Plague, people who catch the plague suffer excruciating pain, and there are horrifying descriptions of it. This, of course, corresponds to the fact that the Gestapo regularly tortured prisoners to make them talk, and anyone who, like Camus, was active in the resistance lived in constant dread not so much of death as of frightful pain.

In many ways, in The Plague Camus showed that he had advanced far beyond where he was when he thought like Mersault, the central character in The Outsider. As I said, he had faced not just death but pain. Also, in The Outsider, Mersault loves no one; Rieux, the central figure in The Plague, loves his absent wife dearly. Moreover, whereas Mersault is a solitary figure, in The Plague one is conscious of a suffering city and of how those who fight the plague work together: Camus himself said that 'if there is an evolution from The Outsider to The Plague it is in the direction of solidarity and participation'. Furthermore, whereas before his arrest Mersault's only purpose in life is to enjoy himself, the main characters in The Plague are dedicated workers for others.

An even greater evolution in Camus's thinking is shown by the change in his attitude towards religion. In The Outsider the chaplain is treated with impatience and contempt, but in the resistance Camus had met a Catholic priest, the Dominican Père Bruckberger, and he had been impressed by him. In the novel Bruckberger is represented by the Jesuit Père Paneloux. Paneloux's basic belief is that the plague is God's will and must be accepted. When things are going well for us, he says, it is easy for us to believe in God and his goodness; at times like those of the plague it is difficult, but we must still believe, and he himself experiences agony as he sees suffering which he believes he must accept. On the one hand, Rieux does not agree with Paneloux but says, in words which express Camus's attitude and which have become famous, 'Until my dying day I shall refuse to love a scheme of things in which children are put to torture' (178); on the other hand, Rieux accepts Paneloux as an ally or co-worker and Camus presents him as an admirable person. After the liberation, he accepted an invitation to address the students in the Dominican house of studies, which Mersault would have regarded as a waste of time.

There is a highly significant way in which bubonic plague is not acceptable as an analogue of the Nazi occupation of France: the plague does not have intelligence, whereas the Nazis did. The novel is mainly about a group of people who fight the plague, in the sense that at some risk to themselves they do all they can to lessen the suffering which it causes; they correspond to people in the resistance in France, but they do not have to be secretive as people in the resistance did. Moreover, Nazism involved moral evil, or evil properly so called, as a plague does not, so that by choosing to use this analogy Camus has avoided facing the problem of moral evil, which was so evident in Nazism.

I must say that if Camus accurately expressed Père Bruckberger's ideas, Bruckberger had read the standard Dominican authors on divine providence (and Paneloux had read Jesuit authors, who said the same things). I for one am convinced, however, that theirs is not a true Christian solution to the problem of suffering and I agree with the rejection of it by Rieux-Camus.

3. *The fall*: moral evil

When France was liberated in 1944, it became known that Camus had written for *Combat* and he quickly became an important commentator in newspapers and a public figure. *The Plague*, when it appeared in 1947, was a huge sucess. In a particular way he was respected as a man of integrity, who could be relied on to tell the truth as he saw it. In short, his public persona was that of a secular saint.

His private life, however, was far from saintly. In 1944, before his wife joined him in Paris, Camus met the actress Maria Casarès, who is known to filmgoers for her performances as the mime's wife in

Les enfants du paradis and as death in Cocteau's *Orphée*. They fell in love, very seriously, and became lovers. They separated when Francine came to Paris and became pregnant, but in 1948 they became lovers again and they continued to be lovers until he died in 1960. He had sexual relationships with other women: one, which began in 1946 and lasted all his life, was with an American, Patricia Blake; another, which began in 1956, was with the actress Elizabeth Sellers (a Frenchwoman who had married an Englishman, hence the name); and another was with a Danish girl known as Mi, whom he met in 1957. All these were going on simultaneously and there were many brief affairs. Casarès seems to have accepted his behaviour but Francine suffered atrociously, experiencing breakdowns, having electric-shock therapy for depression, and even attempting suicide.

In 1955–56 Carnus quickly wrote a short novel, *The Fall*, in which he tried to come to terms with his situation without changing his behaviour. When you begin to read this novel you find that you are in a sleazy bar in Amsterdam and a man whose name is Jean-Baptiste Clamence has come to you and begun to talk about himself. His monologue is the entire novel and to anyone who knows about Camus it quickly becomes obvious that in a sense he is Camus: Herbert Lottman says that Clamence is a 'self-mocking self-portrait' of Camus and Olivier Todd says that 'Camus revealed himself in the character of Jean-Baptiste Clamence'.

He was once, he says, a lawyer in Paris (Camus, it is true, was not a lawyer). Like Camus, he was always polite and he was a good dancer. Unlike Camus, he was unmarried, but like him he had numerous affairs with women: 'I always succeeded with women' (43), he says, and like Camus he often had several affairs going on at the same time. Clamence says, 'I used to specialise in noble causes' (17), he was greatly admired, as was Camus, and he was pleased with himself (17).

Then, says Clamence, he crossed a bridge one night and walked past a girl who was standing there. When he reached the other side he heard a splash and a cry and realised that the girl had thrown herself into the water; but he simply kept going (52). Everyone who knew Camus well knew that the girl stood for

Francine, and that Clamence walking away from the drowning girl stood for Camus refusing to be faithful to her. There we have the problem. What is Clamence's solution, which is to say, what was Camus's?

If I understand the novel rightly, Clamence has decided that all are guilty. We condemn ourselves, he says, and we must condemn all others: 'It is essential to begin by extending the condemnation to all, without distinction'. He says: 'No excuses ever, for anyone, that's my principle at the outset' (96). Yes, he says, I am guilty, but so is everyone else, and therefore 'I am happy – I am happy, I tell you, I won't let you think I'm not happy, I'm happy unto death' (105). It is true that Clamence has radically changed his way of living: he no longer practices law in Paris but buttonholes people in Amsterdam. But his philosophy does not require this of him, and Camus did not retire to a bar.

I criticised *The Plague* on the ground that, while it dealt with suffering as *The Outsider* had not done, it simply did not face the problem of moral evil. In *The Fall* Camus at last faced this problem. Frankly, in spite of what he says through Clamence, I do not believe that he could have been happy with the solution. In my opinion, in *The Fall* Camus presented an utterly false solution to the problem of moral evil, which was his problem. It cannot be solved without repentance on the one hand and forgiveness on the other. Forgiveness is impossible (not difficult, not even extremely difficult, but simply impossible) without repentance and, if ongoing behaviour is involved, not only past actions, a change of life or what we used to call 'a firm purpose of amendment' is necessary.

Certainly Francine was not happy with Camus's solution. She read the novel when it was published in May 1956, if not before, and in June they separated. Camus moved out. There was no divorce and the general public was not told of the break-up. Maria Casarès became his usual partner but when in 1957 Camus was awarded the Nobel Prize Francine, not Casarès. went with him to Stockholm and for the occasion they played the roles of husband and wife.

On 4 January 1960 Michel Gallimard, the publisher, was driving his wife, her daughter and Camus from the south of

France to Paris when he ran off the road and hit a tree. Michel Gallimard died five days later, the two women survived, but Camus, who was forty-six, sitting beside the driver, was killed instantly.

End Notes

1. All pages references to this and the other novels are to the Penguin editions.
2. I have not seen this interpretation of *The Outsider* in any book, but almost everyone interprets *The Plague* and *The Fall* in a similar way, so I feel confident when I propose a similar interpretation of *The Outsider*.
3. Herbert Lottman, *Albert Camus, A Biography* (Garden City: Doubleday, 1979), 562.
4. Olivier Todd, *Albert Camus: A Life* (London: Chatto & Windus, 1997), 342. Francine Camus was still alive when Lottman wrote his book and out of consideration for her he was restrained in what he said about her; by the time Todd's book was published she had died and more could be told.

18

AN INQUIRY INTO MAN'S HISTORICAL UNDERSTANDING

GERARD WILLIAMS

It is recorded in the *Shebet Jehuda* of Ibn Verga that in the year 1142 a Muslim army led by the King Ibn Tamurt appeared in southern Spain. It was decreed that those persons who refused to adopt Islam would have their property confiscated, and would be put to death. Thereupon the Jews and Christians implored the King for mercy. The king replied:

> It is precisely because I have compassion on you that I command you to become Muslim; for I desire to save you from eternal punishment.

Those who were gathered before the palace exhorted:

> Our salvation depends on our observance of the divine Law. You are the master of our bodies and of our property, but our souls will be judged by the King who gave them us, and to whom they will return. Whatever be our future fate, you, O King, will not be responsible for it.

The King answered:

> I do not require to argue with you, for I know you will argue according to your religion. It is my absolute will, that you either adopt my religion or be put to death.

The difference between the record of historical events and their interpretation, understood by those bearing witness to such events, and those who over generations have an account of these events passed down to them, is properly speaking a *theoretical inquiry*. It belongs to the *technical* understanding of the historical discipline. When, if on occasion, moved to inquire *philosophically* concerning man's *historical* understanding, the teachers of this understanding consider it necessary to treat such events in history *figuratively*, it is maintained that this is the only correct method, and must be adhered to. For it is the only strictly objective historical method belonging to philosophy. Indeed, if the religious conflict here outlined arises due to an irreducible paradox which is rooted 'outside' of our historical understanding, then this view is correct. Such conflicts cannot teach us of the phenomena of history as such; for bloody conflict cannot properly be said to arise *because* of historical process. Rather, such conflicts are repeated by subsequent generations and are therefore called 'historical'. They are perpetuated *through* history. It is argued by these teachers of history that it is only through an awareness of this perpetuation that man becomes conscious of his own historicity, and becomes truly conscious of himself. In becoming conscious of himself, he becomes radically independent of all previously held and ultimately a-historical notions, such as divine providence or divine Law. The teaching maintains that in the moment when man becomes consciousness of himself as self-consciousness, he becomes free. Therewith we have a word which demonstrates in speech that which we mean in our utterances about history: *freedom*. In order to understand the 'essence' of history an exceptional man will be moved solely by the action of his intellect to pursue as if through a progressive series of illuminations, the source of the first articulation of this word, the founding action. He will grasp this inaugural movement by exercising his mind freely, unfettered and dynamically, and he will literally possess *it*, decisively, in concrete action. One might be tempted to believe that this is the inevitable fate of man: his natural end and the consummation of his desires in the highest accomplishment imaginable. Such a man will never come to speculate as to whether 'it is good to help one's friends and to harm one's enemies', though he will never doubt that this distinction is necessary to political life. He will understand this distinction exclusively in the light of his historical understanding, that is, retrospectively; he will be swift in his decisions, severe in judgement and ruthless in pursuing his science. He will ensure thereby that others adopt his science, as *freedom*, the object of his science (and it is most assuredly a political science), is naturally desirable, and thus desirable to all men. Surely, he will never doubt that this science has anything of the conviction of a religious belief. This is because the individual who professes such beliefs understands himself as 'outside' or 'beyond' the historical and concrete circumstances of his time. He is beyond all his contemporaries, as he alone understands himself objectively. He alone knows when it is morally condonable to recite untruths.

Such persons (whoever they may be) are correct in drawing these lessons from their teachings. It is correct to assert that religion can teach us nothing of man's historical understanding directly. Furthermore, if religion is ultimately reducible to historical process, because the individual in the course of history is 'liberated' from religion, it is assumed that conflicts of religious belief cannot be understood historically on their own terms; this is because they cannot be understood *literally* as religious, upon 'religious' grounds. A close investigation of the religion based upon this historicist contention uncovers a phenomenon whose founding gesture unfolds historically from an anthropological centre, and whose consequence is an anthropomorphic and subjectively constituted conception of reality. Commensurate with this opinion is the notion that what the religious man believes to be objective and beyond him, the historicist 'knows' to be subjective and beneath him. However, even if the object of this essay were to be a *literal* account of man's nature and beliefs, after a fashion quite contrary to the opinion occasionally voiced by thinkers of history, could these conflicts possibly teach us our nature directly? One doubts it. Indeed, it must be conceded that these conflicts arise according to different inherited beliefs, which contain perchance partial truths of man's nature, and must of *necessity* be treated 'figuratively' from the point of view of an historical consciousness. A sober measure of circumspection is required when judging the purported truth of any accounting presuming to be complete or exhaustive, entailing a claim to absolute necessity. Thus, in consideration of the aforementioned position, we are compelled with reasonable speech to assert that our nature necessarily precedes, or is *literally* prior to, our questioning into its being. Just as the birth of our thoughts, to treat of the foregoing idea metaphorically, is always preceded by the seemingly inscrutable and eternal idea of this birth. Therefore, a philosophical inquiry into man's historical understanding can at best be peripheral, and certainly cannot claim to be exhaustive. Yet the prescient arguments of contemporary thought perpetually announce the exhaustibility of this art of inquiry. The teachers of historicist thought who announce this prospect proclaim that philosophy cannot be considered an eternal possibility available to man; conversely man reaches out towards excellence and self-knowledge born forth in this eternal possibility. It is prudent to discuss the *historicist understanding*, the *object* of the present inquiry, within the context of this disagreement. This understanding dictates that the context of this disagreement is not *philosophical* as it concerns 'philosophy' itself, or put succinctly the *context* of this disagreement is the true object of the inquiry, and is thus *philosophical*.

Historical thought understands itself as an existential account of 'man', whose nature is the product of conscious activity or intellection. The occasionalism which forms the premise of historicism contends that all opinions and beliefs of mankind, as well as their objects, of which these opinions and beliefs are 'conceptions', are the constructions of man, products of his decision-making. 'Intellection' is itself an activity generative of the nature of man through concrete action. This process gives rise to various historical accounts of man's nature, which man then recites to himself over time, in a fashion conditioning which is formative of his beliefs concerning his ultimate end or goal. These accounts are, in turn, made in the last instance compelling by the positive circumstances or constraints, ideological, scientific, geographical, and so forth, of a particular era, under which the originator of these accounts lived and suffered. These constraints mould and form meaning. According to this position, all accounts of man's nature, which point beyond these constraints, are as nothing. All political ends are historically and positively given. They are pragmatic. Democracy, one political construction of man, and the opinions concerning these constructions including those which call themselves 'democratic', consist in the protection of bare and vital desires: the necessities of preservation. These can then be 'legitimated' through an historical perpetuation in defence of the 'natural right' to the freedoms they presuppose. Man's will is sovereign. A liar of supreme cunning once claimed that 'democracy in perpetually leaving itself open to the possibility of its demise, necessitates its demise'. By which he intended to awaken the following suspicion: that as democratic freedoms leave open the possibility of electing a tyrant who *behaves* contrary to democratic ends in the interests of the 'defence' of these democratic-*freedoms*, a democratic society, being the forerunner of a tyrannical regime, *ought* to be willing to 'elect' a tyrant in its defence. Our liar's assumption: man is a pathetic creature, moved by fear, and not be love. Democracy is ultimately tyrannical, as citizens of democracy have been willing in the past to elect a tyrant in order to protect vital interests of self-preservation and self-perpetuation. This is an ignoble lie, as it considers liberal democracy according to the standard set by what is; the vulgarity of fact, and not what *ought* to be, the nobility of truth. Thereupon the lie makes mortal enemies of desire and reason. For where the human will and human reason struggle for rule, and one comes slavishly to follow the other, a science *of* politics makes tyrants out of statesmen. Where this is the case, man is cast into his freedom, as his nature is understood as essentially historical, and his political dialogue as historically constituted. Man is an animal, which may act 'politically' in the interest of its preservation. Thus, the 'freedoms' of historicist thought consist, necessarily, in the negation of man's 'natural self' through the dissolution of philosophy in man's historical understanding. This notion assumes that man's conception of nature is the derivative notion of historical development, the result of free, unconstrained, though formative action. On this basis historicist thought comes to understand itself as self-perpetuating, and thus self-determinate. It is the only truly historically independent and necessary account of man. The origin of this self-determining occasionalism is disclosed in opposition to historical perpetuation. Thus, historical thought consists in the transformation of its own premise in the form of a historically transcendent act of absolute conviction. Furthermore, 'historicist thought' leads necessarily to this conclusion as it concedes, in the *first* instance, that it is *finally* generated through a historically transcendent process of intellection. It leads necessarily to a political theology, which is contrary to liberal democracy, which it cunningly professed to defend. Historicism, in understanding the 'political things' as historically constituted, embodies a radical break with the historical continuity of the dialogue concerning the nature of 'political things'. Historicism then gestures toward the founding of a 'new world' in the name of freedom, independent of hitherto inherited notions, which otherwise become foundational in the further development of those conceptions of political life which remained in the continuity with change and its revolution. Ultimately the revolutionary and independent character of this 'founding freedom' searches out a new set of historically grounded and opposing constraints. These it overthrows, turning eventually against those very forms of democratic political understanding which concede the various relativities of men's opinions, and with which it once was closely related.

Historicism was a critical and rational instrument, a science of reason, and thereby less than the love of wisdom; it was bitter and determined in its pragmatic goal in service to suffering men and women. This goal occasioned the genesis of the philosophical inquiry into man's historical understanding. It was used at different times, in different ways and in different guises, to defend the common good against fundamentalism. Fundamentalisms were schooled in blind commitment to a conception of religious law, which enshrined in the last instance the waywardness of human will. The very existence of this rational instrument suggested that *the rationality* which brought forth nature and the nature-world, and could be seen operating in nature, could also be attributed to the rationality which governed the heavens and was revealed in scripture. It was a human will, and not a divine will that was the true legislator of this rational premise. The highest justification of this thinking, which at one time was persuasive, was shown to be unfounded. He that dared to stand at its head professing a legislative power, binding its coercive necessity, could rightfully be decapitated, as he would consistently act against the freedoms granted to the human will by human reason. However, the legalistic premise set by this law was not itself unfounded, as the law was rational. To disclose the meaning of this legalistic premise in relation to the law's rationality, which is the *inference* from reason to law, necessitated an historical inquiry into the meaning of the rational grounds themselves, as this could not be disclosed by the rational instrument whose sure foundation they established. 'Reason' is a word which, while able to manifest this law of necessity to all men, or so it was thought, can give no account of the necessity which it occasions, in that it *commands*. Rationality or the grounds of this legalistic precedent, were intelligible only through recourse to the historical understanding, to the history of such commands. The ground of man's self-understanding is historical, as the commands of reason are made intelligible only through recourse to history. Thus, man's nature is impermanent and changeable. Change is the result of movement, of action. Historicist thought understands thought and action *synonymously*. The malleability of man's nature is believed to be a literal truth, demonstrable by pointing to 'empirical' events. It transfers the 'meaning' of the rational law across into the sphere of determinate substantial causes.

The relation between historicist thought and this *science* of reason is twofold. It consists, on the one hand, in construing religion as an anthropomorphic attribution of human reason to nature; and, on the other hand, as the reduction of the science of reason to natural science and its positive account of evident *physical* laws. The science of reason distinguishes between symbolic or emblematic uses of language and analogy. It is a critique. It precedes in this distinction-making, in pursuing a uniform account of the rational order in nature and the things belonging to this order, that are not arbitrary, subject to condition or transformation. The science of reason must act in according with its objects, which it infers to be rational. This inference forms the objective of its critique. Its rational object becomes 'symbolic' as it comes to be identified with an instrumental use *of* reason. Rational investigation becomes emblematic of the order which it traces out in the course of scientific progress, which leads to the development and maturation of historical understanding. As comparison analogical or even literal figurations of words resort to, then reason has no 'face'. It has no representation to the public, which can hold it accountable for its judgements. The 'groundwork' of this scientific rationality casts the mould for the substrate of a political rationality. This 'groundwork' contrives to support the idea that as theology corresponds to a scientific rationality, it attributes reason to its ground or 'object' in the form of anthropomorphic utterances, which are finally incompatible with the working out of what this rational anthropomorphism finally dictates, where it formerly forbade 'images' or 'pictorial depictions', that reason itself is an anthropomorphism. This anthropomorphism is derived from a form of 'symbolism', which functions to produce the semblance of reason, its emblematic function in language as it creates 'language' in its 'image'. Thus, as natural science is to 'historicist thought' so is theology to this 'symbolism'. Scientific progress and historical progress come to be spoken of in the same vein. To speak rationally is therefore to use language in a manner 'emblematic' of this scientific rationality. Speaking of a 'scientific rationality' is antecedent to speaking of natural science as the founder of natural laws recognised publicly as physical laws. Natural science then provides the 'models' of physical laws. These are considered actually to govern the behaviour of natural, or rather physical, phenomena: and this behaviour is meaningful exclusively on the basis of this 'signification', in the emblematic correspondence with its 'physics'. This 'physics' is anthropologically generated in accordance with the 'symbolism', in the transference of the meaning of this 'symbolism' into new forms, through its historical recapitulation and refinement as a body of knowledge. (This symbolism consists ultimately in all frameworks of meaning, cultural, scientific, political and religious, which might be deemed in harmony with this modern spirit, the object of anthropology.) It is a reductive method directed towards the disclosure of the necessary axiomatic foundation and systematisation of the symbolic form and its correlate anthropological 'physics'.[1] In transferring this symbolism across from the representation of physical phenomena in natural science, to the activity of physical operations performed on the basis of, or as mechanisms of, this symbolism, the true basis of 'physical laws' comes to be seen as residing in the theoretical framework of this symbolism. It inheres thereby in the historicist's account of intellection.

The term 'intellection' refers, thereby, to the functioning activity of the symbolism, which is also a simultaneously 'self-inherent' and 'self-constitutive' activity, whereby it draws out this 'self-instantiating' 'form' according to the relationship between 'itself' and its intellectual 'object'. The corresponding expression in language has the form of an analogy: being is to consciousness as being is to itself. The likeness of 'the perception of' an object to the 'likening' activity of intellection consists in the determination of the 'symbol' in which the intelligibility of the 'perception' coheres and is made 'meaningful'. These symbolisms are conditioned according to a temporal relation. As 'intellection' relates temporal existence to itself synthetically, it abstracts the 'form', the 'imaging' of this activity analytically. The 'subjective' intellection, the 'perception of' relates itself to itself as 'objective intellect'. The logic of the symbolism consists in the demonstration of the abstraction of the logical form. 'Nature' is made intelligible and thereby categorically evident or manifest through this symbolism. It is given a 'shape' or 'form' and is thus given a logic that is traced out along the lines of the prescient symbolism. In speaking of a 'movement' in history, intrinsically the same 'symbol' and not a 'like symbol' is used, or rather 'functions', as when speaking of the 'motion of a body through space'. Both phenomena proceed from 'experience', and are thus ultimately reducible to the process of intellection. Thus, in transferring the *functioning* of the 'symbolism' to the generation of its emblematic representation in language, it translates an emblematic signification of language into its functional object.

It appears that in pursuing a philosophical account of man's historical understanding, the inquiry moves progressively away from man's natural understanding. It does so via a progressive series of abstractions. In like manner the teachers of historicism assert that at the point in history when historical thought fully emerges and understands itself as contemporaneous with historical progress, nature is comprehensively divined, or revealed. The 'nature of man' is an expression which *signifies* 'the historical essence of man'. Thus the 'nature' of man is defined as the radical independence from nature; man is the being who is radically and absolutely free. The question of man's nature is unnatural, as it constrains him. It constrains him, as this question is rational and nature is irrational. To be free is to transgress the natural law. According to this position 'nature' represents the yoke of meaning which man bears throughout history, which he must cast off if he is to see himself clearly in his unalloyed 'essence'. In the last instance, the root of man's natural understanding is history, *not* nature. Thus, nature appears natural, in its own guise, definitely. Ingratiating wonder, through which the love of wisdom is kindled in the soul of man, is forever extinguished as the position from which the historicist views nature is 'beyond' that which was hitherto considered natural to man. In this 'revelation' of nature's innermost recess, in nature's appearance in its natural 'state', man awaits a 'transference', a carrying across of its meaning into a new form of intelligibility. Therefore, at the centre of historicist thought is a transformation of man's understanding of nature, which awaits a transformation of 'nature' itself. When nature appears natural, mankind has entered upon a new era.

To declare that mankind has entered a new era is not new. Allan Bloom places as the forefront of his introduction to Alexander Kojève's *Lectures on the Phenomenology of Spirit* the following excerpt from Hegel's final speech of his Jena lectures of 1806:

> Gentlemen! We find ourselves in an important epoch, in a fermentation, in which Spirit has made a leap forward, has gone beyond its previous concrete form and acquired a new one. The whole mass of ideas and concepts that have been current until now, the very bonds of the World are dissolving and collapsing into to themselves like a vision in a dream. A new emergence of Spirit is at hand; philosophy must hail its appearance and recognise it, while others resisting impotently, adhere to the past, and the majority unconsciously constitute the matter in which it makes its appearance. But philosophy, in recognising it as what is eternal, must pay homage to it.[2]

This except is placed before Kojève's teaching of the Phenomenology as Hegel still understands himself, in the last instance, to be a philosopher. He is not an 'historicist' by what he says, rather by the action of his argument. However, in its last consequence he demonstrates himself to be a 'historicist', for in welcoming this 'new emergence of spirit' freely and uncritically, Hegel hails the future consequence of his thought's action, and not its argument. This means that the qualitative difference demarcated by the transformation of man's understanding of nature is always evident *in* the transformation. However, the historicist argument articulates this qualitative difference as the outcome of the historical understanding, that is, as the recognition of the transformative power brought forward by historicist thought as this revolutionary aspect. Neither the word 'dialectic' nor the word 'logic' is appropriate here. Similarly, there were those individuals who believed that motion itself is the coming to be and passing away of phenomena in nature, while others believed that motion itself is subject to coming to be and passing away. The latter opinion implicates the former conception of nature, being both logical and dialectical, but the former doesn't imply the latter necessarily, being only logical. The difference between the argument and its action is however discernible only in reference to the latter position. Nevertheless, this does not necessarily implicate a philosophical 'aspect', purely revolutionary in its conception of nature; this aspect is necessarily counterposed by a conservative possibility. A purely revolutionary 'aspect' would necessitate the synthesis of the argument and its action; the word 'synthesis' would then be used polemically in a conception of nature, whereby it ceases to be dialectical and simply contradictory. The opinion: that paradox is unmistakably a form of contradiction, is deeply seductive, for it admits of an anti-philosophical possibility, because it cannot admit of its self as an opinion. To say that mankind has entered a new era, borne out in a purely 'revolutionary' understanding of nature, is to assert that man has transcended history. Man has transcended all meaningful conceptions of nature demonstrable retrospectively, attributed to all previous and all possibly epochal transformations of the philosophical 'aspect'. In paying homage to this purely revolutionary 'aspect', man pays homage to that which is eternal. Such a claim shares the character of myth. For myths, such as the transmigration of souls, to name but one illustrative instance, attempt to *instantiate* – proffering *in* image, though actually describing; and through perennial illustration hope to honour the 'eternal'. It is not so much an attack on philosophy that is here originated, but a seduction of the 'philosophic-spirit' by science. In pursuing this purely revolutionary aspect the philosopher turns-back from his ascent towards the blinding sun. He turns aside from the Socratic question and seeks to describe the sun directly. He believes himself to have apprehended the sun, the ground and the rationality of grounds comprehensively, as he envisions the sun as the analogy of the Socratic question. He seeks its nature in myth. Thus begins the philosopher's 'down-going' from philosophy. All men must, following his lead, adopt this 'prophetic freedom', or stand in dangerous opposition to history and its consequences. Philosophy is at its end, because historicist thought shows us the possibility of the concrete working-out of the problems of philosophy. These are perpetuated *through* history. Philosophy prepares the 'carrying over of its self' into historical thinking as philosophy represents the concrete working-out and solution of the inquiry into the conception of nature, *natural* to man. Philosophy, which once thought to gesture beyond itself, now gestures towards the historical understanding of man's conception of nature as its culmination. Philosophy conceives of itself as mythology. This historicist gestures towards himself and says 'I'.

History represents the comprehensive account of man's conception of nature. The oscillation inherent in turning from one man to another in conversation is understood as itself dialectical, rather than the frame within which the art of dialectic is learnt and exercised. On the contrary, this dialectical oscillation is indicative of man's self-orientated gestures, toward the flux of nature embodied by his will. It is no longer necessary to turn from one person to another, asking after an account of man's nature: rather, we collectively turn toward *the* 'individual', we direct our inquiry inwardly. The 'being' upon which all men hope to found their opinions, and upon which their opinions have hitherto come aground, conforms to this gesture; it is 'willed' into being. The term 'nature' is then a purely *formal* expression through which 'existence' is made progressively intelligible, categorically evident or manifest, through this historically uniform oscillation towards an ultimate unity or basis. The founding mover, the genesis of this restless and violent action, is man's naked existential action. Thus, in attempting to render the word 'man', thereby his nature and the meaning of the name referring to this being intelligible, a 'thought' is called before the mind, in which, or through which, an impression is given, an 'image' of that which man is. In grasping this conception of the relation of thought and image, conjoined in a 'symbol' of man's nature, a feature of history of decisive significance emerges. One of the central differences between Platonic and Aristotelian philosophy consists in the following distinction. Of Plato it might be said, with words of our present historical context, that the nature of man is revealed *in* 'language', where for Aristotle it is revealed consistently *as* 'speech'. However, this distinction must be born out in the light of the historical development, in the light of the sequence of thoughts concerning this distinction. Thereby, it is clearly manifest that Hegel understands Plato according to the second distinction *exclusively*. According to this understanding which is rendered in the light of its historical development, 'freedom' comes to replace 'nature', signifying the era in which nature appears in its 'natural' guise.

On this transition to an era of thought, which comes to understand itself expressly according to this notion of 'freedom' Kojève makes in a 'footnote' to his criticisms of the Platonic-Christian notions of eternity the following observation:

> This conception [of a unique choice...fixed by the relation between the extra-temporal Eternity (or God) and the free agent] comes to light in the dogma of original sin: in Adam, man, in his entirety, freely decides once and for all. Here the act is in time; but it is not *related* to time; it is related to the eternal commandment of God, this God being outside of time. As for the freedom of man properly so called – it is the stumbling block of all theology, and particularly of Christian theology. Even if divine election is a cooperation with man (which is itself quite heretical), human acts are judged all at once by God, so that freedom remains a unique act, situated outside of time and related to Eternity.

The transition to 'historicist thought' consist in understanding 'freedom' as an historically transcendent act, which is at once a unique act of man, and which transcends nature. It transcends the natural law as it is not *of* nature. It is above the conception of nature belonging to nature. Freedom cannot remain a 'unique action' in time: rather it is the active temporal instantiation of historical existence. This transition to historicist thought represents the cultivation of man's 'existential' life, which is phenomenally constituted as freedom. However this freedom can emerge only in the 'unique act' of transcending the historical, or coming to see nature, in its 'natural state' as the outcome of historical transcendence. This represents the transition to a notion of freedom absolutely unique in history. Thus, according to Kojève, Adam must comprehend his nakedness, *before* comprehending the 'uniqueness of his act'. *Contrary* to Kojève man has a natural right to 'Liberty'. Man's nobility consists in this natural right. This natural right belongs to practical philosophy and not to theology, as the concrete explication of that which belongs to man. However it is something else again to declare that it is 'freedom' which determines the natural right to which man then lays claim, concurrently determining the quality of this temporal-existent being, which man is. For surely this is what one must mean when one says that Christianity conceives of 'freedom' as *a unique act, situated outside of time and related to eternity.* This is the corollary of historicist thought, as the historical end can only justify the means, from the point of view of history, which is really to say that historicism is unjustifiable from the point of view of ends as such. The teachers of historicism concede that to make sense *of* man is to comprehend him in and according to his beginnings: man's beginning is the origin of his self-understanding. Only then can one make sense of the ends of man, and seek justification for his doctrines. No position is conceivable independent of its 'origin', its 'inception'. To reiterate: to understand man is to understand him as the originator of the 'symbolism' through which he comes to understand himself. Man comes to understand himself through a philosophical inquiry into his historical understanding. This is to recognise him as the originator of a dialectic of history and nature, through which nature comes to 'appear' in its 'natural' state, and history becomes 'ideal'. In turning to the 'origin' of this 'self-understanding' a question presents itself. It does so immediately. The present inquiry circles about this question, as it is the central presupposition of a philosophical inquiry into man's historical understanding. It concerns the 'status' of the symbolism 'as' a symbolic order in its origin. It is in the direction of an investigation into the 'symbol's' appearance 'as' symbol that the inquiry now turns; turning away from the historical understanding, it subsequently concludes.

The questioning which seeks to understand the 'symbol' as 'symbol' seeks to understand the manner in which the 'symbol' appears *symbolic.* It must concern itself with the process of transference, through which the 'symbolism' conducts the generation of its emblematic representation in language, whereby it translates an emblematic signification of language into its functional symbolic object; such that nature can be 'parted' from its 'appearance'.

The demonstration of the symbolism 'as' a symbolic order consists in its functional aspect. However, its emblematic 'signification' of language can be traced back only to the 'demonstration' of this functional aspect, its abstraction in the form of a symbolic order of meaning, not, however to an account of its *active* functioning. Nature 'appears' natural. Man's conception of nature is thereby transformed, because his conception of nature *becomes* 'natural'. It is 'natural' as it is a conception of nature, which is seen to *belong* to nature and is no longer merely an 'apparent' conception of nature belonging to man. The activity of intellection is itself disclosed *as* the 'representation' of this activity of transformation. Hence, the 'status' of the symbolism cannot be identical with the emblematic system of its functioning, inasmuch as its 'functioning' is inherent in the generative activity of man's conception of nature. Therefore, the 'status' of the 'symbol' presupposes an investigation of the kind of 'being' the 'symbol' is, in and of itself. The status of the symbol necessitates an account of the manner in which the symbol appears *as* 'symbol', the manner in which it appears symbolically, emblematic of the 'language' which it expresses in its generative activity.

The process of transference, through which the 'symbolism' conducts this generation of its emblematic representation in language, consists in the 'anthropomorphic' dimension of the symbol's 'physics', in the anthropomorphic dimension of man's conception of nature. The anthropomorphism of this 'physics' can be discerned only in accordance with a distinction made between those objective realities of the symbolism, whose proper reality, or reality proper to itself, cannot finally be grasped in the process of its translation of 'language' into its emblematic determination as 'appearance'. The correlate expression: the 'appearance' of nature in its natural 'state', presupposes a 'parting' of nature from its 'appearance', where nature is at once discernible, distinct from its appearance and comes to 'appear' as nature herself. The condition of this translation is a relation, which from the point of view of its symbolic representation is irreducible. Its demonstration consists in the *demonstration of its abstraction*, and *not* in the activity of the generative relation.

It is this very tension in confronting a transcendence which resists and simultaneously discloses the ambiguities of the language through which this transcendence might be expressed, that determines the 'status' of the symbol in its symbolic appearance. This context of this ambiguity and inherent difficulties of this translation of the emblematic signification of language into a functional symbolic object corresponds to the inherent difficulties in giving an account of anthropomorphic language in its attributive aspect. The relation of anthropomorphic language to the realities which it grasps in figurative constructions is twofold: there are those realities which can be intimated *only* figuratively, and those which can otherwise be described 'one word' for 'one word', but are conceived of in images, or forms of human semblance. This distinction is experienced keenly by one considering the difference between 'making analogies' and 'drawing distinctions'. It involves the struggle of the human mind in conceiving the reality of a 'pure being', shapeless and in its shapelessness of an absolute sublimity, beyond the reality construed in the image-making language of a graven, created or wrought similitude. Thus, the central question concerning the 'symbolism' of the historicist divination of nature concerns the meaning of the negative expression 'shapelessness'; or rather, in this specific context, the notion of 'appearance', in grasping the reality of the symbol's logic. Indeed, if those realities in their supreme 'actuality', in the ambiguous coincidence of their particular natural 'state' and 'appearance' cannot be described in linguistic figurations, then the term 'anthropomorphism' is itself unreal, the unfounded semblance *of* the human mind.

Thus, the 'symbol' is not generative of the reality which it circumscribes. Rather, the symbol is itself 'real' through its functional circumscription of the 'real' in the form of its 'appearance'. This presupposes an ontology, irreducible to the 'symbol' and its symbolic order. The ontology of the symbolism is thus preceded by a 'conception' of the meaning of the 'symbol's' *appearance* as 'symbol', which presupposes the genealogy of the meaning of this 'appearance'. This genealogy might better be named 'the genealogy of the eidetic determinations of the symbol's character'. It would be incorrect to arouse the suspicion that this genealogy resides in the symbol's own history, rather than in its relation to its 'appearance' as a symbolic order *manifest* in and through history, becoming ever clearer from the point of view of ends, a-historical. The coincidence of the conception of the meaning of the 'symbol's appearance as 'symbol', with its eidetic determination consists in the unity of its analogical relation: being.

The symbol's *appearance* as such is thus concomitantly indicative of a real 'being' *independent* of analogical or symbolic relations. Thus, struggling to put into words an order independent of analogy or symbol, the most precise *word* of effective designation has a history as long as the transformations in its meaning, for to understand it as this designation presupposes its separateness from the history of its transformation. It occurred first to philosophy's founder: the 'idea'.

In the light of this consideration, it appears that the conception of the 'symbol' proper to itself as 'symbol' has been abandoned, which leads to the 'withdrawal' of the language *belonging* to the 'symbol'.[3] That which we name with the word 'idea' exceeds the possibility of 'symbolic' expression. For, the 'idea' is not the 'word' itself. Nor is the idea an effect of the arrangement of words. Rather the idea is that, which is 'named' by a word, which properly speaking is not a name, as it is not decipherable through recourse to a relation of that which it names, or by the substitution of words for words. Yet, we *conceive* of the 'idea' *in* language. The 'idea' is born into language. It is borne out in language, as it transforms the *meaning* of language, in that it changes the 'aspect' of language. For where a symbol can be gestured at in analogous expressions, just as a 'name' can be made intelligible in its relation to the 'object' of its nomination, the 'idea' escapes all 'image-making' of language. We lack the symbol for the 'idea'. Thus, to make an analogy between symbolism and nomination corresponds to a *possible disagreement* of reason; however an analogy between the 'symbol' and the 'idea' corresponds to an *impossible disagreement*. This disagreement has often appeared in history. Often it has been the agent of long and bloody conflict. It remains an agent of such conflict in those places where it has not been understood, by its perpetrators, as having its root in a disagreement of the latter variety, leading inevitably thus: towards *the* object of belief.

Those who teach of historicism may very well assert that when nature appears nature, then mankind has entered a new era. However, we must intuit this thought, allowing its shape to 'spring forth' in what appears a poetical expression of the language appropriate to it:

One, two thousand blossoming epoch have parted us, Beloved,
As is the flower's perishable beauty; by perpetual tides of
light, She thirsts insatiably, yet is barren of refreshing fruits. O
Beloved.

A question might occur to the student of literature: 'Why is the One in
the first strophe related as if grouping the "two thousand" in one-unit?'
or perhaps, 'Why does the poet directly address his "Beloved" for the
first time, vocatively, in the "second" repetition?' However, these are
observations of secondary importance. In pursuing a philosophical
inquiry into man's historical understanding, we approach the natural
limits of the language, which belongs to man, and thus the limits of
what is befitting to philosophical inquiry. We are bereft of the beauty
of that which exceeds our understanding, which we grasp fleetingly
in flashes, as if of gold from behind veils of silver. In this way we come
to understand that when uttering a word in philosophical dialogue,
its meaning should be present as a reality more sublime than the
things of sense, to those who listen, and in listening, understand
of what is being said. In this way, it may be said of an idea, that it,
itself, is *literal*. Thus, in the foregoing passage, within the context of
the whole inquiry particular consideration ought to be given to the
governing function of the preposition 'by'.

End Notes

1. Thus, the term 'anthropological physics' refers to the constitutive function
   of intellection and its symbolisms generative of the anthropological
   construction of a scientific framework, in correspondence with a
   'physics', which becomes formally justifiable against empirical norms.
   An anthropological physics consists in the emblematic constitution of
   the language through which the process of intellection at the centre of
   historicist thought becomes intelligible.
2. A Kojève, *Introduction to the Reading of Hegel: Lectures on the
   Phenomenology of Spirit* (Ithaca and London: Cornell University Press,
   1980).
3. When *everything* is possible, *nothing* is possible – when *everything* is
   changed, '*nothing*' is changed.

19

ENCOUNTERS WITH HOLY WISDOM

DUNCAN REID

Wisdom is radiant and unfading, and she is easily discerned by those who love her, and is found by those who seek her.
    She hastens to make herself known to those who desire her...She goes about seeking those worthy of her, and she graciously appears to them in their paths...[1]

Even after Faust we can imagine the nineteenth century going on, full of enthusiasm for the draining of marshes, but after Dostoyevsky's heroes, there is the unforeseeable twentieth century...[2]

The editors of a recent collection of essays urge us to read Dostoyevsky 'religiously'.[3] By this they mean we should explore the polyphonic religious and theological themes embedded in Dostoyevsky's story-telling. I had been fascinated by Dostoyevsky's story-telling before I met Harry Wardlaw, but it was definitely he who taught me to read Dostoyevsky – whom I remember describing as one of the theological giants of the nineteenth century – if not religiously, then certainly theologically. It is therefore a pleasure and a privilege to be able to contribute this small theological reading of Dostoyevsky to a volume in honour of a thinker who, like Dostoyevsky, has grappled with the crisis of modernity and sought to shed light on it by bringing it into encounter with Christ the Wisdom of God.

1. Dostoyevsky and Sophiology

The 'affinity of soul'[4] between Vladimir Solovyov, the main theorist of the Russian sophiological school, and the novelist Fyodor Dostoyevsky, has often been acknowledged. Soloyov's influence on Dostoyevsky has also been noted, especially with regard to the characterisation and ideas in *The Brothers Karamazov*. To my mind a more interesting question is that of Dostoyevsky's possible influence on Solovyov and his sophiology. We know that Solovyov's older brother Vsevolod acknowledged himself as having been profoundly influenced in his youth by Dostoyevsky: 'He was my teacher and my confessor; he had a very definite influence on me, and I ascribed deep influence to almost every word he uttered.'[5] It would be surprising if something of this influence had not been felt by the younger brother, who became a regular visitor to the Dostoyevsky household in the winter of 1873, and again after his return from abroad in 1877. There had been very little research done on the intellectual exchange between Dostoyevsky and Solovyov, one commentator[6] even dismissing the idea of it, until the recent book by Marina Kostalevsky.[7] An earlier book by Wladimir Szylkarski,[8] which was unfortunately not available to me, seems to have championed the idea of Solovyov's influence on Dostoyevky. A contemporary review by Bernhard Schultze[9] highlights the generic problems in attributing literary influence of one thinker on another, but argues that Dostoyevsky is more likely to have influenced Solovyov. Ellis Sandoz agrees, asserting that 'while Dostoyevsky is sure to have drawn from Solovyov, the principal current runs in the opposite direction.'[10] Sandoz then proceeds to illustrate his position, but (like Schultze) entirely with reference to *The Brothers Karamazov*, especially the three temptations in the Grand Inquisitor story. I have no argument with this, but want to point to what seems a far more obvious point of influence, the figure of Sophia, or Holy Wisdom, as she appears in various places in Dostoyevsky's work.

The figure of Sophia was already alive and well among the Russian people in the nineteenth century. Wisdom themes also surface in various nineteenth century Russian novelists, 'not least Dostoyevsky.'[11] Some obvious older sources of late nineteenth century Russian sophiology are to be found in the Byzantine veneration of Holy Wisdom, especially in Kiev. Bernhard Schultze[12] refers also to the Russian Sophia-icons, reflecting the influence of Cyril, apostle to the Slavs, back through Gregory of Nazianzen to the affirmation of Christ as the 'Wisdom of God' in 1 Corinthians 1:24. We could also mention the Greek icon of St Sophia, venerated as a historical martyr figure, along with her three daughters, Faith, Hope and Love, which in their Russian forms are themselves popular names. Drawing attention to the role of Holy Wisdom in mediaeval Western scholasticism, especially in Thomas Aquinas and Heinrich Seuse (the author of the *Horologium Sapientiae*), Schulze tantalisingly suggests the possibility of Dominican influence in Novgorod, where the most famous Russian Sophia-icon is to be found.[13] The Protestant mysticism of Jakob Boehme is another possible source.[14] However, as Paul Evdokimov points out, Solovyov's most important source is his own personal experience.[15] I want to suggest that among the factors that shaped this experience, alongside the Pauline identification of Wisdom with Christ and the cultural environment of Russian piety, were the Sophia figures in the passages from Dostoyevsky to be examined below. While it may be true that Dostoyevsky 'shared little of Soloviev's Sophiology',[16] the reason may simply be that it was left to Solovyov to develop and make explicit a theme that was already latent and implicit in Dostoyevsky. I want to suggest, in other words, that Dostoyevsky's Sophia-figures may have exercised an imaginative effect on at least two of Solovyov's three mystical encounters with Holy Wisdom, and so worked an influence on his developing sophiological thought.

While Solovyov works preeminently as a philosopher, he sees philosophy as ancillary to religion.[17] Though abstract thinking is useful and necessary, he unhesitatingly gives preeminence to what he calls 'intellectual intuition'. This he explains as 'grasping an idea in the fullness and integrity of its actual objective being, [by] uniting with it inwardly and essentially'.[18] Abstract or rational thinking he sees as a 'transitional state of mind' between sense perception and true intellectual intuition. Solovyov's epistemology privileges artistic creation from the outset as the highest form of knowing because, as he puts it, in artistic creation 'ideas and images ... *appear* to the mental vision all at once, in their inner wholeness'.[19] This will incline him to listen more carefully to artists, including novelists, than even to the 'recent German philosophy' he holds in such high esteem and whose Hegelian idiom he borrows. In a passage Dostoyevsky would undoubtedly approve, Solovyov connects this 'intellectual intuition' to what he calls 'organic thinking', as opposed to 'mechanical thinking'. Where mechanical thinking is the preserve of the 'so-called educated or enlightened people', organic thinking 'belongs, on the one hand, to the true philosophers, and on the other, to the masses of the people'.[20]

Anna Dostoyevskaya's reminiscences give a warm and intimate picture of Solovyov's early visits to the Dostoyevsky home,[21] as well as the developing, though not uncritical,[22] friendship in the late 1870s. In June 1878 Solovyov accompanied Dostoyevsky on his visit to the monastery at Optina, after the death of the Dostoyevskys' infant son Alyosha and ten years after the death, also in infancy, of their first daughter, Sofia.[23] The following year, on 30 October, Solovyov delivered a surprise birthday gift – a photographic reproduction of the Sistine Madonna.[24] Anna Dostoyevskaya and Fyodor Dostoyevsky attended Solovyov's public defence of his doctoral thesis in April 1880. Finally, Solovyov, 'conspicuous for his anguished face',[25] was one of the speakers at Dostoyevsky's funeral at the Alexander Nevsky Monastery in January 1881.

2. Two encounters with holy wisdom

The significance of the names of Dostoyevsky's characters in general,[26] and of the name Sophia – of which Sonia is the Russian diminutive – in particular, has been noted by various commentators.[27] I want to look at two encounters with Sophia characters who at significant points in their stories read from the gospels – two encounters, in fact, with Holy Wisdom. But these two women are not proclaimers of the word, at least not in any conventional sense.[28] Each of them is in a real sense also an embodiment of the Word, an incarnation of Holy Wisdom. They must at least be considered possible sources for Soloyov's theme that he developed in the *Lectures on Divine Humanity*, delivered between 1878 and 1881. Dostoyevsky attended[29] the first of this lecture series, on 26 January 1878, and continued to attend the series 'conscientiously'. In them, Solovyov was to develop his sophiological christology, and indeed they contained the germ of all of Solovyov's mature thought.[30] These lectures were to have a profound influence on the succeeding two generations of Russian intellectuals. But Dostoyevsky had already created the two Sophia-figures we will examine below.

Rodion Romanovich Raskolnikov, of *Crime and Punishment*,[31] and Stepan Tromifovich Verkhovensky, of *The Possessed*,[32] are both closed to the wisdom of self-awareness. Both are encountered by Holy Wisdom, not because they seek her, or because they can in any sense be called 'worthy of her', but solely by God's grace. And both come through this encounter to know themselves, and see through their own previous self-deception. *Crime and Punishment* and *The Possessed* were written in 1866 and 1871–72 respectively, both before the beginning of Dostoyevsky's friendship with Vladimir Solovyov. Dostoyevsky could not have been influenced by Solovyov at this stage. If anything, the influence is more likely to be the other way, and in fact the second of Solovyov's own three formative mystical experiences of encounter with Holy Wisdom, at the British Museum in 1875, comes two years after the beginning of his friendship with Dostoyevsky.

Sonia Semyonova Marmeladova, the central female character of *Crime and Punishment*, has been rightly called the warmest, most tenderly drawn female character in all Dostoyevsky's novels.[33] She is the expression of the gospel claims that what is impossible for human beings is possible for God, that it is to the children of God that the reign of God is revealed, and that the prostitutes will go into that Kingdom before the righteous.[34] Sonia's vulnerability is her strength as she stands up to Raskolnikov's alternating utilitarianism and Napoleonic hybris – both variants on the 'Great Idea' of modernity.[35] Sonia, when she speaks, speaks with clarity and authority, and these qualities in turn come from her having 'the mind of Christ'.[36] There is nothing foreign or forced about this – Sonia's Christlike quality is her own most authentic personality.

The decisive passage, the turning point in the novel, is Sonia's reading to Raskolnikov the story of the raising of Lazarus. Raskolnikov has been taunting Sonia about her faith:

> 'And what does God do for you?' he asked, probing further into her mind.
> She was silent for a long time, as though unable to answer . . .

'Be quiet! Don't ask! You're not worthy!' she cried suddenly. Looking angrily and sternly at him . . . 'He does everything', she whispered rapidly, again dropping her eyes.

A book was lying on the chest of drawers. He had noticed it every time he walked up and down the room. It was the New Testament in a Russian translation. The book was an old one, well thumbed, bound in leather.

'Where did you get that?' he shouted to her across the room. [37]

What follows is the revelation that the book has been given to Sonia by Lizaveta, whom Raskolnikov has murdered, and who had visited Sonia on occasions and read the scriptures with her.

'Where's the place about Lazarus?' he asked suddenly.

Sonia's eyes were fixed stubbornly on the ground, and she did not reply. She stood a little sideways to the table.

'Where is the place about the raising of Lazarus? Find it for me, Sonia.'

But pearls are not about to be cast before swine, and Sonia hesitates.

'Why do you ask? You don't believe, do you?' She whispered softly and as though she were out of breath.

'Come on, read! I want you to!' he insisted. 'You used to read to Lizaveta, didn't you?'

Sonia opened the book and found the place. Her hands trembled, her voice failed her. Twice she tried to read without being able to utter the first syllable.

'Now a certain man was sick, named Lazarus, of Bethany . . .'

Sonia reads on, from 'the eleventh chapter of the gospel of St John, and she read it till the nineteenth verse'.

'*And he that was dead came forth*' (she read loudly and exultingly, trembling and shivering feverishly, as though she were seeing it with her own eyes) 'bound hand and foot with the grave-clothes, and his face was bound about with a napkin. Jesus saith unto them, Loose him and let him go. *Then many*

of the Jews which came to Mary and had seen the things
which Jesus did, believed on him.'

This, though he does not yet realise it, is the anticipation of
Raskolnikov's own resurrection from among the dead. That
resurrection does not begin to take effect for another two hundred
pages. That is the theme of the novel's epilogue, which reads like the
beginning of a new novel.

'Siberia. On the banks of a broad, deserted river stands a town,
one of the administrative centres of Russia.'[38] Here, where Sonia
has followed him, Raskolnikov is 'a convict of the second class'.
'But that', Dostoyevsky concludes his novel, 'is the beginning of
a new story, the story of the gradual rebirth of a man, the story of
his gradual regeneration, of his gradual passing from one world to
another, of his acquaintance with a hitherto unknown reality.'[39]

And what has happened to reach this point of regeneration?
It is the long torturous story of Raskolnikov's inner struggle and
growing self-awareness, of Sonia's demand that he 'Go to the
crossroads, bow down to the people, kiss the earth . . . and proclaim
to the whole world: "I am a murderer!"'[40] What has happened
is Raskolnikov's public display of humility before the mocking
crowds in the Hay Market, with Sonia standing back, watching
but trying not to be seen.[41] She is the wisdom woman of Proverbs
8, standing at the crossroads – though she no longer needs to cry
aloud. Her message has been heard. Raskolnikov's first attempt
to go to the police is pure melodrama. He is about to confess,
when the more pressing news of Svidrigailov's suicide comes in.
Providentially (it would seem) given a way out, Raskolnikov takes
his leave and starts to descend the stairs, when he again catches
sight of Sonia standing in the street, 'pale as death' at his apparent
capitulation to self-interest. Raskolnikov turns back and reenters
the police station. Softly and distinctly he makes his confession:

'It was I – . . .
It was I who killed the old woman money-lender and her
sister Lizaveta with a hatchet and robbed them.'
The assistant superintendent shouted something. People
came running from all directions.
Raskolnikov repeated his statement.

In the closing pages of *The Possessed*, Sophia Matvaevna Ulitina reads three passages to the dying Stepan Tromifovich Verkhovensky. Verkhovensky, an old liberal who has spent the past fifty years in 'isolation from practical life'[42] has set out, on foot, on the open road that goes nowhere and everywhere, on a final pilgrimage 'carrying the banner of the Great Idea'. By a combination of accidents he finds himself travelling with a young Crimean War widow who now sells Bibles to support herself. Verkhovensky, increasingly fascinated with the younger woman, catches a fever and grows delirious. After hearing her read the Sermon on the Mount,[43] he refuses a visit from the doctor but asks: 'read me a bit more, anything you like, the first thing your eye falls upon'. Here she opens to the letter to the Laodiceans in the Book of Revelation. Verkhovensky understands the passage as relating to himself and his past. Yet he has still not given up on the 'Great Idea'.

> 'That – so that's what you've stumbled upon in your book!' he cried, sitting up, his eyes sparkling. 'I didn't know that great passage! Did you hear that? Rather cold, rather cold than lukewarm, rather than only warm. Oh, I'll prove it to them!'

Verkhovensky, in his final delirium, is clutching at straws. He takes comfort in the fact that John the Divine seems to prefer a cold and outright rejection over any lukewarm religious adherence. He clings to his Great Idea, which he is so foolishly determined yet to prove to those who reject it.

Finally Verkhovensky makes a third request. After hearing the call to perfection in the Sermon on the Mount and the rejection of the lukewarm, Verkhovensky asks to be confronted with the division of good from evil, and its consequence:

> 'Now I want you to read me that passage about the swine', he said suddenly.
> 'What did you say, sir?' Mrs Ulitin said. For some reason she was frightened by his request.
> 'About the swine – why, it's in this book all right – *les cochons*. I remember about the demons going into the pigs and getting drowned, the lot of them. Read me that passage, please.

I'll tell you why later. I want to remember it verbatim. Yes, I want it word for word.'[44]

Sophia Matveyevna quickly finds the Lucan passage – quoted in full, as the author reminds us, as the epigraph to the whole novel – and reads it aloud. Verkhovensky's response is an experience of revelation – of seeing himself and his life clearly for the first time.

> 'My dear', Mr Verkhovensky said in great agitation, '*savez-vous*, this is a wonderful, an extraordinary passage and it has been a stumbling block to me *dans ce livre*, all my life ... so I remember the passage from when I was a boy. But now, an idea has occurred to me, *une comparaison*. Ah, so many thoughts keep crowding into my head.'

Verkhovensky is recognising himself, like the madman in the gospel story, as possessed – not by Legion, but by his 'Great Idea'.

> 'You see, it is like our Russia. Those devils or demons coming out of the sick and entering into the swine – they are all the festering sores, all the poisonous vapours, all the filth, all the demons and petty devils accumulated for centuries and centuries in our great, dear, sick Russia ...
> 'It's *us*, us and the others – my son Peter and those around him; and we'll hurl ourselves from the cliff and into the sea and I'll be the first perhaps, and all of us, mad and raving, will drown and it will serve us right because that's all we're fit for. But the sick man will recover and sit at the feet of Jesus and they will look at him in surprise.'

What we have here is a genuine revelation, albeit one that does not simply spring from nowhere: it is touched off from within the tradition, by the reading of the scriptures. Indeed, it is a reading from the word by one who embodies the Word. Verkhovensky, the old idealist, after declaring himself lost, dies repenting and 'in an odour of sanctity'.[45] But only after he has looked the demons in the face. Dostoyevsky, as Boyce Gibson puts it, 'means to suggest that the liberals of the 1840's, including himself, have a good deal to answer for'.[46] For they have fathered the next generation of devils, the anarchists and terrorists of the 1870s. The encounter with Sophia Matveyevna at the end of *The Possessed* is a 'pin-point of light'[47] in what is otherwise perhaps the darkest of all Dostoyevsky's novels. 'Sophia Matveevna', writes Diana Thompson, '[is] the eponym and literal bearer of divine wisdom'.[48] Dostoyevsky is announcing not the end of 'the Great Idea', but its transformation, its transfiguration 'grounded in an orientation towards the eternal'.[49] The formerly possessed man remains, sitting quietly at the feet of Jesus.

Both Raskolnikov[50] and Verkhovensky are in some sense possessed. Both are confronted by a Sophia-figure (and their personal names, Sonia and Sophia, are by no means irrelevant) who reads from the gospels, and thereby announce the good news, if it can only be heard. This moment in each case carries a liturgical allusion: Sophia! is the acclamation used to introduce the gospel reading in the Orthodox liturgy. In both passages, modern secular humanity is confronted with a wisdom that is both older, and younger, than the pretensions of modernity.

3. Sophia as a Christ-figure

Dosoyevsky, it has been noted, does not ask the God-question directly, but indirectly by asking the anthropological question.[51] God is apprehended through the encounter with the human: apprehended, that is, christologically, incarnationally, and in an embodied form. 'The peculiar quality of Dostoyevsky's apologetic lies', according to Vyacheslav Ivanov, 'in the urge, not to found the love of Christ on belief in God, but to arrive through Christ at the certainty of God's existence ... The hidden transcendent reality of God is attested by the directly perceived earthly reality of Christ.'[52] Both *Crime and Punishment* and *The Possessed* are, as Boyce Gibson puts it, stages in the development of Dostoyevsky's anthropology, in which he examines the *alternatives* to a Christian view of humanity, before 'turning the spotlight on Christian anthropology itself'.[53]

Where then is the Christ figure in Dostoyevsky's work, that

gives access to the reality of God? Guardini sees the Christ-figure in Myshkin, the central figure of *The Idiot*,[54] but Boyce Gibson correctly argues that Myshkin is too disembodied a figure to be successfully and truly Christlike.[55] Boyce Gibson prefers to see the Christ-figure in the Christ of the Grand Inquisitor story,[56] a figure who Guardini considers, correctly in my opinion, too detached from everyday life to be real.[57] Alyosha Karamazov is a more likely contender, though even here there are problems, and a newer interpretation would argue that Alyosha is best seen as Christ-like only as a member of his family, in which the three Karamazov brothers *together* form an *imago trinitatis*.[58] Nina Straus argues that in Dostoyevsky's work, it is often a woman who appears as a Christ-figure: 'the image of a woman as a Christ-figure who redeems a "fallen" man, while simultaneously confronting him with her feminist advocacy of sexual equality'.[59] Straus unfortunately fails to pursue this insight in relation to the Sophia figure. Her comment on Myshkin as being 'suffused not with the Father's spirit, but with Sophia'[60] betrays an insufficiently robust image of Sophia. Straus's frequent references to Sonia Marmeladova as a passive 'female holy fool'[61] supports her tendency to assimilate the figure of Sophia into the passive Madonna-image, which she contrasts to the emancipated 'new woman' of Dostoyevsky's Petersburg of the 1860s. This assimilation does justice neither to the Sophia-tradition, nor to the specific Sophia figures in Dostoyevsky's works.

Dostoyevsky's image of Christ is to be seen preeminently, I think, in the two Sophia figures we have looked at here. Other Sophia characters elsewhere in his writings would also be worthy of consideration if space allowed. Both point to Christ the Wisdom of God. Both are examples of Dostoyevsky's 'Sophian vision', as Zander[62] calls it, and this is essentially a christological vision. But there is a fine distinction to be made here, and it is illuminated by Solovyov's distinction between the Logos and Sophia.

> If we distinguish in the absolute in general between the absolute as such (that which absolutely is) and its content, essence or idea, we will find the former directly expressed in the Logos and the latter directly expressed in Sophia, which is thus the expressed or actualised idea. And just as an

> existent being is distinct from its own idea but is at the same
> time one with it, so the Logos, too, is distinct from Sophia
> but is inwardly united with her. Sophia is God's body, the
> matter of Divinity, permeated with the principle of divine
> unity. Actualising in himself, or bearing, this unity, Christ, as
> the integral divine organism, both universal and individual, is
> both Logos and Sophia.[63]

Sophia, in other words, is the Logos actualised in bodily form,
not simply 'once for all', but again and again in the ongoing life
and experience of the Christian community. The desire of the
Logos is to be embodied, and this, Solovyov would seem to be
saying, occurs constantly in the Sophia-figures of this world.[64]
Solovyov expresses his christology through his sophiology,[65] and
the most obvious immediate source of this idea for Solovyov is in
the Sophia-figures of Dostoyevsky's novels.

Sophiology was, according to Schultze, always methodologically
more 'artistic and intuitive ... than discursive'.[66] It should not
surprise us that it might draw on literary as well as philosophical
sources. Although it is set out in the language of Hegelian
philosophy, its more immediate sources are the Sophia icons of
the eastern church and, I suggest, the Sophia characters of the
novels of Dostoyevsky.

There is a difference though. Dostoyevsky never romanticised the
Sophia figure in the way Solovyov arguably, and his followers clearly,
did.[67] There is a romanticism to be seen in some of Dostoyevsky's
commentators – Guardini and Zander, for example – which does
not quite ring true to Dostoyevsky himself. Neither Sophia Ulitina
nor Sonia Marmeladova is romanticised by Dostoyevsky. The first is
a widow who supports herself by door-to-door book selling, who
has the strength of character to confront Verkhovensky with his own
lifelong self-deception. The second is a prostitute, with the strength
of character to resist Raskolnikov's feverish illusions about himself.
True, they are both 'meek ones' (Guardini) or 'humble ones' (Zander),
but this meekness never means non-resistance, and this humility
never means acquiescence. It may mean a certain vulnerability in
each of them, but it is never weakness – in fact there is an enormous
enduring (which again does not mean 'long-suffering') toughness

about these two wisdom women.[68] In this sense Dostoyevsky perhaps stands closer to our post-Romantic age than some of his mid-twentieth century commentators. One reason for this may be that Dostoyevsky's anthropology is, as Nina Straus argues, a gendered anthropology, with *Crime and Punishment* the novel where Dostoyevsky discovers for himself and works out the politics of gender.[69]

4. Dostoyevsky and contemporary Theology

Dostoyevsky's genius was, in part, that he looked honestly and discerningly into the heart of darkness that lies within each of us, and within our human culture. He was granted a vision, like Dante's vision of Hell, into the coming century, and he did not return unscathed from the experience. For this reason, Dostoyevsky's characters at times seem to lurk in the shadows of much twentieth century theology. 'Even if we had not learned it from Dostoievski', says Barth, 'the experiences of our own day have surely taught us that we can no longer have any illusions as to what is dormant even in the heart of the average man...'[70] And after Dostoyevsky, as Berdyaev put it, we can no longer 'imagine the nineteenth century going on, full of enthusiasm for the draining of marshes'.[71] Something has changed in the cultural landscape, something of seismic proportions. Though the European world – and in the last decades of the nineteenth century that meant the whole world – may have looked secure and self-assured, this self-assurance was in the early years of the new century rapidly to appear increasingly hollow. Dostoyevsky had somehow discerned the crisis of modernity, the end of modernity.[72] This is why Eduard Thurneysen, writing after the catastrophe had become plain for all to see, could liken Dostoyevsky to 'our expressionists' in his prophetic insight into the crisis looming on the horizon of his own age.[73] Behind Dostoyevsky's post-modern fascination with the incongruous there is an underlying sense of apocalyptic dread. It would be a mistake to confuse this with mere conservatism. Dostoyevsky's hostility to revolution is not, as Berdyaev points out, the hostility of someone with vested interests in the old order.[74] 'Genuine prophecy always sounds a little indecent to those whose minds are closed to its truth', says René Girard. 'Was it not indecent, in 1871, to suggest that the sincere and politically correct Russian revolutionists would end up with Stalin and Beria?'[75] Rather, Dostoyevky shares the apocalypticism of the New Testament and the early Christians. And like any true prophet, Dostoyevsky takes no delight in the message he is called to proclaim.

Most theological references[76] to Dostoyevsky tend to focus on a single issue, that of suffering and human evil as the basis for protest atheism, and on a single passage, the conversation between Ivan and Alyosha Karamazov in which Ivan tells the story of the Grand Inquisitor. What I want to suggest here is that Dostoyevsky (by way of Solovyov and perhaps von Balthasar) may have provided an impetus for the emergence of a whole new theme in contemporary theology, that of Sophia or the Wisdom of God. Because there is another side to Dostoyevsky's genius. Though not unscathed by his vision of the crisis of modernity, this 'explorer of Hell'[77] refuses to lend death any final dominion. For this crisis is brought into confrontation with Holy Wisdom. In the two passages explored above, it is the Sophia figure who redeems, in each case, the lost representative of modernity.

Paul Valliere argues convincingly that sophiology was intended to be the bridge between Orthodoxy and the modern world.[78] It was, in other words, the late nineteenth century Orthodox response to the problem of Christ and culture. Holy Wisdom for Solovyov was always ill-defined, and so his interpreters have read him in a multiplicity of ways. But in 1935 it was the one of the very few contemporary matters on which the Moscow Patriarchate and the Russian Orthodox Church in Exile (based at that time in Karlovci, in Yugoslavia) could agree, both issuing condemnations of the sophiology of Bulgakov – and by implication, of Solovyov – in that year. (Perhaps significantly, the following year saw the reemergence, at the Pan-Orthodox Conference at Rhodes, of Palamism as another sort of Orthodox response to the culture of the West). Bulgakov himself, as a member of the faculty of St Sergius in Paris, came under neither the jurisdiction of Moscow nor Karlovci, and although no condemnation was issued by his own diocese, he was advised to reconsider his views. This strange consensus between these bitterest of opponents saw the effective disappearance of sophiology from the Russian intellectual scene, both within the Soviet Union and in the various Russian *émigré* communities.

Recent theological recoveries of both the personification of Wisdom[79] and the Wisdom literature[80] have often occurred at the point where theology is most deeply and strenuously engaged with the issues of the contemporary world. So far, however, these newer contributions have rarely if ever drawn on the Russian sophiologists, or even noted their pioneering contribution. The influence of sophiology is also strangely absent in those areas of theology that might be expected to welcome it as an ally. The link between the theological critique of modernity and the Russian sophiological school is to be found in Dostoyevsky.

End Notes

1. The Wisdom of Solomon 6:12-1. I am grateful to Denis Edwards for drawing this passage to my attention.
2. N Berdyaev, *Dostoyevsky* (New York: Meridian, 1934/1957), 74–75.
3. George Pattison and Diane Oenning Thompson (editors), *Dostoyevsky and the Christian Tradition* (Cambridge: Cambridge University Press, 2001).
4. David Magarshack, *Dostoyevsky* (London: Secker and Warburg, 1962) 62. Sophiology, a religious philosophy developed by Solovyov (1853–1900) and several others, was highly influential in Russia and Russian expatriate communities during the late nineteenth and early twentieth centuries.
5. Cited in Anna Dostoyevsky, *Dostoyevsky Reminiscences* (London: Wildwood House, 1976), 431.
6. EH Carr, *Dostoyevsky, 1821–1881* (London: Allen and Unwin, 1931), 277.
7. Marina Kostalevsky, *Dostoyevsky and Soloviev: The Art of Integral Vision* (New Haven: Yale University Press, 1997).
8. Wladimir Szylkarski, *Solowjew und Dostoejewskij* (Bonn, 1948).
9. Bernhard Schultze, 'Solowjew und Dostojewskij', in *Orientalia Christiana Periodica*, 15, 1949, 202–7.
10. Ellis Sandoz, *Political Apocalypse: a Study of Dostoyevsky's Grand Inquisitor* (Baton Rouge: Louisiana State University Press, 1971), 11.
11. Schultze, 'Hauptthemen der neueren russischen Theologie', in W

Nyssen *et al* (editors), *Handbuch der Ostkirchen*, Bd 1 (Düsseldorf: Patmos, 1984), 356.

12. Schultze, 'Hauptthemen der neueren russischen Theologie', 349. See also Deidre Good, *Reconstructing the Tradition of Sophia in Gnostic literature* (Scholars Press, 1987), 57–9.

13. Schultze, 'Hauptthemen der neueren russischen Theologie', 357.

14. But note Bulgakov's criticism of Boehme (and Berdyaev), on the grounds that the Sophia symbol is not essentially a virgin figure, which might suggest disdain for the flesh, but rather a mother figure (Bernice Rosenthal, 'The Nature and Function of Sophia in Sergei Bulgakov's Prerevolutionary Thought', in J Kornblatt and R Gustafson (eds), *Russian Religious Thought* (Madison: University of Wisconsin Press, 1996), 164, 169). See also Deidre Good, *Reconstructing the Tradition of Sophia*, 14–22.

15. Paul Evdokimov, *Christus im Russischen Denken* (Trier: Paulinus, 1977), 131.

16. Kostalevsky *Dostoyevsky and Soloviev*, 110.

17. Vladimir Sergeyevich Solovyov, *Lectures on Divine Humanity*, edited by Boris Jakim (New York: Lindisfarne Press, 1995), 76, fn 2; 80; 82. Cf Bernhard Schultze, 'Hauptthemen der neueren russischen Theologie', 360. Cf Bernice Rosenthal, 'Nature and Function of Sophia in Sergei Bulgakov's Prerevolutionary Thought', 160.

18. Solovyov, *Lectures on Divine Humanity*, 60–1.

19. Solovyov, *Lectures on Divine Humanity*, 62. Kostalevsky, *Dostoyevsky and Soloviev*, 61–2, notes the literary influences on Solovyov's descriptions of his mystical experiences.

20. Solovyov, *Lectures on Divine Humanity*, 90.

21. Anna Dostoyevsky, *Dostoyevsky Reminiscences*, 223–4.

22. Judith Kornblatt and Gary Rosenshield, 'Vladimir Solovyov: Confronting Dostoyevsky on the Jewish and Christian Questions', *Journal of the American Academy of Religion*, March 2000, 68/1, 69–98. See also David Goldstein, *Dostoyevsky and the Jews* (Austin and London: University of Texas Press, 1981), xxiii, 37; Anna Dostoyevsky, *Dostoyevsky Reminiscences*, 431.

23. Anna Dostoyevsky, *Dostoyevsky Reminiscences*, 294. The letter Dostoyevsky wrote to his wife about this pilgrimage is published (in Russian) in NF Bel'chikova and VF Pereverzeva (editors), *Pis'ma FM Dostoevskogo k zhene* (Moscow and Leningrad: Gosudarstvennoe Izdatel'stvo, 1926), 233–4.

24. Anna Dostoyevsky, *Dostoyevsky Reminiscences*, 325–6.

25. Anna Dostoyevsky, *Dostoyevsky Reminiscences*, 361.

26. A Boyce Gibson, *The Religion of Dostoyevsky* (London: SCM Press, 1973), 143; Richard Peace, *Dostoyevsky: An Examination of the Major Novels* (Cambridge: Cambridge University Press, 1971), 170ff.

27. Romano Guardini, *Religiöse Gestalten in Dostojewskis Werk: Studien über den Glauben* (München: In Kössel, 1964), 49 ff; LA Zander, *Dostoyevsky* (London: SCM Press, 1948), 67; Kostalevsky, *Dostoyevsky and Soloviev*, 111.

28. There is a sense in which the Word cannot be proclaimed in a conventional sense in Dostoyevsky, whose 'art does not require listening to sermons, for our age cannot tolerate them' (Girard, 137). Diana Thompson (in Pattison and Thompson, *Dostoyevsky and the Christian Tradition*, 69–70), citing Bakhtin, offers a reason why our age can no longer tolerate sermons: 'Modern man does not proclaim; he speaks. That is, he speaks with reservations', and Dostoyevsky gives expression to his Christian worldview in this modern idiom.

29. This was the occasion of a famous misunderstanding between Dostoyevsky and Tolstoy. See Anna Dostoyevsky, *Dostoyevsky Reminiscence*, 290–1, 364.

30. Kostalevsky, *Dostoyevsky and Soloviev*, 81.

31. Fyodor Mikhailovich Dostoyevsky, *Crime and Punishment* (Harmondsworth: Penguin, 1961).

32. Fyodor Mikhailovich Dostoyevsky, *The Possessed* (London: Signet, 1962).

33. Guardini, *Religiöse Gestalten in Dostojewskis Werk*, 61.

34. Guardini, *Religiöse Gestalten in Dostojewskis Werk*, 66.

35. See Bruce K Ward, *Dostoyevsky's Critique of the West: The Quest for the Earthly Paradise* (Waterloo, Ontario: Wilfrid Laurier University Press, 1986), especially 35–61.

36. Guardini, *Religiöse Gestalten in Dostojewskis Werk*, 85.

37. Dostoyevsky, *Crime and Punishment*, 339.

38. Dostoyevsky, *Crime and Punishment*, 543.

39. Dostoyevsky, *Crime and Punishment*, 559.

40. Dostoyevsky, *Crime and Punishment*, 536.

41. Dostoyevsky, *Crime and Punishment*, 536–542.

42. Dostoyevsky, *The Possessed*, 648.

43. Dostoyevsky, *The Possessed*, 668.

44. Dostoyevsky, *The Possessed*, 670.

45. Boyce Gibson, *The Religion of Dostoyevsky*, 144.

46. Boyce Gibson, *The Religion of Dostoyevsky*, 128.

47. Boyce Gibson, *The Religion of Dostoyevsky*, 145.

48. Thompson, in Pattison and Thompson, *Dostoyevsky and the Christian Tradition* 77. Thompson's very perceptive reading of this whole passage is to be found on pages 77–82.

49. Ward, *Dostoyevsky's Critique of the West*, 180.

50. Berdyaev, *Dostoyevsky*, 96.

51. Berdyaev, *Dostoyevsky*, 24, 74–5.

52. Vyacheslav Ivanov, *Freedom and the Tragic Life: A Study in*

Dostoyevsky (London: Harvill Press, 1952), 114.

53. Boyce Gibson, *The Religion of Dostoyevsky*, 98. Svidrigailov's suicide in *Crime and Punishment*, is, according to Boyce Gibson's reading of the novel, the logical conclusion of his godless life. Individualism and atheism – the hallmarks of modernity – go together, and both are ultimately self-defeating.

54. Guardini, *Religiöse Gestalten*, 383.

55. Boyce Gibson, *The Religion of Dostoyevsky*, 109.

56. Boyce Gibson, *The Religion of Dostoyevsky*, 183–7.

57. Guardini, *Religiöse Gestalten*, 180–90.

58. David Cunningham, 'Trinitarian Rhetoric in Murdoch, Morison and Dostoyevsky', in G Sayler and R Detweiler (editors), *Literature and Theology at Century's End* (Atlanta: Scholars Press, 1995).

59. Nina Pelikan Straus, *Dostoyevsky and the Woman Question: Rereadings at the End of a Century* (New York: St Martin's Press, 1994), 7.

60. Straus, *Dostoyevsky and the Woman Question*, 62.

61. Straus, *Dostoyevsky and the Woman Question*, 58. Cf 32, 145, 152.

62. Zander, *Dostoyevsky*, 60.

63. Solovyov, *Lectures on Divine Humanity*, 108. Solovyov, in a footnote, is careful to point out he is using the terms 'body' and 'matter' in a distinctive and technical way. Earlier he had also defined 'idea' in distinction to 'concept' (61, fn 3). See also Paul Valliere ('Sophiology as the Dialogue of Orthodoxy with Modern Civilisation', in Kornblatt and Gustafson, *Russian Religious Thought*, 181) on the relationship between Sophia and Christology.

64. I take it this is what Florensky means when he identifies Sophia with created grace. See Schultze, 'Hauptthemen der neueren russischen Theologie', 352.

65. Evdokimov, *Christus im Russischen Denken*, 131.

66. Schultze, 'Hauptthemen der neueren russischen Theologie', 349.

67. Eg the mystical-chivalric 'order' of Sophia instituted by Solovyov's nephew and others. See Solovyov, *Divine Humanity*, xiii, fn 9.

68. Boyce Gibson, *The Religion of Dostoyevsky*, 106.

69. Straus, *Dostoyevsky and the Woman Question*, 22.

70. Karl Barth, *Church Dogmatics* (Edinburgh: T&T Clark, 1932ff.), III/4, 413.

71. Berdyaev, *Dostoyevsky*, 74–75.

72. Berdyaev, *Dostoyevsky*, 60, 74–5, 147, 182. cf Guardini, *Religiöse Gestalten*, 285. It is this crisis of modernity, I believe, that George Steiner pinpoints as occurring in Central European and Russian culture and speculative consciousness during the decades between the 1870s and the 1930s as 'one of the very few genuine revolutions of spirit in Western history and which defines modernity itself' (*Real Presences*

[London: Faber and Faber, 1989], 93).

73. Eduard Thurneysen, *Dostojewski* (Zuerich: Gotthelf-Verlag, 1948), 30.
74. Berdyaev, *Dostoyevsky*, 135.
75. René Girard, *Resurrection from the Underground: Feodor Dostoevsky* (New York: Crossroad, 1977), 160.
76. Eg Barth, *Church Dogmatics* II/1, 88; II/2, 542; III/4, 139, 413, 676; IV/1, 609; W Pannenberg, *Systematic Theology* (Grand Rapids: Eerdmans, 1994) II, 164; J Moltmann, *Theology of Hope* (London: SCM Press, 1967), 168; Moltmann, *The Crucified God* (London: SCM Press, 1974), 220–1; Moltmann, *The Spirit of Life: A Universal Affirmation* (London: SCM Press, 1992), 105, 126. Hans Urs von Balthasar appears to be one of the few major theologians who also refer to the redemptive theme in Dostoyevsky. Von Balthasar comments, *inter alia*, on our themes of the influence of Dostoyevsky on Solovyov (*The Glory of the Lord: A Theological Aesthetics* [Edinburgh: T&T Clark, 1986–91] II, 19; III, 298, 342) and wisdom (V, 143, 188–203). See also J Moltmann, *The Church in the Power of the Spirit* (London: SCM Press, 1977), 114; and *The Way of Jesus Christ* (London: SCM Press, 1990), 196.
77. Ivanov, *Freedom and the Tragic Life*, 122.
78. Valliere, 'Sophiology as the Dialogue of Orthodoxy with Modern Civilisation'. Solovyov's frequent references to modern scientific advances in the *Lectures on Divine Humanity* substantiates this claim, in my opinion.
79. See especially Elizabeth Johnson, *She Who Is: The Mystery of God in Feminist Theological Discourse* (New York: Crossroad, 1992). Also Denis Edwards, *Jesus the Wisdom of God: An Ecological Theology* (New York: Orbis, 1995) and Patricia Fox, *God as Communion: John Zizioulas, Elizabeth Johnson and the Retrieval of the Symbol of the Triune God* (Collegeville: Michael Glazier, 2001).
80. Norman Habel, *The Voice of the Earth in the Wisdom Literature: The Earth Bible.* Vol 4 (Sheffield: Sheffield Academic Press, 2001).

20

'THE SELF AND ITS DESTINY': TS ELIOT, EMILY DICKINSON, BARNETT NEWMAN AND WS MERWIN

Patrick Hutchings

In his elegant essay and collection of Readings entitled *The Self and its Destiny in Christianity*[1] the Revd Professor Wardlaw distinguishes the Old Testament 'self definition' of a Jew as 'being one of Abraham's children', from the New Testament, 'Who am I?' where the self is established by our obeying Christ's injunction 'follow me'. In Wardlaw's essay the philosopher's self never appears: he relies, correctly, on our commonsense sense of self, and, as a theologian, concentrates on its *destiny*. Comfortingly he concludes that this is: salvation.

As a – mere – philosopher writing in a *Festschrift* for a theologian, one feels very much on the margin. Even the Angelic Doctor, who was a very great philosopher, thought this trade to be housemaid to theology. And so it may have been, until the Enlightenment. Since then, it has been the case that philosophy has challenged the authority of theology, and eroded the notion of – the sense of – the self, and of its fellow the soul. In Postmodern times (and Post-Post) the self has become a mere 'site' for the play of linguistic forces, ('wall to wall language'), and of social determinations.

The self was notably eroded by Hume in *A Treatise of Human Nature*, 1739, Book I, Section VI, 'Of personal identity',[2] where, in search of his identity, Hume finds a lot of things in his mind, but his self-identity not among them:

> For my part, when I enter most intimately into what I call *myself*, I always stumble on some particular perception or other, of heat or cold, light or shade, love or hatred, pain or pleasure. I never can catch *myself* at any time without a perception, and never can observe any thing but the perception.

And, a little later:

> Our eyes cannot turn in their sockets without varying our
> perceptions. Our thought is still more variable than our
> sight . . . nor is there any single power of the soul which remains
> unalterably the same perhaps for one moment. The mind
> is a kind of theatre where several perceptions make their
> appearance; pass, re-pass glide away . . . . There is properly no
> *simplicity* in it at one time, nor *identity* in different . . . .

The man who mistook his wife for a hat was mad: but Hume's
mistaking himself for a theatre is misguided. He is not a building,
but the sometimes elated, sometimes melancholy, but permanent
caretaker and spectator of whatever comes, not into 'the' mind (*the*
mind?), but into *his*. One may weary of spectatorship, but it is laid
upon us: *ie*, on you, me, him, her, and whoever. 'What is your name,
N or M?'

Hume loses sight of Hume himself who is taking the inventory
of what is to be found. He reminds me of a scholar surveying his
books, files, papers, and not noticing that what gives *sense* to this
united – and possibly ill-arranged – array is the scholar to whom
all this collection means something. When the scholar dies, all the
books become secondhand merchandise, and the papers are either
archived – or dumped. To the Po-Mo person one would remark, à
propos this: the scholar in his study is a site within a site: the self is
a prime site, without which not *this* study, but another would be
instanced in the real. We are not, quite, made by language and social
determinations: these, equally, depend on what we make of them. It
goes both ways: the self is pulled – but can push, as well.

Kant famously saves the self by promoting it to being a
Transcendental Ego, a condition of experience, but not itself
experiencable. Or not to philosophers. Some poets and artists catch
this transcendental butterfly if only for a moment, in aesthetic nets,
which still the creature for observation, but do it no injury. We shall
consider some examples below, looking at poems by TS Eliot, Emily
Dickinson and WS Merwin.

Kant's self-as-individual has an 'immortal' but to him inscrutable
destiny: 'God freedom and immortality' are, notoriously, off the

Critical map.[3]

Animula

TS Eliot's *Animula*[4] is bookended at one side by Dante (a Thomist poet) and at the other by Cardinal Mercier's *A Manual of Modern Scholastic Philosophy*, the American edition of the English translation, 1916, on which TS E[liot] wrote a brief 'Shorter Notice' in the *International Journal of Ethics*, 1917. Thus when Eliot writes, ' 'Issues from the hand of God, the simple soul' ' we have the indication that this is a quotation, and the ineluctable feeling that 'simple' has a double meaning. The Dante reads:

Esce di mano a lui,	From his hands who
che la vagheggia	fondly loves her ere she
prima che sia, a	is in being, there issues,
guisa di fanciulla che	after the fashion of a
piangendo e ridendo	little child that sports,
pargoleggia,	now weeping, now
l' anima semplicetta,	laughing,
che sa nulla, salvo	the simple, tender soul,
che, mosa da lieto	who knoweth naught
fattore, volentier	save that, sprung
torna a ciò che la	from a joyous maker,
trastulla.	willingly she turneth to
	that which delights her.[5]

From this we may take that 'simple' means at once 'simple-substance' and 'as yet not, fully, knowing person' or '*infans* and naïve'. In the Catholic philosophy of Dante's time (and still, among Thomists) the soul is created directly by God, to be the form of whatever matter-as-person it informs.[6] We now know that the *materia signata* apt for *a* soul is already 'programmed' by DNA, and will, further, be affected by culture, experience – and its own free choices. God, unlike Leibniz, has no trouble in distinguishing one 'simple soul' – sense one – from another: to Him indiscernibles are not identical. . God knows souls before their issue, and the issue at the end of their being here. When Animula – the person, a now-becoming empirical *self* – 'Issues . . ./ to a flat world of changing light and noise', s/he issues into William James's 'great big, buzzing, bumbling confusion', and becomes unconfused when she can recognise '. . . running stags around a silver tray': though she as yet still 'Confounds the actual and the fanciful', and is content with the trifles. Culture supervenes on childhood, 'behind the *Encyclopedia Britannica*'. Then, inevitably 'Issues from the hand of time the simple soul / Irresolute, selfish, misshapen, lame, / Unable to fare forward or retreat' and so, unhappily on into a self-history at once unique and with banal precedents. In the end 'Leaving disordered papers in a dusty room', as in my figure of the Scholar whose room of books and papers is *his*, his-*self's*, but to his heirs an incomprehensible concatenation of unrelated print and scribble.

Eliot's Anglo-Catholic theology comes into the open in the line, 'Living first in the silence after the viaticum'. Life's only sense is life eternal. So: Eliot's final, paradoxical line 'Pray for us now and at the hour of our birth', where the *Ave Maria* is misquoted to give us the double sense of 'birth': infusion of a soul into a psychosomatic shell; issue of the soul – and resurrected body – into the presence of God.

Of born-again-ness in the Evangelical sense, one would not expect TS Eliot to write. The general experience of Baptism, Eucharist (Marriage? Holy Orders?) is implicit in the simple sacrament of 'Viaticum'. 'Issues from the hand of God, the simple soul', into, *first* life's journey: *then* into Salvation. The poem's feel is of cool Anglo-Catholicism, with a Thomist ring to the 'mechanics' of the thing. Soul-as-unique-armature-of-self is the model. The self is denied any final ordering before death, 'disordered papers in a dusty room': hereafter the sense of all can be read, presumably.

But the destiny of the soul, for Eliot, as for Dante, is all. As it is for the notable Reformed writers to whom Harry Wardlaw directs us in his essay-with-readings.

Emily Dickinson: *The Single Hound*

Far more Protestant than Eliot is Emily Dickinson. And, given her Puritanism and her brushes with Transcendentalism, rather curiously Protestant. ' 'Consider the lilies of the field' is the only commandment I have kept.'[7] And she was no attender of church services. But her total sense of inwardness strikes a Catholic reader as quintessentially Protestant.

One of the great aesthetic cruces of the aesthetic phenomenology of the self is Dickinson's *The Single Hound*, from which I shall quote only part: Section I outfaces Hume:

> I
> Adventure most unto itself
> The Soul condemned to be;
> Attended by a Single Hound –
> Its own Identity[8]

Hume is outfaced not simply by assertion, but, I would argue by a *sense* of self, a sense of identity, strong enough for capital 'I'. In a paper on Barnett Newman's 'zip' paintings[9] I made a one-off argument for Newman's 'zips' as interruptions of a large chromatic field intended to read '*you* are here: attend to *you-yourself*'. Newman 'authorises' this ascription of intension by his remark 'The self, terrible and constant, is for me the subject matter of painting' (1965).[10] The great non-figurative paintings are not about the everydayness of persons – even those who stand, 'I am here', before the 'zips'. They are about the 'I' of each such person, taken out of the everyday commonplace.

Where the I – for Barnett Newman himself – stands is: in the synagogue:

> Here in this synagogue, each man sits, private and secluded in the dugouts, waiting to be called, not to ascent a stage but to go up to the mound, where, under the tension of that 'Tzim-Tzum' that created light and the world, he can experience a total sense of his own personality before the Torah and His Name.[11]

The phrase 'a total sense of his own personality' is breathtaking. Barnett Newman seems to suggest a personal religious experience as of a *totum simul*? That, even in a synagogue one might achieve the 'total sense of his own personality' is fairly doubtful. But what Barnett Newman would have the worshiper have, is of course the *ideal* of the self: a Boethian *totum simul* in which all experiences of a self are collected and resolved. This one hopes for – if at all – hereafter. And its closest analogue – and prefiguring – are certain moments in a psychoanalysis, and or in the literary phenomenon of ekphrasis.[12]

Barnett Newman had already written, à propos a particular synagogue which he had in mind, puzzlingly:

> In the synagogue ceremony nothing happens that is objective [of course no Eucharist as Transsubstation]. In it there is only the subjective experience *in which one feels exalted* ....

This subjective experience of exaltation (which I have italicised) Newman has elsewhere identified with the Sublime, in his seminal essay 'The Sublime is Now'.[13] Barnett Newman's remarks about the synagogue go on:

> 'Know before whom you stand' reads the command. But the concern seems to be not with the emotion of *exaltation and personal identity* called for by the command, but with the number of seats and clean décor...'[14]

The particular synagogue about which Barnett Newman is writing fails in the purpose which Newman would have such a place of worship fulfil. His own 'zip' paintings may very well bear a reading, on one hand 'feel your-*self*', and on the other, 'know before whom you stand'. The first reading, having stood in front of many Barnett Newmans, I would endorse. The second I would be sympathetic to, provided that the 'know' in 'know before whom you stand' is less than the knowing which Moses had. Barnett Newman would have taken this qualification as read, even as he makes claims for an 'eternal moment' of self-identity.

There are – perhaps – two exaltations: the mere one of 'I-am-I-ing'; and 'I stand in the presence of 'He who Is, the I AM of Exodus''. Such, anyhow, seems to be the subtext.[15]

Barnett Newman stands in his own text as a son of Abraham

and a man of the late Enlightenment, between the old religion, and the eighteenth century, and contemporary, sublime. There is a curious parallel between Barnett Newman's paintings and his ideal-synagogue experience. He may, like Mark Rothko, intend that we have before his paintings, a full religious experience.[16] That we can, one may contest.

Dickinson's *The Single Hound* II, III and XXV

Dickinson similarly polarises *The Single Hound*, in that it is at once *identity*, and being-with-something-transcending that very identity:

II

> The Soul that has a Guest,
> Doth seldom go abroad,
> Diviner Crowd at home
> Obliterate the need,
> And courtesy forbid
> A Host's departure, when
> Upon Himself be visiting
> The Emperor of Men![17]

The 'soul's Guest' here might suggest that the reclusive Dickinson entertained 'The Emperor of Men' constantly, as might a contemplative. However the home-centredness of Emily Dickinson is a great problem for her biographers and critics, and to call her a 'contemplative' would be vastly to oversimplify.[18] What is interesting is the move from – mere – empirical self to some putative being-with a more Absolute self.

The transition from simple – 'philosophers' – self to one engaged with respect to God or Christ as destiny seems seamless and effortless (if perhaps unorthodox), in Dickinson; and in Barnett Newman. Are these special cases – leading to one's being a special pleader? Or does self as self *imply* destiny?

Dickinson's third section of *The Single Hound* is enigmatic, and needs more unpacking than we can give it here. It reads:

III

Except the smaller size, no Lives are round,
These hurry to a sphere, and show, and end.
The larger, slower grow, and later hang –
The Summers of Hesperides are long.

In the end it's all the same, the richer fruit of the Hesperides fall too – and must. The 'sphere' of final self-containment and self-comprehension is not here but – if at all – hereafter only.

Section XXV is matter indeed to our present considerations. It reads:

> XXV
> There is a solitude of space,
> A solitude of sea,
> A solitude of death, but these
> Society shall be,
> Compared with that profounder site.
> That polar privacy,
> A Soul admitted to Itself:
> Finite Infinity.

The line 'Finite Infinity'[19] represents both the soul's present state – finite even though immortal, and so in *that* way infinite: and 'infinite' as to 'content'. The 'infinity' here is double: pointing, (1) towards Destiny as Wardlaw would have it; and (2) towards the – secondary – benefit of destiny, as when in a *totum simul*, the self becomes 'round', (see Dickinson's poem III), as no sublunary lives are. In the *totum simul* are, in full detail, the empirical self's 'contents', its experiences and aspects as these are reduced to a comprehensible unity. This is a unity implicit in the soul's 'simplicity' as it is 'issued', but which unity is never given in the life which follows birth: only in the life which follows hereafter.

It is embarrassing to one's reading of Emily Dickinson that her faith in any hereafter wavered. She carefully kept clear of the religious revivals which occurred from time to time in her native Amhurst. Enthusiasm was not for her, even if ecstasy was, very much. And Dickinson could manage private interpretation, and a religion of *one*, herself its sole believer and ultimate synod.

Self without Destiny: Pascal's **Divertissements**?

For Sartre and most Existentialists, there is no God and no immortality, and the only 'destiny' lies in the mere praxis of project after project. Even the notion of 'mere project' seems to be one as of a diminished destiny. Does personal identity not only make sense of its person's experience, but have its own final sense, not in a complete biography, but this biography read as destiny? One puts this as a question: one is not sure that it is a rhetorical one.

If Harry Wardlaw says more about the self's destiny than about the self, is it because as a Protestant pastor he so well knows the answer to our – rhetorical? – question that he overlooks it. As, further, he takes the philosophers' self for granted, as a simple necessary condition of destiny? If so, one is tempted to mark Destiny with a capital 'D'.

Freud, Heidegger and other gloomy thinkers have us living towards death, as if it were the project of projects. With Karl Barth, Wardlaw has us already projected towards a destiny with God.

But Wardlaw would complicate the Anglo-Catholicism of TS Eliot with something that seems to a Catholic, essentially a Protestant earnestness:

> ...the resurrection is not simply a transition of the immortal soul from one state to the next. It is, in quite a fundamental way a raising of life out of death; and just as judgement is the way to salvation, so death is the way to eternal life. This is the destiny which is set before us in Christ, and this is the hope in which Christians, 'look for the resurrection of the dead and the life of the world to come'; [as reads] the Nicene Creed.[20]

WS Merwin's 'Soul' and His 'Self' – Enigmas or Revelations?

The poet-as-soul addresses his soul in a series of questions without questions marks, since one is not speaking to another, but an identity questions itself:

TO THE SOUL

Is anyone there
if so
are you real
either way are you
one or several
if the latter
are you all at once
or do you
take turns not answering
is your answer
the question itself
surviving the asking
without end
whose question is it
how does it begin
where does it come from
how did it ever
find out about you
over the sound
of itself
with nothing but its own
ignorance to go by[21]

The lines 'are you / one or several' just possibly reflect medieval questions about the 'active intellect' into which the poet does not go: his strategy perhaps is merely to try to drive a wedge into the unity which is strong enough to speak in question-mark-less-questions to itself. So: 'is your answer / the question itself / surviving the asking / without end'. One is inclined to respond, 'yes, it is'. The poet asks of *his* question, 'whose question is it', writing not quite as the poet but as the soul of the poet: where the soul's 'hand' must be the poet's. And the primal *fissure* of self is not duality but self-reflexiveness, without which consciousness itself (its-self), would be nothing. The secondary fissure is that the present slides into memory, and may not always be able to be recovered.

The poem concludes 'how did it ever / find out about you / over the sound / of itself / with nothing but its own / ignorance to go by'.

Merwin's soul is, like *animula*, a simple soul, as yet without predicates whose self-naming would fracture the ignorance. Ignorance is what is 'had' where things are not named. But the soul – as 'simple' – is self-aware, a kind of existence without predicates: its consciousness of itself is a consciousness only of existence. This existence sans predicates presses the limits of intelligibility, but does not transgress them. The poet gives us a sense, aesthetic if not conceptual, of the soul's simplicity – and its power of self-reflection, writing, as he must, as Animula, adult and not infans, but eloquent. The whole poem is an aesthetic idea enacting a kind of glimpse-of-itself-by-the-soul: it is of course an aesthetic idea forged by the person WS Merwin. In TS Eliot's terms it tries to ask – and succeeds in asking/answering – '*Animula* how were you when *simple*?' And, notice the prime 'simple' of pure soul is fractured – even in Merwin's poem – by the need for predicates and un-simplicity as a condition of saying anything. Even about the totally *simple*. Merwin's masterly spareness brings off an utterance, and a sense, prima facia impossible of achievement. What we are offered here is at least a Kantian aesthetic idea; though I would reckon it an aesthetic apprehension of what – under Critical rules – cannot be apprehended. It is.

Merwin's self in 'To Myself' is the ideal unity of a self's experience which does not appear – even to itself – as an empirical given. Merwin's 'myself' is caught up in a Humean bind: the self 'pretend[s] to be time' when ideally it is – or has the destiny to be – a *totum simul*, making sense/completed narrative of the particular self's experiences: 'you who always the same / but pretend to be time . . .' The destiny/Destiny is sameness all-at-once-comprehending all-this-self's-times.

TO MYSELF

Even when I forget you
I go on looking for you
I believe I would know you
I keep remembering you
sometimes long ago but then
other times I am sure you
were here a moment before
and the air is still alive

> around where you were and I
> think then I can recognise
> you who are always the same
> who pretend to be time but
> you are not time and who speak
> in the words but you are not
> what they say you who are not
> lost when I do not find you[22]

The poem is – in part – about the self's secondary fissure, its being spread across a number of presents, along a life, and, doubtful, memory-line. 'You who are always the same', '...pretend to be time', because time is an absolute condition of our existence.

The syntax of the last six lines is forged, especially in the last three, into a grammatical knot, not easily untied. It reminds one of Donne, and baroque wrought-iron, while being so laconic and simple. Consider 'you are not time and who speak / in the words but you are not / what they say you who are not / lost when I do not find you'. Here it is a matter of teasing out (1) the intrusive 'they'; and (2) of unknotting the 'nots'. 'You who are not time [but] speak in the words of time (and speaking words is a function of time), *are.*' 'But you are not, what *they* say [i.e. that you are not]: 'you who are not-lost when I do not find you', no matter what '*they*' say. One might venture this analysis:

> ...but you are not
> what they say you {who} are [:] not [.]
> lost when I do not find you.

In the second quoted line we can get: 'what they say who you are, i.e. not'. That is: 'who or what you are is zero'. This reads if we transpose the {who} and add a 'what' as if implied. The 'not' in bold works twice; (1) As in 'what they say you who are not' as 'what they say, oh you who are not' – which apostrophic assertion of not-being Merwin's whole poem denies. This since, (2) the second tone of 'not' belongs to 'you who are not-lost when I do not find you'. Despite the text's 'not/lost' we can read 'not-lost'. And what we can read here, we must:

since the poem seems an enactment of not-lost-ness. The 'who' {who} becomes less puzzling when we see how it can *slide* between: 'you who are not' *(false)* and 'you who are not-lost *(true)*. The 'not' is double but not dubious, since Merwin's – just – conclusion is that: 'you {who} are not-lost when I do not find you': here the {who} is simply elided in the sense that we may read it or ignore it, taking the text as either apostrophe or plain assertion. Or *both*. The search has no end, so 'you' are not *found*: but 'you' are always there, in *the seeking itself*.

One can analyse this text, but not paraphrase it. Its indeterminacy of grammar is something within which one can determine – even so – a tension of meanings, which resolve into a determinate meaning, 'you . . . are not lost'.

Merwin holds at the centre of his high quest as Hume did not. Merwin's point is that: *you are not nothing as often alleged* by 'they', where Hume etc. are *'they'*. Merwin is 'myself-to-myself'. He routs the conspiracy against self, by enacting an aesthetic finding of it. *'They'* can go fish: and will catch nothing. He in a sense *knows* what he is trying to catch in the trying itself. That the total self as ideal unity is not in time to be found as a *totum simul* is an empirical fact which does not count against the possibility – 'ideally' – of finding – out of time – the rounded whole: Dickinson's, '. . . no lives are round / These hurry to a sphere and show, and end', suggests, as do Merwin's lines, an idea of the all-enclosed-sphere knowing itself as such. The sphere is a *totum simul* figure. Merwin gives us an aesthetic feel as of self. But Dickinson's 'and end' *ie* the ending of lives, is the necessary condition of their becoming 'round' in the required sense. And though, 'The Summers of the Hesperides are long', they are not endless. All ends in a ball. Destiny is the *terminus ad quem* of human/spiritual being. The semi-Puritan Dickinson points this up. Merwin, our contemporary, gestures towards it, more coolly even than Eliot.

In these Po-Mo post Po-Mo days, 'readings' are the way in which things go. I am reading Merwin – and to some extent Dickinson – through the Thomist fame: 'The soul is part of time existing above time in eternity; it contains nature, but surpasses the physical principle of motion measured by time.'[23]

Coda

The poets, by showing us the inwardness of felt-consideration of first *soul* then *self*, make of the Empiricist's failure a kind of success. Deep as Eliot, Dickinson and Merwin, one would find the standard undergraduate tutorial questions about soul and personal identity not inviting the usual dusty Empiricist answers – but issuing in an affirmation of: if not here, then hereafter soul and self, *given*. That is to say – if you let it – theology can well out of 'mere' philosophical problems, taking the empirical unavailability of the quite necessary idea of self-in-a-*totum simul* not as a dead end, but as a pointing beyond.

The philosopher on the margin of theology wriggles his way – with the help of poetry and aesthetic ideas – *in*. If only just. Full talk of destiny as Destiny, in which the totum simul is a mere incident, is the proper business of theology.

End Notes

1. *The Self and Its Destiny in Christianity,* by Harry Wardlaw, in the 'Religious Systems' series HUR203/4, Deakin University, 1990.
2. *A Treatise of Human Nature*, edited by LA Selby-Bigge, Oxford, at the Clarendon Press, 1888 etc, Sect VI, 'Of personal identity' 251*ff*.
3. God, freedom and immortality, see *The Critique of Pure Reason*, by Immanuel Kant, Bxxx and B7 Kemp Smith's translation (London: Macmillan), 29 and 46.
4. *Animula*, in TS Eliot, *Collected Poems 1909–1935*, (London Faber & Faber, 1936), 111–112.
5. *La Divina Commedia*, by Dante Alighieri, Italian edited by H Oelsner, English translations by JA Carlyle, Thomas Okey and PH Wicksteed: see *Purgatorio*. Published London, JM Dent & Sons, 1899–1901: edition of 1933 (and '38); Girone III, *Purgatorio* Canto XVI, 85, 196–197. See also Canto 86.
6. St Thomas Aquinas, *Summa Theologica*, *Prima Pars* Q.90, Art 2 and 3; Q118, Art 2. *Prima Secundae* Q3, Art 7 (reply to 2nd Objection); Q9, Art 6. The key quotation for our present purposes is '... the rational soul cannot be produced by a change in matter, it cannot be produced, save immediately by God', *cf Prima Pars* Q90 articles 2 and 3. Dominican translation Vol IV, 245 *ff* (London: Burns Oates & Washbourne, 1922, etc).

7. See *The Life of Emily Dickinson*, by Richard B Sewall, 1974. Edition used, First Harvard University Press pb, 1994, 23.

8. *Emily Dickinson: Selected Poems*, with intro by Christopher Moore, Gramercy Press, New York, Avenel, New Jersey 1993, quotations from Dickinson are from 175 to 184. *The Single Hound* text in the Gramercy Press volume is from Martha Dickinson Bianchi's 1914 edition. Bianchi was Emily's niece.

   The three-volume *Critical Edition of Dickinson* edited by Thomas H Johnson, (Cambridge, Mass: The Belknap Press of the Harvard University Press, 1951) says of Bianchi's edition, 'The text of *The Single Hound* is refreshingly accurate.' See Vol 1 xvii. So it is surprising that 'Adventure most unto itself', does not occur in the 'Index to First Lines' of the *The Poems of Emily Dickinson (Reading Edition)*, edited by RW Franklin (Cambridge, Mass: The Belknap Press of Harvard University Press and London, 1999). This omission is tiresome since the *Critical Edition* gives the line; but the poem is #822 'Stanza', 4; so 'Adventure most . . .' is not a *first* line. Richard B Sewall's biography of Dickinson, see above, warns us, 195, Note 3, against Bianchi's views on ED 's biography. However, to one who has become used to her compilation of ED 's poems – almost certainly not intended by ED to go so together in this array – there is a –gratuitous? – sense of rightness. The poem 'There is a solitude of space . . .' is #1696 in the Harvard *Reading Edition*.

9. 'Barnett Newman: The "Zip" and Specious Presents, or (Specious?) Presence. What Am I Doing Here?', by Patrick Hutchings, *Literature and Aesthetics*, Vol 13, No 1 (2003): 71–87.

10. See the second title page Harold Rosenberg's *Barnett Newman*, NY, NY, Harry N Abrams Inc publishers, edited by John P O'Neill 1978 cf reprint of 1994; title page #2 reads 'The self, terrible and constant, is for me the subject matter of painting' BN 1965. See too, loc cit '"Angst is dead", Joseph Albers', message to the author, late 1960s.'

11. From 'Recent American Synagogue Architecture' in *Barnett Newman: Selected Writings and Interviews*, edited by John P O'Neill, text notes and commentary by Mollie McNickle, intro by Richard Shiff (New York, NY: Alfred A Knopf, 1990), 180. For the explication of the expression 'Tzim-Tzum' in this Note (or Appendix) I am beholden to my friend and erstwhile colleague Dr Ian Weeks who pointed my reading in the right direction.

   The notion of *Tsimtsum* occurs notably in the Kabbalistic writings of Isaac Luria, sixteenth century. The following paragraphs may serve as an account:

   > Luria's theory based upon the doctrine of *Tsimtsum*, one of the most amazing and far-reaching conceptions

ever put forward in the whole history of Kabbalism. *Tsimtsum* originally means 'concentration' or 'contraction', but if used in the Kabbalistic parlance it is best translated by 'withdrawal' or 'retreat'. The idea first occurs in a brief and entirely forgotten treatise which was written in the middle of the thirteenth century and of which Luria seems to have made use, while its literary original is a Talmudic saying which Luria inverted. He stood it on its head, no doubt believing that he had put it on its feet. The Midrash – in sayings originating from third century teachers – occasionally refers to God as having concentrated His Shekhinah, His divine presence, in the holiest of holies, at the place of the *Cherubim*, as though His whole power were concentrated and contracted in a single point. Here we have the origin of the term *Tsimtsum,* while the thing itself is the precise opposite of this idea: to the Kabbalist of Luria's school *Tsimtsum* does not mean the concentration of God *at* a point, but his retreat *away* from a point.

The text continues a little later:

> God was compelled to make room for the world by, as it were, abandoning a region within Himself, a kind of mystical primordial space from which He withdrew in order to return to it in the act of creation and revelation. The first act of *En-Sof*, the Inifinite Being, is therefore not a step outside but a step inside, a movement of recoil, of falling back upon oneself, of withdrawing into oneself. Instead of emanation we have the opposite, contraction. The God who revealed himself in firm contours was superseded by one who descended deeper into the recesses of His own Being, who concentrated Himself into Himself, and had done so from the very beginning of creation. To be sure, this view was often felt, even by those who gave it a theoretical formulation, to verge on the blasphemous. Yet it cropped up again and again, modified only ostensibly by a feeble 'as it were' or 'so to speak.'

From: *Major Trends in Jewish Mysticism,* by Gershom Scholem, foreword by Robert Alter (New York, NY: Schoken Books, 1946), 260–261. There is an article on Gerhard/Gershom Scholem by Cynthia Ozick in *The New Yorker,* September 2, 2002: 143–48: the *tsimtsum* is mentioned 145, col b 'In the beginning – Indeed before the beginning – God's luminous essence filled the pleroma, the stuff of nothingness that was everywhere. Then God performed an act of *tsimtsum*, self-limitation, in order to make room for Creation . . .'

12. See *Ekphrasis or the Illusion of the Natural Sign*, by Murray Krieger (Baltimore and London: Johns Hopkins University Press, 1992).

13. See 'The Sublime is Now', Barnett Newman *op cit* above, 170–173.

14. 'Recent American Synagogue Architecture', *op cit* above, Note 11, 180–182. Italics added.

15. Of Barnett Newman's subtext we make remark that his exaltation in the synagogue and the exaltation of a viewer of a Newman 'zip' work as a double. But Newman escapes Samuel Taylor Coleridge's so unfortunate conflation of *cogito ergo sum* and the 'I AM' of Exodus. See my 'ST Coleridge and the Desolation of Aesthetics', *Philosophical Studies* (Ireland), Vol XV, 1966. How Barnett Newman's tact works is by letting us make, and dialectically unmake, a connection, between our self and Absolute Selfhood. Where Coleridge plunges, Barnett Newman carefully insinuates. '[We] can experience the vision and feel the exaltation of "His trailing robes filling the Temple"'. This is how Barnett Newman's synagogue essay ends.

16. Rothko, see Robert Rosenblum's *Modern Painting in the Northern Romantic Tradition* (London: Thames & Hudson 1975), 215.

17. Emily Dickinson, Gramercy Press edition 175*ff*.

18. Emily Dickinson's 'home centeredness', her idiosyncratic religious beliefs, her reluctance to publish and so on are all themes in Richard B Sewall's already cited, and quite admirable *Life of Emily Dickinson*, qv.

19. The phrase/line 'Finite Infinity' of the Gramercy Press edition is missing from Franklin's Harvard edition, which – rather fussily – substitutes a simple dash for the end of poem 1696. The full *Critical Edition* by Thomas H Johnson allows the line. See Vol III, poem 1695, 1149. 'No autograph copy of this poem is known. The first seven lines follow the transcript made by Sue [Susan Dickinson] (HSTs) who did not there copy down the final line. The last line is taken from the published text . . . . Publication SH (1914), 27: LL 1924) 196.' *Note* 'There is a solitude of space' is # 1695 in Johnson's *Critical Edition*, but 1696 in Franklin's *Reading Edition*.

20. Concluding section of Wardlaw's essay in the Deakin booklet.

21. 'To the Soul', WS Merwin, *The New Yorker*, February 5, 2001: 40.

22. 'To Myself', WS Merwin, *The New Yorker*, June 2, 2003: 46. Both poems are reproduced with the author's most kind permission, and with the permission of his agents.

23. Opusculae, a, Exposition de Causis, lect 9. More easily to be found in the late Mgr Thomas Gilby's *St Thomas Aquinas: Philosophical Texts* (Oxford: Oxford University Press, 1951), extract no 531, 197.

21

NAMING THE CREATOR AND FACING THE CONSEQUENCES

NORMAN YOUNG

To contribute to this volume of essays in honour of the Revd Professor Harry Wardlaw is both a pleasure and a privilege. Harry and I both took up our Professorial appointments at the beginning of 1964, he at Ormond and I at Queen's, and we have been colleagues and firm friends ever since. Our decision to combine our classes and to share the teaching anticipated the wider integration of the Presbyterian and Methodist theological halls, which in turn led to establishment of the United Faculty of Theology less than a decade later. Over the years Harry's creative intellectual dialogue with the thought of Paul Tillich has been widely known and appreciated on three continents by colleagues and students. Therefore in this essay, while I return to a topic that has long preoccupied me, I do so here informed particularly by one aspect of Tillich's most characteristic methodological theme, *viz* that of correlation.

Tillich maintained that 'the answers implied in the event of revelation are meaningful only in so far as they are in correlation with . . . existential questions.'[1] Applying this to the doctrine of creation, or better, to belief in God as creator, means that significant theological discussion must address issues involved in our human existence. This correlation is not a matter of bringing to bear an already formulated and immutable body of revealed truth. It implies a relationship between the divine and the human in which revelation is an occurrence within historical event. In this paper, therefore, after a brief introductory section, what is involved in believing in God as creator will be considered in four specific situations.

*

To believe in God as free and purposive creator is to believe that hope for the future is warranted and that direction for the present can be found. But in order to give content to such hope and direction we need to be able to say more than that 'God created'. Revelation that gives rise to the affirmation, 'God, creator of heaven and earth' needs to be correlated with questions that emerge in human existence. Consequently, faith that gives rise to a way of life needs to be able to give this God a name, to say who this God is, what are God's intentions and how these are to be brought to fulfilment. This cannot be extrapolated from variations on the theme 'God created out of nothing'. Judaism goes on to affirm that God is the one who remains faithful to the covenant and calls for faithfulness from the covenant people, while Christianity goes on to declare that the creator-God is one whose creative word was incarnate in Jesus Christ and whose life-giving Spirit creates anew.

As far as religious *theory* is concerned, this is just another instance of the widely recognised circular nature of theological reflection – no doctrine is complete in itself, each informs the other. But approached with the question of religious *practice,* how one is to live faithfully in the world of the creator and covenant God, another circle becomes evident. Israel's first belief in God as creator was as creator of them as a nation, a people who had been no people, called out of captivity, guided through the desert, directed toward the promised land. Since this God would stand by the covenant people, they were ensured of protection from the gods and rulers of hostile nations. This confidence was shored up further as they came to believe that their God was none other than the one almighty creator of the heavens and the earth and all the nations. What now was their place among the nations? No longer God's only-*created* people, but still God's only-*chosen* people through whom all the nations would be blessed, and given the law so that through this covenant people of God all could know the creator's will for the whole creation. The sequence of belief, therefore, was from God the creator of the nation to God the creator of the heavens and the earth. But to know *how* to live in the created world, back around the circle to their belief in the creator as God of the covenant.

The same connection between belief in Creator-God and Covenant-God, in this case God of the new covenant in Jesus

Christ, is clearly present in Christian faith as well, and here too the interconnectedness is evident in both theory and practice. The Creed begins with an affirmation of belief in God as Creator and immediately goes on to Jesus Christ, incarnate Son. But which comes first in practice? Looking at the world around us, would we conclude it was the work of an orderly, much less compassionate creator? Influential theologians as far apart as John Henry Newman and Karl Barth did not think so. Newman thought that looking into the world for signs of the creator was like looking into a mirror and not seeing your own face. Barth maintained that the world is recognisable as God's creation only as we begin with God's new creation in Christ. In any case, whatever the sequence of belief and experience, it remains clear that in order to live in the world with faith, hope and love we need to believe both that there is a purposive Creator so that there is some point in seeking purpose in the creation, and that the Creator's intention for the creation is conveyed to people through a self-revealing covenant in which the Creator is named.

*

What then are the consequences of knowing the name of the creator and covenant God, remembering that in Judeo-Christian context a 'name' is more than an extrinsic label for person, since it conveys the reality of one's very nature and being?

The most obvious consequence is that those to whom such insight into the nature, being and purpose of God have been given are called to shape their lives according to that purpose. Such expectation is not an arbitrary demand imposed simply to reinforce the Creator's authority but is an insight into the way of life that is most creative, 'for the best', not only for us but for the whole created order. However, at the same time we have to face the fact that, from whatever varied motives, people over the centuries have acted out destructive distortions of these insights, and we are left to deal with the consequences. Sometimes the distortions and their consequences are addressed by reconsidering views of Creator-

God and of Covenant-God in their own right, at other times by re-reading one in the light of the other. Four examples follow, two dealt with rather briefly, the other two more extensively.

First, it is clear from the Old Testament witness itself that from time to time the calling of Israel was interpreted as granting her a privileged place superior to all other peoples and nations, and that Israel's Covenant-God would destroy her enemies and prosper her cause no matter what. Against this, various writers called Israel back to her God-given vocation, to be a light to the nations, the one through whom all peoples would be blessed. The prophets declared that if Israel disobeyed her Lord she would not be spared punishment and exile, and that invoking 'the Temple of the Lord, the Temple of the Lord' was blasphemous and would prove ineffective. As well, and employing parable and irony to great effect, the Book of Jonah corrects the misreading of belief about the Covenant-God by appealing to the consequences of believing in the Creator-God. Why should God rejoice in the destruction of Israel's enemy? After all, God had created not only Israel but the people of Nineveh also. They were close to the Creator's heart too, and so were their cattle!

Richard Niebuhr maintained that the sequence described above involves a persistent dilemma:

> Faith in the One cannot become incarnate short of the realisation of a universal human community in which all relations are part of the covenant with the Faithful One; but neither can it become incarnate unless in an intensive way every part of human existence – from religion to eating and drinking – is brought into relation with him.[2]

What Niebuhr cites here as a dilemma ought to be seen more positively as the challenge to recognise the inter-relationship between believing in God as creator and deciding how responsibly to live in the created world – in one sense, the task of correlation. Clearly this challenge is by no means confined to those within the circle of Jewish faith. Nor is it easily met. The next example confronts us with the most notorious instance in recent history of perverse understanding of God as creator. But whereas in the first example prophetic voices faced the situation by proclaiming the universality of the Creator's care, in the next, faithful prophets affirmed the particular revelation in which the Creator's purpose is known.

Second then, in Germany in the late 1920s belief in God as creator was invoked to assert that in the rebuilding of the nation under the Nazi regime, God's creative spirit was evident. People were called upon to recognise that out of the chaos of civil unrest following World War I a new order was emerging, and to identify this as a sign of God's working within the life of their nation. Out of despair was growing hope. Out of the weakness, disillusionment and aimlessness of youth was evident a rising strength, idealism and purpose. Not surprisingly the German Christian movement that supported these views found ready endorsement from within the churches.

Only later, in the 1930s, did it become clear how these views were being distorted to justify the Nazi blueprint for a greater Germany, and the policy of eliminating those who did not fit their criteria for being fully human beings. Only when purges became more frequent, persecution of Jews more evident, and churches themselves subject to more restrictions with some of her leaders imprisoned, did opposition solidify. Those who led the opposition did so by appealing to the second article of the Creed as interpreter of the first. What is genuinely of the Creator-God could be discerned, it was insisted, only by re-examining the terms of the covenant in the light of God's re-creative word in Jesus Christ. Naming the Creator then as the Lord and Father of Jesus Christ had the most profound consequences. It led to the founding of the Confessing Church in Germany in 1934,[3] the establishment of a clandestine seminary for training its pastors, the termination of the appointment of some theological professors involved in the founding of the Confessing Church (among them Karl Barth), the internment of some pastors, and an identifiably Christian stream within the ongoing opposition to Hitler in Germany, some of whom were involved in the plot to assassinate him (notably Bonhoeffer) which cost them their lives.

Third, over the centuries we have seen that God's call to a

particular people to be a 'light to the nations' has been interpreted as giving the covenant people the role of 'enlightener of the nations'. So long as this is understood modestly as 'sharing insight into God's purpose for all' it can be defended. However, once it develops into asserting a people as 'only-enlightened among the nations' and is allied to a view of God's favouring this people, especially with a grant of sole tenure to a land, we have to face consequences that are far-reaching, on-going and devastating. Some of the most destructive horrors in human history, from crusades and holy wars in the past to Arab-Israeli conflict and Islamic-fundamentalist campaigns in the present, have fed on this conviction of being the most enlightened and with God-given right of dominion. We see its most recent manifestation in the alliance of American far-right Christians with the hawks in the Bush administration, where justification for invasion and pre-emptive strike is couched in overtly religious terms – enemies are characterised as 'the axis of evil' and the name of God constantly invoked in the cause. 'God bless America!'

Most Christians from whatever country will be able to recognise the ill effects of this notion of God's granting superiority to a particular nation, race, culture, or gender. The British must assess the extent to which colonial expansion depended in large measure on this view, and those from the British Methodist tradition as I am need to acknowledge that some of Charles Wesley's verse shows that he was by no means immune to the 'God who made thee mighty, make thee mightier yet' syndrome.[4] Americans acknowledge how influential in dealing with the original inhabitants was the view that God had given white settlers the land. For my part, I need to testify to the destructive consequences of that view in Australia.

In the early days of settlement here it was a view widely expressed by Christian leaders, full of optimism and hope,[5] and it still persists, albeit in a secular version. Potential for destructive consequences was enhanced by the British law under which Australia was settled in the eighteenth century, declaring the area *terra nullius*, ie, legally unoccupied. This not only left Aborigines with no land rights whatsoever, it also reinforced the view that they were so primitive as to be of no account, if not actually sub-human. It also contributed to the justification for the virtual extermination of Aborigines on the island of Tasmania in the nineteenth century. Significantly, those to be thus dealt with were usually referred to not only as savages, but as *heathen* savages. From the presumption of God-given superiority of the settlers, it followed that when Aboriginal culture did not conform, it could be swept aside. Aborigines, it was noted, did no paid work, had no purpose-built housing, no significant monuments, no discernable boundaries, tended no flocks, did not till the land. It therefore seemed, from the perspective of the settlers, that by imposing their way of life they were doing the right thing, not only for the land but for its ancient people too. So when the final conflict came, as it did inevitably when Aborigines saw what was happening as no less than stealing their land, the view that Aborigines were less than fully human lent legitimacy to the settlers' recourse to the superiority of arms.[6]

No one these days would justify the slaughter that followed, but is the reasoning that made it possible over and done with? We are still coming to terms with the way Australian churches actively co-operated with the Government in its policy of forcefully removing mixed race children from their Aboriginal families and placing them in church-run institutions to be brought up as 'white'. No doubt many of these children have benefited from better health and enhanced opportunities that schooling and higher education can bring. But evidence from the Royal Commission[7] conveys in harrowing detail the ongoing psychological damage done to many by this policy. The claim that this was done for the best of motives is probably true, but those motives themselves depend upon the presumption of superiority on the part of those implementing the policy.

In the twenty-first century the Australian Government places in mandatory detention, usually in remote and inhospitable areas and behind razor wire, all asylum-seekers landing on our shores without visas. They are classed as illegal immigrants, and this inhumane policy is defended, at least partly, by the less-than-subtle suggestion that they belong to an alien religion and inferior culture. (British or American citizens who overstay their visas and are therefore also illegal immigrants receive no such treatment!) We need no reminding that just before a recent Federal election, a hitherto unpopular government became overnight favourites with

Australian voters. What turned out to be false accusations were made that some Afghani asylum seekers on boats off the Australian shore threw their children overboard in an attempt to blackmail the navy into letting them proceed. 'We don't want those sort of people here' our Prime Minister declared, over and over again, and the majority of the electorate agreed.

In the case of asylum seekers, Australian churches have campaigned against the policy of compulsory detention and have condemned the technique of demonising people in order to justify their being treated inhumanely. Although not always articulated, this campaign is based on belief in God as creator who has equal regard for all people, *and* in the Covenant-God who calls us to care especially for those most in need. On the same grounds the churches have vigorously supported moves (recently successful) to grant Aboriginal land rights.[8] They have also, collectively and as individual churches, said an official 'sorry' to the Stolen Generation (which the Government steadfastly refuses to do) and have made some restitution, moving closer to full reconciliation.

Fourth, since the 1960s it has been widely recognised that one of the consequences of believing in God as creator has been a distorted conclusion about the authority God has given humans over the rest of creation.[9] The commands in the Genesis story, 'be fruitful and multiply, fill the earth and subdue it, have dominion . . .' have been interpreted as giving humans the right to exploit the rest of creation for their own purposes.[10] So much has been written since about the relation between religious belief and ecology that there is no need to rehearse it further here. I simply raise the issue because setting right the erroneous religious interpretation that leads to such destructive consequences involves *both* (a) re-examining the doctrine of creation in its own right, *and* (b) understanding it in the light of God's new covenant in Jesus Christ, and in both cases facing the consequences.

(a) That giving humans 'naming rights' is no justification for unbridled exploitation becomes clearer with further reflection on what is implied in 'being made in the image of God'. That means, among other things, being given the capacity and responsibility to image or reflect God's being and attitude toward the rest of creation. This relation can be expressed in terms of proportion

– God is to humans as humans are to the rest of creation. Since the fact that God is our creator does not mean that God exploits us for God's benefit, so our God-given role does not imply permission to exploit the rest of creation for our benefit.

What then does being in the image of God, as the rest of creation is not, imply? Having freedom and reason and so not bound to act just on instinct? Yes. But more profoundly, using both freedom and reason to *be creative.* Alone of all the species, humans share God's creative capacity, not to create *ex nihilo* of course, but certainly to be inventive and to bring into being that which is genuinely new.

To sustain, replenish and renew the creation then is our vocation as humans. To do this we are called and gifted by God's spirit, but not just to keep everything the way it was in the beginning. That kind of ideological primitivism is designated unfaithfulness and ingratitude in the New Testament. Remember the servant who preserved his one talent by hiding it in the ground? We are called and empowered to be creative by developing the potentialities of creation to enhance the health and fruitfulness of the earth and the well-being of all God's creatures. So the question we have constantly to face is not *whether* land should be developed and resources tapped but how much should be used and how much left in its natural state, and in what ways development should best proceed, and from what motives and for whose benefit.

So, reconsidering the doctrine of creation, and of humans made in the image of God, challenges the notion of God-given right to exploit and despoil. How then *should* we live in our earthly environment, obedient to the will and purpose of the Creator-God? To answer that we reconsider the doctrine of new creation and of humans remade by the Covenant-God.

(b) The New Testament proclaims in various ways that in Jesus Christ new creation is already dawning. Within the church this has been understood largely as the salvation of individuals, with images of a renewed earth projected to the end-time.[11] There are, however, conclusions to be drawn from this belief in Jesus Christ that relate to our caring for the environment here and now. Some of these have been superficial. One popular song of the 1960s called people to follow Jesus as leader of the counter-culture – he was bearded and unemployed, lived in a nomadic commune, wore homespun clothes and ate organic food! There are, however, at least two theological insights with far more profound implications.

First, in the light of Christ we believe that we are justified by grace through faith alone. That is often viewed as a theological abstraction with little down-to-earth relevance. Consider, however, the everyday meaning of 'justifying ourselves'. Establishing our own importance is a large part of that, doing and saying things that back up the status we want to claim. Despite what we profess about being justified by God's grace, we Christians spend a great deal of time and effort justifying ourselves by works, and those imbued with the so-called Protestant work ethic are particularly susceptible. Years ago RH Tawney wrote his influential *Religion and the Rise of Capitalism,* whose thesis was that the amassing of capital and possessions for their own sake developed largely because of a misconception that these would be evidence of being numbered among God's elect.

However we assess Tawney's original thesis, people today who may think not at all about justifying themselves in *God's* eyes are nevertheless greatly concerned about how other *people* regard them. There can be no doubt that this is one of the main motivating forces in accumulation for the sake of accumulation, conspicuous consumption far beyond even the most extravagant need, exercising the power of wealth to show who is the greatest. This goes on not just at individual but also at communal and national level as well, and there can be no dispute that all this contributes to the most serious depletion of natural resources.

Second, to believe in Jesus Christ is to know that we are all one people on earth created by God, all of us sisters and brothers of Christ. Consequently, as one family the whole human race is called on to take responsibility and to care for each other. We are called to be neighbour. Who is our neighbour? Whoever is in need, the parable of the Good Samaritan teaches us, and that includes those we cannot see, those distanced by space and also by time. Not only those in other countries but also future generations as yet unborn, these are neighbours. Consider, without elaboration, some of our most urgent environmental issues:

- Building nuclear power plants without safe waste disposal being in place
- Misuse of herbicides and pesticides
- Dumping of toxic industrial by-products
- De-afforestation and over-cultivation
- Heedless waste of water resources
- Build-up of gases that lead to global warming

So often responses take a short-term and short-range view. 'Things won't get bad enough to harm me.' 'Dump it anywhere so long as it's far away.' 'Environment friendly costs too much money.' 'Signing up to the Kyoto protocols is not in the national interest.' Consequently toxic chemical waste accumulates at an alarming rate in rusting containers in Melbourne's western (poorer) suburbs. Uranium miners in Kakadu National Park sought permission to flush radioactive waste down-river because holding tanks were not big enough. Four-fifths of water for irrigation is wasted by evaporation because it flows through open channels. Are there no alternatives? Well yes, there are. High-temperature incinerators could be built to dispose of chemical waste safely. Additional holding tanks could be built at Kakadu. Water for irrigation could flow through enclosed pipes. Australia could sign up to the Kyoto limits on greenhouse gases. All of these alternatives, of course, would be very expensive, and no Australian government has yet been willing to raise taxes, nor any company to lower corporate profits, sufficiently to pay the cost.

However, once again the parable of the Good Samaritan gives us a lead. In stopping by the roadside to tend the one wounded by bandits he ran the risk of attack from the same marauders. In binding up the wounds he used some of his own provisions. In providing for the future he dug into his own pocket. So whether it is reversing the effects of environmental degradation in our own land, or providing alternatives for those countries whose livelihood depends on degrading their own, we cannot avoid the challenge of helping to meet the costs, as individuals, as churches and as nations. This too is involved in facing the consequences of naming as Creator the God and Father of our Lord Jesus Christ.

Where any are in Christ, there is new creation.

End Notes

1. Paul Tillich, *Systematic Theology*, Vol 1 (Chicago: Chicago University Press, 1951), 61.
2. H Richard Niebuhr, *Radical Monotheism and Western Culture* (London: Faber, 1960), 61.
3. The first Synod was held at Barmen on 29 and 30 May, 1934. Its Declaration affirmed that the actions of the Creator-God in nature and history could be discerned only in the light of the revelation in Jesus Christ.
4. See especially his 'Hymns and verses on patriotism', part II of *The Unpublished Poetry of Charles Wesley*, edited by Kimbrough and Beckerlegge, Vol 1 (Nashville: Kingswood Books, 1988), 59–140.
5. For example, J Dunmore Lang, Church of Scotland minister who became minister of Scots Church, Sydney, and later elected to the Legislative Assembly, expressed the view of many earlier leaders when he wrote, 'I believe it [Australia] is destined, in the counsels of infinite wisdom, to be the seat of one of the first Christian nations of the world.' *The Coming Event*, 39.
6. All this, it should be noted in defiance of instructions from British Parliament, consistent with those given to settlers in other new colonies. Eg, 'You are to endeavour by every possible means to open an intercourse with the natives, and to conciliate their affections, enjoining all our subjects to live in amity and kindness with them.' *Historical Record of New South Wales*, Vol 1, part II, 52. Quoted in J Woolmington, editor, *Aborigines in Colonial Society* (Melbourne: Cassell, 1973), 2. My attention was first drawn to this by my son Paul Young in an unpublished essay, 'Was the extermination by the British settlers of the Aboriginal Tasmanians inevitable by 1830?' He sets out in detail what hallmarks of British culture were lacking that led to the judgement that Aboriginal culture was deemed so primitive as to be of no account.
7. The so-called 'Stolen Generation' Report, chaired by Sir Ronald Wilson, former High Court judge and President of the Assembly of the Uniting Church in Australia.
8. Some decades ago, when the House of Lords was the final Court of Appeals for Australians, the Methodist Church funded an appeal for Aboriginal land rights, which foundered on the *terra nullius* clause.
9. Lynn White, Jr, in his article 'The historical roots of our ecological crisis' (in *Science*, Vol 155, March 1967: 1203 ff) was a prime mover in the debate that followed.
10. Charles Birch, in an address to the WCC Assembly in Nairobi in 1975, noted that the other directive in that chapter, *viz.* 'replenish the earth' has largely gone unheeded.
11. Only comparatively recently has Paul's passage in Romans, about

the created universe waiting with eager longing for its release, been interpreted as committing people of faith here and now to the task of redressing human devastation of the environment. CFD Moule was an early exception. *Man and Nature in the New Testament* (London: Athlone, 1964).

22

IN DEFENCE OF FIG LEAVES:
A TANGENTIAL REFLECTION ON THE
SEXUALITY DEBATE IN THE UCA

SANDY YULE

It is a privilege and a pleasure for me to contribute to this *Festschrift* volume in honour of my teacher and friend Harry Wardlaw.[1] To God be the glory.

I first met Harry when he came to College Church, Parkville, as parish minister. I was in Ormond College studying philosophy and then entering the Theological Hall for education and training as a Presbyterian minister myself. Harry took up his appointment as Professor of Theology in 1964 when my class was beginning its second year. I was one who felt very happy at this development. In our first year, we had been taught theology by Professor Dudley Hopkirk, whom I remember as a kindly man whose lectures had first been written in – some said – the 1930s. Whatever the truth of this ecclesiastical legend, I was still struggling with the theological questions raised for me by four years of study in philosophy and by my experience of the Australian Student Christian Movement (ASCM). I was therefore not very receptive to clear-cut theological teaching which seemed overly simple to me.

In those years, the Theological Hall conducted internal examinations during the year, leading up to final external examinations from the Melbourne College of Divinity. I duly took note of warnings from my senior colleagues and wrote answers to the internal exam that were based upon my lecture notes. In the external Theology paper, however, I wrote answers from my own philosophically oriented reflections. I was not pleased to learn that my mark for the external exam was fifty per cent, significantly less than my internal mark, and that Professor Hopkirk had been the examiner. One friend commented at the time that fifty per cent was the lowest mark available before a second examiner would have had to be called. I tell this story to illustrate the depth of welcome that I personally felt for Harry's appointment as Professor.

Harry did not let me down. No one could complain about getting cut and dried answers from Harry's lectures. I mainly remember them as an intense monologue in which Harry would establish a question and then address it, occasionally coming to a clear and persuasive statement which he offered as a reliable basis for further intellectual exploration. I remember the long shadow of Søren Kierkegaard, both in Harry's approach to the task of thinking theologically and to the choice of questions. We started with the possibility and the reality of divine revelation to us finite creatures – and it must be said that we hardly ever departed very far from this theme. I did not experience this as a limitation, so much as a firmly based initial uncertainty on which to build an intellectual approach to Christian faith and life. Harry encouraged me to take the risk of avoiding premature closure about important questions. He also showed me how to appreciate the level of genuine progress made in a sustained piece of reflective thinking. For this – and for many more things, especially friendship – I thank him.

In the spirit of the saying that the most sincere form of flattery is imitation, my offering to this *Festschrift* takes the form of a tangential reflection on the long-running debate about Christian teaching on homosexuality. This debate continues to be of central importance in the life of the Christian churches. It profoundly touches our sense of human and personal identity. It raises awkward and uncomfortable questions about biblical teaching and about past Christian understandings and practices. It raises questions about God's purposes for us and our world. Ultimately, it raises questions about our understanding of God.

This debate has challenged me at many different levels over many years[2] and is showing no signs of getting any easier, despite my best efforts at reaching well-based theological conclusions. I recognise that I have the possibility of entering this debate at a detached and intellectual level because I am a happily married father of two and grandfather of one. Also, I have heeded the prudential counsel of the church in which I grew up about avoiding promiscuous sexual involvements because they compromise personal integrity. My experiential base for thinking about these questions is therefore mostly centred on traditional Christian family life and what I have received from the imaginative and/or biographical accounts of others. Yet it is also true that I can learn from what I receive from those whose experience has been very different from my own.

Perhaps the most important thing for me to acknowledge is that the voice of heterosexual males has been historically privileged in this discussion. There are many dimensions to this historical privilege, but my point is that the mere fact of this privilege makes the speech situation unequal. This was brought home to me recently when I read an account of a session of a workshop on violence. In this session, the group was divided into two, the men and the women. All participants were then provided with paper and pens and invited to make a list of the things that they did every day in order to avoid sexual harassment and assault. The group of men reportedly all scratched their heads and looked blank. The only positive response recorded was to stay out of jail. They were all finished within five minutes. The group of women wrote pages of detailed accounts of habitual actions and strategies which they found it necessary to use.

This anecdotal report brought home to me the profoundly different reality in the general experience of men and women on this matter. My point here is that something of the same kind of difference – a difference that affects all aspects of our lives – exists between heterosexual and homosexual men, and probably also between heterosexual and homosexual women. Admittedly, there will be many other people who find themselves somewhere between these clear-cut identities, like men who happen to be unusually fearful of predatory sexual attack or people of bisexual orientation. Still, the general point is that this is a situation of inequality of standing. Apart from anything else, it is hard to find genuinely common ground. It also seems important for the privileged to show care for those less privileged.

Elizabeth Stuart, a Senior Lecturer in Religious Studies at the University of Glamorgan, is a theologian who writes from a feminist and lesbian perspective. Her sardonic comments on the efforts of male theologians such as myself in this debate are worth hearing.

> Those of us who are lesbian, gay or bisexual have sat on the
> sidelines watching scholars tackling each other for the ball of
> our lives. When the fundamentalist gets hold of it he kicks it
> into the goal marked 'perversion deliberately chosen, explicitly
> condemned by God's word, get cured or get out of the Church'.
> When the conservative gets hold of it he kicks it into the goal
> marked 'not deliberately chosen, probably born that way, but
> activity still condemned by God's word – it is OK to be it, not OK
> to engage in genital acts'. The angst-ridden liberal kicks the ball
> back and forwards, up and down the pitch; finally he stands in
> the middle and declares that, whereas scripture and tradition
> undoubtedly condemn homosexual acts, they did not know
> as much about homosexuality as we do today; so although the
> Church has a duty to uphold the idea of heterosexual marriage,
> because that is what scripture and tradition do, homosexual
> relationships might be looked upon as falling short of this
> ideal but not sinful as such because they can't help it. He then
> scuttles off the pitch before the crowd and the players can get
> him. The radical bounces the ball up and down on his head,
> doing amazing tricks whilst he explains: 'Yes, marriage is the
> ideal, but lesbian and gay people are perfectly capable of
> marriage' . . . He awaits the adoration of the crowd but the only
> sounds are of splatters of rage coming out of the fundamentalist
> and the conservative, and the anxious perspiring of the liberal
> in the changing-room . . . He turns to the crowd: 'What *do* you
> want, then?' he shouts in exasperation. And with one voice
> the answer booms: 'Can we have our ball back please?' We are
> tired of other Christian people kicking around the ball of our
> lives . . . Lesbian and gay people are the latest in a now fairly long
> line of people claiming the right to do theology for themselves
> about themselves.[3]

There is a fundamental question of principle asserted here, that it is
improper for one group of people to theologise in such a way that
they unilaterally define the reality of the lives of other people. This
seems an acceptable principle to me, both in terms of natural justice
and in terms of the nature of theology. Our human theologies seek to
express God's truth. Where we are dealing with the reality of people's
lives (and ultimately, I believe that this also holds for the reality of our
own lives), we should, as a fundamental matter of truth, recognise that

God is the judge and not ourselves. We should therefore respect the right of others to inform us of how they believe they are before God. We should also attend to anything that they might want to tell us about their spiritual discernment of our situation. This does not end all questions, but it offers a better chance of success in the theological task than individual theologians universalising their intuitions. This respect for others requires us to engage with others in the task of articulating our understanding of God.

In terms of Stuart's typology of male theologians, I recognise all too much of myself in the liberal. Perhaps this is my moment for re-emerging from the changing-room. I see value in emphasising the need for humility in this whole matter. The theological condemnation of sodomy, generally understood today to refer to same-sex genital activity, has a very long history in Judaeo-Christian tradition, though the word itself is apparently not found before the eleventh century in Latin usage.[4] It is a word formed for purposes of condemnation. Church people from generations up to and including my own have to ask: Can it really be true that this condemnation is not from God? Even to use the word is to conjure up the shades of Christian inquisition of the lives of those suspected of heterodox faith and practice, an inquisition all too often backed by the authority to torture and kill. Liberality in holding back this authority seems to me not such a bad thing.

The most serious question for Christians here is probably that of God's judgement. One of the important divisions in this debate is between those who believe that we already know what God's judgement is and those who do not so believe. If we do know, it is a matter of unfaith if we shirk our responsibility to witness to this judgement. If we do not, it seems quite wrong to condemn people different from ourselves (who do not obviously harm others) in the name of God. I stand with those who genuinely believe that we do not know how God judges homoerotic friendships. I say this on the basis of a careful study of the relevant passages of the Bible and of church tradition. It also seems important to remember the words of the Sermon on the Mount: 'Judge not, that you be not judged' (Matthew 7:1 NRSV). God is the judge of each of us and our conversation within the church should continue to take this as a starting point.[5]

An important prior question we should ask in thinking about God's judgement is who this 'we' may be. When we intentionally include people of homosexual orientation within the bounds of this 'we', the nature of the question is likely to change. People who are existentially involved in the relationships under consideration deserve respect in two important ways. They have a distinct authority in relation to the lived experience under question which the rest of us – I believe – must acknowledge. They also have the right to a care for their privacy in matters of self-disclosure. We all know about the prevalence of self-serving and self-justifying dynamics when our own case is under scrutiny. As Christians, we have well developed ways of testing the spirits to see if they be of God. My conclusion is that it is impossible to enter into this debate without a lively sense of our need for divine guidance and assistance in discernment.

Our spiritual forebears knew about homosexuality. They mostly had a simple answer to it, which was a general rejection of homosexual behaviour as a possibility for Christians. To let one voice speak for this majority view, we can turn to what Karl Barth has to say in the *Church Dogmatics*.

> ... everything which points in the direction of male or female seclusion, or of religious or secular orders or communities, or of male or female segregation – if it is undertaken in principle and not consciously and temporarily as an emergency measure – is obviously disobedience. All due respect to the comradeship of soldiers! But neither men nor women can seriously wish to be alone, as in clubs and ladies' circles. Who commands or permits them to run away from each other? ... It is well to pay heed even to the first steps in this direction.
>
> These first steps may well be symptoms of the malady called homosexuality. This is the physical, psychological and social sickness, the phenomenon of perversion, decadence and decay, which can emerge when man refuses to admit the validity of the divine command in the sense in which we are now considering it. In Rom 1 Paul connected it with idolatry, with changing the truth of God into a lie, with the adoration of the creature rather than the Creator (v.25).
>
> ... there follows the corrupt emotional and finally physical desire in which – in a sexual union which is not and cannot be genuine – man thinks he must seek and can find in

man, and woman in woman, a substitute for the despised partner ... Naturally the command of God is opposed to these courses. This is almost too obvious to need stating ... But the decisive word of Christian ethics must consist in a warning against entering on the whole way of life which can only end in the tragedy of concrete homosexuality ...

The command of God shows him irrefutably – in clear contradiction to his own theories – that as a man he can only be genuinely human with woman, or as a woman with man. In proportion as he accepts this insight, homosexuality can have no place in his life, whether in its more refined or cruder forms.[6]

There is much here that is obviously helpful. The requirement that men relate to women and men (and women to men and women) in order to find their humanity is an appropriate challenge to all areas of same-sex preference. This is particularly helpful to the church in assessing gifts for Christian ministry. It does seem clear that men who despise women and women who hate men are not well placed to convey the Christian gospel. Well roared, old lion. So why might we feel a need to go beyond Barth's categorical rejection of physical homosexuality?

The basic reason why I feel the need to withhold assent from this rejection is the claim advanced by homosexual people who are Christians. These people tell us that they are called by God into Christian obedience and that, for them, part of the expression of that obedience is through a loving friendship with another person of the same sex. On Barth's terms, this is an impossibility if homoerotic activity is involved. Yet we are finding significant numbers of people in the life of our churches who are dedicating their lives to proving the viability of this way of life for homosexual people called by Christ. The advice of Gamaliel to the Temple Council in Jerusalem about dealing with the first Christians has resonance here. 'If this plan or this undertaking is of human origin, it will fail; but if it is of God, you will not be able to overthrow it – in that case you may even be found fighting against God' (Acts 5:38–39).

I recognise that for many Christians, the fact that it is part of our sinful human condition to prefer our own way to God's way means that they find it hard to credit the possibility of Christian vocation for practising homosexual people. Still, this is for me the fundamental issue for the church. Is there a genuine vocation from God for certain individuals into a form of Christian identity different from those traditionally accepted? Nancy Duff[7] presents an approach to this question in terms of vocation.

> Drawing on the doctrine of vocation and the freedom of God, I contend that while most human beings are called by God into heterosexual relationships and some are called into the celibate life, still others are called into homosexual relationships. This affirmation of faithful, homosexual unions does not challenge the essential value of the male-female relationship (as some fear that it will) any more than the affirmation of celibacy does.[8]

For Christians, living in the light is important. We cannot afford to refuse to know what is true. Whatever the consequent difficulties, Christians must, it seems to me, accept the need for the genuine 'coming out'[9] of homosexual people. We should do so in the same spirit that we welcome all honest confession of what we have done and who we are. The differences among Christians which are still proving divisive relate not to 'coming out' as such, but to how Christians should respond to it. Conservative evangelicals see 'coming out' as a confession of a certain kind of sinfulness, so that the appropriate response is aimed at the overcoming of what is seen as sinful homosexual activity. Many liberal Christians consider the wrongness of some activities involving homosexuality to depend upon features such as promiscuity or the exploitation of children rather than homosexuality as such. Many liberals are happy to criticise promiscuity and exploitation by anyone, whatever the sexual orientation involved, but not to criticise sexual orientation. Both groups claim theological and biblical support for their view.

Before going into the arguments for these opposing positions, I want to look more closely at the matter of fig leaves. Fig leaves have had a bad press. They are regarded as a pathetic attempt at modesty where covering up has become impossible. They are generally thought to add to the embarrassment of nakedness through their inadequacy as covering and through the shame displayed by the attempt to cover up. Excuses that are too threadbare to be effective are sometimes referred to metaphorically as fig leaves. I can imagine that you are wondering about my choice of title. What's to defend? How could fig leaves be excused, let alone defended?

Fig leaves play a significant role in the story of creation and fall in the early chapters of the book of Genesis. They relate to the theme of human nakedness and shame. In the world created by God, the humans were naked and were not ashamed (Gen 2:25). After eating of the fruit of the tree of the knowledge of good and evil, they knew that they were naked and they were ashamed. To overcome their shame, they tried to hide their nakedness by sewing together fig leaves as aprons (Gen 3:7). They then hid from God. These are the only actions recorded in the wake of their eating of the forbidden fruit, so that this sense of shame would seem to have a primal significance. Perhaps we can say that the sense of shame both expresses and seeks to conceal their new-found sense of vulnerability and separation from God.

The dialogue between God and Adam and Eve in hiding is well known. In it, the close connection between eating the fruit of the tree and knowing that they were naked is again central (cf Gen 3:10–11). God pronounces judgement on the serpent, Adam and Eve (Gen 3:14–19). Just before expelling the humans from the garden, he gives them garments of skin (Gen 3:21). We may wonder from where the skin came. We should also note that God gives them no other help for life outside the garden. This gift confirms their initial judgement that being naked in a fallen world justifies a need for covering. The garments given by God are real covering of a more permanent value than the aprons of fig leaves that they made for themselves.

What seems to me to emerge from this aspect of the story is that covering for our human nakedness is indeed needed in a fallen world. Nakedness is our true condition before God. In the original state of unbroken unity with God, our nakedness is of no account. In the absence of evil, of powers acting contrary to the will of God, nakedness is not an occasion for shame. It does not create damaging vulnerability. In a broken world which does know the action of evil powers, or powers separated from their source which is God, nakedness does mean damaging vulnerability. Our shame and anxiety in the face of our vulnerability are proper responses to our condition. God's gift of clothing shows that this is so. This gift can also stand as a sign of God's care and love for the disobedient humans.

This line of interpretation probably came to me from Dietrich Bonhoeffer, who presents this matter of shame about nakedness as a primal consequence of our fallen condition. It is noteworthy that in his *Ethics,*[10] shame at nakedness stands at the very beginning of the discussion. For Bonhoeffer, Christian ethics relates to the overcoming of the damage caused by the knowledge of good and evil.

> The knowledge of good and evil seems to be the aim of all ethical reflection. The first task of Christian ethics is to invalidate this knowledge ...

Already in the possibility of the knowledge of good and evil Christian ethics discerns a falling away from the origin. Man[11] at his origin knows only one thing: God. It is only in the unity of his knowledge of God that he knows of other men, of things, and of himself. He knows all things only in God, and God in all things. The knowledge of good and evil shows that he is no longer at one with this origin.[12]

This radical reading of the story of the Fall (Gen 1–3) seems to me to be faithful to the story in seeing that sin is the departure from God. The act which expresses this departure consolidates the break, but it is the separation from God which is crucial in Bonhoeffer's account, not the act on its own. It is plausible to think that Bonhoeffer is correct in questioning the acceptability for Christians of this assumption of the freedom and autonomy of humans in decision making.

> In the knowledge of good and evil man does not understand himself in the reality of the destiny appointed in his origin, but rather in his own possibilities, his possibility of being good or evil. He knows himself now as something apart from God, outside God, and this means that he now knows only himself and no longer knows God at all; for he can know God only if he knows only God. The knowledge of good and evil is therefore separation from God. Only against God can man know good and evil.[13]

It is important to look more deeply into the links that Bonhoeffer posits between separation from God, knowledge of good and evil, awareness of nakedness and shame. Our created state is one of nakedness. When we are at one with God, this nakedness is no problem. When we are not at one with God, this nakedness causes us shame because it witnesses to the brokenness of our relationship with our origin, God. 'Shame is man's ineffaceable recollection of his estrangement from the origin; it is grief for this estrangement, and the powerless longing to return to unity with the origin.'[14] Only then can we also talk about vulnerability to attack from hostile powers.

> 'They made themselves aprons' [Gen 3:7]. Shame seeks a covering as a means of overcoming the disunion. But the covering implies the confirmation of the disunion that has occurred, and it cannot therefore make good the damage. Man covers himself, conceals himself from men and from God. Covering is necessary because it keeps awake shame, and with it the memory of the disunion with the origin, and also because man, disunited as he is, must now withdraw himself and must live in concealment. Otherwise he would betray himself.[15]

For Bonhoeffer, shame (unlike remorse or guilt) is a direct sign of our fallen human condition. Remorse and guilt relate to the particular actions, choices and situations in which we can see the inadequacy of our individual histories. Shame arises from the primal reality of our separation from God and resists other explanations, according to Bonhoeffer. Our human desire for covering is therefore to be respected as a proper response to our condition.

Fig leaves were well in place in the world in which I grew up. Sexual matters in general were well covered by discretion, tact and respect for privacy. Of course, there was gossip, sex education and the occasional scandal, but there were limits in place that were observed, at least within my experience. Today, there seems to be little left of these cultural agreements about limitations on what should be publicly revealed, at least within Australian society. I can feel in myself a nostalgic desire for the apparent order and certainties of the church of this pre-liberation era. Still, I recognise the illusory character of my nostalgia. I concur with the judgement expressed by Walter Wink,[16] that it is inadequate to 'long for the hypocrisies of an earlier era.'[17]

Even raising these questions about sexuality and covering up our nakedness seems risky and uncomfortable to me, as I acknowledge that my natural tendency is to avoid having to talk – even indirectly – about things sexual. Also, I am quite uncomfortable about supporting censorship, even self-censorship. Still, natural limitations respected and accepted by all present are quite different from imposed limits on discourse. We continue to live with all kinds of contextual limitations on what constitutes appropriate communication and interaction, even as these shift and change from time to time.

A further reason for discomfort stems from my knowledge that what I am socialised to find normal is experienced as oppressive by some others. Does my comfort with culturally accepted fig leaves simply reflect my relatively sheltered upbringing and the particular attitudes of my parents? For me, fig leaf culture has worked benignly because there were not too many discrepancies between the public and the private realities. I know that this has not been the case for all too many of my contemporaries. The socially accepted limitations on the invasion of privacy that were in place in my youth have been widely condemned because they have provided shelter for such unacceptable things as child abuse. The power of the media to reveal scandalous secrets rests upon the genuine benefit of such revelation to society as well as to the people involved. Horrendous domestic oppression can be overcome when other people become involved. Yet even in this area, there remain difficult ethical considerations, as anyone wrongly accused of child abuse can attest. I conclude that we are torn between divergent impulses here, the impulses of respect for privacy and concern for victims of covert oppression.

It seems highly plausible to think that homosexuality, as an orientation of some members of all societies, has always been with us. Yet I have no real memories of any awareness of homosexuality before adulthood. I do remember stories about the behaviour of one or two of my fellow students who were expelled from school. This relative innocence is unlikely to be true for most people growing up in Australia today. I recognise that it was also not true for those of my contemporaries for whom the traditional gender roles were unhelpful or even destructive. For these people, I can appreciate the genuine liberation of 'coming out', of not having to keep their own emotional reality hidden. I am not among those who regard it as offensive that people confront others with their difference. Offence can occur when the difference comes to be used as a weapon of attack and rejection; yet the assertion of the reality of difference does seem to be required where there is unjust discrimination and prejudice. I cannot find it within me to recommend a return to the expectation that homosexual people live in 'the closet'.

Still, we should ask whether this affirmation of 'coming out' is culturally possible only for those of us who share the humanistic, liberationist assumptions of contemporary left-wing Western culture. Some of my friends from communities whose culture is not Western have helped me to see that God may dwell in light but that our lives are lived in a mixture of darkness and light. It is all very well for me to want to live without keeping secrets, but this does not give me the right to shout out the secrets of others. Similarly, I may hope for a world in which people can own up to identities traditionally frowned upon – or even despised – without suffering rejection and condemnation, but we obviously do not yet live in such a world, or even such a church. We should also remember that some cultures do not have words for many aspects of sexuality that can be expressed in English. There is a general taboo on talking about many aspects of sexuality. I conclude that we have yet to learn how these fundamental cultural differences are to be successfully negotiated in cross-cultural communication. This is a particular problem for the Uniting Church in Australia because of our multi-cultural reality and our commitment to collective oversight of church life through inter-related councils and the full sharing of all information relevant to an issue.

Writing from the perspective of the social sciences and his own pastoral experience, Robert Albers[18] makes a helpful distinction between discretionary shame and disgrace shame.[19] Broadly speaking, discretionary shame relates to socially approved acts protective of privacy. A more commonplace word might be 'modesty'. A person described as 'shameless' would be someone seen to be lacking in discretionary shame. Disgrace shame relates to the public uncovering of a person caught in socially disapproved actions and attitudes. This distinction seems to me broadly acceptable in phenomenological terms. It is helpful in providing us a road map for the renegotiation of cultural and social disapproval.[20]

Homosexual behaviour has historically been disapproved within societies influenced by Judaeo-Christian traditions. For a person to be publicly identified as homosexual has therefore been a matter of disgrace shaming. Since about 1972, what can be called the gay liberation movement has promoted a strong challenge to this culture of disgrace shaming. One central aspect of this campaign has been the encouragement of 'coming out'. The aim of gay liberation within the subsequent furore, discriminatory action and counter-action and discussion has been to remove the disgrace from homosexual identity. This aim has met with considerable success within Australian society since 1972.

One consequence of this situation has been that society in general and the churches in particular have had to reconsider the basis for rejecting homosexual identity. In terms of the attitudes of the European Enlightenment, it seems hard to condemn homosexual behaviour between consenting adults. How do they harm anybody? If they do harm to themselves, is that not their free choice? Are homosexual people completely free to choose this identity or is it somehow given to them without the possibility of developing another sexual orientation? These seem the most significant questions guiding the public debate in Australia. The emerging secular consensus in Australian public life, which can be seen in various kinds of anti-discriminatory legislation, would seem to be that adult homosexual people do not harm others through consenting sexual behaviour and that at least some of them do not have a real possibility of choosing another orientation. Whatever we may think of this within our church discussions, we need to recognise the current situation in the general community.

Those wishing to maintain a hard line against the acceptance of homosexual people as fellow citizens have found it very difficult to mount convincing counter-arguments. Indeed, it could be argued that secular society has tacitly or openly accepted the Enlightenment view for adults and is in the process of redrawing the traditional line more narrowly, with a focus on paedophilia. Within the churches, the main barrier to an easy acceptance of the Enlightenment position has been the existence of a small number of biblical texts which do seem to enshrine a divinely sanctioned condemnation of homosexual behaviour (notably Leviticus 18:22, 20:13 and Romans 1:26–32). There are a few other texts which have some relevance, though these probably do not really contribute to a condemnation of homosexuality as such.

> It is not clear whether 1 Cor 6:9 and 1 Tim 1:10 refer to the 'passive' and 'active' partners in homosexual relationships, or to homosexual and heterosexual male prostitutes. In short, it is unclear whether the issue is homosexuality alone or promiscuity and 'sex for hire'.[21]

One of the important questions highlighted by this debate has been that of the authority of the Bible. For me, the church is wise to remain unconvinced by voices that dismiss the biblical witness as irrelevant to present-day issues. It is important to respect the normative role of scripture in witnessing to God's revelation in the history of Israel and in Christ. Yet we must also recognise the difficulty of interpreting scripture correctly. The terms in which its witness is made are deeply historical in origin and meaning. I accept that scripture is inspired by the Spirit of God, but would add that interpretations also require a like inspiration. As Paul says, 'Our competence is from God, who has made us competent to be ministers of a new covenant, not of letter but of the spirit; for the letter kills, but the Spirit gives life' (II Cor 3:5–6). In this whole question, we are seeking to know God's will; for this, spiritual illumination is crucial. I conclude that we are required to engage earnestly with the Bible in seeking to know God's will, not just for the letter of the law, but for the word of God to our situation. For this, the whole Bible is potentially relevant, not simply a few isolated texts.

Later tradition associates the sinfulness of Sodom with homosexual lust, based on Genesis 19:1–11, though to use this story to justify condemnation of all forms of homosexual activity is, despite subsequent Christian assertions, highly implausible, as Walter Wink, among other commentators, has suggested.

> Some passages that have been advanced as pertinent to the issue of homosexuality are, in fact, irrelevant. One is the attempted gang rape in Sodom (Gen 19:1–29). That was a case of ostensibly heterosexual males intent on humiliating strangers by treating them 'like women', thus demasculinizing them. (This is also the case in a similar account in Judges 19–21). Their brutal behaviour has nothing to do with the problem of whether genuine love expressed between consenting adults of

the same sex is legitimate or not. Likewise Deut. 23:17–18 must be pruned from the list, since it most likely refers to male and female *prostitutes* involved in Canaanite fertility rituals that have infiltrated Israelite worship; whether these males are 'gay' or 'straight', a mature same-sex love relationship is not under discussion.

If Wink's interpretation is accepted, we need to question the basis of much of the mediaeval condemnation of sodomy, which is where our modern attitudes would seem to have been significantly shaped.[22] The biblical story makes it clear that the sinfulness of Sodom and Gomorrah was so grave that God sent two angels to destroy these cities and, as later belief had it, to cover the area with the salt waters of the Dead Sea. If this sinfulness was based upon the general practice of same-sex intercourse, then the belief that God is uniquely offended by this practice would seem to have some basis. If we do not accept this reading of the story, but instead focus on the inhospitality and attempted victimisation of strangers as the evidence of sinfulness, the sense of same sex intercourse as a uniquely offensive behaviour in the eyes of God becomes much less plausible.

In discussing the Leviticus texts, Wink acknowledges the clarity of the rejection of male homosexual acts, with the punishment of death. He understandably takes refuge in the New Testament. With regard to the Romans passage, he presents the case that Paul thought that the people whose behaviour he was condemning were by nature 'straight', so that their homosexual acts were indeed contrary to their nature.[23] This is a possible narrowing of the force of the passage, though we should acknowledge that Paul is making a very general case about human sin with this as a flagrant example. Marion Soards[24] gives a more traditional interpretation of this passage.

> As Paul discerned and declared God's relationship to humans, homosexual acts were outside the boundaries of God's intentions for humanity. Homosexuality was one vivid indication of the real problem of sin, and Paul states bluntly that all humans are sinners. On the matter of homosexuality, we should see clearly that the biblical understanding of homosexuality is univocal (although this issue is at most a minor concern). Homosexual activity is not consistent with the will of God; it is not merely a

sin but evidence of sin, and there is no way to read the Bible as condoning homosexual acts.[25]

I do not feel as confident as Soards that this is the only way to read the Bible in relation to this question. I am more impressed by the large areas of silence and the evident distortions in some of the traditional interpretations. I conclude that both liberals and conservatives have an almost persuasive reading of these texts, though this brief survey can hardly be taken as the last word on such a weighty question. Soards largely acknowledges the areas of silence, but claims that biblical statements all go in one direction. He goes on to discuss the pastoral implications of his general conclusions about homosexuality.

> While the church cannot offer approval of homosexual activity, the church can also not deny the validity of faith in less-than-perfect humans. If approval of one's homosexual behaviour becomes a condition for one's joining the church, then the church faces an insurmountable problem; for Christians seeking to recognise and to honour the authority of the Bible will insist that no such approval is possible. If there is no demand for approval of homosexual activity, there is no reason to deny church membership to the homosexual who takes his or her place along with other forgiven sinners in the corporate body of Christ.[26]

I would read this to mean that the church should offer full acceptance of people prior to any discussion of what behaviour is or is not acceptable within the community of believers. I think Soards makes an important point in resisting requests for specific approval by the church for homosexual activity. Who made us judges of the sexuality of others? If we can indeed reduce the significance of the debate to a conversation about acceptability within the community of faith, we can go on to ask whether this matter is not primarily between the individual and God. If we do reach this conclusion, I think it then becomes a responsibility of the church to defend this understanding of the situation. Conservatives need to be restrained from seeking the expulsion of homosexual people as such (i.e. without citing further causes) from the church. Homosexual people need to live with an ambiguous welcome if the church finds itself unable to provide a clear word of affirmation for homosexual activity. We are left with a continuing tug-of-war between homosexual people wanting affirmation and conservatives not able to affirm.

This is clearly a recommendation for an unstable, holding pattern in the life of the church. This may be as well as we can do in our generation on this issue. We are dealing with a monumental cultural shift in the life of the church and we should not expect to achieve settled judgements, let alone comfortable arrangements, in our lifetime. We are, I believe, the 'guinea pig' generation in this matter. This is why I think we need to review our disdain for fig leaves. For what my analysis seems to leave us with, liberal and conservative alike, is a set of fig leaf aprons. Walter Wink offers us a careful, serious and honest interpretation of the biblical material which opens the way for full acceptance and inclusion of homosexual people in the life of the church. Marion Soards offers us a pastorally caring but principled resistance to affirming homosexual activity as possible for Christians. Whatever our conclusions, we should follow – not our own preferences but – the Holy Spirit's leading in our attempts to discern the will of God. When the fig leaves of our devising prove effective and reliable for covering, we receive a kind of confirmation that God is blessing our work.

The focus of this paper has been on general Christian teaching about homosexuality and the inclusion of openly homosexual people in the life of the church. When ask about the possible ordination of such people, further considerations come into play which would require another paper. Briefly, it seems to me that the church should have no problem about special friendships, though these may affect the fittedness of some people for ordination, as previously suggested. It may also affect the availability of people for specific roles and responsibilities in the life of the church, as we see with many married ministers. Can we leave the matter of sexual dimensions of special relationships to the relatively private realm of the people themselves and their relationship with God? How these friendships are presented more publicly, particularly when the sexual dimension is salient, is rightly of concern to the wider church. Still, the heart of our struggle is with the unresolved and humanly unresolvable tensions within the Christian community when homosexual relationships are in question.

If we take our cue from Bonhoeffer, we might come to recognise that our cultural attitudes towards homosexuality are inevitably based upon our human knowledge of good and evil. If we do seek to invalidate our knowledge of good and evil as Bonhoeffer suggests, we probably wipe out most of our cultural markers for acceptability and rejection, whether conservative, liberal or radical. These markers return once we try to interpret biblical teaching about God's self-revelation, but they do so under the shadow of God's judgement, not our human judgement. This seems to me to bring us all to a common level before God. None of us have standing in the presence of God apart from God's gracious call into fellowship on the basis of the life, death and resurrection of Christ and the forgiveness of sins. Considerations such as these seem to me to lie at the heart of the arguments for an inclusive attitude to church membership. They also point in the direction of a Christian responsibility to care for those who are different and vulnerable because of the difference.

Staying close to the theme of God's judgement about human sinfulness, we can remember the gift of clothing which went with the expulsion of Adam and Eve from the garden of Eden. It seems obvious that nothing can be hidden from God. It seems that God supports the hiding of nakedness from others, human and non-human. We can go on to think that when we encounter another in mutual or one-sided nakedness (physical and/or metaphorical), we come objectively closer to the perspective in which God knows us and others. Such encounters are clearly marked out as specially significant. They represent occasions on which our clothing, God-given or self-fabricated, is no longer present. Such occasions would seem to be part of God's blessing upon us when God is present and honoured. When our particular nakedness leads to our rejection, God is not to be thought of as truly absent, but we come into the area indicated by the phrase 'divine judgement'. As followers of Christ, we need a special sensitivity to the likeness to Jesus on the cross of those under human condemnation, whose covering has been stripped from them.

I have already put forward the plea that Christian discussions attend to a wide range of biblical passages in seeking direction in our present struggles. Recently, I was required to comment on the reading for that morning, Luke 5:33–39. In this passage, Jesus is asked about his disciples eating and drinking instead of fasting and praying. Jesus replies in terms of the presence of the bridegroom with them, that is, his own Messianic presence, which requires celebration. Luke then attaches seemingly different sayings to this story, about not tearing a piece from a new garment to patch an old (a stupid thing to do!) and not putting new wine into old wineskins. He is clearly seeing the coming of Jesus as a new thing which requires new forms of reception and response. So new wine must be put into new wineskins, as anyone who wants the wine to stay within its container would agree. So we are led to the thought that the Holy Spirit can lead us to new things in the life of the church and that the containers for this newness must themselves be renewed. This seems to be saying that God is on the side of the new.

But then the text goes on to say something rather puzzling, at least, in the majority of manuscript sources. It comments on the foregoing that no-one after drinking old wine desires the new, but concurs in the judgement that the old is better. This makes sense when we reflect that storing wine is usually for years so that it may mature. We prefer to drink the mature wine. The history of this text may give us an unexpected window on the struggles in the early church between those emphasising the newness of Christ and those emphasising the continuity of Christ with God's covenant people, the Jews. I note that one of the early witnesses lacking the text favouring the old is Marcion. I conclude that the text shows us our need to welcome and accommodate the genuinely new that God brings us. It also shows us that our human comfort is served by the time matured – but only if we have been successful in providing appropriate fresh covering for the new. This sounds to me like a call to take up the sewing kit and gather fig leaves.

John's Gospel offers us some suggestive themes for this work, particularly that of friendship. 'I do not call you servants any longer, because the servant does not know what the master is doing; but I have called you friends, because I have made known to you everything that I have heard from my Father' (John 15:15). Christian friendship is firstly with Jesus, but surely then also with all the others who share in this friendship with Jesus. There can be modern equivalents to idolatry where our friendships block us from friendship with those outside our closed circle, whether the circle is formed by nation or race or gang or household or gender or even the special friendships of marriage or marriage-like relationships. The gospel challenges all of us to follow the call of Christ beyond these more limited loyalties, important as they are. Within friendship, there is a necessary privacy which derives from the basic structure of our human experience. We cannot truly make public the inner reality of friendship. The emotional element and the sharing of lived experience resist effective public naming, let alone full truthful disclosure.

We may want to recommend that homosexual relationships be reframed in our thinking and our public statements in terms of friendship, which is a suggestion that I personally favour. This is a fig leaf of a policy which will be met with contempt by those for whom homosexual relationships are anathema. Yet we may find that the spiritual depths touched by the reality of friendship convey to us, in time, the recognition that it is God who meets us here with a covering for our nakedness that we cannot despise.

Selected bibliography

Albers, Robert. *Shame: A Faith Perspective* (New York: The Haworth Pastoral Press, 1995).

Balch, David (Editor). *Homosexuality, Science and the 'Plain Sense' of Scripture* (Grand Rapids, Michigan: Eerdmans, 2000).

Barth, Karl. *Church Dogmatics* III:4. Translated by GW Bromiley and TF Torrance (Edinburgh: T&T Clark, 1961).

Bonhoeffer, Dietrich. *Ethics*. Edited by E Bethge, Translated by NH Smith (London: Fontana, Collins, 1964).

Brawley, Robert (Editor). *Biblical Ethics and Homosexuality* (Louisville, Kentucky: John Knox Press, 1996).

Jordan, Mark. *The Invention of Sodomy in Christian Theology* (Chicago: The University of Chicago Press, 1997).

Seow, Choon-Leong (Editor). *Homosexuality and Christian Community* (Louisville, Kentucky: John Knox Press, 1996).

Smith, Robin. *Living in Covenant with God and One Another*

(Geneva: World Council of Churches, 1990).

Soards, Marion. *Scripture and Homosexuality: Biblical Authority and the Church Today* (Louisville, Kentucky: John Knox Press, 1995).

Stuart, Elizabeth. *Just Good Friends: Towards a Lesbian and Gay Theology of Relationships* (London: Mowbray, 1995).

Wink, Walter (Editor). *Homosexuality and Christian Faith* (Minneapolis: Fortress Press, 1999).

End Notes

1. A slightly abbreviated version of this article has been circulated electronically within the Victorian Synod of the Uniting Church in Australia.
2. I can claim to have been present at the beginnings of this debate in the Uniting Church, at least in terms of questions about the ordination of openly gay people. I was minister in the Uniting Church of Fitzroy when one such candidate presented herself for ordination in 1981. I was also a member of a working group on this issue for the Yarra Valley Presbytery in the period 1981–84.
3. Elizabeth Stuart, *Just Good Friends: Towards a Lesbian and Gay Theology of Relationships* (London: Mowbray, 1995), 1–2. The main theme of her book is a reflection on what the experience of gay and lesbian people can contribute to Christian theological reflection on friendship (God's friendship for us and our friendship with each other).
4. Cf Mark Jordan, *The Invention of Sodomy in Christian Theology* (Chicago: The University of Chicago Press, 1997), 1. Jordan shows how the word *sodomia*, sodomy, came into use as a sub-category of the sin of *luxuria*, luxury or the love of pleasure. In mediaeval usage, it had a shifting range of meanings that could sometimes include masturbation and/or sexual intercourse with animals.
5. It has been suggested that the mere fact that this matter has so exercised churches around the world is a sign that God is calling us to rethink it. Elizabeth Stuart quotes the World Council of Churches study (see bibliography) approvingly in this sense (Stuart p.xvii).
6. Karl Barth, *Church Dogmatics* III:4. Translated by GW Bromiley and TF Torrance (Edinburgh: T&T Clark, 1961), 165–66.
7. Nancy Duff is Associate Professor of Reformed Theological Ethics at Princeton Theological Seminary, New Jersey.
8. Nancy Duff, 'Christian Vocation, Freedom of God and Homosexuality', in *Homosexuality, Science and the 'Plain Sense' of Scripture*. Edited

by David Balch (Grand Rapids: Eerdmans, 2000), 261–277.

9. 'Coming out' refers to homosexual people making their sexual orientation publicly known. This process of difficult and dangerous self-revelation can obviously apply to many other kinds of people. Cf P Campolo, 'In God's House there are Many Closets', in *Homosexuality and Christian Faith*. Edited by W Wink (Minneapolis: Fortress Press, 1999), 97–104.

10. Dietrich Bonhoeffer, *Ethics*. Edited by E Bethge, Translated by NH Smith (London: Fontana, Collins, 1964), 17–26.

11. I note that this text consistently uses masculine forms in a general sense, contrary to our contemporary sensitivities. I thank Duncan Reid for pointing out that this may be a matter of the translation rather than the original German.

12. Bonhoeffer, *Ethics*, 17.

13. *Ibid*, 17–18.

14. *Ibid*, 20.

15. *Ibid*, 21.

16. Walter Wink is Professor of Biblical Interpretation at Auburn Theological Seminary.

17. Walter Wink, 'Homosexuality and the Bible', in *Homosexuality and Christian Faith*, 45.

18. RH Albers, *Shame: A Faith Perspective* (New York: The Haworth Pastoral Press, 1995).

19. *Ibid*, 7–15.

20. There are many other perspectives on our general experience of shame. These perspectives sometimes assimilate shame to guilt, in that they identify specific aspects of ourselves which are culturally rejected. I find it plausible to follow those such as Albers who distinguish shame from guilt in terms of the distinction between act and being. We can experience guilt when we recognise that our own action has been wrong in some respect. Once we start to consider ourselves a bad person for doing such things, our experience moves into the area of shame. Disgrace shaming occurs when this unacceptable aspect is brought into the light of public attention. This shaming of individuals and groups can be seen to be socially constructed. The power of the shame would seem to be given by the intensity of the social repudiation of the negative aspect that is rejected. This power would seem to be negotiable, as it can conceivably be withdrawn when social and cultural values are redefined. This general concept of shame is anthropologically based. As such, it is quite distinct from the perspective offered us by Bonhoeffer.

21. Wink, 34. Cf DB Martin, '*Arsenokoites* and *Malakos*: Meanings and Consequences', in *Biblical Ethics and Homosexuality*. Edited by RL Brawley (Louisville, Kentucky: John Knox Press, 1996), 117–136. Martin

does not accept the meanings given by Wink. Martin claims that we cannot be sure of the meaning of the word *arsenokoites* due to the small number of extant occurrences of it in ancient literature. His suggestion is that it could refer to some kind of economic exploitation by sexual means. *Malakos*, by contrast, clearly means 'effeminate'. Martin argues that neither word provides an unambiguous condemnation of homoerotic behaviour as such.

22. This is the central concern of Mark Jordan's study of this process. Cf M Jordan, *The Invention of Sodomy*.

23. *Ibid*, 34–37.

24. Marion Soards is Professor of New Testament Studies at Louisville Presbyterian Theological Seminary.

25. Marion Soards, *Scripture and Homosexuality: Biblical Authority and the Church Today* (Louisville, Kentucky: John Knox Press, 1995), 23–24.

26. *Ibid*, 76.

HOW DOES PAUL KNOW WHEN TO WINK WITH BOTH EYES AND WHEN TO JUMP WITH BOTH FEET?

Nigel Watson

One of the many things that I admire about my old friend and long-time colleague, Harry Wardlaw, is the hospitality of his mind. However wrong-headed, pig-headed or obtuse the view of his dialogue partner may be, Harry always gives it his careful and respectful attention. In grateful recognition of Harry's hospitality of mind, I offer him, and the other readers of this book, the following study, which examines the co-existence in the thought of St Paul of tolerance and intolerance.

A word of explanation of the title of this essay. There is a residential college of the University of Otago in Dunedin, New Zealand, called Knox College. Knox College was modelled on Ormond College in Melbourne and St Andrew's College in Sydney. The Master of Knox College for several decades around the middle of last century was a man called Hubert Ryburn. He was sometimes asked, towards the end of his tenure of the position, how he had managed to stay on as Master for so long. What was the secret? 'The secret of being Master of Knox College', he used to say, 'was knowing when to wink with both eyes and when to jump with both feet'.

That remark is very relevant to this paper, because there are times when Paul, in his letters, seems to wink with both eyes, and there are times when he seems to jump with both feet.

1. Jumping with both feet

We probably find it easier to recall passages in which he jumps with both feet, passages of denunciation. An outstanding example is

Gal 1:6–9, where Paul expresses his amazement that the Galatians should be deserting so quickly the one who had called them in the grace of Christ (clearly, an allusion to himself) and turning to a different gospel – not that there is another gospel. The paragraph ends with the solemn words: 'If anyone proclaims to you a gospel contrary to what you received, let that one be accursed!'

2. Winking with both eyes

Now set alongside the passage just quoted from Galatians Paul's appeal to 'the strong' and 'the weak' which runs from Rom 14:1 to 15:13, the tenor of which is summed up in 15:7, where Paul writes, 'In a word, accept one another as Christ accepted us, to the glory of God'.

Why does Paul react with condemnation in the one situation and with a plea for mutual acceptance in the other? In other words, why does he jump with both feet, when writing to the Galatians, and wink with both eyes, when writing to the Romans?

3. Paul's tolerance in Philippians

There is another instance of Paul seeming to wink with both eyes in the first chapter of his letter to the Philippians. In Phil 1:14, Paul informs his readers that his imprisonment has been of benefit to most of his fellow Christians in the place from which he is writing. It has given them confidence to speak the word of God fearlessly and with extraordinary courage.

Some, Paul continues, proclaim Christ in a jealous and quarrelsome spirit, but some do it in goodwill. The latter are moved by love, knowing that it is to defend the gospel that I am where I am; the others are moved by selfish ambition and present Christ from mixed motives, meaning to cause me distress as I lie in prison. What does it matter? One way or another, whether sincerely or not, Christ is proclaimed; and for that I rejoice (Phil 1:15–18).

Fee remarks in his commentary at this point that 'most of us know this passage so well that we tend to overlook how surprising it is.'[1]

Some of those who have been emboldened by Paul's imprisonment to speak the word of God fearlessly are proclaiming Christ from mixed motives, being motivated, at least in part, by a jealous and quarrelsome spirit and by selfish ambition, hoping to cause Paul distress as he lies in prison. The actual words that Paul uses to describe the unworthy motives of these people are *phthonos, eris* and *eritheia*. These are words that occur elsewhere in Paul, all three in Gal 5:20–21 and two in Rom 1:29. Both of these passages are lists of vices which are the hallmarks of those who will not inherit the kingdom of God. How can Paul be so magnanimous in Philippians towards people who are exhibiting qualities which he condemns so strongly in Galatians 5 and Romans 1?

4. The problem in a nutshell

We have noted one passage where, if anywhere, Paul jumps with both feet, Galatians 1; and two, Romans 14–15 and Philippians 1, where he seems to wink with both eyes. How are we to make sense of this apparent contradiction? How can Paul, at certain times, castigate his opponents in caustic and virulent language and, at others, be quite untroubled by differences of belief or practice?[2]

To answer this question, we need to consider more fully the different situations which Paul is addressing in these three passages.

5. The situation in Galatia

Galatians first. The stern word of Paul to the Galatians which was quoted a moment ago was aimed at newcomers into the community who were telling the Galatians that faith in Christ was not enough. They were evidently propagating the same view as was held by the people whom we read about in Acts 15:1, who came down from Judaea to Antioch and declared, 'Unless you are circumcised according to the custom of Moses, you cannot be saved' (cf. Gal 3:1–5; 5:6). We can surmise that the newcomers in Galatia argued that circumcision was the mark of every male member of the people of God, and that they appealed to Genesis 17 to support their position. Those who would be part of the people of God must observe circumcision, along with the rest of the law (cf. Acts 15:5).

But, as Paul sees it, this is to call in question the sufficiency of the work of Christ. Hence his anathemas.

6. The situation in Rome

But what about the situation which Paul is addressing in Romans 14 and 15, where he appeals to 'the strong' and 'the weak' to accept one another? Two historical questions need to be addressed, first of all.

First, are Paul's comments directed to a real problem in the Roman church, about which he has heard reports, at least in broad outline, or are his comments directed to a hypothetical situation? Most recent commentators take the view that Paul is addressing a real problem. I cite, for example, CEB Cranfield, John Ziesler, James DG Dunn and NT Wright. One exception to this consensus is Luke Timothy Johnson, who argues, mainly on the grounds that Paul's description lacks specific detail, that he is generalising on the basis of his experience of the Galatian and Corinthian controversies.[3] Even Johnson, however, concedes that the problem probably did exist in the Roman community in some fashion. In any case, Paul makes clear what his approach would be to such a situation, should one arise.

The other historical question is what sort of people Paul has in mind, when he speaks of 'the strong' and 'the weak'. According to 14:2, the strong believe in eating anything, while the weak eat only vegetables. Again, according to 14:5, the weak judge one day to be better than another, while the strong judge all days to be alike.

Most recent commentators take the view that these two groups held different attitudes towards the Jewish law, particularly its prescriptions concerning clean and unclean foods and concerning the Sabbath and other holy days. The prominence of the notion of uncleanness in 14:14 points strongly in that direction. It is true that the Torah does not prescribe abstention from meat, but there is plenty of evidence that many Jews at this time chose to be vegetarians, so as to avoid the possibility of eating food tainted by idolatry.[4]

However, it would be an over-simplification to identify 'the weak' with Jewish Christians and 'the strong' with Gentile Christians. 'The weak' probably also included some Gentiles who had been attached to the synagogue as proselytes or godfearers, while 'the strong' also included some Jews, like Paul himself.

As we have already noted, Paul's response to the situation of tension between these two groups is to plead with them to accept one another, to welcome one another (15:7). His own theological sympathies are all with the strong. He explicitly associates himself with their point of view. 'We who are strong', he says in 15:1. And yet he can say to this group, 'If a person is weak in their faith, you must accept them, without attempting to settle doubtful points' (14:1f).

Not: 'Your differences of opinion are scandalous, you must resolve them at all costs'; but 'Accept one another' – a plea for mutual acceptance, for tolerance.

To understand this tolerance of his, which, at first sight, contrasts so strongly with his anathemas in Galatians, we need to ascertain as clearly as we can the attitude that 'the weak' took towards 'the strong'. Paul urges 'the weak' not to be censorious towards 'the strong'; and 'the strong' not to be contemptuous of 'the weak'. In 14:3 he writes:

> Those who eat must not despise those who abstain, and those who abstain must not pass judgement on those who eat; for God has welcomed them.

Several commentators remark on how contemporary these attitudes are. However, it appears that, however much 'the weak' disapproved of the laxity of 'the strong', they had not called in question their Christian standing. They had not said to them, in effect, 'Unless you live as we do, you cannot be saved'.

As Cranfield puts it:

> The weak, while neither thinking they were putting God in their debt by their obedience nor yet deliberately trying to force all other Christians to conform to their pattern, felt that, as far as they themselves were concerned, they could not with a clear conscience give up the observance of such requirements of the law as the distinction between clean and unclean foods, the avoidance of blood, the keeping of the Sabbath and other special days.[5]

To sum up the difference between the intruders in Galatians and 'the weak' in Romans, the former had, in effect, called in question the adequacy for salvation of faith in Christ alone, whereas the latter had not.

7. All things to all men

We may note, in passing, that the tolerance that Paul calls for in Romans 14 and 15 was evidently reflected in his own dealings with Jewish and Gentile communities. In 1 Cor 9:20f he writes:

> To the Jews I became as a Jew, in order to win Jews ... To those outside the law I became as one outside the law ... so that I might win those under the law.

The implication is that, when evangelising Jews or working with Jewish communities of believers, Paul followed the Jewish calendar and dietary laws, but ignored such Jewish requirements, when working with Gentiles.

8. Paul's magnanimity in Philippians

And now for Philippians, and Paul's extraordinary magnanimity towards the people who were proclaiming Christ in a jealous and quarrelsome spirit, moved by selfish ambition, hoping to cause Paul distress as he lay in prison. Who were these people? Most commentators assume that they were either Judaising Christians who advocated some measure of obedience to Jewish beliefs and practices or else Christians of more liberal convictions who were envious of Paul's successes and trying to undermine his influence. It is hard to see how the first view can be right. Paul does not accuse them of false teaching or of preaching a perversion of the gospel. So some form of the second view seems more likely. Calvin shows historical acumen in observing that there would be many ways of annoying the Apostle that do not occur to us, owing to our ignorance of the circumstances. However, we may imagine a situation comparable to that which Paul faced in Corinth and, as Beare suggests, 'suppose that the admirers of some unknown Apollos are jealous for their learned and eloquent leader'.[6]

Whoever these people were, one thing is clear: the furtherance of the gospel is all that matters for Paul. Beside that, everything else pales into insignificance. As Fee observes, 'Paul is a man of a single passion: Christ and the gospel'.[7]

It would surely have given Paul greater satisfaction, if he had been persuaded that these other people were motivated by a similar passion instead of the mixed motives that he discerned in them. Nevertheless, it was better that Christ be proclaimed from mixed, and even in part unworthy, motives than not at all.

Another passage in which Paul shows an equally impressive lack of concern for his own reputation is his closing exhortation to the Corinthian church in 2 Corinthians, where he writes:

> Our prayer to God is that you may do no wrong, not that we should win approval; we want you to do what is right, even if we should seem failures . . . We are happy to be weak at any time if only you are strong (2 Cor 13:7, 9a).

To paraphrase what Paul is saying, in the light of the wider context: If only the life of your community is repaired, I, Paul, will gladly renounce the use of my apostolic authority to discipline you, even if this means that the reputation for being weak still clings to me. What matters is that you should do what is right, not that I should refute any criticisms that have been made of my apostolic style. I am glad not to have to show my strength by exercising discipline, if you prove not to need it.

In other words, Paul will be happy to wink with both eyes at any slurs that may be cast on his weakness, so long as the Corinthians put their life as a community in order.

In his controversial book, *The Cost of Authority: Manipulation and Freedom in the New Testament*, Graham Shaw devotes a chapter to 2 Corinthians and in it accuses Paul of self-congratulation, deviousness, flattery, manipulation and, in the last two chapters of the letter, of 'the most aggressive assertion of power'.[8] Shaw's one-sided assessment of Paul contrasts most sharply with Paul's own magnanimity, and indeed with the magnanimity exemplified by my old friend and long-time colleague, Harry Wardlaw.

End Notes

1. Gordon D Fee, *Paul's Letter to the Philippians* (Grand Rapids: Eerdmans, 1995) 118.
2. I am here echoing Richard Longenecker's statement of the problem in his essay, '"What does it matter?" Priorities and the *adiaphora* in Paul's dealing with opponents in his mission', in Peter Bolt and Mark Thompson (editors), *The Gospel to the Nations* (Leicester: Apollos, 2000) 147.
3. Luke Timothy Johnson, *Reading Romans* (New York: Crossroad, 1997) 196–99.
4. See James DG Dunn, *The Theology of Paul the Apostle* (Grand Rapids: Eerdmans, 1998) 682, note 46.
5. CEB Cranfield, *The Epistle to the Romans* (Edinburgh: T&T Clark, 1975–79) vol II, 695.
6. FW Beare, *The Epistle to the Philippians* (London: A&C Black, 1959) 59.
7. Fee, *Philippians* 125.
8. *The Cost of Authority* (London: SCM Press, 1982) 101–25.

24

FORGIVENESS OF ENEMIES

JC O'NEILL

Harry Wardlaw, old friend, fellow student, onetime colleague, was also, all too briefly, my minister. As minister of College Church, Parkville, he delighted us all by bringing a sensitive and imaginative philosophical mind to his preaching from the Bible. I have chosen in his honour to attempt to solve an exegetical problem that has far-reaching philosophical implications.

In Mark 11:25 Jesus is reported to have taught, 'And when ye stand praying, forgive, if ye have ought against any: that your Father also which is in heaven may forgive you your trespasses' (AV). That seems to command unconditional forgivness of enemies. The philosophical problem is this. Is it possible to forgive someone who does not think they have done a wrong that needs forgiveness and who does not want forgiveness? Is not forgiveness a benefit sought of the person they have harmed by a person who realises that they have done wrong? If I seek forgiveness from you, I acknowledge I have done wrong; I have made what restitution I can (always inadequate); I am willing to do penance in ways you suggest; and I resolve to avoid that sin in the future. Furthermore, I cannot demand that you forgive me. You may have reason to bind me rather than to loose me. How then can a victim forgive an enemy who thinks they were fully justified in inflicting the harm they did inflict? Forgiveness requires repentance.

In so arguing, I am going against a popular conception of what true religion requires. The father of a daughter blown up by terrorists and the wife of a rabbi blown up by terrorists say in public that they forgive their loved-one's murder, even though the perpetrators believed they were using legitimate means to further a righteous cause.

If the saying of Jesus in Mark 11:25 contradicts this logic, I, as a follower of Jesus, would have to suspect that my philosophy was defective.

Does Mark 11:25 imply that, even if those against whom I have a complaint that they have wronged me do not think they have done wrong, I should forgive them? Is that the condition of my asking God for his forgiveness with any hope of success? Does the petition for forgiveness in the Lord's Prayer entail that I must first have forgiven even those who have wronged me who believe they did right?

Surely not. I a sinner come before the heavenly Father repentant. The prayer has involved or will involve my contrition, my making restitution, even fourfold, my resolution to avoid and to resist temptations to repeat the offence, my willingness to accept specific penitential requirements and my acknowledgement I am dependent on God for an answer to my prayer for forgiveness, and that the answer could be no or not yet. I do not think forgiveness is unconditional or it would not be a true prayer for forgiveness.

If that is so, then the person who has wronged me cannot be granted my forgiveness unconditionally. The logic of the saying is that I cannot expect from God something I am not prepared to grant to others. But just as I am not asking God to forgive me though I do not really want forgiveness, I am not expected to forgive those who have wronged me although they do not really want forgiveness.

Peter asks how may times he should forgive his brother, who sins against him: Seven times?; and Jesus replied, Seventy times seven (Matt 18:21–22). The Lucan parallel, Luke 17:4, says explicitly, 'And if seven times a day anyone sin against you and seven times a day he turn to you saying, I repent, forgive him'. The same plea for forgiveness must be implicit in the Matthaean account, for the issue is, how many times should a request for forgiveness be countenanced, not, how often should someone put up with offences without retaliation.

There is a verse in one of the *Testaments of the Twelve Patriarchs*, Testament of Gad 6:7, which seems uncompromisingly to teach that the wronged person should forgive a persecutor even if that persecutor persists in shameless wickedness: 'And if he be shameless and persist in his wrong-doing, even so forgive him from the heart and leave to God the avenging' (TGad 6:7; RH Charles,

The Apocrypha and Pseudepigrapha of the Old Testament in English, Vol II: *Pseudepigrapha* (Oxford, Clarendon, 1913), p 343). This verse is quite out of keeping with the preceding verses and with other passages in the *Testaments of the Twelve Patriarchs*. Their refrain is, treat your enemy well so that that enemy will repent, and if he repent, forgive him (TGad 6:3,6; TBen 5:4; cf. TGad 7:5 of God).

Our present text of TGad 6:7 contains a number of variants which indicate that an over-zealous scribe has produced a startlingly extreme version which can scarcely represent the original. The words *even so* indicate that a change has occurred in the enemy's outlook which calls for a corresponding change in attitude on the side of the person wronged. But our present text emphasises the persistence of the offender in the evil. However, there are two variants for the verb *he persists* in evil; one of these reads *he stands up against* evil. I conjecture that an original *and if there is compassion* took the prefix from the following verb to produce the opposite, *and if he is shameless*, converting the following verb into *if he persists* in evil. This conjectured reading of the verse would then fit the context: 'And if there is compassion and he stands up against evil, even so forgive him from the heart and leave to God the vengeance'. In a similar way, a scribe probably turned the simple, 'He loves the righteous as his own life' of TBen 4:3 to 'He loves those who do unrighteously as his own life'. Ancient scribes, like modern journalists, love paradox.

Nothing I have said implies the weakening of the command to love our enemies and to do good to those who despitefully use us (Matt 5:43–48; Luke 6:27–29, 31–35; Rom 12:14, 17, 19, 20, 21; 1 Cor 4:12; 1 Thess 5:15; 1 Peter 2:23; 3:9; Did 1:3; Justin Apol I 15:9; Dial 96:3; POxyrh 1224; 2 Clem 13:4; Polycarp Phil 12:3). The hope is that the generous treatment of wrongdoers will help them to recognise that what they thought right was wrong and that, if wrong, they should repent.

No doubt there is also a therapeutic effect on the injured party of blocking out the wrong done, but forgetting is not forgiving. Tertullian interpreted Jesus as teaching those wronged to consign offences to oblivion, even the offences of those who did not seek forgiveness. Not to forgive offences but to forget them (adv. Marc. iv:35.3).

Nor does anything I have written preclude our praying, with our

Lord and with Stephen, that God would have mercy on our persecutors and forgive them (Luke 23:34; Acts 7:60; GospHebrews Hier. ep. 120:8.9; cf. MarZutra in Meg. 28a; T Bab K ix. 29,30; CG Montefiore, H Loewe, *A Rabbinic Anthology*; repr. with a Prolegomenon by Raphael Loewe (New York, Schocken Books, 1974), extracts No. 1510, 1282). These prayers assume that God's forgiveness is dependent on repentance on the side of the wrong-doers, but they recognise that the victims of sin do not know whether or not the offenders are fully aware of the wrong they do, and perhaps that very ignorance may suffice for forgiveness to be granted. But it is also a prayer that God will give time and grace to ignorant sinners to know what they have done, to receive the benefit of the prayers offered on their behalf, and to repent, as Judah was given time and repented (TJud 191–4). Our forgiveness of others, like God's forgiveness of us, depends on repentance.

Further Reading

Jacoby, Jeff. 'Repentance Comes First.' *Boston Globe*, 15 September 2002, E11.

On which see Neuhaus, Richard John. *First Things*, December 2002, 91–92.

Martin, Troy. 'The Christian's Obligation Not to Forgive.' *The Expository Times* 108 (1996–97), 360–362.

Walsh, Patricia. 'Forgiveness'. *The Oxford Companion to Philosophy*. Edited by Ted Honderich (Oxford: Oxford University Press, 1995), 284.

Wilson, John. 'Why forgiveness requires repentance.' *Philosophy* 63 (1988): 534–535.

25

TRULY THOU ART A GOD WHO HIDEST THYSELF

**Based on a sermon preached for the New College
150th anniversary service of thanksgiving on
Friday 5 July 1996 at the parish church of St
Andrew and St George, Edinburgh**

DAVIS MCCAUGHEY

ISAIAH 45:15: Truly thou art a God who hidest thyself,
O God of Israel, a Saviour.

A cry of astonishment, or acceptance, or both: these words may
have been a gloss written in the margin as a comment, later taken
into the text, words wrung from a bystander, when the oracles
concerning Cyrus had been read in public. Or perhaps words put
there by the anonymous poet-prophet whom we infelicitously call
Deutero-Isaiah. Yahweh has raised up Cyrus to re-build Jerusalem
and set Israel free: a pagan monarch acting for the redemption
of Israel. This is an unprecedented assertion: no longer simply
a God on the side of Israelites, supporting them in battle, no
longer even God using the enemies of Israel to chastise his people
– Assyria, the rod of God's anger – but a redeeming act, through
the triumph of a Persian autocrat. Such a suggestion wrings from
the bystander what has been called an 'Amen'. 'So be it, thou art
a God who hidest thyself, O God of Israel, a Saviour.'

Today, two and a half thousand years later, there are still
men and women of faith prepared to say their own Amen, of
astonishment and acceptance, of wonder and praise: Truly thou art
a God who hidest thyself, O God of Israel, a Saviour. God has done
great things for us, greater than we could ever have hoped for or
foreseen, whereof we are glad.

And yet, and yet: to leave it at that would risk complacency, and
its statement be banal. On this anniversary occasion we are not
met calmly to record change, blandly to remind each other that

some things are different and others remain unaltered. We are not even met honestly to acknowledge both success and failure. Those of us whose study of theology has fallen within the second half of the twentieth century as it galloped like an apocalyptic horseman to its end, need hardly to be reminded of the ambiguous character of those years. Taken as a whole the twentieth century was a time in which human skills and compassion reached out to meet human suffering with previously unknown scientific and technical aids, and at the same it was a century which began with a World War which in the words of a recent historian 'was a machine for brutalizing the world' and left as part of its legacy men who 'gloried in the release of their latent brutality'. It is a world of which human beings have with accelerated speed learnt new secrets of nature, and have exploited the environment to threaten the healthy survival of the human race, the animal kingdom and the beauty of nature. I need not go on: you can illustrate for yourselves. It should be no surprise to us if some deeply sensitive, indeed believing men and women would be prompted to put as their gloss on the history of our times: 'Truly thou art a God who hidest thyself'. What they are talking about is no longer simply an inability to understand, an acknowledgment with any half-decent agnostic that God is incomprehensible – 'a paltry humourless and sterile insight' in the mouths of Christian apologists as it has been called. The gloss in this case is neither in wonder nor praise, but the cry of the victim: 'Truly thou art a God who hidest thyself'.

About sixty years ago, when students of Harry Wardlaw's generation were finishing their schooling and preparing themselves for university studies, two men of unusual understanding had gone through experiences which formulated this question afresh: the Christian, Dietrich Bonhoeffer, and the Jew, Elie Wiesel.

In July 1944 Bonhoeffer in prison in Tegel was writing about how Christian men and women were required to live in the world as though there were no God. 'God would have us know that we must live as men and (and women) who manage our lives without him.' God will not allow himself to be reduced to a working hypothesis. 'The God who lets us live in the world without the working hypothesis of God is the God before whom we stand continually.' Then he reminds us that 'God lets himself be pushed out of the world on to the cross'. Here indeed is the God who hides himself: not simply one who is hidden from us by finiteness, stupidity or insensitivity, but one who hides himself, perhaps to have us understand afresh how he deals with the world.

Bonhoeffer constantly reminds us that God is no longer to be understood in triumphalist terms; and in consequence that we must appreciate afresh the scale and intensity and complexity of human responsibility. He is not just reviving a thought of Nietzsche, or anticipating the briefly fashionable concept of the death of God. In his often-quoted words he says

> The God who is with us is the God who forsakes us. The God who lets us live in the world without the working hypothesis of God is the God before whom we stand continually. Before God and with God we live without God. God lets himself be pushed out of the world on to the cross. He is weak and powerless in the world, and that is precisely the way, the only way, in which he is with us and helps us. [Bonhoeffer quotes Matthew 8.17 – 'he took our infirmities and bore our diseases' and comments that those words make it quite clear that Christ helps us, not by virtue of his omnipotence, but by virtue of his weakness and suffering.]

In the twentieth century we have learnt to discard a triumphalist view of God as surely as Deutero-Isaiah taught Israel no longer to invoke Yahweh as their leader in battle but to recognise the hidden hand in the actions of a triumphant pagan, with the corollary that Israel was to be God's faithful, perhaps suffering servant. We have discarded a triumphalist view of God as surely as we reject the triumphalist Church architecture of another age, however much we may admire its strengths and the ingenuity of its arts, it is for another age, not our own.

In particular, however, we have been taught, not least by Bonhoeffer, to reject a Christian, certainly a religious triumphalism in ethics. We are to take the secular with a new seriousness, because God takes it seriously. He deals with the lawyer as a lawyer, with the medical scientist as a doctor, with the business man or woman in the creation of wealth and employment, with the craftsman in the use of his labour, with the social worker or scientist in the alleviation of poverty, with the housewife as a housewife, and with the househusband as a househusband. In a tradition that goes back to Aristotle, every human occupation has its own *telos*, its own end, and its own *techne*, its own means of dealing with its own problems; and within those traditions God is hiding himself. Certainly those traditions have been formed by many elements, Jewish, Christian, Greek, Roman and Arab, as well as good common sense, and the conditions imposed by our several callings. But those so-called secular callings are not necessarily enhanced by being surrounded by an aura of religiosity. Progress in the development of an ethic or way of life appropriate to a profession or trade is made by people in those occupations understanding the best in their own tradition of applied learning or craftsmanship, understanding from within the moral terms on which alone their callings work. Our part as Christians is to listen and help men and women to realise in their own lives Bonhoeffer's paradoxical statement: 'before God and with God we live without God'. Our care is to avoid re-introducing God simply as the working hypothesis of other people's lives – a denigration of his role, and a diminishing of his reality.

Mary Lavin the Irish writer of short stories has recently died. She once rejected the idea of a conventional plot in the short story, and argued that for her writing 'is only looking closer than normal into the human heart whose vagaries and contrarieties have their own integral design'. Someone commenting on that said, 'She is the sculptor who refuses to impose her shape on the stone but searches instead for the shape latent in the material'. Our lives are at best short stories. Even the lives of our institutions – 150 years of New College – are short stories in the long purposes of God.

Perhaps we too are being taught to live those short stories that are our lives, without the support of the conventional plot. Perhaps we must search afresh for the shape latent in the substance of our age. Jesus, you remember, rejected the conventional religious plot of his day. His parables are for the most part about non-religious events which disclose to men and women through the vagaries and contrarieties of human life how they stand before God, at once hidden and revealed. They enclose and disclose God's presence.

Yet there are the longer stories, the older stories, within which our short stories gain a greater significance. The God who hides himself is remembered as 'the God of Israel'; but even here, especially here, we must be careful not to take refuge in the conventionally religious. The figure of Elie Wiesel checks us.

About the same time as Bonhoeffer wrote his letters from prison, the boy Elie Wiesel lost his mother and young sister, taken off to be incinerated in Auschwitz. Later his father died when they were being moved to Buchenwald. He survived that house of death, that Holocaust, to tell the tale. For long he could not tell it, his attitude summarised in two phrases: '. . . one who was not there can never understand it, and one who was there can never communicate it'. Yet, for the benefit of the rest of us, Jew or Gentile, he has made the attempt, through autobiographical writings, novels and tales, and most recently in his memoirs, *All Rivers Run to the Sea*. For him too, with a depth of experience mercifully denied to most of us but experienced by millions of Jews, God is the one who hides himself.

> Perhaps I may someday come to understand man's role in the mystery Auschwitz represents, but never God's . . . [he writes]
> Was I later reconciled to him? Let us say that I was reconciled to some of His interpreters, and to some of my prayers. If men killed other men, if they massacred Jews, why should Jewish man stop praying? Those prayers do not always coincide with reality, and surely not with truth. But so what? It is up to us to modify reality and make the prayers come true. As the Rebbe of Kotzk affirmed: '*Avinu melkainu*, our Father, our King, I shall continue to call You Father until You become our Father.

Elsewhere he says: 'Sometimes we must accept the pain of faith so as not to lose it'. And we think again of Bonhoeffer, writing shortly before his own death, of God who lets himself be pushed out of this world on to the cross.

Both Bonhoeffer and Wiesel lived within a tradition of faith and of prayer. Neither gave up praying. God hides himself from those who believe in him, in those who can address him as 'Thou'. Otherwise the phrase 'Truly thou art a God who hidest thyself, O God of Israel' is meaningless. The question becomes acute at these very places which we share with Judaism. He is the God of Israel.

What would we know of faith and its hazardous character were it not for the faith of Abraham? What would we know of a God who required obedience were it not for the obedient and impetuously disobedient servant Moses? What would we know of a chosen people, were it not for the faith and faithlessness, the obedience and disobedience of Israel and Judah? What would we know of a people's obligation to seek for justice and its toleration of injustice were it not for the prophets? What of the heights and depths of suffering and separation from God, were it not for Job and Jeremiah? What of a people seeking to address God, to live before him in the joy of praise, and to struggle in the agony of finding him absent, if it were not for the psalms? What of the requirement to use our brains (and common sense) and our tendency toward folly if it were not for the wisdom of old Israel?

'Truly thou art a God who hides thyself, 0 God of Israel.' But it does not stop there. '0 God of Israel, a Saviour?' A phrase pregnant with memory, but also with hope.

Bonhoeffer speaks of God who lets himself be pushed out of the world on to a cross: not for irrelevance but for salvation. But *what does that mean*?

Those of us who sat in William Manson's class will never forget his insistence that salvation is an eschatological term. The last word will not be frustration but fulfilment, not the absence of God but his presence, not blame and shame but forgiveness, reconciliation and life. Our present calling as Christians is to live by that reality, grounded in that hope. John McIntyre at the end of his admirable book on soteriology throws out a challenge to us all. Any understanding of the death of Christ which does not issue in, demand, and effect forgiveness is ultimately inadequate. At the end of the twentieth century the world's greatest need and the message of the cross of Christ meet: the human heart, human beings organised into groups, be they nations or classes or genders, human history itself cries out for forgiveness.

WH Auden in an early poem written during the Spanish Civil War understood all too well the twentieth century, or at least the despair and sorrow at its heart.

The stars are dead; the animals will not look:
We are left alone with our day, and the time is short and
History to the defeated
May say Alas but cannot help or pardon.

An Australian historian defined his aim, to look at the story of his people with the eye of pity. Well it is better to pity other members of the human race than to despise or exploit them. It is better to say Alas to the defeated than indifferently to pass them by. But our hope goes further. It speaks of help and pardon: help here and pardon at the end. But not only at the end. The one who hangs upon the cross not only offers but also demands forgiveness. He required his followers to pray for forgiveness, even as we have forgiven others. In John McIntyre's disturbing closing words: 'by refusing to forgive we may actually be preventing the forgiveness of God from reaching others, and so bringing the purposes of God to frustration'. We cannot afford 'to ignore the final finishing touch given (to the effectiveness of salvation) by human agency'. The risen Lord who hid himself upon the cross lays an almost overwhelming weight of responsibility upon men and women, whom he sets free to enter into his work.

We began with the God who hides himself. We end there too with the ancient Christian cry *Ave crux, spes unica*; Hail the cross, the only hope. So we face the future. God grant us grace in our personal lives to come to terms with the one thus hidden. God give us understanding in our intellectual lives to perceive his significance for all our disciplines, God give us faithfulness in our ecclesiastical lives to show forth the reconciling love of the redeemer. And God grant to the family of humankind a century of greater peace and compassion than we have known.

Thou, 0 Lord, art in the midst of us, and we are called by Thy Name. Leave us not, neither forsake us, 0 Lord our God.

And to Him be the glory.

26

ON PILGRIMAGE AND AT HOME: REFLECTIONS ON FAITH AND GLOBAL CIVILISATION IN HONOUR OF RUTH AND HARRY WARDLAW

JOHN F KANE

It is, of course, little more than a cliché to speak of our times in terms of the many processes of globalisation. It is likewise almost a matter of banal self-evidence to refer to my own nation as the sole global 'superpower'. Yet many draw from this fact about economic and military power a far more questionable inference: that the US is somehow also the centre of an emerging global civilisation.

Clearly we cannot know how the historians, philosophers and theologians of the future will understand our era – where they will locate the crucial centres of both force and spirit which will have shaped that global civilisation which for us remains a matter at once both of great hope and of great fear. For my part, whatever the present significance of the US as a centre of many of the lines of force moving us inexorably, for better and worse, into global interdependence, I seriously (and sadly) doubt that my nation has the spiritual resources that transform our global future into something other than that vast commercial and mechanical wasteland about which we have been warned by writers as different as TS Eliot and Karl Jaspers. I suspect, rather, that some of the cultural and political forms that may serve to humanise our global future are currently (by fits and starts) emerging from the earlier defeats and the present struggles of post-imperial Europe – struggles to shape both structures and shared beliefs that might order the internal relations of a post-national economy and external relations with a re-emerging Muslim world.[1]

I also suspect, though I risk further cliché in saying it, that some of the more significant spiritual resources for our global future will emerge from what are marginal places on the map of global power. Yes, I do mean from the poor of the 'underdeveloped' world. Yet I also mean from countries and cultures of relatively minor geo-political significance which nonetheless represent boundary situations between the major centres of power and the vast masses of humanity – countries like Canada and Australia.

Now this may seem a strangely abstract way to begin a reflection intended to honour two Australian friends. Yet I can think of no better nor more realistic way to understand and honour the lives of Harry and Ruth Wardlaw.

I first met Harry and Ruth in Canada where Harry was Visiting Professor in the doctoral program in religious studies at McMaster University in Hamilton, Ontario. It was Harry who introduced me to the thought of Karl Jaspers, especially the latter's wrestling with the question of religious truth as that question has of late been raised in a context of growing awareness of religious pluralism and, unfortunately, also of continuing intolerance and violence. Jaspers had, of course, brought attention to the notion of boundary situations, and to the idea of truth as an existential or conceptually-transcending faith which opened for us at the many boundary or limit situations of our lives – perhaps especially today in the boundary embodied by that other whom we meet in what Jaspers called 'the loving-struggle' of deep difference and dialogue.

As a Catholic, I soon realised that Harry's interest in Jaspers was itself a development of his early doctoral work on Kierkegaard and, more broadly, of the Kantian foundations which have provided such fertile ground for modern Protestant understandings of faith. For as Christian faith has been challenged and delimited, first by the still expanding and quasi-imperial boundaries of science and secularisation, and then by other often hostile and antithetical faiths (political as well as religious), it has often responded (as my own church frequently has) by raising high the battlements of orthodoxy, expelling the stranger in our midst, and seeking to guard the substance of faith in a safe homeland of tradition. To their great credit, however, many Protestant churches and thinkers have responded in a fundamentally different way. They have been willing once again to leave the security of faith's homeland and take up the way of the pilgrim – sustained by both memory and hope, memory of the past richness of faith, yet hope for new forms of faith that might emerge as one crosses boundaries onto new terrain. This is true, moreover, though in different ways, as much for the Barthian elements of modern Protestantism as for its more liberal forms.

As I came to know Harry and Ruth and learned of their family's many trips – to Scotland and Ireland, to Basel, to the US as well as Canada – I began to understand a regular (and seemingly very Australian) pattern of pilgrimage. Yes, there has been a sustained pilgrimage of thought: to the resources of Kierkegaard and Barth as well as those of Buri and Jaspers, to the Scotch and Swiss and German homelands of the Reformation's original pilgrimage, to the foundational modern expressions of that pilgrimage in Kant and Hegel, and to the now prototypical political and economic elaboration of that pilgrimage (for better and worse) in North America. Yet this was not simply an intellectual journey. Rather, for Ruth and Harry and their family it has been a deeply personal journey into an ever broadening experience of our world, a journey whose faith has blossomed in a network of deep and enduring friendships that crisscross the globe, sustained both by memory and hope, especially hope for those forms of faith which, while yet inchoate, are already lived in the love of friendship and mutual hospitality.

It was not, however, until my wife and I, with our children, first experienced that hospitality during an extended sabbatical in Australia – in Harry and Ruth's own home and in the community of Ormond College's Theological Hall – that I also began to understand another dimension of the lives of these modern Christian pilgrims. Yes, of course, I saw how their Protestant pilgrimage across boundaries was also lived at home: in work towards the founding and development of the Uniting Church of Australia, and in the Protestant, Anglican, and Catholic communion of the United Faculty of Theology in Melbourne – of which I and my family were such beneficiaries, and in which Harry's own philosophically informed faith played such a major role, especially in relation with the participating Jesuits. Yet in the Uniting Church and this United Faculty, and especially in the Wardlaw household, I came to see how much the strength and hope required for pilgrimage was grounded and sustained by the at once tenacious and yet gently embracing roots of home.

I must, I suspect, immediately note that many among contemporary Australians might, as would many in the US, respond with ironic chagrin, or even contempt, to the notion of finding deep roots and a sustaining sense of home in either of our homelands – so much have our countries and cultures been ravaged by modernising and deracinating forces. Yet I believe it to be nonetheless true that sustaining 'habits of the heart'[2] do remain in the patriotic and religious roots of both our cultures. And, at least for me and my family, it was especially with the Wardlaws and, through them, with friends in the philosophical and religious 'community' (the word is not misused) of Melbourne that we came to experience anew the meaning of hospitality and home during an important part of our own pilgrimage into the complex and changing reality of our world. In common worship, through both word and sacrament, through afternoons on the sunny shores south of Melbourne and evenings blessed both by Australian wine and intense conversation, we came to experience that paradoxical combination of being at once on pilgrimage and at home, a situation which seems both inescapable and necessary for the contemporary experience of faith.

Even as I write these words about our time in Melbourne, I suddenly recall another evening, years before, during a cold Canadian winter at the house which Harry and Ruth, by their warmth, had converted into a real, if temporary, home. My Presbyterian wife, in good Protestant fashion, has questioned the idea of canonised saints to which, somehow, the conversation had turned. To her surprise, and my own, it was the Wardlaws who sprang to defense of the idea and the practice – both as a matter of the lived experience of the Christian Church over the centuries, and as a still very much needed way of embodying the substance of faith.

And so it has gone down the decades, this conversation between our families and our many mutual friends. It has been a constant and loving struggle between 'protestant principle' and 'catholic substance'. Yet a struggle no longer neatly identified by inherited positions, and continually broadened by new elements of both substance and protest carried by those many other forms of life – forms of both faith and thought – which globalising processes have brought inescapably onto our paths.

I cannot name the substance of the new forms of faith which seem almost simultaneously to both emerge and recede in the constantly renewed dialectic of pilgrimage and return, boundary crossing and remaining home. Yet like many others I can recognise the real thing when I see it. And I have seen it – this lived and living unity of pilgrimage and home, of catholic substance and protestant principle – in the lives of Ruth and Harry Wardlaw. For such witness and friendship I join my family and so many others in plain and simple gratitude.

It is, after all, one of the great wonders of our time that, dark though the path often is, sacraments of grace continue to arise along the way.

End Notes

1. For one historically and theoretically informed account of this struggle, see Nicholas Boyle's *Who Are We Now? Christian Humanism and the Global Market from Hegel to Heaney* (Indiana: University of Notre Dame Press, 1998).
2. The reference, of course, is to *Habits of the Heart* (Berkeley: University of California Press, 1985), that already classic study of contemporary US culture by Robert Bellah and his colleagues.

LIST OF CONTRIBUTORS

REV ROBERT ANDERSON is Emeritus Professor of Old Testament at the Uniting Church Theological Hall within the United Faculty of Theology, Melbourne.

REV BRUCE BARBER is former Dean of the United Faculty of Theology, Melbourne.

REV DR WESLEY CAMPBELL is a Minister of the Word in the Uniting Church of Australia.

REV DR JOHN COWBURN SJ teaches Philosophy at the Jesuit Theological College within the United Faculty of Theology, Melbourne.

DR LOUIS GREENSPAN teaches in the Department of Religious Studies at McMaster University, Hamilton Ontario.

DR JOHN HOWES taught philosophy at the University of Melbourne and held the chair of Philosophy at the University of Cape Town.

MR PATRICK HUTCHINGS is a Senior Fellow in the Department of Philosophy at the University of Melbourne.

PROFESSOR JOHN KANE teaches Religious Studies at Regis University, Denver Colorado.

REV CATHERINE LAUFER teaches at St Francis Theological College within the Brisbane College of Theology. She is a doctoral student at Monash University, Melbourne.

The late *REV DR DAVIS MCCAUGHEY* was Master of Ormond College Melbourne, Moderator of the Uniting Church of Australia, and Governor of Victoria.

DR GRAEME MARSHALL is Principal Fellow in Philosophy at the University of Melbourne.

REV PROF CHRISTIAAN MOSTERT is Professor of Systematic Theology at the Uniting Church Theological Hall within the United Faculty of Theology, Melbourne.

REV DR FRANK NICHOL is Emeritus Professor of Systematic Theology and sometime Principal of Knox Theological Hall, University of Dunedin.

The late *PROFESSOR JOHN O'NEILL* was Professor of New Testament at the University of Edinburgh.

REV DR ERIC OSBORN is Emeritus Professor of Church History at the Uniting Church Theological Hall within the United Faculty of Theology, Melbourne.

REV DR DUNCAN REID is Dean of the United Faculty of Theology, Melbourne.

PROFESSOR DR DIETRICH RITSCHL is the former director of the Ökumenisches Institut in Heidelberg. He has been visiting professor at the United Faculty of Theology in Melbourne on a number of occasions.

REV DR GEOFFREY THOMSON is Professor of Systematic Theology at Trinity Theological College within the Brisbane College of Theology.

PROFESSOR GARRY TROMPF teaches in the Department of Religious Studies at the University of Sydney.

MRS RUTH WARDLAW is a retired medical social worker.

REV DR NIGEL WATSON is Emeritus Professor of New Testament at the Uniting Church Theological Hall within the United Faculty of Theology, Melbourne.

The late *PROFESSOR MAURICE WILES* was Regius Professor of Divinity at the University of Oxford.

MR GERARD WILLIAMS is doctoral student at Deakin University, Melbourne.

REV DR MARGARET YEE is Chaplain to Nuffield College, Oxford, and Honorary Associate Director of the Ian Ramsey Centre, Oxford.

REV DR NORMAN YOUNG teaches at Yarra Theological Union in Melbourne and is Emeritus Professor of Systematic Theology at the Uniting Church Theological Hall within the United Faculty of Theology, Melbourne.

REV DR SANDY YULE taught at Sia'atoutai Theological College in Tonga and is National Secretary for Christian Unity in the Uniting Church of Australia.

INDEX